With the
Weathermen

subterranean lives

CHRONICLES OF ALTERNATIVE AMERICA

Bradford Verter, series editor

ADVISORY BOARD
Gerald Early
Ann Fabian
Helen L. Horowitz
Regina Kunzel
David Roediger

Subterranean Lives reprints first-person accounts from the nineteenth and twentieth centuries by members of oppositional or stigmatized subcultures; memoirs by men and women who lived, whether by circumstance, inclination, or design, outside of the bounds of normative bourgeois experience. They include tramps, sex workers, cultists, criminals, drug addicts, physically disabled people, sexual minorities, bohemians, revolutionaries, and other individuals who have survived on the margins, within the interstices, and across the boundaries of American society. Each volume presents either a book-length memoir or a selection of shorter texts in their entirety, together with an introduction and notes.

The Road, Jack London
   Todd DePastino, editor
The Hasheesh Eater: Being Passages from the Life of a Pythagorean,
   Fitz Hugh Ludlow
   Stephen Rachman, editor
With the Weathermen: The Personal Journal of a Revolutionary
   Woman, Susan Stern
   Laura Browder, editor

With the Weathermen

The Personal Journal
of a Revolutionary Woman

Susan Stern

Edited and with an Introduction by

Laura Browder

Rutgers University Press
New Brunswick, New Jersey, and London

Library of Congress Cataloging-in-Publication Data

Stern, Susan, 1943–1976.
    With the Weathermen : the personal journal of a revolutionary
woman / by Susan Stern ; edited and with an introduction by Laura
Browder.
        p. cm. — (Subterranean lives)
        Includes bibliographical references.
        ISBN 978-0-8135-4092-4 (hardcover : alk. paper)
        ISBN 978-0-8135-4093-1 (pbk. : alk. paper)
        1. Stern, Susan, 1943–1976.   2. Feminists—United States—
Biography.   3. Women revolutionaries—United States—Biography.
4. Weatherman (Organization)   I. Browder, Laura, 1963–   II. Title.
    HQ1413.S68A36   2007
    322.4' 2092—dc22
    [B]   2006039166

A British Cataloging-in-Publication record for this book is available
from the British Library.

With the Weathermen first published by Doubleday & Company, Inc. in
1975. All rights to the work remain with the estate of Susan Stern.
    Introduction to this edition copyright © 2007 by Laura Browder

    Book design by Karolina Harris
    Visit our Web site: http://rutgerspress.rutgers.edu
    Manufactured in the United States of America

Contents

Acknowledgments   vii

Introduction   ix

With the Weathermen   1

Explanatory Notes   383

Acknowledgments

Thanks to Bunny Raymond for generously making Susan Stern's papers available to me—and most of all for sharing her memories of her daughter Susan. Thanks to Roger Tannenbaum for making this new edition of his sister's book possible. Thanks to David Courtwright for making the connection. Many thanks to Melanie Halkias, who began as my Rutgers University Press editor on this project, and to Kendra Boileau, who saw the project to its conclusion: I very much appreciate the care and attention each of you gave to this. Thanks to Brad Verter, for his unflagging enthusiasm, keen editorial eye, and ability to find anyone, anywhere. Thanks to my writing group: Carol Summers, Dorothy Holland, Janet Winston, Sydney Watts and Abigail Cheever. Your suggestions and comments helped me enormously. And, as always, thanks to Allan Rosenbaum and to our children Nina and Leo, for everything.

Introduction

Woman of the Weatherman, indicted member of the Seattle Seven,
ex-felon, underground fugitive, brainless slut, porn film star, bride
with a lavish social wedding, possessor of two master's degrees,
daughter of wealth.

Thus began the *San Francisco Examiner*'s profile of Susan Stern in
the wake of her controversial 1974 memoir, *With the Weathermen*.
Stern's life was one of contradictions, and the political memoir she
published a year before her death described that contradictory life in
a way that drove critics of all political persuasions crazy.

Drugs. Sex. Revolutionary violence. From its first pages, Susan
Stern's memoir provides a close look inside Weatherman (also
referred to as the Weathermen and the Weather Underground
Organization, or WUO), one of the best-known and most controversial political groups of the late 1960s and 1970s. It challenges conventional notions of female autobiography in its treatment of the
traditional markers of female experience. And it provides glimpses
of the ways in which women in the 1960s and 1970s reconfigured
their sense of what was important in their lives—not marriage and
babies, but revolutionary action, sexual liberation, drug-taking, and
collective living. It offers a definition of revolution that is not just
about politics but also about lifestyle.

This is not to say that *With the Weathermen* should be read merely as
a historical document or sociological curiosity. It is certainly one of the
best accounts we have of a woman's evolving political consciousness

as she grapples with some of the major issues of her time, in the context of a group that was notorious and reviled both within and without the left. However, it is also an autobiography in a classic American tradition: an account of rebirth into a new identity. As a conversion narrative, it echoes the turn-of-the-century accounts of immigrants eager to proclaim their ethnic selves dead and to celebrate their rebirth into an American identity.[1] It sounds most of all like the memoirs of unbelievers who have found God, but in this case, Stern celebrates her birth, not into Americanness or faith, but into a life of heightened violence, sexuality, and drugs.

Moreover, Stern's memoir brings together two seemingly incompatible traditions: that of evangelical Christianity (the confession of a life of sin) and Maoist discipline. Weathermen, as Stern detailed in her memoir, routinely engaged in many-hours-long, brutalizing criticism/self-criticism sessions, modeled after those in Mao's China, in which collective members would be viciously attacked by their comrades for a variety of personal and political sins until they confessed their unworthiness. However, these sessions were designed for internal consumption only: Stern aired this dirty linen in public.

A book that received a great deal of attention when it was first published, *With the Weathermen* seemed to serve as a referendum on the place of rebellious youth in American society and on the meaning of political activism during that period. Responses by feminist critics offer us a window into the period's debates over what real feminism was all about—and whether there was a place in the women's liberation movement for a street-fighting, go-go dancing militant. Conservative critics voiced their disgust at having their worst impressions of radical students confirmed. And left-wing critics accused Stern of playing into the hands of conservatives by presenting the political activism of the time as being a little bit about ending the Vietnam War, and a lot about sex, drugs, and mindless violence. All in all, Stern managed to upset a lot of readers of her time—while offering later generations of readers a window into one kind of 1960s and 1970s radicalism. No matter how upsetting it may have been to readers anxious to defend Weatherman politics, readers looking to excoriate feckless youth, or readers searching for a feminist role model, the book provides us with a gritty portrayal of life inside a movement.

WEATHERMAN IN CONTEXT

To understand the genesis of Weatherman, and the group's dedication to a revolutionary strategy that included, at various points, assaulting police, vandalizing stores, and bombing government buildings, it is necessary to trace an important shift among the leaders of the left. In the mid-1960s many activists made a conscious decision to abandon the nonviolent strategies of an older generation of social reformers in favor of more confrontational tactics.

Violence as a revolutionary strategy did not develop in the United States until the late 1960s, in large part because victimized innocence proved to be such a powerful spectacle. Martin Luther King Jr.'s strategy of nonviolence helped cast the civil rights movement as a moral drama, and the brutality of segregationist tactics against nonviolent marchers provided compelling political theater. During the Birmingham civil rights marches of 1963, public opinion turned in favor of the civil rights movement when television audiences saw the spectacle of police commissioner Bull Connor setting police dogs and fire hoses on the thousands of children who were marching through city streets. As one of King's lieutenants, Andrew Young, told the parents of the young protesters, however, "We must not boo the police when they bring up the dogs." Rather, "We must praise them. The police don't know how to handle the situation governed by love, and the power of God."[2] Although many civil rights workers armed themselves in self-defense against the attacks of white supremacists, they did not publicize this fact for fear that doing so would lessen public support for the movement.[3]

However, by the time of King's death, the civil rights movement and other progressive groups had become increasingly militant. The embrace of armed self-defense and the escalating violence of the American left began as a direct response to the violence, both governmental and extra-governmental, aimed first at civil rights activists and then at other leftists. At the beginning of the decade, white student activists had joined black civil rights organizers in

Mississippi to foster voter registration efforts during 1964's Freedom Summer. Members of the predominantly white Students for a Democratic Society (SDS) had joined with the predominantly black Student Nonviolent Coordinating Committee (SNCC) to follow Reverend Martin Luther King Jr.'s dictate that only through nonviolent protest could activists vanquish white supremacy and bring equal rights to African Americans. But as King noted, turning the other cheek is a very difficult burden to bear, and years of unceasing bombings, shootings, and beatings by hardcore segregationists inevitably took their toll. For many activists, King's assassination in April 1968 was the final straw, breaking their faith in nonviolence.

In the late 1960s, the most prominent group of African American activists was not linked to the church-based movement that had been epitomized by King, but the Black Panther Party (BPP), whose founding in Oakland, California, in 1967 was heralded by its members marching into the statehouse in Sacramento, fully armed. Explaining this action—which was undertaken to protest a proposed gun-control law—Party leader Huey Newton insisted that "the time has come for Black people to arm themselves against this terror before it is too late."[4] This was more than a defensive move. As *The Black Panther* newspaper put it: "Revolutionary strategy for Black people in America begins with the defensive movement of picking up the Gun, as the condition for ending the pigs' reign of terror by the Gun."[5] This was a far cry from Martin Luther King Jr.'s "I have a dream" speech.

The Black Panthers galvanized white students like Susan Stern, who saw their political skirmishes as being coterminous with leftist struggles the world over, including anti-colonial movements in Africa and Latin America. Also inspirational were the May 1968 Paris uprisings, in which 800,000 high school and college students, teachers, and workers took to the streets demanding an end to the De Gaulle regime and protesting police brutality—a movement that spread until ten million laborers, roughly two-thirds of the French workforce, went on strike, paralyzing the nation for two weeks.

Most of all, however, the student left looked to Vietnam. The war that would result in 58,000 American casualties and millions of Vietnamese dead would not be over until 1975, but as the 1960s neared their conclusion, few Americans believed that it was winnable, and many believed that it was deeply immoral. The Tet offensive of January 1968, in which 80,000 Viet Cong guerrillas launched assaults on every major city in South Vietnam—including Saigon, where they blew a hole in the wall of the American embassy—made it clear to many Americans that the United States was not, in fact, advancing triumphantly, despite constant government assertions to the contrary.

While Americans of all ages and many occupations engaged in war protests, colleges and universities were widely regarded as particular sites for the concentration of radical activism. White and black students alike had applauded President Lyndon B. Johnson's signing of the Civil Rights Act of 1964 and the Voting Rights Act of 1965, and his championing of what he famously termed a "war on poverty." However, by 1968 another war had come to overshadow Johnson's focus on issues of domestic equality. American students, dismayed by the growing violence of the Vietnam War and appalled by the assassinations of Malcolm X, Che Guevara, Martin Luther King Jr., Robert F. Kennedy, and other progressive leaders, were nevertheless affected by the martial spirit, and in frustration abandoned the peaceful tactics of their predecessors. By the end of 1968, hundreds of major student protests had taken place at American universities— and there were more to come. The nonviolent activism of the early 1960s was, if not entirely over, now merely one approach to protest— and an approach that an increasing number of students and young radicals eschewed in favor of armed confrontation.

Weatherman—which later became the Weather Underground— had its genesis in a 1969 rift within Students for a Democratic Society (SDS), a group that gained most of its strength and membership through the free speech movement at Berkeley in the early 1960s, and which found its greatest influence as the most powerful antiwar group on American campuses. Of the schism, Stern wrote, "Weatherman had been born, and SDS had died, taking with it a decade of valiant revolutionary struggle and burying the strongest white radical group since the Communist Party of the thirties. Now instead of a half-million members and supporters across the country, SDS

Weatherman represented a few thousand at the very most" (chapter 4). Activists and scholars during the time of Weatherman's formation and since then have debated whether the group was a cause or a symptom of the student left's fragmentation. What was very clear, however, was that the group, with its flamboyant tactics and outré beliefs, represented a direction very different from that of the student groups that had preceded it, which were tied philosophically to the peace movement and the civil rights movement. To many, Weatherman represented a new era of nihilism and despair. Though not all observers pinned the blame for the growth of radical violence on Weatherman, most were unified in their conclusion that as a strategy, violence did little to advance the progressive causes that occasioned their protest in the first place.

For those who were swept up in the torrent, however, Weatherman represented the fulfillment of years of frustrated striving. As Stern wrote, "With the advent of the Big Split [within SDS] there was only one reality in my life. Weatherman. I fell in love with a concept. My white knight materialized into a vision of world-wide liberation. I ceased to think of Susan Stern as a woman; I saw myself as a revolutionary tool. Impetuously and compulsively, I flung myself at the feet of the revolution and debauched in its whirlwind for the next few years . . . my family, my past all faded into dreary insignificance. For the first time in my life that I could remember, I was happy" (chapter 4). A new lifestyle (revolutionary debauchery, a heady mixture of sex, violence, and political theory), a new identity (goodbye friends and family), a new fantasy (the white knight of political activism, rescuing her from bourgeois anomie): in Weatherman Susan Stern was transformed.

Stern was a key player in the Seattle collective. Possessed of boundless energy, she seems to have been everywhere that major action was taking place: at the Days of Rage in Chicago, at the Ave riots in Seattle, at the Weatherman 1969 Flint War Council. She was a defendant in the well-publicized trial of the Seattle Seven, who were charged with trashing an ROTC building in a case that drew national attention. Her memoir provides a detailed account of life inside the group. Perhaps most gripping, beyond her detailed descriptions of daily life inside the collective, are her analyses of the group's—and her own—attraction to violence.

Weatherman embraced theorist Regis Debray's idea of exemplary violence—the notion that the underclass could be inspired to foment revolution by the example of a small cadre of activists committed to spreading disorder through riots, bombings, and other acts of depredation.[6] They admired the work of anti-colonialist theoretician Frantz Fanon, who in his influential essay "On Violence" derided the revolutionary value of nonviolence and instead advocated that

> the violence which has ruled over the ordering of the colonial
> world, which has ceaselessly drummed the rhythm for the
> destruction of native social forms and broken up without reserve
> the systems of reference of the economy, the customs of dress and
> external life, that same violence will be claimed and taken over by
> the native at the moment when, deciding to embody history in his
> own person, he surges into the forbidden quarters.[7]

Violence, wrote Fanon, was not only tactically necessary in order to overthrow an oppressive regime, but was also personally transformative: "At the level of individuals, violence is a cleansing force. It frees the native from his inferiority complex and from his despair and inaction; it makes him fearless and restores his self-respect."[8] For Weatherman, the ideal of transformative violence became a central focus, to the extent that its leaders came to admire mass murderers and celebrate white infanticide—an approach far beyond what Debray and Fanon ever advocated.

Weatherman believed that only acts of armed protest could succeed in ending the war in Vietnam, and one of their earliest and most well-known actions, the Days of Rage, brought widespread publicity to the group. In preparation for this event Weatherman appealed to the white youth of America to come to Chicago during the weekend beginning October 8, 1969, to "bring the war home." The city had been the site of mass protests during the Democratic National Convention the previous year. Weatherman called for youth to return to the scene "to turn pig city into the people's city."[9]

As Susan Stern wrote, in detailing her preparation for the Days of Rage, "In one month's time we had handed out almost a million leaflets in at least two hundred different places swarming with potential revolutionary youth. We had learned how to use guns. Carrying pieces that we could shoot, in some fashion or another. I had carried a .22 caliber revolver tucked into the waistband of my jeans, plus a whammie slingshot stuck into my back pocket. We had all learned to make Molotov cocktails, but to my knowledge we had never used any. We could recite verbatim the ABC's of racism in America, the history of the Vietnam war, and sundry other political raps" (chapter 8). She and her comrades may have been unpracticed in the use of the guns, slingshots, and Molotov cocktails they carried, but they were important props for the confrontational form of political theater they practiced—and their "political raps" formed the script to the drama.

The Weathermen predicted a storm of tens of thousands, but the Days of Rage turned out to be a drizzle, drawing only a few hundred activists who smashed storefront and car windows and rioted in the streets, and got beaten by the cops in return. But the tremendous impact belied the modest numbers: Weatherman became instantly notorious as the most revolutionary faction of the New Left. With many Weathermen severely injured, though, the group subsequently deemphasized massive violent street actions. The leaders of Weatherman—Mark Rudd, Bill Ayers, Bernardine Dohrn, and Jeff Jones—still encouraged youth to rise up, loot, and otherwise disable small businesses, banks, and military recruitment centers. But they cautioned that these measures would be less effective than more explosive overtures.

As Mark Rudd and Terry Robbins wrote in an early statement, Weather should be "a movement that fights, not just talks about fighting. The aggressiveness, seriousness, and toughness . . . will attract vast numbers of working-class youth."[10] Cathy Wilkerson, a founding member of Weatherman, recalled in an interview that the group "was trying to reach white youth on the basis of their most reactionary macho instinct, intellectuals playing at working-class toughs."[11] Weatherman leaders, many of them from privileged backgrounds, shared a romanticized vision of white working-class youth: what Weathermen found when they encountered random groups of the young white workers whom they idealized was that these kids simply did not find the theory of exemplary violence compelling. While radical groups like the Black Panthers sought alliances with GIs fighting in Vietnam, Weatherman referred to U.S. soldiers as "pigs." In many instances like this, Weatherman seemed more interested in celebrating violence than in winning converts to the revolution. While their strategy was certainly theoretically grounded in their desire to engage in guerrilla struggle against an enormously powerful military-industrial complex, the theory that they embraced did not lead them to effective forms of activism.

Most alienating of all, though, was Weatherman's professed admiration for mass murderer Charles Manson and his "family" of devotees who, in 1969, in the hopes of igniting a race war, embarked on a killing orgy that ended in the grisly deaths of seven people in the L.A. area. Many observers, appalled by the Manson murders, saw in them a death knell for the idealism of the 1960s. But at Weatherman's War Council, held later that year in Flint, Michigan, delegates reveled at the news. As Stern reports, "Almost everybody in the Bureau ran around saluting people with the fork sign [to symbolize the fork the Mansons left in the belly of one of their victims] . . . There was a picture of Sharon Tate up on the wall, in tribute to Manson's murder of the star in her eighth month of pregnancy" (chapter 11). It was incomprehensible to most people why Weatherman would celebrate the spree killings of a white supremacist or advocate white infanticide (another stated position of the group during this time). However, Weather leadership saw the Manson cult as youths engaging in a guerrilla theater of violence against the wealthy and powerful.

Weatherman promoted an outlaw image with such stunts as helping LSD guru Timothy Leary escape from prison in 1970. And the group's commitment to violence remained strong even after three Weathermen accidentally blew themselves up while manufacturing bombs in one member's Greenwich Village townhouse—

bombs they had intended to plant at an army dance at Fort Dix, New Jersey.

The townhouse fiasco, the indictment of twelve Weather leaders on counts related to the Days of Rage, and the death of Black Panther leader Fred Hampton at the hands of the police hastened implementation of a decision made at the 1969 War Council: to go underground. From this point on the organization would be known as the Weather Underground Organization (WUO). After the townhouse incident, the organization decided to avoid human targets in favor of such institutional targets as the Capitol building, banks, military recruitment centers, and police barracks.

However, although its leaders made the decision to blow up buildings rather than people, Weatherman continued to support groups that others on the left shunned, such as the Symbionese Liberation Army and the Black Liberation Army, revolutionary organizations that robbed banks, organized kidnappings, and staged assassinations of government officials and cops, both black and white.

Despite these few alliances on the left, the group was despised by many radicals and liberals who shared Weatherman's opposition to the Vietnam War but found many of the group's other positions and tactics incomprehensible. As Susan Stern writes, "The majority in Seattle and across the country were violently opposed to Weatherman. Weatherman was the single biggest unifying factor in the Movement since the outbreak of the war. . . . I couldn't resist their appeal. Their flagrant arrogance, their contempt for everyone around them. I thought they were remarkable; I knew I belonged there" (chapter 6). Both the hostility Stern sensed from the group and her intense desire to be included suffuse her memoir. She herself seems conscious, throughout the text, that her feelings are those of a high school girl longing to belong to the coolest clique.

Central to Stern's attraction to the group, as well, was her own experience of the transformative quality of violence and of sex. Weather saw physical transgression as a means of not only political change but also social metamorphosis, particularly for women. The 1969 Weather essay "Honky Tonk Women" celebrated women's transfiguration through violence:

Completely transformed from passive wimps, afraid of blood or
danger or guns, satisfied with the limitations set on us by hated
slave relationships with one man, we became revolutionary
women—whole people struggling in every way, at every level, to
destroy the dying pig system that has tried to keep us and the rest of
its leadership under its total control.

Giving up "hated slave relationships with one man" meant adhering
to the Weather imperative to "smash monogamy," even, or especially, if it meant breaking up longstanding personal relationships.
Weatherman promoted "wargasms," or group sex, and Weather
leaders often demanded that group members sleep with others in
their collective in rotation, in order to depersonalize sexual experience. In short, Weatherman insisted that women stop attaching
meaning to the personal relationships that had traditionally defined
their lives. For Weatherwomen, the focus of many feminists on such
issues as better child care, reproductive freedom, and equal wages
was misguided and downright selfish. As "Honky Tonk Women"
concluded, "We demand—not 'Bread and Roses' to make our lives a
little better and shield us from struggle a little more—but bombs
and rifles to join the war being fought now all over the globe to
destroy the motherfuckers responsible for this pig world."[12]

This dismissal of "Bread and Roses" concerns, as well as Weatherwomen's "more revolutionary than thou" stance, offended many
feminists, who saw Weather's focus on violence as a reproduction of
the aggressive patriarchal structures that were responsible for society's ills. In an influential essay, feminist Robin Morgan criticized
Weatherwomen for rejecting "their own radical feminism for that
last desperate grab at male approval that we all know so well, for
claiming that the *machismo* style and the gratuitous violence is their
own style by 'free choice' and for believing that this is the way for a
woman to make her revolution."[13]

THE EROTICS OF LIBERATION
Susan Stern, however, found personal and political liberation in the
very aspects of Weatherman that so many feminists and leftists

deplored. For Stern, sexuality, feminism, and revolutionary violence were inextricably intertwined. Many feminists of Stern's day, such as Marge Piercy and Barbara Haber, scathingly critiqued the mistreatment of movement women under the guise of sexual liberation which, they argued, offered men more power rather than granting women true sexual freedom.[14] As one veteran of the movement recalled, "Women, in many instances, lost the right to say 'no,' accused instead of being 'uptight.'"[15] In contrast, Stern presented herself as a sexual aggressor. While she writes frankly about her disgust with the sexual expectations of SDS men—"They would drop into small-town U.S.A. with their grinning good looks and their political palaver and just like any other superstar attract a bunch of shining little groupies"—and her own disinclination to meet those expectations—"I couldn't stand the thought of being just another piece of ass to SDS men" (chapter 5), Stern is equally open about her own strong sexual desires and needs.

Most provocatively, Susan Stern insisted that the lifestyle others deplored as nihilistic was at the heart of her liberation. By defining herself as a feminist while detailing the ways she used her sexuality for pleasure, profit, and power, Stern defied conventional understandings of women's empowerment. Whereas many of her sisters decried the sexual exploitation of women, Stern supported herself much of the time through topless dancing and performing in pornographic films. Even her revolutionary comrades "were appalled that I would go-go dance . . . at a time when the Movement was in a crisis over Women's Liberation." Never one to smooth over difference when she could highlight it and provoke discussion or confrontation, "I chose to ignore what everyone was saying and took an aggressive 'who cares' attitude. Instead of hiding the fact that I worked at the Dunes [a local strip club] I flaunted it. Before work, I'd prance around the house in a miniscule G-string. Everyone in the house was too intimidated to stop my outrageous activity" (chapter 5). Stern used every means possible to provoke, intimidate, and throw her audience off balance, all in the interest of increasing her own personal power.

She had a deep understanding of political theatricality in many contexts. Reflecting on her trial as one of the Seattle Seven, for example, she called the court "a movie set," and noted that the jury regarded her and her fellow defendants as "part of the evidence . . . as they might a pornographic movie" (chapter 15). When she discovered, during the trial, that she was pregnant, her lawyers attempted to dissuade her from having an abortion by limning the image she would create: "It will look good to have you come in, glowing and pregnant, maybe with some knitting" (qtd. in chapter 14), one of them told her. Stern ultimately went ahead with the abortion: this was her life, and her show, and she would control it.

Just as sex for Stern was sometimes a means of aggression, so violence could be a means of female bonding. Her experience is common to many of the women she meets in her affinity group. Affinity groups, writes Stern, were "small groups of people, highly mobile, who could use guerrilla tactics on the streets" (chapter 2); hers was preparing for a violent demonstration in 1969 on University Avenue ("the Ave") in Seattle: "We wanted to fight. The women had waited for a chance to assert leadership all summer; the Ave riots provided the opportunity" (chapter 5). Her collective saw the protests, which lasted for three days, as a great success: not only were they disruptive to the status quo, but they were also evidence of the strength of female leadership and of the women's physical courage. More important, in Stern's view, was their effect on the women of the group: "The major thing that came out of the Ave riots was a heavy corps of street-fighting women. The nights of rioting and fighting together had made bonds among the women that years of talking had not done . . . Nothing but action, running in the streets, actually fighting with the pigs could have released such a pent-up force. We were tasting the macho strength that characterizes men, but we felt it keenly as women. Eyes glowing, we looked at each other warmly. Like a sweet perfume in the air we breathed in our first scent of sister-love" (chapter 5).

The sister-love came about through their shared experience of violence: this was a far from gentle vision of sisterhood, though one embraced by a number of feminists on the left. A feminist journal of the time, *Dragon*, published instructions on making pipe bombs,[16] and produced a special issue on "Women and Armed Struggle"; around the same time, the authors of *The Woman's Gun Pamphlet* expressed the hope that "G.C.R. (Gun Consciousness Raising) groups will spring up all over." Armed women, they wrote, could empower women to "escape from ties with men and male institutions . . . men are afraid of women and a woman with a gun in her hand is indeed a wonderful fright."[17] The debates on whether feminists should engage in violence, or whether women were inherently nonviolent and thus superior to men, raged throughout the late 1960s and 1970s.

While Stern's attitudes toward violence and sexuality are striking, her memoir offers much more than her revisionist take on feminism. As her editor noted when he was in the process of acquiring her manuscript, "No one who 'ran with the Weathermen' has ever written a book, and so Susan Stern's will be the first inside look at what was surely the most amazing radical group in America in decades." What attracted him to the work was the way "she gives a picture of life inside the Weatherman collective that makes you think of Orwell and of [Arthur Koestler's] *Darkness at Noon*—the 'stalinoid' stress on thought-reform, the tyranny of double-think."[18] The practices that horrified him included the criticism/self-criticism sessions that lasted for hours and were designed to break down collective members' defenses—their very personalities, in fact—and remake them in a revolutionary mold. As Stern wrote,

> The key to the hours of criticism was struggle. Struggle was the only way to produce change; change was growth. To purge ourselves of the taint of some twenty-odd years of American indoctrination, we had to tear ourselves apart mentally.
>
> With an enthusiasm born of total commitment, we began the impossible task of overhauling our brains. Out all the garbage our parents and schools taught us—in all the wisdom of Mao, Ho Chi Minh, and Che Guevara—OVERHAUL! That's what we attempted to do in a few short weeks. Turn ourselves inside out and start all over again. Fearless and unmindful of the dangers involved, we plunged into the process. (chapter 6)

This process of self-destruction and self-creation, and the relentless self-examination it demanded, made Stern's autobiographical voice more self-critical than most, and in ways that sometimes made reviewers uncomfortable. She was always willing, and even eager, to acknowledge the more personal, less political motives for her actions, in much the same way that members of the collective had.

RADICAL AUTOBIOGRAPHY

Susan Stern's autobiography falls uncomfortably between genres. In it, Stern refuses to employ what Irene Gammel calls the "confessional form" of women's autobiography—the frames and practices that, as Gammel puts it, "systematically foreground and reproduce victims."[19] Yet even as Stern refuses to be a victim (or a victimized former revolutionary), she also declines to present herself as a committed unambivalent revolutionary.

Stern's book was published during a period in which several high-profile women radicals were issuing autobiographies, including Angela Davis, who published her memoir shortly after her acquittal on charges of kidnapping, conspiracy, and murder in the attempted release of black activist George Jackson.

Like Stern, Davis belonged to an unpopular political group—in her case, the Communist Party U.S.A., an organization that had historical resonance for many readers of her autobiography but by the 1970s was completely irrelevant. In other contexts, Angela Davis did not shy away from incendiary remarks. In one interview from the 1970s, she explained that "for the black female, the solution is not to become less aggressive, not to lay down the gun, but to learn how to set the sights correctly, aim accurately, squeeze rather than jerk and not to be overcome by the damage. We have to learn how to rejoice when pigs' blood is spilled."[20] However, in her autobiography she presented herself as a disciplined, intellectual revolutionary, far from "rejoicing" at the sight of spilled blood. In fact, her autobiography was a book appealing enough (in both senses of the word) to mainstream audiences to be selected for the Book-of-the-Month Club. Davis kept the focus of her book on political events and largely eschewed a personal tone. Rather than end with a reflection on her life, she concluded her autobiography with a list of U.S. political prisoners and the exhortation that "across this country, there are hundreds and thousands more like Reverend [Benjamin F.] Chavis, Donald Smith and Marie Hill. We—you and I—are their only hope for freedom."[21] She insisted that her experience as a political prisoner was only one among many: in her autobiography, she was not interested in herself as self, but rather as political example. Moreover, she steered clear of criticizing any of her political comrades.

Stern, on the other hand, aired a great deal of dirty laundry in her memoir, and was as unsparing of herself as she was of others. It is instructive to compare Stern's treatment of her Weather experience with that of Weather leader Bill Ayers, who in 2001 published his memoir, *Fugitive Days*, about his time in Weatherman and the Weather Underground. While Stern never steered clear of chastising herself or Weatherman, Ayers presented an uncritical view of the group and glossed over acts of violence (many of the most dramatic of which took place only after Stern left the group). In Ayers's book—perhaps because of the legal issues involved—he places a great deal of emphasis on the fragility of memory and is coy about specifics. After each of the Weatherman's most controversial acts, he recalls a chance encounter with ordinary citizens who support what he is doing: in the case of the Days of Rage, he flees the police only to be rescued by a homeless man, Brother Red, who takes him to the hobo encampment and nurses him and a couple of Weather companions through the night. "At dawn, Brother Red told us we looked to him like angels now, glorified and risen up. You've been severely tested, he said, in a preacherly voice, and found worthy."[22] Similarly, Ayers reports that once his working-class landlord hears a radio report of a WUO plot to bomb the Pentagon he spontaneously compares the action to the Boston Tea Party.[23]

Ayers's autobiography, written decades after the events he describes, is suffused in nostalgia; Stern's is immediate and unsentimental. Yet it clearly bears the mark of one of the most notable features of the Weatherman experience: those endless criticism/ self-criticism sessions that took place in Weather collectives, and the notion that it was necessary for true revolutionaries to remake themselves in order to better serve the revolution. If this practice was, as Stern wrote, personally destructive, it perhaps helped her to produce an autobiography in the classic American vein. Ironically enough, the tradition of the self-made man—exemplified first and most famously by Benjamin Franklin, whose autobiography detailed the steps he took to most perfectly perform the role of the successful individual, and echoed by hundreds of years of autobiographical tradition, on through Lee Iacocca—found full flower in Susan Stern.

In *With the Weathermen*, Stern presents herself in each new incarnation as having been a tabula rasa, reinscribed continuously and very deliberately with the marks of her new identity:

> Now, for the first time in my life I had something to talk about, and people listened to me, especially women. I studied their reactions. I found that if I talked a certain way, and smiled a lot, and looked straight at them when I talked, that they listened better. I found it was best to talk very firmly and without hesitation, as if I was an authority on the subject . . . I talked incessantly. And as I talked, I grew. And as I grew, I thought more. And as I thought more, I read more widely. As I read more widely, I felt a new sense of pride which quickened my step, raised my head firmly in the air, and gave my voice a resonance and force that had never been there before. I bought a new pair of glasses, with thin gold rims, round and tinted pink, and I began using make-up again. Off came the sloppy jeans and on went the miniskirt and knee-high boots, and I developed my Style. Zip, zap, I was a new Susan Stern, and, honey, when I walked, I threw back my head and moved with determination. People moved out of my way as I strode through them. When I entered a room, I did so with a flourish, and people looked at me, and God damn it, when I talked, they listened, finally they listened. (chapter 1)

In this passage, Stern makes clear how studied her transformation was, how carefully she gauged not only her own performance but also the reactions of her audience to the way she presented herself. Stern's self-conscious fashioning of a new identity, her focus on everything from her posture and the way she carried herself to her clothing—her determination to shed what she saw as the uniform of the women's movement—is only the first of many transformations she undergoes in the course of the book.

Yet her real "birth," as she terms it, comes not in this extended performance of her new self, but in the first moment of rage that she fully expresses, in the aftermath of the SDS men's resistance to the women's focus on women's liberation. At a meeting on women's liberation, a topic the SDS men dismiss as trivial in comparison to racism or war, Stern, as chairwoman, "dressed to the teeth for the occasion and flying on speed," begins to speak: "I put my hopeless marriage and its demise on a silver platter and danced around and around with it." When her husband attempts to interrupt, she shouts him down: "backed by three years of bitterness and frustration I screamed 'Fuck you—sit down and shut up, it's my turn now.' He sat down stunned, and I felt a surge of power in my body that I had never felt before. And that was the very first moment of my life!" (chapter 1). For Stern, the ability to understand and represent her personal experience in the context of a larger political truth is deeply empowering—and her propulsive rage is the quality that makes her understanding, and the transformation it leads her to, possible.

Her next epiphany comes during the Democratic National Convention in Chicago in 1968. Against the backdrop of police and protester violence, surrounded by cops with clubs, rifles, and gas masks, and jeeps festooned with barbed wire to protect their drivers against attack, she lies on a blanket, recovering from a strained ligament she got while marching, and has a revelation:

I lay down shuddering on a piece of blanket, and looked at the clouds gauzy in the blue sky. I thought about bullets ripping through flesh, about napalmed babies. I thought about Malcolm X and lynching and American Indians. Lying there, sweating from doses of speed and terror, I thought about Auschwitz, and mountains of corpses piled high in the deep pits dug by German Nazis. I closed my eyes tightly, but tears oozed from under my lids and rolled off my face.

A new feeling was struggling to be born in me. It had no name, but it made me want to reach beyond myself to others who were suffering. I felt real, as if suddenly I had found out something true about myself; that I was not helpless, that life meant enough to me to struggle for it, to take chances with it, to thrust out and wrestle with it. I thought about all the years I had been strangling my misery as I turned the other cheek. Now it would be different; now I would fight. (chapter 2)

Her anger and sorrow at the injustices of history propels her forward, in this case, into a more personal epiphany. In deciding to fight for the powerless, she is able to become more powerful herself. Yet even in this moment, she refuses to present her revelation as unadulterated analysis: these visions, she remarks, and the profound resolutions they inspired in her, were obtained while she was "sweating from doses of speed and terror."

Her personal rage, her individual self-fashioning, will not be enough: she needs the connection to the past and the future to sustain her. Like fellow Weatherman David Gilbert, who first recalled being sensitized to injustice through learning about the Holocaust,[24] Stern also connects to her Jewish identity. In fact, her disconnection from her father, from whom she is estranged, is based in part on his inability to find a way out of racism through his Jewish identity: "Thinking Jewish made me think about my father and my childhood. I suddenly understood that I resented my father not only because he had tormented me for the first twenty years of my life, but because he was a capitalist, and he was very prejudiced. I don't know what he really learned from the massacre of six million Jewish human beings in Germany. He hated any other color, but even if you passed the color test, he certainly hated all other religions" (chapter 8).

Her background is the reason movement leader Mark Rudd, "somewhat like a king talking to a peon," dismisses her: "There was no way to escape the fact that I was white, female, from a wealthy family, Jewish, had been married, was well educated, had been a ghetto schoolteacher, etc.," she wrote in a letter. "The obvious reaction to Rudd's contempt for me never crossed my mind; he was from a similar background" (chapter 2). However, she herself soon feels that the background which once defined her choices is a distant memory, having nothing to do with her current identity: "Careening from meeting to meeting, from demonstration to demonstration, from man to man, I wondered how I had lived a middle-class existence for so long. I knew that that part of my life was over. I would never again know how to be or want to be Susan Stern—student, housewife, potential mother" (chapter 3).

Stern thus experienced her personal journey as a form of loss. Distancing herself from her past, she loses the ability to inhabit her former self; she no longer knows how to be the Susan Stern she once was. Her revolutionary transformation leads to a kind of personal amnesia, and then finally to an obliteration of her physical past:

> I sat out in front of Sundance and tore up my life. All the photos of my youth taken out of my album, one by one, tore up and into a big garbage can. Then my scrapbooks. Then all the poetry I'd written, notebooks filled with the odyssey of my adolescence, with the panic scribbles of those endless, sleepless nights of my youth. . . . Love trinkets, old letters, all traces of Susan Harris Stern shredded and into a foul garbage can.
>
> Joe sat beside me the entire time, begging me to save some of it, telling me there would come a time when I would want it all. But he didn't know that I was about to jump off, make a clean break, split. Soon there would be no more Susan Stern. She would be dead, and the person she had been would have another face, another color hair, another name, another past. She would invent it, build it, engineer it to be exactly what she wanted it to be, what she had never been. A past of fiction, a life of science fiction. Susan Stern Sham would end finally, finally she would end. (chapter 13)

This, then, is a form of revolutionary suicide, a willful self-immolation. Even though she speaks of inventing a new self, of rising from the ashes of her former life like a resplendent phoenix, what the reader is finally left with is not a triumphant rebirth, but a deliberate erasure of self. Unlike the old self ("Susan Stern Sham") this newly engineered self would supposedly be authentic.

Yet in the end she could not fully eradicate herself, could not subordinate personal relationships in the way that Weatherman insisted was necessary in order to be an effective revolutionary. Her libido, she felt, was one of the factors that distracted her from her political goals. As she told one interviewer about her decision to go underground and why it failed, 'I went off with a shotgun, two handguns and a coffee pot in one valise, but I was the only one without a man. I didn't want to share. After three weeks I surfaced, sex-starved. That's why I am such a poor revolutionary and such a poor Weatherman.'[25] Although she frames her failure in terms of sexual starvation, it's clear that she could have had all the sex she wanted, if only she had been willing to have that sex in the way the organization deemed appropriate, by "smashing monogamy." The fact that she didn't, that the props of coffeepot and weaponry were not enough to enable her to play the role she had accepted, suggests that she was unsuccessful in her attempt at self-erasure. And, of course, the very act of writing and publishing an autobiography is an assertion that contradicts the self-negation for which she strove: every autobiography is a survivor's story.

With all the changes in identity that Stern underwent and detailed in her memoir, she sometimes seemed difficult to pin down. Perhaps the clearest self-portrait she produced was her memoir, but it is possible that another image she created of herself was just as memorable, just as controversial, and, in a certain way, just as true. In 1970, shortly before Stern made her preparations to go underground, she and a female friend painted a mural on the wall of their collective house, while tripping on acid:

I noticed some oil paints and paintbrushes scattered on a table, and decided that what that living room needed was a symbol of liberated womanhood. Together, the other woman and I painted an eight-foot-tall nude woman with flowing green-blond hair, and a burning American flag coming out of her cunt! One graceful arm was raised in a fist; the other held a shotgun. Her breast was crisscrossed with a bandoleer. A caption beneath her said LONG LICKS OF LUST!

It was the first thing you saw when you entered the Sundance house. It dumfounded the Ithaca men, and infuriated all the radical women. No one could understand exactly what I had tried to represent. Perhaps in my acid frenzy I had painted what I wanted to be somewhere deep in my mind; tall and blond, nude and armed, consuming—or discharging—a burning America. (chapter 13)

Was this blonde woman posed as Miss America, with a bandoleer replacing her sash, a rifle her bouquet, and a raised fist her wave to the adoring crowd? Or was this the statue of liberty, carrying a gun as torch? Her height suggested overwhelming power, and her hair was green as well as blonde: this vision was both dream and nightmare. This aggressively sexual, violent woman who threatened to consume a country in flames was simultaneously a vision of a woman giving birth to a new nation. This vision of both nationhood and destruction, of maternity and erotic horror (the vagina dentata), psychedelically inspired and painted as home décor, offered Stern's housemates her vision of the revolutionary American woman, circa 1973.

COMPOSITION AND CRITIQUE

However spontaneous and outrageous *With the Weathermen* might seem, it was a carefully crafted, thoroughly researched literary document. Susan Stern began writing her memoirs while in jail serving time for contempt of court in the Seattle Seven trial. She described her writing process to her mother in a letter: "first I write in the morning, then I read (I am reading the classics, with female protagonists to help me with one of the chapters in my book; Tolstoy, thackery [*sic*], hardy, nabokov, lewis) . . . sleep until one-thirty when we are unlocked again; then I type until four on my book." Stern, who originally envisioned the memoir as covering not just her time in Seattle, but also her marriage to Robby Stern, a year spent in New York, and her work at Columbia SDS, had high hopes for the book: "if it is actually published, it will be the first chronical [*sic*] in America of a white American woman and her political experiences—for that reason, I expect to have little difficulty publishing it."[26]

Stern's papers reveal that she did a great deal of revision as she wrote the work, first in response to the queries of her agent, David Obst (whose long list of editorial suggestions included such things as "Expand on your head trip at the time") and then in response to the urgings of her Doubleday editor, Tom Congdon, who wrote in an internal memo to a senior editor that her manuscript was "damned good—but so raw a mess of badly-typed single-spaced raw material that I could not bring myself to ask you to read it." As Congdon wrote, he was having her revise the work so that "the book itself will be lively but less ideological, with all the emphasis on story-telling. I think I can get the stories out of her without the aid of a ghost-writer. She's willing and works hard, and catches on quickly."[27]

It is clear that Stern did a great deal of work to confirm and supplement her recollections. As she described the process to an interviewer,

> The majority of the book was set down from memory . . . but then because I realized there had to be some kind of reality to it, I did six months of research in New York, San Francisco and here in Seattle.
>
> I went to ex-Weathermen who had kept things like leaflets and newspapers. They were very helpful then, but none of them like the book now. I actually did interviews. I interviewed ex-Weathermen, people who had been friendly with Weathermen, people in RYM II [Radical Youth Movement II, a rival group resulting from the split in SDS that launched Weatherman], altogether I did 30 or 40 interviews. I also read all the literature I could get my hands on about that time. I read the two books out on Weatherman and biographies, like that dreadful biography of Diana Oughton.[28] I even read *The Strawberry Statement*, you know, "We ain't marchin' anymore." All that helped a great deal.[29]

However, Stern's attempts at total honesty ran into legal problems. "Dear Susan," began one letter from Stern's editor at Doubleday, "I'm attaching herewith the eleven page libel report from the Doubleday lawyers." As one of the lawyers for the press wrote in a letter to the contracts manager there, "The book itself, to put matters in

context, is one big libel problem. Its narrative focuses on 'revolutionary' activities—destruction of property, physical assault of police—
that are at worst criminal and at best obnoxious to current standards
of society. The woof to this warp is the continuous description of a
lifestyle shared by all the major characters that includes drug taking,
extramarital sex, bomb making, thievery, arrests and terms in jail.
Each statement that related an identifiable living person to one of
these activities is libelous."[30] Indeed, three of the principal characters
depicted in Stern's book threatened legal action.

Contributing to the controversy engendered by Stern's book and
her tendency to make provocative comments was the promotional
campaign launched by her press to accompany the book's release—
one that situated Stern as a generational spokeswoman. Doubleday's
publicity release was headed by three photos of Stern, which were
also used to illustrate the book: her formal wedding portrait, a shot
of her being led away in handcuffs, and a picture of a smiling, long-
haired Stern in a moment of repose. "THESE ARE THE FACES
OF SUSAN STERN," read the caption. "Ten years have elapsed
since Bradford Bachrach took this glowing photo of Stern on her
wedding day. During those ten years not only the face of Susan Stern
but the faces of thousands of America's young people have under-
gone many changes. And so have their hearts and minds."

The transformation of young women from debutantes and brides
to wild-eyed, promiscuous revolutionaries was very much in the
public consciousness in July 1975, just two months before the capture of heiress-turned-kidnap victim-turned bank-robbing revolutionary Patty Hearst. Appealing to those outside of revolutionary
movements and those baffled by them ("Susan Stern tells it like it
was for her and for many of the other kids who joined the movement in search of a better world and who were cruelly hurt by the
experience, hurt and disillusioned") the release also stressed the feminist aspects of Stern's journey: "It will shock many to learn that
male chauvenism [sic] was as prevalent in the movement as it was in
the world outside. Women were cast in traditional roles, brewing
coffee, sharpening pencils, making love (or just 'making out') with
the movement men who were also the leaders and policy makers.

Only when it came to standing on the barricades and going to jail . . . were women considered equals."[31] By casting Stern's journey as a feminist and revolutionary odyssey, the press opened the door to a barrage of reviews attacking Stern for the quality of her feminism and the nature of her revolutionary activities—and the connection between these two causes.

Although Doubleday may have highlighted the provocative aspects of Stern's book in its publicity campaign, Stern herself added to the controversy. She told Doubleday that she "would welcome all appearances and interviews,"[32] and made outrageous comments whenever she had an opportunity. When she appeared on the Seattle *Today* show, viewer comment ranged from disgust ("Susan Stern is a horrible person! It's good you had her on because she is an advocate of all that we real American's [sic] are against"; "I never heard so much crap on this show before! That woman should be locked up") to guarded interest ("How do I get in touch with Susan Stern?"; "What's the name of Susan Stern's book?")[33]

Reviews of *With the Weathermen* were decidedly mixed. Some reviewers praised Stern's "unblinking clarity," lauded the autobiography as "an honest, painful portrait and not a work of sensationalism,"[34] and admired *With the Weathermen* as "a most absorbing and interesting book about radical youth by one of the most dedicated of them."[35] *People* magazine declared it one of six books readers should take on summer vacation. However, Stern herself pointed out in an interview that the attention her book was getting was comparable to another famous female outlaw of the time: "It's like all the publicity surrounding Patty Hearst . . . *Time* and *Newsweek* probably kept breaking sales records as long as they kept Patty Hearst's picture on the cover. People are bored, and they're fascinated by sensation and romance."[36]

Yet how reviewers felt about the work seemed, in large part, to depend on how they felt about radical youth in general, and about Weather in particular—and these were subjects on which few reviewers were neutral. Daily newspaper reviews tended to be written by those who had nothing but disdain for leftist youth movements. The *Columbus* (Ohio) *Evening Dispatch* summarized Stern's life contemptuously: "born Harris in 1943 of prosperous Brooklyn parents later divorced, attended Syracuse University, had one abortion before marriage in 1965, divorced in 1970 with a second abortion, became an activist revolutionary after SDS membership and thereafter eagerly joined any demonstration anywhere for any cause whatever." This description, with its focus on her prosperous upbringing, premarital sex, abortion, and divorce, paints Stern's politics as symptomatic of her personal pathology and the cultural breakdown it seems to embody. In this description, Stern's politics are beneath contempt, merely another outgrowth of her criminal tendencies: "She cheerfully admits gross shoplifting, extensive supermarket thievery, check and credit card forgery, persistent and recurrent addiction to drugs: a cavalcade of sickness, foolishness, amorality and utter irresponsibility."[37]

By describing her revolutionary activities as a personal existential quest, rather than a sober process of political awakening, and by foregrounding the "thrills" that she experienced, Stern offered ammunition to critics on both the right and the left. However, she also offered a personal truth that was shared by many during that period. The enormous popularity of Arthur Penn's 1967 biopic *Bonnie and Clyde*, which presented the couple as romantic desperadoes, popularized the image of the sexy, existential outlaw. What surprised many older leftists of the period, including those who remembered the 1930s gangster couple as violent psychopaths, was the way in which this image would be linked, most famously by the Weathermen, to revolutionary politics, so that engaging in mindless violence, wearing cool clothes, and embracing a hedonistic lifestyle could be defined as political activities. Susan Stern's revolution seemed above all to be about her existential experience: as she confessed, even if she had been aware of her shortcomings as a political thinker and activist, she wouldn't have let this knowledge dissuade her from her life as a revolutionary.

Unlike other former revolutionaries (such as the ex-Communists whose self-abasing memoirs flooded the publishing market in the 1950s), she tries to hold fast to her ideals, and faults herself and her fellow revolutionaries for failing to live up to them satisfactorily. When she took herself to task for being insufficiently knowledgeable about the causes she championed, or interrogated her own need for fame and attention, and when she reflected honestly about her work as a go-go dancer and her consumption of massive amounts of drugs, she gave ammunition to critics who were only too eager to trash her as a spoiled brat on a criminal rampage. In a sense, her autobiography was a neo-conservative's dream: she seemed like a poster child for what was wrong with youth. As Peter Prescott sniffed in *Newsweek*, "Dragging a man to her mattress every night became as imperative as ending the war in Vietnam, as offing honky pigs."[38]

Stern's book appeared at a time when there were several high-profile radicals who came from privileged Jewish backgrounds. Thus, reviews in the popular press were often tinged with anti-Semitism. Several reviews took the tone of the California *Canyon Crier*, which explained that "Once a Jewish princess, Stern became a terrorist."[39] Jewish publications, on the other hand, tended to place Stern's narrative in the context of questions about Jewish political identity, wondering, for example, whether her behavior was motivated by her reaction to ethnic slurs: What did Stern's activism express, asked the *Women's American ORT Reporter*? "Was it perhaps a desire to dispel the 'Pampered Princess' myth?"[40]

Yet even as conservative book reviewers dismissed Stern for her class privilege and her criminality, feminist critics and critics on the left attacked her as an example of the macho politics they detested. Within the community of Weather Underground members and sympathizers, the reaction to Stern's book was one of dismay. On the eve of Stern's cross-country publicity tour to promote her book, the Mother Jones Brigade of Seattle released a two-page manifesto and asked sympathetic media to reprint it in its entirety. In it, the group complained that "we have enough garbage to deal with from the pigs without having to answer this bullshit from our supposed sister."[41] A review in the magazine *Win* written by some of Stern's former associates identified Stern's account as a naïve and treasonous work:

The effect this [portrayal] has on anyone who has had no contact with the left is to make us seem insane, pop star adventurers, self

indulgent children of the middle class. To place revolution far from
the lives of the majority of people is one of the betrayals of this
book. It is no accident that *The New York Times Book Review*,
Newsweek, and *People* magazine have given the book a lot of
coverage—because it fits right into their strategy of counter
insurgency: to attack us from within, to trivialize the sources of
struggle, to undermine the integrity of our lives.[42]

These critics were doubtless responding to Stern's characterization
of her comrades as "Stalinoids," "Mansonites," and "automatons,
unthinking tools parroting the Weatherman line."

Indeed, on her publicity tour for the book Stern often made statements that were bound to infuriate left-wing critics. In one San
Francisco newspaper profile she called herself a "tireder, older and
wiser revolutionary," and was, as the journalist pointed out, "quick
to acknowledge that drugs and sex first attracted her to the movement" and that "lack of a bed partner nipped her underground
life."[43]

Despite—or because of—the contradictory identity Susan Stern
expressed in her mural and her memoir, *With the Weathermen* is a
book that still demands to be read, as gripping narrative, as (debat-
ably) feminist odyssey, and as political bildungsroman. Stern's
painful honesty may make a reader wince, at times, as it did reviewers when it first appeared, but it is an invaluable addition to the
canon of political memoir, of 1970s cultural documents, and of
American autobiography.

Despite the stir it caused when it first appeared, *With the Weathermen* was never reprinted—this volume presents in its entirety the
text of the Doubleday edition. Susan Stern died at thirty-three, on
July 31, 1976, of cardiac arrest. Her death certificate noted that the
heart attack occurred after she "took [a] sauna after drug & alcohol
ingestion."[44] Although she did not die immediately, she suffered
irreversible brain damage and her family discontinued the use of her
respirator after a week. Although Universal Pictures optioned the
book for a movie, and Berkeley purchased the paperback rights, neither of these plans came to fruition. It is quite possible that without

Stern's nearly inexhaustible energy—and without her dramatic presence—to keep these projects afloat both the studio and the publishing house lost momentum. In any event, Stern's controversial and incendiary memoir sank into obscurity.

NOTES

1. See, for example, Mary Antin's classic autobiography, *The Promised Land* (Boston: Houghton, Mifflin, 1912).

2. Taylor Branch, *Parting the Waters: America in the King Years 1954–63* (New York: Simon and Schuster, 1989), 763.

3. Lance Hill, *The Deacons for Defense: Armed Resistance and the Civil Rights Movement* (Chapel Hill: University of North Carolina Press, 2004), 2.

4. David Hilliard and Lewis Cole, *This Side of Glory: The Autobiography of David Hilliard and the Story of the Black Panther Party* (Boston: Little, Brown, 1993), 122.

5. *The Black Panther*, April 25, 1970. Reprinted in *The Black Panther Speaks*, ed. Philip S. Foner (New York: J. B. Lippincott, 1970), 19.

6. Regis Debray, *Revolution in the Revolution?: Armed Struggle and Political Struggle in Latin America* (New York: Monthly Review, 1967).

7. Frantz Fanon, *The Wretched of the Earth* (1961; New York: Grove, 1968), 40.

8. Ibid., 95.

9. Kathy Boudin, Bernardine Dohrn, and Terry Robbins, "Bringing the War Back Home: Less Talk, More National Action," in *Weatherman*, ed. Harold Jacobs (Berkeley: Ramparts, 1970), 177.

10. Mark Rudd and Terry Robbins, "Bring the War Home," *New Left Notes*, July 23, 1969, quoted in Jacobs, *The Way the Wind Blew*, 32.

11. Quoted in ibid., 43.

12. "Honky Tonk Women" reprinted in Jacobs, ed., *Weatherman*, 319.

13. Robin Morgan, *Goodbye to All That* (Pittsburgh, Pa.: Know, Inc., 1971), 2.

14. See Ruth Rosen, *The World Split Open: How the Modern Women's Movement Changed America* (New York: Viking, 2000), 144–148.

15. Sara M. Evans, "The Rebirth of Feminism," in *Long Time Gone: Sixties America Then and Now*, ed. Alexander Bloom (New York: Oxford University Press, 2001), 198.

16. *Dragon* 1 (August 1975), Bay Area Research Collective, 22.

17. Women's Press Collective, *The Woman's Gun Pamphlet,* 1, 2, 4.

18. Memo from Tom Congdon to (recipient whited out), February 7, 1973, Stern archives.

19. Irene Gammel, ed., *Confessional Politics: Women's Sexual Self-Representation*

in Life Writing and Popular Media (Carbondale: Southern Illinois University Press, 1999), 8.

20. Reprinted in M. F. Beal and Friends, *Safe House: A Casebook Study of Revolutionary Feminism in the 1970's* (Eugene, Ore.: Northwest Matrix, 1976), 130.

21. Angela Davis, *Angela Davis: An Autobiography* (New York: Random House, 1974), 399.

22. Bill Ayers, *Fugitive Days: A Memoir* (Boston: Beacon, 2001), 175.

23. Ibid., 262.

24. Varon, *Bringing the War Back Home*, 29.

25. Mildred Hamilton, "An Old Rebel Finds a New Way," *San Francisco Examiner*, August 14, 1975, 2, "Scene" section.

26. Susan Stern to Bunny Raymond, letter dated April 15, 1972, Stern archives.

27. Memo from Tom Congdon to (recipient whited out), February 7, 1973, Stern archives.

28. Harold Jacobs, ed., *Weatherman* (Berkeley: Ramparts, 1970). This was a compilation of documents issued by and about the organization. Among the other publications available on Weatherman at the time of Stern's interview were Worker-Student Alliance (U.S.); New England Free Press; Weatherman (Organization), *Documents on SDS and the Split* (Boston: New England Free Press, 1969); Bruce Franklin, *The Lumpenproletariat and the Revolutionary Youth Movement* (Boston: New England Free Press, 1970). Stern would undoubtedly have been outraged by a book that came out shortly after her own: Larry Grathwohl and Frank Reagan, *Bringing Down America: An FBI Informer with the Weathermen* (New Rochelle, N.Y.: Arlington House, 1976). It is unsurprising that Stern hated Thomas Powers's, *Diana: The Making of a Terrorist* (Boston: Houghton Mifflin, 1971). As the title suggests, Powers did not admire Weatherman's revolutionary commitment. Moreover, Stern would hardly have agreed with Powers's assessment that "most women in the movement were touchy to the point of hysteria about their dignity" (79).

29. Walt Shepperd, "Weatherman to Waitress," *Berkeley Barb*, August 8–14, 1975, 12. *The Strawberry Statement: Notes of a College Revolutionary*, by James Kunen (New York: Random House, 1969), was a tremendously popular account by one of the leaders of the Columbia University student protests.

30. Letter from Satterlee & Stephens, lawyers, to Kenneth William Lang, August 7, 1974, Stern archives.

31. "News from Doubleday," Publicity Department/Doubleday & Company, undated press release, Stern archives.

32. Doubleday author's questionnaire, March 24, 1973, Stern archives.

33. "Audience Reaction Recap for Tuesday, June 24, 1975," King AM FM TV, related by switchboard operator, Stern archives.

34. *The Booklist*, 5, no. 72 (September 1, 1975): 8.

35. Aaron Michelson, *Best Sellers* 35 (August 1975): 129.

36. Shepperd, "Weatherman to Waitress."

37. Charles M. Cummings. "Lame Apologetics for Radical Youth," *Columbus* (Ohio) *Evening Dispatch*, July 13, 1975, 11.

38. Peter S. Prescott, "Stormy Weather," *Newsweek* 85 (June 30, 1975): 64.

39. "Among the Publishers with Stephen Ongstreet," *Canyon Crier* (Calif.), undated clipping, Stern archives.

40. Roslyn Lacks, "Again, the 'Jewish Princess,'" *Women's American ORT Reporter* (May–June 1976): 4, 16.

41. Mother Jones Brigade, "Stern's Book Opportunistic," Stern archives.

42. Review of *With the Weathermen*, *Win* 11, no. 34 (October 16, 1975): 21–22.

43. Hamilton, "An Old Rebel Finds a New Way."

44. Death certificate for Susan Stern, State of Washington Department of Health.

With the Weathermen

With the Weathermen

The Personal Journal
of a Revolutionary Woman

Susan Stern

Doubleday & Company, Inc.
Garden City, New York
1975

For Marty, El Ray, and the Underground

CONTENTS

1. Leaving   August 1966—June 1968   11

2. Chicago   August 15—20, 1968   28

3. New York   September 1968—June 1969   45

4. Weatherman   June 21—24, 1969   62

5. Seattle   July 26—August 15, 1969   75

6. Handle-Vandals   August 20—September 2, 1969   87

7. Children's Crusade   September 2—October 5, 1969   110

8. Days of Rage   October 8—11, 1969   134

9. Last-Ditch Effort   October 20—November 15, 1969   154

10. Disintegration   November 16—December 20, 1969   180

11. War Council   December 27—31, 1969   201

12. Kicked Out   January 1—February 2, 1970   213

13. Sundance   February 2—April 16, 1970   232

14. Seattle 7   April 16—November 22, 1970   261

15. Trial   November 23—December 14, 1970   289

16. Jailtime   December 14, 1970—June 29, 1972   332

Afterword   369

Appendices   371

Chronology   377

"Oh no," said the little man, "I'm the WHETHER man, not the WEATHER man, for after all, it's more important to know WHETHER there will be WEATHER than what the WEATHER will be," and with that, he released a dozen balloons that sailed off into the sky. "Must see which way the wind is blowing," he said, chuckling over his little joke and watching them disappear in all directions.

The Phantom Tollbooth
1961 © Norten Juster
Random House, Inc. New York, 1964

"One day," said Bernardine Dohrn, "you'll wake up and look out your window. And there, on your front lawn will be a great flaming W and you will know the time has come for you to be a WEATHERMAN!"

It was my first drive from the East Coast to the West Coast. In the next few years I would make the journey many times and each time it would be just as splendid. "America is such a beautiful country," I told my husband, Robby. "Well worth saving."

The rising and falling of the young and wild Pacific Northwest greeted my eyes like no scenery I'd ever seen. Everywhere were green-blue fir trees and lush golden-green foliage, endless mountains and valleys sparkling under a clear blue sky. It was vast and pure and vividly beautiful. I had the strange sensation that I was coming home after a long absence.

I looked at Robby from behind my sunglasses as he drove, his powerful hands handling the wheel confidently, effortlessly as he did everything. He was humming along with the radio, smiling to himself.

I loved him so much. My sun rose and set on the broad shoulders of Robby Stern. His soft brown eyes, the expansive sweep of his gestures, his ruddy glow captivated me. He was so exciting compared to me and my own lackluster life that I was grateful to him for having chosen me from all the other women he could have had.

We plunged through a short tunnel, and surrounding us were the seven hills of Seattle. The waters of Puget Sound sparkled to the left of us as we drove toward the University of Washington, and beyond the water, sprawling, snow-capped, were the Olympic Mountains.

"Aren't the mountains beautiful, Robby?" I said, and he nodded yes without lifting his eyes from the road, and hummed more loudly.

I felt suddenly depressed. Robby hadn't spoken to me for several hours. But then, we really hadn't talked much during the year we'd been married. In a sense we were moving to Seattle to make a fresh start. He would go to law school, and I would go to the School of Social Work, and somehow, everything would work out and our marriage would be saved. We had told each other we were leaving the East to escape my family and the strangling hold of my miserable childhood. But I knew we were running in desperation from the unhappy rut of our life together.

That first night in Seattle, Robby and I walked around the University District. On the corner of Forty-second Street and University Way, which was known as the Ave, were the hippies, laughing and milling around in front of the Coffee Corral. I had never seen a hippie before, and here there were dozens of them. The only person who came close to looking like these people had been an oddball art student who lived in a turret at Syracuse University; he had had long hair and wore a lot of beads and bright colors.

Feeling alien, I clutched Robby's arm as we walked through the mellow crowd. Everyone looked young, happy, and peaceful, and they were beautiful, with all that flowing hair and those pretty necklaces. Incense and other smells, pungent and thick, hung in the air as we walked through the brilliant cluster.

The first part of my year in Seattle was taken up with settling into the new city and into the School of Social Work. Robby and I moved into a two room apartment on Capitol Hill. For three weeks we decorated the apartment, fished, and explored Seattle. Then school began at the end of September.

Almost immediately we fell into a routine. I went to school, held a job, cleaned the house, cooked, and helped Robby type his papers. Robby went to school. As time wore on I wore thin. It seemed to me grossly unfair that we should both go to school, and then I first had to do all the housework while he relaxed and watched the news or studied. We both considered housework shit work; why did I end up doing it all?

As the dark, raining winter months passed, I became nervous and morbid. I would go on long crying jags before Robby ever came home, and fly into a rage the minute he entered the apartment. I found fault with everything he did, but would accept no criticism from him concerning anything I did. The more miserable I made our home, the more insecure I became. The more Robby withdrew from me, the more I craved his love.

Although I was among the top students at the School of Social Work, I compared myself to Robby and convinced myself that I was stupid. I compared myself to Robby in all ways and always came out inferior. But I had grown up thinking I was stupid and ugly. I had grown up lonely and envious of people like Robby to whom friends and grades came so easily.

During that winter Robby and I attended Free University meetings off campus.[1] This was the extent of the political activity in Seattle, 1966. Robby soon began to dominate meetings; although I always attended them with him out of fear of missing something important, I was known mostly as "Robby Stern's wife."

In March, coinciding with the spring break, Robby returned to his home in the East to face his draft board. When he came back to Seattle he brought with him a quarter ounce of marijuana.

I exploded when he presented it to me. I believed all the bad stereotypes about Reefer Madness. I was convinced that with marijuana lay the road to drug addiction, insanity, imprisonment, if not death. Infuriated, I ordered Robby to leave the house. He left so rapidly he forgot the marijuana. After a couple of hours curiosity got the better of me and I tried some. It was rare that I wasn't stoned after that.

A few days later we decided to have a trial separation. Our marriage was bad for both of us. Maybe if we separated for a time we might feel better about each other. I moved into the Magic Mountain, a commune run by Marguerite, a woman involved in the Free University.

Although I was excited about moving into the Magic Mountain, I was devastated without Robby. My world had revolved around him for so long that I wasn't interested in anything else.

I wandered around in a daze for the first couple of weeks, hanging out in the University District, walking up and down the Ave, not talking to anybody. Someone at a hippie coffee shop told me about the Spring Moratorium Peace March in San Francisco. Bored and depressed, I decided to go, hoping that the change would help me forget Robby.

There were over fifty thousand people on the march, which wound for blocks slowly toward Golden Gate Park, a profusion of signs, color, and excitement. I was amazed that so many people were against the war; we had seemed such a small group of anti-war activists at Syracuse.

I went with the throng to Kezar Stadium to listen to the speeches, but I got bored and tired, and wandered out, following a group of hippies to a broad meadow which curved into a hill bordered by trees. In the meadow below the hill, hippies were playing Frisbee, chasing dogs, and kissing. The sun was brilliant; it was melting me like butter. There was a Mexican serape on the grass near me. I slipped it over my head. It felt like a cocoon. I was so tired. And sliding down on the grass, snuggling in the serape, I fell asleep.

I woke with the sun hot upon me, to the sound of tom-toms, guitars, and flutes around me and the scent of marijuana and incense thick in the air. Sitting up I was amazed to find myself in the middle of a group of hippies. They had been playing their music and smoking dope while I was sleeping. Noticing that I was awake, one of the men came over and offered me a toke from a joint. The serape, he said, belonged to him. I began to apologize, but he stopped me, and gave me more dope instead.

I joined the group. They began singing a freedom song, and without thinking about it I sang with them, my voice soaring rich and beautiful in the sun, at home with the familiar words. "Hey, that's too much. You've got a lovely voice," a smiling girl said to me. I smiled back gratefully. I was so happy.

Without any effort, without knowing who I was or wasn't, this casual group of people had made me happy. I felt like I belonged. For the first time in my life, I felt I belonged somewhere. I looked up at the hill, over which the sun hung, already turning orange. "Where am I?" I asked. "This is Hippie Hill," someone answered. "Ain't it beautiful?" Almost reverently I agreed.

It's not that I resolved that afternoon on Hippie Hill to become a hippie; I simply decided not to be straight any more. When I returned to Seattle, I threw most of my clothes into a valise, and went to the Ave and bought myself a long skirt and an old blouse several sizes too large for me. With a thin piece of leather I gathered the blouse at the waist, peasant style. I got my ears pierced and wore long, dangling, vividly colored earrings. I let my hair curl naturally. I went without make-up. I gave up shoes and underpants. Getting myself a brilliantly colored shawl, I flung it over my shoulders when it got chilly.

I got myself a job singing in between sets at a local jazz gallery. It wasn't much, but every time I passed the Longrilin, I saw my name up there: FEATURING SUSAN STERN, blues singer, and I knew Robby would see it every day as he went home.

Sometime in early May I took my first acid trip. I swallowed the orange tablet at the Magic Mountain and sat in a chair and waited for something to happen. Marguerite and the rest of the house waited with me. After an hour I was convinced that acid didn't work on me. Just as I was about to get upset about this, I felt a strange feeling in my vagina. Almost like a buzzing. Then like a pressure, growing and humming. And it felt hot and wet down there.

Confused, I went to the bathroom to check out my vagina. The feeling was spreading throughout my entire body. In waves it washed over me, almost like separate little electrical impulses. I took my hands and pressed them as hard as I could against my jeans. Then I splashed some cold water on my face; it tickled coolly. As I rose from the sink, I caught sight of myself in the mirror. Egads! my face was expanding and contracting. It looked like a balloon that someone was blowing air into and then letting it out again. Every time some new air came into my head, my nose would get very big and my lips and eyes would seem about to bulge out of my head. Instead of being mortified because I looked so funny, I thought it was hysterical, and bent over unable to control my laughing.

I had brilliant thoughts during my trip, but before I could talk about them new ones charged into my mind. It seemed I was thinking about a thousand miles per hour. All my thoughts were fragmented; pieces of them floated like slivers of glass through my brain.

The only reality was the throbbing in my vagina. As the first few hours of the trip wore on everything became one big palpitating vagina. I sat in the same chair wordlessly for several hours, letting people wait on me.

The only time I got a hint of what that other acid trip, the bummer, would be like, was when Marguerite started crying about how life had abused her. For a few minutes the entire character of the room changed. It became dark and cold. I began to shiver. I could see cold gusts of wind passing over the room like a shadow. And the furniture suddenly became sharply angular and menacing. Then Marguerite and her tearful eyes left the room and like the sun reappearing from behind a cloud, the room was bright and radiantly warm again.

I never saw the world the same after that first trip. The conclusion I came to was that I had been taking myself too seriously all my life. Acid did for me what no other person or experience or drug had done before or since. It taught me how to see and think in a new dimension. The only bad part about acid, I soon discovered, was coming down. Eventually the glow faded and the living room once again smelled of cat shit and sweat and was dark and dingy. Reality waits at the end of every trip. And you come down every time.

That was the spring of silent vigils, when anti-war activists in Seattle stood together immobile for an hour each day. Standing in the rain day after day, I began to resent the role of pacifist. We weren't touching or threatening the people who manufactured the arms or airplanes sent to Vietnam, or those who made the decisions about the war. Dissatisfied as I was, I was proud that at least I was taking a stand, even if it was a silent one in the rain.

In June I moved back into my old apartment with Robby. We missed each other and decided that our marriage hadn't been so bad after all.

That summer was the Summer of Love. Robby and I reveled in it. It was beautiful while it lasted. From June through August the days were warm and clear. Several times a week Robby and I took acid and sat together on a section of the campus we called Hippie Hill. At night we'd wander in the crowds lining the Ave, smoking joints and chatting. We no longer knew everyone in the University District, for hundreds of people had come from other parts of the country because Seattle was now a "scene."

And pursuing us all, with dogged determination, was that grim reaper—The System. Unable to beat the flower children, it joined us. Shops opened wherever hippies gathered to cater to the new styles. Suddenly the Ave was flooded with heroin and speed. The acid became bad, cut with other chemicals such as strychnine and belladonna, which were highly dangerous. The police materialized en masse and harassed the growing hippie hordes. "More protection," cried the hip young merchants who were cashing in like mad on the fads the new culture introduced. And all too happy to comply, the police overran the Ave.

The amount of speed and smack grew, but never were the pushers arrested. And the dead faces of the wilting flower children became stark as their money disappeared into their ever demanding veins, and they were thrown out onto the streets because they couldn't pay rent, and they began to get sick because they were starving. The police harassed those who sold cannabis.

They imposed curfews on the streets and closed down the haunts where underage people could hang out. But the heroin dealers and speed freaks were older for the most part; they were immune to the curfews.

Robby and I and everyone else ignored the symptoms of decay and played flower child instead until it was too late on the Ave as it was too late in Haight-Ashbury.

Still the culture flourished, on the surface at least. Even as the system closed its strangle hold on the Summer of Love, Robby and I cherished it. We had found, we thought, a new way of living, an alternative to the system we despised. We had cultivated love and beauty in a society that thrived on hate and deceit. We had said good-by once and for all to the establishment, to our parents' way of doing things, to middle-class life, to upward mobility, to capitalism, to money, property, war, and double standards in sex, to laws that were unfair and oppressive. We believed in Timothy Leary. "Turn on, tune in and drop out," he said, and all around us we watched the flower children ardently follow his advice. We decided that living alone was too middle-class; besides it was too expensive. We wanted to live communally.

Our commune was not built on love or common interest but solely by accident. I had begun to play in a band, so the guitarist moved in. A few days later he brought home a friend of his named Jay. "Jay is a cook," he told us, and straightaway, Jay began turning out magnificent, mouth-watering meals. Then a few days later a shy, brooding girl moved in. In this haphazard manner our commune grew to eight people.

In August Robby and I hopped a train to Chicago to attend the New Politics Convention.[2] Most of the Convention consisted of endless debates between the black militant caucus which controlled the majority of the votes, and the white liberals who were horrified by the black militants. The important thing about the New Politics Convention for Robby and me was that we came in contact with other white radical organizers, among them Students for a Democratic Society (SDS).[3] We were impressed by their spirit and polemic and decided to join SDS when school resumed in the fall.

I didn't want to start my second year in the School of Social Work, but Robby was adamant about it, so I returned reluctantly. My first year had been alienating, but my second year was a fiasco. I was contemptuous of the students and professors for their liberalism and for their straight life style, which I had so recently discarded. I knew after the first month of school that I would never be a social worker.

That year SDS did a lot of leafleting and educational work around ROTC and the Black Student Union on the University of Washington campus. We went to endless meetings of liberal groups formed by white students to deal with black problems. Black students would show up at those meetings, and I would shrink as they told us what a bunch of honkies we were. I had been through it all before at Syracuse, when white people had been asked to leave CORE. During the winter SDS got involved with the Black Panthers.[4] They were always calling our house asking for cars or money.

Sometime prior to Christmas we moved our commune into a new house. It was located on Woodlawn Avenue, not far from our first commune. It had five large bedrooms, a paneled living room, a large, homey kitchen and a large dining room. Downstairs there was a full basement, large enough for the band I sang with to practice in.

Robby and I grew very close to Jay who turned out to be a gem among human beings. He was one of the most selfless people I ever knew. He was a shy man, but once you got to know him, all you saw was his wide smile and his open friendly face and laughing eyes filled with a vital lust for life.

Things between Robby and I didn't improve in our new house. We argued constantly. Many times we argued at the dinner table. Jay, who loved us both, would look from one to the other, his face strained. Sometimes three weeks went by and Robby and I didn't fuck.

There were nice times as well. The pleasurable parts that go along with living with other people. The making of group meals with Jay as Chief Chef. There were lavish dinners that took hours to eat, with all of us singing the Fugs in a different key. There were political disputes, growing more heated, with Jay becoming more interested in them. And there were the Friday night horror movies, and watching TV and eating until three o'clock in the morning. Still, I knew that my marriage was failing, and I was terrified whenever I thought about Robby's leaving me.

Sometime in the beginning of 1968, when I had just turned twenty-five, my misery found expression in a book by Betty Friedan, *The Feminine Mystique*.[5] I discovered that millions of American women felt the same way I did. Just think of it—millions of women tired of being mothers, tired of being wives, tired of being mistresses, tired of doing laundry, tired of cooking, cleaning, sewing, serving, chauffeuring, mending, shopping and suffering the daily tantrums not only of their children, but of their men as well. Millions of women reading Betty Friedan and muttering in their homes over coffee, over the ironing board, over dinner, over dishes, and under their men, "I'm not alone. Others feel like I do. Others want out out out, NOW."

In Brooklyn, in San Francisco, in New Orleans and Portland, women began to stir and breathe, to moan new words: freedom; liberation; independence; employment; unemployment; divorce; birth control. *Political*, and with a gallop, the Women's Liberation Movement was born. And yours truly was one of its first babies.

For the next few months all I thought about was Women's Liberation. I talked about it everywhere to everyone. I read what little there was to read on the subject. It was the first time in my life that I'd ever taken a personal interest in anything.

Not long after I read *The Feminine Mystique,* Flo Kennedy, a black lawyer from New York, came to Seattle at the invitation of Robby's law school. Although a lot of her interests centered about the law, she was also a feminist, and a member of the National Organization of Women (NOW), which had been organized by Betty Friedan. It was impossible not to love the affable and stunning woman, who had an amazing amount of energy and could talk for hours. I will never forget the sight of her in my bed when she first woke up, asking me if her false eyelashes were still on okay.

False eyelashes or not, she was one of the first people to talk to me seriously about Women's Liberation. "What!" she exclaimed in horror. "You don't have a woman's organization in Seattle yet? Well, what in hell have you been doing?"

Bolstered by Flo's encouragement, I began to think about organizing a woman's group in Seattle. I discussed it with other Movement women, and we finally decided upon a series of weekly classes, with a lecture followed by discussion. I then hoped to organize a woman's group out of the class participants.

The class ran for eight weeks, and was very successful. Out of it grew Radical Women. The group wasn't as successful as the classes, because we could never agree on our goals. Most of the differences lay between young, action-oriented women, and older, education-oriented women. Even though political dissension made the meetings hopelessly tedious, two good actions did come out of Radical Women during its early months.

One of these was a demonstration against a Playboy bunny appearing on campus for Homecoming Weekend. Barkers standing outside the student union building (HUB) screamed "Ladies, come see Lorna Dune . . . see what she has that you don't have. Gentlemen, come get an eyeful of Lorna, what you want, what your girl friend doesn't have." Lorna held court with the men and women separately.

Several Radical Women attended Lorna's visit with the campus women. We sat down with everyone else, but soon after Miss Dune minced onto the stage, six of us pulled paper bags over our heads and joined her, chanting a litany for her. We were about to make a quick exit, when several jocks galloped on stage and grabbed us. I was suddenly crushed in a half nelson, and some jock whispered harshly in my ear as he strangled me, "You fucking dike," and I was dragged off stage and thrown down a small flight of steps.

I didn't get hurt, but Beth Allworth, one of the other women, didn't fare so well. Beth bit the jock that grabbed her, and he retaliated by smashing her in the eye before he catapulted her down the stairs.

We left the auditorium to the sound of female college students screaming shrilly, "You horny bitches. What you need is a good fucking, then maybe you won't hate men so much." I couldn't help agreeing that I needed a good fucking, but I knew Beth didn't because she was sleeping with my husband.

Now, for the first time in my life I had something to talk about, and people listened to me, especially women. I studied their reactions. I found that if I talked a certain way, and smiled a lot, and looked straight at them when I talked, that they listened better. I found it was best to talk very firmly and without hesitation, as if I was an authority on the subject. I also found that my personal experiences were what interested other women most. Others related to my life and marital experiences, shaking their heads and saying, "Yes, that's exactly how it is with me. Oh my God, I'm so glad you understand."

I talked incessantly. And as I talked, I grew. And as I grew, I thought more. And as I thought more, I read more widely. As I read more widely, I felt more secure in my knowledge. As I felt more secure in my knowledge, I felt a new sense of pride which quickened my step, raised my head firmly in the air, and gave my voice a resonance and force that had never before been there. I bought a new pair of glasses, with thin gold rims, round and tinted pink, and I began using make-up again. Off came the sloppy jeans and on went the miniskirt and knee-high boots, and I developed my Style. Zip, zap, I was a new Susan Stern, and, honey, when I walked, I threw back my head, and moved with determination. People moved out of my way as I strode through them. When I entered a room, I did so with a flourish, and people looked at me, and God damn it, when I talked, they listened, finally they listened.

Together we women stood in those early days of liberation and groped for better ways of bringing our lessons to other women, hopefully to all women some day. And we did it, every step of the way, in spite of the men, and not because of them.

Beth and Robby continued to see each other. It was nothing serious, but while it lasted, I suffered. One night we all went to a party together after an SDS meeting. I asked Robby to dance with me, but he said he was too tired. Dejected, I went into another room to get something to drink, and when I returned, Robby was dancing a slow dance with Beth. Choking back tears, I hitchhiked home.

That night I asked Robby to find himself another place to live. He didn't argue at all. I guess he was relieved that I was finally taking a stand. Maybe that's what Beth was all about.

Calmed by the inevitable, I turned to my master's thesis, burying myself in work. The work was tedious and unrewarding. To continue at the pace I set for myself, I had to have chemical reinforcement. Jay, who liked speed himself, complied by supplying me with methedrine. For three months I used speed daily, taking it orally. By the end of the quarter, I was addicted to it. Depressed, nervous, overworked, emotionally spent, I was the perfect candidate for drug addiction.

Two weeks before the spring quarter ended, Seattle SDS had its first Regional meeting. The purpose of the meeting was to develop a summer strategy, but because of the women, the main theme soon became Women's Liberation. The women decided to hold their own General Assembly to which all the men were invited. The men were infuriated, saying that a General Assembly to discuss Women's Liberation was a waste of time, that the meeting should be devoted to discussions about war and racism. But the men could hardly refuse to come.

I was chosen to be Chairwoman for the General Assembly. I was dressed to the teeth for the occasion and flying on speed. When I stood to speak, I waved a clenched fist in the air, spit as I spoke, and, hardly pausing to catch my breath, I put my hopeless marriage and its demise on a silver platter and danced around and around with it. Startled by the force of my language, and the rage that accompanied it, the restless movements of the men stopped. When Robby had heard enough and couldn't take it any more, for he was no worse than any other man, he attempted to interrupt me, and backed by three years of bitterness and frustration I screamed, "Fuck you—sit down and shut up, it's my turn now." He sat down stunned, and I felt a surge of power in my body that I had never felt before. And that was the very first moment of my life!

A week later I decided to leave Seattle. I was scared to death about leaving. Yet I felt I was on the brink of something great and otherworldly, and like a child, I was eager to grasp, touch, sniff, hold, and understand absolutely everything.

My female friends shook their heads in wonder as I prepared to leave. They were envious of me because I was escaping. And the men looked at me with new respect, because I was daring to do something out of the ordinary. My master's completed, my good-bys said to all my friends in a flurry of parties given for me, sometime in early June, Jay drove me to San Francisco.

Although Haight-Ashbury was still a "happening," I rarely went there. Although be-ins and music festivals took place that summer, I never went to them. I was too lethargic. During the day I lay on the grass in Washington Square, playing my guitar for the drunks, or just staring at the sky. At night I played my guitar and sang in cafes on Grant Street. Many people made offers to help me with my music, but I wasn't interested. I just sang the blues and lived a blah existence.

I went to Berkeley, just after the riots supporting the Paris revolts.[6] The riots sounded great, but I didn't like the professional politicos who tried to cash in on them afterward. I hung around the Peace and Freedom Party Office, but I thought their politics were fucked. But they were running Eldridge Cleaver for President, and I supported the Panthers, so I tagged along to rallies.[7]

I wandered around Berkeley, trying to find a niche. Volunteers were needed to help with all the free centers popping up and down

Telegraph Avenue. Raggedy hippies sat idly in the sun, or on the wall in front of Sproul Hall. The Hare Krishnas danced every day, pale orange and reeking of incense. It all seemed dull to me; it had all happened last summer. After a week of hanging around there, more depressed than ever, I returned to San Francisco.

I decided to look for work. One night, as I leafed through the classified, a friend suggested that I try topless dancing. She had just quit her job, and she thought that I could get it that night. "Topless dancer," I mused. It certainly would be something different. What a thing to write home about! I could see the headlines . . . "New Jersey girl murdered; found strangled in her topless dancing outfit in a forsaken apartment . . ." I was utterly titillated by the thought of being a topless dancer, and even more excited when I learned it paid three dollars an hour.

The Bunny Club was about the smallest bar on Broadway, the strip in North Beach that caters to honky tourists who want a gaudy night life, and to lonely sailors docked in San Francisco harbor for a day or so, and to young women on the make, and pimps searching for whores for their stables. Broadway is a mixture of lowly Mafia types, highbrow Smith and Vassar girls who never made it to Hollywood, welfare mothers who dance in the dozens of topless joints to support their half-dozen children; heroin dealers and addicts and hundreds of indescribably lonely, wretched, empty people who wander the streets night after night, leaning against the plush orange-red doors open like mouths, lurching into glittering windows plastered with photos of women of every shape and hue, all with naked breasts sticking out, falling low, full and pointed with silicone, and small and perky like mine, so soon to join the throng on the bill posts.

Putting on gobs of make-up, teasing my short hair until it looked about three times as long, penciling in my eyebrows thick and black and my lips white and shiny, donning dark stockings, hanging inches of earrings from my drooping lobes, and finally spraying the whole thing with some God-awful reekingly sweet perfume, I minced on my stiltlike heels down Stockton Street to Broadway, and at about four-thirty in the afternoon, entered the sleazy red-black entrance of the Bunny Club.

I walked up to the bar and asked the bartender, a thickset Italian, if there were any topless jobs available. He eyed me slowly and thoroughly up and down, told me to take my clothes off and show him what I could do. I felt calm, very calm. I was like a piece of steel. My hands as they pried off my miniclothes were ice cold. I swiftly took off everything but a pair of mesh black bikini panties with a fringe, which I had purchased for the job, and as the bartender dropped some coins into the juke box, I climbed onto the little platform and began to dance. I moved my body slowly and steadily, all the time staring at the bartender (I couldn't see him very well because I had taken my glasses off) who I felt was watching me closely. I danced three songs one right after the other. When I got down from the platform, the grinning bartender told me to come back and start work at eight o'clock that night. I would work from eight o'clock to two o'clock in the morning, five nights a week.

The thing I most remember about working at the Bunny Club was how boring it was. Night after night, without interruption, I had to put on all that make-up, paste a smile on my face, and dance for six hours. I danced three numbers, and then two other girls each danced three numbers, and then it was my turn again. In between my dancing, I sat in the darkest corner I could find, but inevitably some lonely sailor would ask the bartender to ask me to have a drink with him, and it was part of my job to do so. Many times these men would offer me all the money they had if I would sleep with them. But I always said no, although it was tempting enough to be a prostitute. I just couldn't stand the thought of kissing any of them.

The men who came into the bar were disgusting, but I felt sorry for them anyway. The whole place was like a pile of dying fish, all caught in the same net.

While I was in San Francisco, Huey P. Newton's murder trial began.[8] The police had begun harassing the Panthers long before 1968. Panther leadership was thrown in jail on every kind of phony charge. But the Panthers never stopped hawking their newspapers or working on their breakfast programs. I had been drawn to the Panther line immediately; their military posture appealed to me, and the picture of Huey Newton sitting in his wicker chair, with his beautiful face looking deadly serious, captured my imagination. If anyone could bring the system to its knees, I thought, it would be Huey P. Newton. Handsome, brilliant, charismatic, young and fearless, he was a dazzling figure for black youth to follow. And since there was no white leadership like Huey, then white youth had to follow him as well.

The Panthers set the tone for revolution in America at the end of the sixties. All the slogans, most of the theory, the gravitation toward Mao Tse-tung, the militaristic approach, all came from the Black Panthers.[9] They didn't just pick up the gun; it was indigenous to the black community. But they coined the fact for us that "Power comes from the barrel of a gun." They gave white radicals a focus for their sprouting hatred—the pigs. As they began to grow, the pigs pounced on them in deadly earnest; Panthers were shot and murdered and jailed. By the time Huey's trial began, many of the top leadership was dead or behind bars.

Although thousands of people screamed "Free Huey Newton by any means necessary," Huey stayed in jail. After a week of demonstrations, the crowds had dwindled to a few Black Panthers. Depressed and disappointed, but not really knowing what else we could have done, I decided to leave San Francisco and go to Los Angeles.

In L.A. I worked at the L.A. SDS Regional Office, doing total shit work. The days were hot and breezeless. I was depressed and bored.

Then one day I slumped into the airless office, and there, surrounded by the staff, was a wildly gesturing man, who was hollering so loudly that his neck muscles stood out at the beginning of each word; and every word was punctuated by the rapid shaking of a very long, bony finger. But the finger and vocal cords of this man were peanuts compared to his eyes; never have I seen a couple of burning pools of emotion and intensity such as those eyes. They seemed to dart right out of his long face, darkly flashing. This strobe-eyed, screaming individual was Mike Klonsky, National Secretary of SDS, who in his gravelly Los Angeles truck driver's voice was telling the staff about "Dis here demonstration in Chicago that's coming up in a week or so, and youse guys had better be there cause this is da bigges' thing yet in radical history."

Mike Klonsky embodied a riot. His whole appearance was so entrancing to me that I couldn't talk or think about anything else but the Democratic Convention from that moment on.

Klonsky spied me swaying hotly in the background, and after he finished his rant, he came up to me, always being on the lookout for new SDS recruits. We conversed for a few minutes; or rather, Klonsky harangued, and I looked at him with total absorption. He smiled, being sensitive to my receptive radical vibes, and mentioned that it might help my political education if I came to the Democratic Convention in Chicago.[10] Then he cocked an inquiring eyebrow at me. I told him I had no idea what I was going to do but that I would keep it in mind.

Klonsky called the Regional Office the following week to speak to one of the staff members. He pressed me again to come to Chicago. "You'll learn more in three days in Chicago than you'll learn in three months at the Regional Office," he said. Again I told him I'd consider it.

I doubt that seeing Klonsky by itself could have pulled me out of my rut in L.A. But I was so bored and the prospect of a national demonstration in Chicago sounded exciting. And Chicago was on the way to New York, and I hadn't been home for two years. Maybe it was time to go back for a visit. I made up my mind to leave, put some clothes into a valise, left my car and most of my belongings parked on some street, and flew to Chicago.

The demonstration to which I was flying had been billed by the Yippies as a Festival of Life versus the Convention of Death.[1] It was to be a head-on collision between the old way of life and the new, between young and old, left and right. Jerry Rubin and Abbie Hoffman, Yippie leaders said, "The mission is to freakout the Democrats so much that they disrupt their own convention."

The National Mobilization Committee (Mobe) declared the week of demonstrations to be largely anti-war, and were very serious about disruptive, nonviolent protest.[2] Initially SDS hadn't supported the demonstrations, but in July, it became apparent that it was going to be a big event. Klonsky began to encourage SDS organizers from around the country to go to Chicago, with the sole purpose of reaching the McCarthy kids.[3]

From the beginning my encounter with SDS was with the leadership. It was with the leadership that I identified, and from leadership that I learned. To the masses of SDS and to the outside world, I was considered a top organizer.

That first night in Chicago, before the action began, there were already more than two or three thousand people milling around Lincoln Park, fucking in the bushes, blowing joints down by the lake, talking quietly in groups or couples. There were hundreds of young couples with long hair and beautiful bangles, representatives of the hippie counterculture. Mixed in with them were the clean-cut, collegiate-looking McCarthy supporters. These young students would learn the most from the week of demonstrations.

The night was warm and breezy, and bright with a full moon and splashes of clouds flooding the sky. In the distance, around the lake, I could see the lights of Chicago, sense the press and clamor of a big industrial city. But in Lincoln Park the night mellowed the city noise, and walking around I could only hear laughter and light-hearted conversation, singing and clapping, panting love-makers and the vibrating beat of tom-toms pounding through the night.

Hundreds of people were hungry and I stood laughing and smiling and dishing out spoonfuls of stew-type glop and rice and loaves of bread, and everyone smiled back at me through the filmy night. I felt part of a great whole, a feeling that would grow on me as the days of the demonstration passed. I felt at home and serene among the smiling youth that had come to Chicago to protest the war, to dance the sundance of freedom. A feeling of tenderness for my nightfriends surged up in me and beaming, I attracted a huge crowd of people who helped me ladle out the stew and eat it. It never occurred to me to worry about where I would spend the night. I never felt alone there, although I knew no one in Chicago but Klonsky, and he was nowhere to be found. I felt very strong and at ease; I was happy and at peace with myself.

In that frame of mind I bumped into Mike James. Mike was an organizer with JOIN, a group that worked with street kids and Chicago greasers. He had once visited Seattle to talk with SDS about the problems of organizing greasers. I had been very much attracted to him then. Now he was both surprised and pleased to hear that Robby and I had separated, and he asked me if I would like to get together with him while I was in town.

Next morning, after showering and eating, I walked from the dark house where I had crashed, out into the white-hot August Chicago. A meeting was going on at the Sedgwick Center, a church recreational center which had been donated to SDS as a meeting place and central clearinghouse during the demonstrations. Although I was a newcomer, no one resented my presence. I listened absently to discussions of how to handle SDS housing, when suddenly the room exploded, as a swarthy, handsome young man began arguing. The man was talking fast and loud, with a heavy Brooklyn accent, and shaking his arms up and down while he talked, swinging his large head from side to side. He seemed to talk with his teeth clenched, and he was so loud and persistent that no one could interrupt him. When the chairman tried to quiet him, he stood up and began talking even louder, jabbing into the air at the chairman with his finger. His talk was so rhetorical that I could hardly understand him. He refused to let anyone else talk until he finished, and his tone was at once so commanding, and contemptuous that everyone else in the room was more or less intimidated into silence.

After the willful young speaker sat down, the chairman hastily called the meeting to an end. As I sat there trying to figure out what would happen next, the volatile finger jabber stalked up to me, and casting a sneering glance in my direction, asked me out of the side of his mouth what I thought. I stuttered something incomprehensible; I had the feeling it didn't matter what I said, he would have reacted the same way. He immediately began to argue with me in the same volcanic tones he had used previously. Once again his eyes narrowed and he was off and running. I was unimpressed and repulsed by his heavy-handed manner, and after a few minutes of his finger waving and spitting in my face, I excused myself and walked outside.

People were going to the Hotel Hilton, where the McCarthy supporters were staying, to leaflet there, and try to talk to them. I asked to go along, and wouldn't you know it; in my car was the loudmouth, still talking away a mile a minute. Since the car was overcrowded, I ended up in his lap, where he almost squeezed me to death in a lovely pair of brown arms. He continued to mumble in my ear with a whoosh of sweet breath. After a while he broke off his monologue, and asked me my name. After telling him, he informed me that his was John Jacobs, but he was called J.J.

I never made it inside the Hilton that day, for no sooner had I gotten out of J.J.'s lap and out of the car, than I saw Klonsky running toward me, with his eyes shining. We talked casually for an hour, and then he asked me if I'd like to see the SDS National Office. I went there with him, but only stayed a few minutes. I was uncomfortable the entire time I stayed. Everybody in the office was so chilly and serious they scared me to death.

Klonsky and other members of the NO staff, and SDS organizers from across the country met at the Sedgwick Center that night before we headed off to Lincoln Park and the first night of action. The feeling of excitement was overwhelming. I felt breathless. I had goosebumps. My stomach was all tied up in knots and I was edgy and giddy from the several hits of speed I had just taken. Sudden noises and motions made me tremble and start, and the jittery laughing and rapping of everyone else just added to my speed-induced frenzy.

Finally it was time to go to Lincoln Park. I followed behind Klonsky, and the New York Motherfuckers, who were the downright dirtiest, scuzziest, and loudest group of people I'd ever laid eyes on.[4] They always said that "SDS should talk less and drink more," and they lived their philosophy; everyone was roaring drunk and stoned when we left the Sedgwick Center that evening.

It was about eight o'clock, but it was still light outside. We walked in a small group swiftly to Lincoln Park, which was a very different scene from Sedgwick Center. The Center had a political, businesslike air about it; phones ringing constantly, "sharp struggle" over tactics and other political issues; piles of leaflets and underground newspapers; and official-looking, serious people concerned with bail, medical care, housing, march permits, and legal aid, constantly conferring. In contrast, the park was like a big be-in. Everyone was placidly smoking dope, making love, and wandering around listening to spontaneous "bands" playing on garbage cans, park benches, and tom-toms, and halfheartedly participating in some of the discussions going on.

In the center of a big circle of people sat Abbie Hoffman, loudly discoursing on SDS. He was highly critical, because SDS had not supported the demonstration until two weeks before it happened, and then only a small number of the broad SDS membership actually came to Chicago. He was also very critical of SDS because they worked on campuses instead of on the streets where the "people" were.

My sympathies were definitely with SDS, probably because all my political work had been on campus, and probably because I was still much too middle-class to accept the Yippies' utter contempt of everything Establishment. So I immediately resented Abbie Hoffman, sitting there in that ring of youthful admirers, pontificating against SDS. There was an air of pomposity about him that I found distasteful, and time and subsequent meetings haven't altered those initial flashes.

Plainclothes policemen, newspapermen, FBI agents, uniformed pigs proliferated the crowd, walking about with their walkie-talkies under their jackets. There were eyes everywhere. Undercover agents peered out from under shaggy manes of hippies; others posed as newspapermen, photographers, bikers, medics, and food venders. The only people you could really trust were those you knew.

This was my first street action and I was nervous. The speed had me quivering, and as Klonsky and I threaded our way through the crowded park, every noise, every motion made me jump. But I felt *good*. I could feel my body supple and strong and slim, and ready to run miles, and my legs moving sure and swift under me, and the hot sun growing pale as night came on cooling my sweat and fanning my perfume into my nose. I was ready to riot. And my feeling was buzzing through thousands of other young, strong people, who, laughing and singing, were building up momentum for the kinetic stomp through the Chicago Loop.

There were several speeches, one brief one by Bobby Seale of the Black Panthers. He ended his speech by wishing "power to the people."

About an hour later we began to move. From all directions the stoned and smiling flower children, the crew-cut and Oxford-shirted McCarthy students, the tie-and-jacketed Humphrey supporters, the stockinged and high-heeled sorority girls, the leather-jacketed greasers, helmeted bikers, springy walking, hotly dressed black dudes, ragamuffin hippies, baubled love children, and tense, urgent radicals streamed in spectacular color and rhythm out into the streets of Chicago chanting, "Take the streets," "The streets belong to the people," "Ho, Ho, Ho Chi Minh, Vietnam is gonna win," "Freedom now," "End the war in Vietnam"; screaming, laughing, jeering at spectators, giving the peace sign, the finger sign, the fist sign, in glorious profusion the Yippie action romped and glittered on toward the downtown section of Chi-town, the Loop.[5] After the first ten minutes everyone was on the streets and the traffic was stalled honking and groaning as the colorful youth threaded its way between the cars, and finally a huge crowd began to run down the streets of the August night.

All I could see were oceans and waves of running, chanting people around me, and glowing lights and neon signs flashing hotly, and the street lights flipping by above me, and the restaurants, movies, stores, and bars zipping by, and couples walking, looking dazed and terrified as we surged upon them. It was muggy-hot, and I was dripping sweat, but the breezes coming from Lake Michigan cooled me continuously. I began screaming chants with the crowd, until I couldn't scream any more. My arms were flung out in fists above my head and I pumped the air with them; I was boiling, singing, dancing, erupting with the spontaneous surge of freedom, of having the streets. Yes, I felt it, I knew it—crash—a gigantic rock hurled past my nose and a big bank window fell like billions of icicles. "End the war in Vietnam," "Power to the people"; smash—a spectator who tried to stop a man from throwing a rock was jammed up against a wall and bashed with a fist and he fell like a sack of potatoes. More rocks. The sound of shattering glass everywhere. Destroy the capitalists' property or else take it for the people. We gobbled up the night in a singing roar, violent and wild, saying clearly that we were on the side of the Vietnamese, on the side of freedom—and then the pigs were on us.

They closed in from all directions; from every street they came running, with their clubs stretched out before them like hardons; and they came smashing: heads, not windows; noses and teeth, not windshields; flesh and blood, not steel and glass. Blood streamed and spattered on me and I could hear the sickening thud of the club followed immediately by the crunch of breaking bones. In front of me, almost in slow motion, I saw a burly pig swing with all his might across the face of a pretty young man, and I saw the nose cave in and

I saw the teeth spill out of his mouth, and I felt the sickness rolling in me, and I stopped and puked.

Once a pale and terrified pig raced up to me, and for a second his club hovered in the air, and he stared at me, and then, screaming wildly, he backed away. Did I look like a witch, blood-spattered, with vomit hanging from my mouth in mucous streams, dirt-smeared, tears streaming down my face, hot, sweaty, and angry beyond despair? I wanted to kill.

The fighting went on not more than ten minutes, although it seemed like hours, and little by little the crowd thinned. I split down a side street, and hiding in an alley, tried to clean off my face with spit. As I sat there I could hear sirens and screams in the distance. A light breeze was still blowing, and I leaned my head against the building and listened to my heart pump.

I gradually became aware of a dull pain in my left leg behind my knee, where the leg bends; within a few minutes, the pain was unbearable, and I decided to find some help. I hopped on my right foot for a couple of blocks, and exhausted, sat down on the sidewalk near a traffic light. After it changed a couple of times, a man on a motorcycle came by, and gave me a ride to the Sedgwick Center.

About midnight Mike James came in. He was glowing with descriptions of his sojourns that night on the street. Mike offered to show me Chicago on the back of his motorcycle. Instantly my exhaustion vanished, and I felt like a new woman. I hobbled out and put on a helmet, and then slid in back of the chunky James.

The bike was big and smooth. The night was light and sultry and Mike knew every inch of Chicago, which he loved as much as I loved Seattle. We drove all over finally stopping at a funky little bar where a country-western band was playing and greaser-worker types and women with teased hair and heavily penciled eyes and high heels hung out, dancing and flirting. I drank some wine and drank in Mike James, until, at dawn, we returned together to the old house where I was crashing. We went into one of the large empty rooms, fell onto a bare mattress and made beautiful love.

The next two days passed swiftly. My leg continued to hurt me, and I went to have it examined at one of the Red Cross trucks stationed in Lincoln Park. A young medic told me that I had strained a ligament, and that I would have to stay off my leg for at least a week until it began to heal. I was horrified. I would miss the entire demonstration. People were sympathetic but firm; I would endanger myself and everyone I ran with if I went out into the streets and couldn't run fast; besides, some people were needed to handle the phones at the Center, and to take care of housing and bail. I was elected.

Thursday, the day of the big march to the amphitheater dawned hot and breezeless. I drove from the Sedgwick Center to Grant Park with J.J. and his brother. We parked several blocks from the park under a railroad trestle. We were rather quiet and tense. On the way downtown, we had driven past the amphitheater, and it looked like a scene from a war movie. There were a tank and several gigantic guns that may have been cannon; there were at least a dozen large army trucks and a militia of jeeps; rows of soldiers stood surrounding the building itself, and dozens were stationed at the periphery. All stood at attention and all were armed. It was frightening and we shivered as we passed by. There was no doubt in our minds that if the march ever got to the amphitheater there would be a tremendous bloodbath.

There were already thousands of people in Grant Park when we arrived. Hundreds of park benches had been set up in front of an outdoor amphitheater, where march officials would be speaking later. The usual mellowness of previous park scenes had vanished. Although the suited and high-heeled McCarthy kids could still be seen, the hippies and Yippies and other commie-type freaks were not quite as bedecked and bedangled and baubled as they had been three days ago. Dozens of people limped and leaned on canes or crutches; many more were bandaged in one place or another. Hundreds nursed cuts and gashes. People looked tired and serious.

Surrounding the immediate area around the amphitheater were rows of helmeted, riot-geared pigs, standing in formation, with their clubs gripped in front of them with both hands. Behind the pigs were troops with gas masks on, their rifles slung over their shoulders. There were jeeps with barbed wire strung around the top of them, so that nobody could attack the driver. There were army trucks and all kinds of military equipment. There were also small deployments of National Guardsmen in groups of twenty or thirty, standing in formation or marching.

I lay down shuddering on a piece of blanket, and looked at the clouds gauzy in the blue sky. I thought about bullets ripping through flesh, about napalmed babies. I thought about Malcolm X and lynching and American Indians.[6] Lying there, sweating from doses of speed and terror, I thought about Auschwitz, and mountains of corpses piled high in the deep pits dug by German Nazis. I closed my eyes tightly, but tears oozed from under my lids and rolled off my face.

A new feeling was struggling to be born in me. It had no name, but it made me want to reach beyond myself to others who were suffering. I felt real, as if suddenly I had found out something true about myself; that I was not helpless, that life meant enough to me to struggle for it, to take chances with it, to thrust out and wrestle with it. I thought about all the years I had been strangling my misery as I turned my cheek. Now it would be different; now I would fight.

As I lay on the grass thinking so deeply, a scuffle began not far from me. Somebody had attempted to lower the American flag, and replace it with a Vietcong flag. The pigs had intervened, and hand-to-hand fighting had resulted. I stayed where I was and watched as the fight grew.

Within a few minutes it had spread to include several hundred people and almost as many pigs. Suddenly a metal object about twice as large as a baseball whizzed through the air and landed a few yards from me with a pffft and immediately the air was foggy with tear gas. I began choking and gagging. At the same time my eyes burned and teared, and I had to squeeze them shut. I was gagging so badly that I fell on my knees, retching, clawing at my throat; I couldn't breathe.

All around me I could hear the shrieks and moans of the gassed people. I couldn't seem to move, and just stayed where I was, getting sicker, until I was plucked from my dark retching and dragged off to a point where the air was less poisoned. J.J. had run through all that tear gas and pulled me from the worst area, and pressed a cool wet rag over my scorched eyes. We found out later that the tear gas used that day had been developed especially for riots; it was known as CS gas and had a special chemical in it that induced nausea and vomiting and severe stomach cramps. It was known to be lethal to anyone with asthma, a weak heart or bad lungs.

Many of the people gassed had been McCarthy kids, who had just been sitting listening to speeches. They looked sullen. The glow was gone from their eyes and so was the rose from their scrubbed cheeks. They had been unjustly treated, and were pouting like spoiled children.

About one o'clock we began to leave the park in a line that stretched for several blocks. Suddenly the line stopped. A half hour passed, and people began to sit down in their places. Whispers—the pigs are coming; no—they are arguing about the parade permit. Rennie Davis was talking to the Chief of Pigs.[7] To march or not to march—that was the question. Finally we started moving, but those of us at the end of the line never knew if we had obtained permission to march or not. It didn't really matter anyway.

J.J. and I and a few others began to run alongside of the march, trying to reach the front. It took us quite a while to get there, and by this time people were in a dither of excitement and anticipation of heavy street fighting. We wanted to turn all this momentum downtown, away from the amphitheater.

There were some bullhorns at the front of the march, and I grabbed one and screamed into it about the pigs and tanks at the amphitheater, about the bloodbath; how there was nothing but open space there, no protective alleys to run down, or back streets to hide in. About thirty people began to turn toward downtown Chicago, when a diminutive black girl called Charlie Brown came flipping from the line and shrieked in a magnetic voice, "To the amphitheater," and with a yelp, the line became a mob and surged in the direction of the amphitheater. J.J. and I had no choice but to follow.

We must have run for several blocks, before the people in the front ran smack into a line of pigs. J.J. and I ran holding hands so that we wouldn't be torn away from each other in the chaos. But as the front ran against the rows of pigs, the people behind them turned around and began running back the way we had just come. They were terrified, screaming, whitefaced, eyes glazed; I had never seen such wild fear. They catapulted into J.J. and me, and our hands were torn apart. He was pulled with the crowd who was still heading toward the pigs, and I was pulled back by the part of the crowd running from them. That was the most frightening thing; being pulled along helplessly by the terrified, out of control mob, right into another army of pigs.

And they were smashing. Up and down with methodical persistence went those clubs, and blood began to spill, and the shrieks and moans of terror filled the air.

The police encircled about fifty of us, pressing us together in a smaller and smaller circle. The people around me began to kick and struggle like wild horses; I was punched and battered as they threw themselves about. I saw a bus drive near us, and to my horror, more police came out. I looked from the bus into the wild eyes of a pig. He was holding his club like a baseball bat and his lips were pulled back over his teeth, and he was giggling like a maniac. He was as scared as I was. I stared at him for a moment, and then he swung his club across my chest. The blow wasn't hard, but it was enough to knock me down.

I crawled among the falling and screaming people and right between the legs of a pig who was twisting the arms of a young girl and under the pig bus to the other side where, to my complete amazement, there was absolutely nobody to be seen. Limping, I began to run in the direction of the amphitheater until, a block away, I saw more fighting.

Every step was agony shooting up from my leg to the top of my shoulder. The pigs were only a half a block away now; I could see their faces as they ran straight toward me. They looked crazy and frightened. I ran to the right, and flattened myself against a building and continued to move slowly toward them. Suddenly I heard my name—I couldn't believe it. And right through the line of pigs came J.J. like a brown bullet. I was never so happy to see anybody in my life. He grabbed my hand, and half carried, half dragged me in back of an old warehouse.

After a while we gathered our courage and J.J. and I and a small group of people we had picked up along the way crept out onto the streets again, and headed for the Hilton. Several thousand people were gathered in front of the Hilton, milling around in the gathering dusk.

For a couple of hours there were minor skirmishes. But mostly everybody stood waiting for night to fall and give protection to our activities.

While we waited, the march of the poor people on their way to Washington and Resurrection City passed by.[8] The poor people wound their way down Michigan Avenue, walking quietly beside covered wagons pulled by swayback mules. They walked with solemn dignity, their heads held high, looking in wonder at us dirty, cheering radicals who lined the sidewalks and jammed the park to greet them as they passed. Tired, old, young, exhausted, eager, smiling, crying they came, fulfilling the dream of Martin Luther King. The whole group had an air about them of pilgrims going to the Holy Land. "I have a dream," King said. Luckily he was dead and could not see the dream wallowing in the mud, filth, and despair of Resurrection City as the nation's poor stumbled up the steps of the nation's Capitol and were received with the withering sounds of silence and not even a token attempt at understanding.

We began to shrill like the Algerian women.[9] Up Michigan Avenue, searing up to the top floor of the Hilton, to the dignified, benign and honeysuckle-rosed McCarthy, to the fat-paunched, heaving, pasty-faced Humphrey, to their compatriots and campaign supporters, to the youth who believed in them. The cries rose and fell, waking up the night, waking up the blood, waking up the hearts of youth who had grown depressed and fallow in the great universities, and with a vibrating scream, the children of America exploded and the streets were filled with streaming bodies, and once again we were fighting.

Cars were stalled everywhere, honking, their petrified drivers and occupants gagging and crying from the tear gas. And up on the top floor of the Hilton, the air conditioner carried into Humphrey and McCarthy the noxious fumes until those two venerable candidates were puking and gagging like the rest of us. And out on the streets more of their children were getting their heads cracked open.

J.J. and I ran miles that night before ten o'clock. As the battle continued, a pattern became clear. The people would mass, then race into the streets throwing rocks, and the pigs would attack with clubs and those awful-looking jeeps protected by barbed wire. These jeeps were used viciously; the driver would simply drive into a cluster of people and mow them down.

Around one o'clock that night, exhausted but exuberant, J.J. and I returned to my crash pad. We took a boiling shower together, tumbled into bed, made love, and fell asleep immediately.

I hadn't wanted to spend the night with J.J. at all, but he had done so much for me that day, I felt almost obligated to sleep with him. There was something obnoxious about him; like an insecure and lonely kid, coming on so tough, hoping that no one would guess how miserable he was. When I thought of J.J. then, and for the next year, I would think of a young punk whose occasional brilliance couldn't quite make up for all his other irksome characteristics. At the same time, there was something about J.J. that required respect; maybe it was those blasts of genius that would cut through hours of Movement rhetoric in a minute, so startlingly clear and cogent, that no one could begin to argue with him. Maybe it was the fact that he showed a street mentality that was undeniably unique; he never deserted anyone, no matter how much the danger to himself. And if he talked tough, then at least his actions matched his theory. This was not always true of all SDS heavies. All too frequently there were leaders who willingly formulated great theories about fighting in the streets, and then stayed off the streets when the fighting began.

There was another day of demonstrations following the Hilton Massacre, but to me they were insignificant. I vaguely remember a Candlelight March led by Dick Gregory and dominated by older pacifists.[10] I scorned them ruthlessly at the time. Their peace march was an affront after the butchery of the past few days. They were marching in the blood of my friends and peers; their peacefulness was like a slur in the face of the spirit and courage of the previous day's activity.

I was invited to a National Interim Committee (NIC) meeting of SDS officers, following the Democratic Convention. I was enthusiastic about going, because I was stunned by some of the SDS people I'd met from around the country, and I considered it an honor to be in their presence. Also, I was caught up in a sexual frenzy. All I could think about was fucking. First Mike James, then J.J. had let loose a torrent of libidinal drives in me. At the NIC would be lots of men— tough, handsome, virile SDS men. As fucked up as it seems, as embarrassed as I am to admit it, sex motivated most of my political ventures for the next few months.

During the car ride to Indiana, where the NIC was meeting on a farm, someone explained to me that it was composed of eleven people, all of whom were National Officers elected by SDS membership during the annual June National Convention. Some of the NIC members were NO staff. The NIC was largely responsible for decision making in SDS.

The National Office that year consisted of Mike Klonsky as National Secretary, Bernardine Dohrn as Inter-Organizational Secretary, and Fred Gordon as Educational Secretary. These three people were responsible for running the NO. Among the other eight people on the NIC that year were Mike James, who had been on the NIC for three years, Carl Oglesby, one of the earlier SDS National Secretaries, and a man who I didn't know yet named Chip Marshall, an SDS organizer at Cornell University who was now doing regional traveling in the Niagara region. Mark Rudd, now a national figure because of his role in the Columbia University strikes, was an alternate to the NIC.[11]

I felt like a groupie on my way to Indiana. Gee, I was going to mingle with the stars. The Movement was my milieu, and people like Rudd and Oglesby were the superstars of the Movement.

I was totally exhausted when I arrived at the farm in Indiana, and sick from constantly taking speed. I remember little of that first day, except that I was trying hard not to collapse in the middle of a Great Debate between Klonsky and someone else. I finally crept out of the meeting room and up a flight of stairs. In the hallway was a bare mattress, on the floor. I lay down on it, shivering and shuddering, longing for sleep. My eyes were closed but I became aware of a presence leaning over me. I opened my eyes to the warm, homely and concerned face of Carl Oglesby. He was gently covering me with a blanket. Then he kissed me on the cheek. I couldn't talk; just looked up at him, gratefully. Then I fell into a deep sleep.

I woke up late the next morning. Everybody was sitting in practically the same place, as if the meeting had gone on all night. I discovered I had to shit, and decided to do it outside.

Outside, deep yellow sunlight, golden fields of grain, and pea-green trees. Everything was rich and warm. I started down a dirt road, and several hundred yards from the house, I ducked into the grain and crouched. I had just finished when a man came walking down the road, whistling. He was tall and kind of stooped. Every once in a while he'd stop whistling and carefully taking aim, he'd throw a rock at a tree. Then he'd bend down, pick up another rock, whistle and amble a bit, and then stop and throw the rock with great absorption. He turned when he heard me coming out of the grain.

He smiled. I got the impression of everything being too long, almost awkward. Too much arms, too much legs, too big a head, too much eyebrow. He looked like the kind of person who might trip over his left foot.

The rock-throwing whistler had an engaging smile. "Who-r-y?" he asked amiably. I told him my name. He had steely blue eyes that seemed to go right through me. "From Seattle, eh?" he said. I was surprised. As if reading my mind . . . "I've heard of your husband, Robby." Of course. Robby. I should have known.

"Who are you?" I asked in a timid voice. The man razed me with his steely blues. On his face was an unmistakable look of contempt. I was seething with resentment just looking at him.

"Mark Rudd," he said testily. Then he turned immediately and began whistling again. I felt I was expected to follow him.

So this is the famous Mark Rudd. This cocky kid!

In his rather scornful manner, somewhat like a king talking to a peon, he questioned me closely concerning my thoughts on the days of the Democratic Convention. But no matter what I said, Rudd turned it around so that I felt like a creep. There was no way to escape the fact that I was white, female, from a wealthy family, Jewish, had been married, was well educated, had been a ghetto schoolteacher, etc. The obvious reaction to Rudd's contempt for me never crossed my mind; he was from a similar background. But instead of thinking the obvious, I took Rudd very seriously and felt as debased as I used to feel when my CORE and SNCC friends put down white Movement people as liberals. Feeling totally shattered in front of the regal Rudd, I was relieved when he suggested that we return to the NIC meeting.

Some of the discussion at the NIC included criticism of the National Office's participation in the Convention demonstrations. Instead of sticking to organizing, Klonsky and others had encouraged SDSers to form "affinity groups"; small groups of people, highly mobile, who could use guerrilla tactics on the streets. Some of the people on the NIC resented the fact that the NO had organized with greater militancy than had been expected.

As the meeting progressed, I slowly became aware that nobody in the NO agreed with anybody else. Klonsky and Bernardine Dohrn, who wasn't there, agreed more closely than either of them did with Fred Gordon. No one agreed with Fred Gordon, because he was with the Progressive Labor Party (PL), a faction within SDS. It got confusing after a while. But one thing became clear. As in Seattle, whoever talked loudest and fastest always won the argument. In Seattle it had been Robby; at this NIC it was definitely Klonsky or Rudd. Other people had other roles, but those two and a few others dominated.

Rudd, whom people listened to with total respect, was flippant and cocky when arguing. Amazingly, everything he said was brilliant. Then there were a few hippie women who spoke. They were barely listened to. Oglesby would smile musingly, Klonsky would twiddle his hair or his fingers, Rudd would pace around the room banging on objects, other women who knew better would look embarrassed. I would sit expectantly, waiting for some revolutionary gems to fall from the mouths of these fearless women who dared to speak at meetings; most of their offerings were procedural, and not very substantive.

That evening was good old fun. Lots of wine and dope. Oglesby had a good country-and-western voice and played the guitar. He sang, and we all sang with him. When I began to sing, people stopped and listened; it was the only time I had been noticed the entire day. J.J. never left me alone. He hung around wherever I was; I thought it was absurd. There were times when he was so nice to me that I wanted to kick him. In the past I've found it very hard to respect people who liked me too much. I had such a low opinion of myself; they had to be really dumb to like me. So I resented J.J. for being so nice to me. When he spoke in front of the group, it was like an earthquake. He never stopped until he had finished what he had to say. I was always amazed that he could think fast enough to string his thoughts together so brilliantly.

When the NIC ended, somebody drove me to O'Hare Airport, and I caught a plane to New York. My mother would be waiting for me at the airport, which had been changed from Idlewild to Kennedy in my absence. I had been away two years.

My first couple of weeks in New York I had to scrounge to stay alive. I crashed on floors and couches, slept in Grand Central Station one night, and lived off the hot dog venders. I saw my parents only briefly.

At first I tried to stay away from SDS. I worked for Liberation News Service collating their news packets.[1] One day, in the middle of September, they sent me to report on a registration day demonstration at Columbia University. When I got there, the only person I recognized was Mark Rudd. He was sitting beneath a statue, slumped in the position of Rodin's The Thinker, and he looked tired and depressed. He eyed me as I approached. Immediately I was intimidated. I don't know why Rudd had such control over my self-esteem. Klonsky was just as authoritarian, yet he made me feel as if I had some contribution to make to the Movement, no matter how meager.

Rudd was very concerned about the registration demonstration and wasn't very talkative, so I meandered off to observe it for myself. It was an abysmal failure. A small group of students rushed the iron door of the gym, where registration was in progress, and the Columbia administration closed registration for the day. It was continued without incident the following day.

I stood there wondering exactly how I was going to report such a farce, when a slender man with olive skin and dark eyes approached me, smiling. He introduced himself as Jose. We stood there and talked for a while. He told me about an International Students Conference being held at Columbia that night, where radicals and Communists from student groups around the world were meeting to share ideas and experiences. He suggested that I might find it interesting. Taken with Jose, I told him I'd come.

At the International Students Conference we heard stories from Palestinian guerrillas, Parisian students, SDS organizers from West Berlin, and representatives from other European countries and several South American countries. As I listened to the stories of building seizures and street fighting in Paris and Berlin and Mexico City, I realized that they weren't any different from the Democratic Convention. Everyone was fighting for the same thing all over the world; freedom, and an end to war and poverty.

Jose and I spent the next couple of days together. We made love casually; mostly we talked. He told me about the Columbia Strikes of the previous spring and about some of the expectations SDS had for the coming year at Columbia. It was obvious from what Jose said that SDS wanted to close down the campus, repeating the successful strikes of the spring before.

At the time I met Jose, I was very uncertain about my future. The two months in California had confused me politically; I hadn't been able to relate to any group. In Berkeley everyone was too intellectual, and in Los Angeles everyone was too tedious. Also, I wasn't sure if my involvement with SDS had been because of Robby or because I was really interested in doing political work. Now that we were separated, I didn't know if I wanted to be active. All this I told Jose, struggling to find a place for myself in life that had some meaning.

It was through Jose that I met most of the people in Columbia SDS. He took me to a meeting in the Student Union Building after a couple of days and introduced me to the two other men who, along with him, more or less controlled SDS at Columbia, with some occasional outside guidance from Rudd and J.J. and Bernardine Dohrn, when she was in New York. They were known as the Big Three. It was also through Jose that I found a place to live.

Although I had been at Columbia only two weeks I had already made a life for myself. I began spending time at the New York

Regional Office. Jose and several others from the Columbia SDS hard core would go down to the Regional Office for meetings about the Election Day demonstration. Going to the Regional Office was always a hairy experience for me; practically everyone intimidated me. Mark Rudd was generally there; he would corner me and ask me questions, sometimes about Robby, sometimes about what I was doing at Columbia. I never overcame my dislike for him; I also never felt that he approved of me.

One day I was at the Regional Office, waiting for a meeting to begin, when a woman I had never seen before walked in. She was not so much beautiful as she was commanding; there was something in the way she carried herself that exuded authority. She had large breasts, which were partially exposed because her blouse was half unbuttoned. She wore no make-up, and her straight hair fell in wisps around her shoulders. Her eyes were clear and steady, but not unfriendly as she gazed at me and in a tone that assumed an answer asked me who I was. I introduced myself. She introduced herself. Her name was Bernardine Dohrn. Here was the woman I had been hearing about for so long.

After a few minutes of desultory conversation, she moved on to more pressing matters. My meeting her, as casual as it was, thrilled me. The way she spoke and moved; such control, such self-assurance, such elegance. She immediately became a symbol of what I hoped to become. At the same time I felt helplessly inadequate in the face of all that splendor.

Once the meeting began, Bernardine stood on one side, and said little. Yet her presence seemed to dominate the room. Many times the men would glance at her quickly before they started to speak. Some men just stared at her openly. The few times she spoke she was quietly forceful. Although she didn't appear to choose her words carefully, they made such sense, they seemed like a prepared speech. I barely took my eyes off her the entire meeting. J.J. was there, but he was noticeably cooler to me this time. It was rumored that he and Bernardine were lovers. My immediate reaction was "What's a splendid woman like that doing with that kid?" But at that meeting J.J. seemed more poised than I had ever seen him. As brusque as always, when he spoke he did so with a brilliance that was undeniable.

Organizing for Election Day, I also got to know some of the Newsreel people. Newsreel was a group who made movies about the Movement. Several people from Columbia would truck down to Newsreel and meet with other New York groups to discuss strategy for the Election Day demonstration. The New York Motherfuckers would sporadically attend these meetings, adding a little color, and passing around wine and marijuana.

Columbia SDS had begun organizing in early October around the elections in November, as did SDS chapters across the country. The slogan of the organizing was "Vote in the streets, vote with your feet," and it was seen as direct opposition to Nixon's campaign slogan for law and order. Out of the organizing around the elections came the Columbia People's Street Theater.

The Street Theater was the most significant work I did during my stay in New York. We wrote at least three plays, after hours of political discussion, argument and analysis. These plays we performed for almost every college and high school in New York, and on all major street corners as well.

The best play the Street Theater did was called *Under the Pig Top*. The play was a major organizing tool for the Election Day demonstration. It was so effective we performed it everywhere we could and gave the script to anyone interested in reading it. Our motto was a familiar one that year: THAT IS ONLY THE START, WE'LL CONTINUE TO FIGHT!

The manner in which we presented the politics of the play was both funny and serious. Wherever we performed, crowds of people milled around us. The crowds grew so huge at times that the pigs would disperse the group. We always incorporated this into the play.

I went to meetings constantly. They were largely governed by the Big Three. Occasionally J.J. or Rudd or some of the Regional Office staff would come to a meeting, but the Columbia chapter resented national or regional interference and it was the Big Three who chaired meetings and articulated the primary political issues.

Organizing for the Election Day demonstration, I felt I was part of a vast network of intense, exciting and brilliant people. I was amazed at the genius in SDS. I was galvanized by the energy. I went to every SDS meeting, worked endlessly on every rally, demonstration, and open forum we organized. I was learning all the time and loving it. Enthralled as I was with political activity and political people, I couldn't understand why everybody didn't want to be in SDS. Nothing in my life had ever been this exciting. Careening from meeting to meeting, from demonstration to demonstration, from man to man, I wondered how I had lived a middle-class existence for so long. I knew that that part of my life was over. I would never again know how to be or want to be Susan Stern—student, housewife, potential mother.

Besides the meetings I found time to be a Regional organizer, and traveled to high schools, community colleges, talking about the Election Day demonstration, and after they were over, about the war and racism. I did mountains of shit work. I wrote leaflets, typed them, mimeoed them, and passed them out. I performed with the Street Theater throughout the fall and winter in all five boroughs of New York, at all hours of the day and night. And I loved every minute of it. I had all the excitement and activity I had ever yearned for.

During all those months I kept my mouth shut and listened and learned. In spite of all I learned I still couldn't talk at meetings, even of the hard core. I would think of something to say and then my heart would start pounding madly and I would feel like gagging and keep my mouth shut. It always amazed me when a man would stand up and say just what I'd been thinking. I realized that I could have said it just as well, but I still felt powerless to speak until the year was almost over.

Just before Election Day, Jay came from Seattle. I was never sure why he came, but I wasn't happy about it. With him he brought memories I had been diligently suppressing. Also, I considered New York my turf, and I didn't want anybody from Seattle intruding on it. I didn't want to be responsible for introducing Jay around; I didn't want to help him find a place to live. In short, I didn't want to be his friend.

When I think back to that time, I am disgusted with myself. I was caught up in the worst of possible Movement tendencies—elitism.

In New York it was all business and little play, and Jay's sweet dis-
position was overshadowed by stronger personalities who used their
extensive educational backgrounds like levers against people who
weren't as well educated. He could never keep up his part in an
argument, or even a discussion with Jose or other SDS heavies; he
hadn't read a lot of books, and he didn't know a lot of big words. He
knew a lot about life, but in New York that meant nothing. After a
couple of weeks, unable to make any friends at SDS, and probably
feeling my aloofness, Jay went to work at *The Guardian* newspaper
as a delivery boy. I rarely saw him after that.

As hard as we worked for the Election Day demonstration, it was
a fiasco. Thousands of people turned out for the rally downtown,
but then instead of rioting we ambled in orderly fashion up the
street, chaperoned by pigs on foot and horseback. Paddy wagons
were parked on all the street corners, and there were almost as many
uniformed pigs present as demonstrators. That night, during the
election returns, people tried to start something. But the pigs were so
well prepared and so methodical, that no one could do anything.

The Election Day demonstration seemed prophetic for SDS at
Columbia that year. While campuses were closing like Venus's-
flytraps on administrations across the country, Columbia continued
with business as usual.

Part of the problem with Columbia SDS, and everywhere else,
was that it was operating at 50 per cent of its potential. Women were
almost systematically excluded from anything but a secondary role
throughout the fall and into the winter. When we did begin to force
the male leadership to share the radical burden with us, the inexpe-
rience of the women, and the uncertainty with which the male leadership reacted to the growing strength of women, weakened the
entire chapter drastically.

Toward winter it became clear to all factions of SDS that women
intended to be seen and heard. It was gradual and painstaking but
relentless. Women began to attend meetings in clusters, to sit in
groups, and to raise their hands simultaneously in response to arguments. All too frequently we would sit with our hands dangling in
the air, waiting patiently to be recognized, while the chairman looked

over us, or around us, or through us, and called on some man who made a twenty-minute speech with two minutes' worth of substance.

The mounting fury of the SDS women was finally reflected in action in January, when two demonstrations were organized and led primarily by women. Both actions essentially failed, but they did give SDS women a taste of leadership.

The first action was against Marine recruiters coming to Columbia. I did my first reconnaissance for an action; I checked out all the escape routes in a building. The plan was to gain entrance to the Marine recruiter's office, overwhelm him by sheer numbers, tie him up, and carry him out to Lowe Plaza and leave him there in front of the students. But the recruiter canceled, and we never got a chance to carry out our action. We took this as a victory, until a few days later the recruiters showed up off campus.

So we tried to off the recruiters again. They were now housed in a building called Casa Hispanica. The women and their cohorts unsuccessfully tried to lob stink bombs into the windows of Casa Hispanica, but the bombs fell short; the streets around 116th Street and Broadway smelled like rotten eggs for several days, and so did some SDSers. And someone who had been assigned to short-circuit the electrical system of the building got stoned instead. So what might have been a very good attack on the recruiters fizzled into a small mob raging and cursing outside Casa Hispanica.

During my ten-month stay in New York, I attended two SDS National Council (NC) meetings. The first was in December in Ann Arbor, Michigan.

After the long, uncomfortable drive, during which we had two accidents, we arrived at the NC exhausted. Everyone there looked fresh and invigorated. The convention was chaotic. People were everywhere, waving pamphlets, hawking leaflets, and debating strenuously. There were rows of tables with every kind of Movement literature imaginable covering them.

People from the Movement remember me with some disdain for my NC wardrobe, which consisted of a black miniskirt that barely covered my ass and some sleazy blouse that barely covered my breasts, high-heeled boots, earrings and make-up. Nearly everyone else was in the inevitable unisex outfit. Movement threads consisted of tight blue jeans and a blue jean shirt, and little variation. The major issues of the meeting were racism, the "women question," and the position of youth in the revolution. At the plenary where the council met as a whole before breaking down into workshops, the writers of the various resolutions submitted them to the SDS delegates and members at large. Then each proposal was debated for hours, and finally the delegates voted for or against them.

Mike Klonsky erupted with his usual flair, and presented a resolution entitled "Toward a Revolutionary Youth Movement" (RYM). The RYM proposal shifted SDS away from organizing students and toward organizing youth as a group by itself, with special emphasis on working class youth. Passage of the proposal would be decisive in moving SDS from the campuses and into the streets. It was this orientation that also laid the basis for Weatherman.

The last two days of the NC dragged on. Arguments between PL and the remainder of SDS were continuous.[2] I got lost in the endless rhetoric. I got tired of the constant repetition over issues I barely understood. My insight was dim. The brightest time of the NC for me was meeting two friends from Seattle and hearing all the gossip from the city I still considered home.

NCs usually end joyously, I was told by a friend. This one was no exception. At the end of the last plenary, the chairman called for contribution for the National Office. While people went up and down the aisles collecting money, half of SDS stood singing loudly and chanting Ho Ho Ho Chi Minh, while the PL faction stood opposite chanting Mao Mao Mao Tse-tung. On both sides the chants got louder and soon we were standing on chairs and screaming our heads off.

I was so naïve. It was easy to get angry at PL, to return to New York feeling elated because our major resolutions had passed, especially Klonsky's RYM proposal. So easy, and so fatal. It was the warming-up exercises for the June Convention when SDS would cleave itself in half and begin its slow, painful death.

The first few months I lived in New York I had money left over from a wedding gift my father had given me, but that soon ran out. In November and December I began to support myself illegally. I stole most of my food from chain supermarkets, which were still buying scab grapes. I ate meat every night; I was an expert thief. To pay my rent, I had other means of getting money. I cashed phony checks. I would get a bank account in a phony name and dress in clothes I had stolen from the most exclusive department stores. I would go back to those same exclusive department stores to cash my phony checks. Coming from a rich family, I had always shopped in these stores. It never felt as though I was doing anything illegal. I belonged there. I knew how to smile at the salesgirls and look them right in the eye totally innocently while I cashed a phony check. Occasionally I'd take my mother or grandmother along while I did my stealing. They looked very respectable and middle-class. "Such a lovely girl," the ogling saleswomen would say to my beaming mother or grandmother. And while they talked about how lovely I was, I stuffed a sixty-dollar sweater into my pocketbook, or a bottle of Joy perfume into my pocket.

Once I was walking down Broadway, and I found a check for $150 just lying in the street. It was a pay check, made out to a woman. I forged a signature, and walked into the first bank I came to. The teller said, "Do you have an account here," and I said, "Yes." Then as she took my check and started leafing through the bankbooks, I looked around and froze. There were two pigs standing right behind me. I watched the teller leafing through the bankbook, and remained standing at the counter, feeling faint. After a while she returned to the counter, smiled at me, and said, "Here's your money." I couldn't believe it! She was black and I don't know if that had anything to do with it, but out of the hundreds of banks in New York, I couldn't have picked the one where the woman whose pay check I cashed really had an account. I was sure I was going to jail right then. I should have gone to jail many times. I was so lucky. And so arrogant. After a time I was convinced that I would never be caught.

To supplement my stealing, my biggest scam was what I ironically dubbed *"flesh."* I had an agency that knew me only as Susan. When I needed money, I gave them a call. They would get me a body-painting job, or a topless job, or arrange for me to make a dirty movie. Each job would take only a few hours and it paid very well.

People may be horrified that a bonafide Women's Liberationist obtained money in this manner, but when it came to paying for the endless leaflets, no one hassled me about where the money came from. The Movement came first. It didn't matter how I supported my habit. And, to be really honest, I never saw anything wrong with my topless dancing, or my body-painting experiences. They were certainly more exciting and less dehumanizing than secretarial work, and they paid about ninety times better. My "flesh" work, my stealing, was all to make time for my radical activity.

The factionalism within the chapter increased, yet SDS appeared to be growing. *New Left Notes*, the SDS newspaper, *The Guardian*, and other underground papers declared its growth across the country. Colleges with SDS chapters were constantly erupting.

I had plowed through the heavy ideological debates with enthusiasm during the fall because I thought we were building to close down the campus during the winter. But the winter was half gone and nothing had happened. SDS persistently planned for the Big Event, but somehow the plans seemed hollow, and the winter months dragged on.

We slowly began to leave the campus, gravitating to the high schools. For weeks I traveled to predominantly black high schools in the Bronx, and stood freezing while handing out leaflets. But nothing much came of our organizing. The only time we got a response was when the Street Theater performed.

In March SDS successfully seized two buildings, and had a one-day strike against Columbia. To ensure the success of these actions, the chapter had spent a lot of time organizing in dormitories, classrooms, and at rallies. The major demand for these actions were open admissions to Columbia for all Third World students. It was an exhausting month, but many students were organized when it was over.

Then on March 25, the Columbia chapter piled into several derelict cars and began the long trek to Austin, Texas, and the spring NC. I could barely contain myself. I was so nervous, because I had heard through the SDS grapevine that Robby was also attending the council meeting.

Almost as soon as I arrived in Austin, Robby approached me, and we sat down not at all awkwardly and had a nice, polite conversation in which he told me that he had been living with another woman for months, was very much in love with her and was very happy. That made it much easier for me to relate to him; he now belonged to someone else. I found I was not as upset as I thought I would be.

As an overture of casual friendship, Robby took me to a meeting of the Michigan-Ohio and New York Regions. The meeting was dotted with familiar faces, but there were many new people. Everyone was very excited and appeared to be very together. They were talking about SDS people going to major cities for the summer, forming collectives, and seeking employment in factories where they could work with young workers.

I listened dully at first. Then the excitement in the room caught me. I looked around at the faces. All young, beautiful, all forceful, including the women. A sandy-haired man with gold-rimmed glasses and an engaging smile got up and introduced himself as Bill Ayers.[3] Then he began to talk quietly but dynamically. The room was captivated as he enthusiastically explained the concepts of collective, cadre, exemplary action and white fighting force.

"If the working class won't come to us," he said, glowing, "then we'll go to the working class. In the factories, in the bars, at the laundromat, on the army bases, at cab stands and on baseball diamonds, we'll be there and we'll be talking. We'll be everywhere, rapping it down about youth, and how this motherfucking country is dying, but we are just beginning to live. We're going to work this summer and study and organize and then we are going to bring the revolution out into the streets."

Carl Oglesby was the only one standing in the room. "Listen," he said urgently. "You can't just get a job in a factory for the summer and think that a man who has been struggling on his job for twenty years is suddenly going to leave and go out into the streets with you. You're young, from wealthy backgrounds. You can always go back to school, on to some luxury job someday. The worker has shit, and still won't have anything after you get bored working in the factory for a few months, decide he's counterrevolutionary, and go back to your ivory-tower radicalism again. Please listen to me. . ." but most of the people in the room ignored him.

"From here on in there's no middle, Oglesby," someone shouted from the group. "Only one side or the other," and they went on with their discussion. Oglesby slumped out, looking defeated.

Oglesby had been one of SDS's first presidents. Well, he had had his turn, I thought, now they would get theirs. Who would come next, convinced that theirs was the only way?

Most of the meeting was one battle after another between PL and the remainder of SDS. The National Office had come to this council prepared, and the three important resolutions that were debated were passed in favor of the NO, making PL more antagonistic than ever.

I met three other people at the Austin NC who would have a great impact on my life in the next year. The first was Michael Justesen, a Seattle-born man who, at eighteen, was already considered an important part of the leadership of SDS at the University of Washington. Robby introduced him to me proudly. We talked about Ayers's proposal, and about the burning of an ROTC building on the U of W campus. Mike was very hopeful that a major strike could be organized on the campus before spring quarter ended.

Mike was tall and gangly; his hair jutted out at unexpected places, and his eyes were hidden behind thick glasses. His angular face was roughly handsome, but he never looked at me when he talked. His eyes stayed on his shoes. There was something so cynical, so deadly serious about Mike, despite his youth, that it almost put me off. At the same time, there was a quality of great patience, making him seem old and gentle. I liked him from that first meeting, and was impressed by his quiet brilliance when he spoke.

I also met Joe Kelly and Chip Marshall there for the first time. While lounging in the big room where the plenary was convening, a boy who looked about sixteen came waltzing up to me and said, "Hi, Kate," mistaking me for a girl who lived in my apartment.

"I'm not Kate," I told him.

"So you're not Kate. Well, who are you?" He smiled and two great dimples appeared on either side of his mouth. Curly hair sprang all over the place in a sort of Afro, and blue eyes twinkled above rosy cheeks in his boyish face.

"I'm Susan Stern."

"I'm Joe Kelly, from Cornell," and he began a stream of commentary about the Convention that went on for ten minutes. I couldn't help laughing with him. Joe was so merry it was contagious. While we were talking, Chip Marshall, a Niagara Regional organizer in SDS at Cornell came and stood near us. Joe introduced us; a faint sign of recognition crossed Chip's face. We had seen each other around. Chip, unlike Joe, was not very talkative. He seemed very interested in the debate in the plenary, and was staring at each speaker, frowning. Every once in a while, he would pace back and forth, or shake his head. He had dark hair and a grand mustache, and was powerfully built like an athlete. He walked like Charlie Chaplin.

Suddenly Chip went bounding off in the direction of the mike. Joe gave me a huge bear hug, and went flying after Chip. I felt as if I had known him for a long time. (Only a year later Joe, Chip and I would be co-defendants in a conspiracy trial.) Threads run a patchwork quilt across the country, connecting in the strangest places.

The months following the NC, Columbia SDS was in a frenzy. We were spread out all over the place, trying to organize everybody, and not succeeding. We had alienated the majority of high school students primarily because we told them they had bad politics, and they didn't like our supercilious attitude even if we were right. We also hadn't made contacts with kids on the street.

At the end of April, SDS seized Philosophy Hall. In trying to keep the pigs out of the building, I did my first real damage to one of them; I threw a Coke bottle, which hit him across the forehead. He staggered back looking stunned. I waited to feel nauseated as I saw the red ribbon of blood deepen across his face and begin to drip down his nose. But I felt exhilarated. I wasn't frightened. I stayed in front of the action. For once the odds were with us; there were about twenty security guards and about thirty of us. We beat them back.

The seizure of Philosophy Hall had been the Big Event we had been waiting for all year, but again, it didn't happen. Our major demand was for full open admissions for Third World students. The black students felt that we would ruin their chances of getting open admissions if we continued to hold the building. They had their own ways of dealing with the administration; that year it was primarily talking, and through established boards and committees. Philosophy Hall was our last real chance to cause a confrontation that year on the Columbia campus, and it didn't happen. But on May 1, still not willing to give up, SDS seized two buildings—Math and Fayerweather Halls and kept them for a day and a night. The takeover of Math Hall was organized as a cadre action; telling no one of our plans, the hard core simply did it early in the morning. Then we notified the campus that a building had been taken, and asked others to join us. People stood outside all day and looked at the building, calling to people inside. By evening a citation for contempt of court was served against the leadership. All night we debated whether to stay or not. A feeling of defeat hung over everybody. Finally, toward dawn, we left. Beaten, depressed, miserable and confused, we slowly left Math and Fayerweather. It was desolation row.

Jose and several others went to jail for a month. I cried along with everybody else when we found out that they were actually going to jail. White students went to jail for a month while Black Panthers were killed.

Just about the time the Columbia SDS leadership went to jail, the New York Lawyers Guild came out with a pamphlet entitled *The Bust Book*. This was a very detailed manual to Movement people about their rights when busted, and what procedure they should follow under such circumstances. By the spring of 1969, it was obvious that the Movement was in for a reign of repression. One of the authors of the *Bust Book* was Kathy Boudin.[4] She was very friendly with Karen Clark, one of my roommates. That was always a source of pain to me.

At different times, as the year had passed, Kathy had come to my apartment. At first she had come to visit in general. As time passed, it became clear that she was coming to see Karen.

Toward the end of spring, when there was a sudden hot spell, Kathy Boudin invited Karen to spend a few days at a friend's town house in Greenwich Village while the parents were out of town. I was crushed that I wasn't invited. Once again I wondered what it was that differentiated me from Karen in the eyes of a woman like Kathy whom I admired for the same reason I admired Bernardine Dohrn. They had a strength and self-possession that I hoped to achieve someday. I equated this quality common to all of them with real liberation.

The rest of my apartment was finally invited down to the town house for dinner and a midnight swim. Karen looked right at home there; I felt out of place. The two superior women seemed to exclude me. Their grasp of theory, and their own sense of identity put them in a different realm. I wondered if I'd ever know enough to contribute as they did to the revolution.

Kathy overwhelmed me. No matter how much she ignored my approaches to her, I wanted to be around her any way I could. So when I heard her talking to Karen about needing someone to oversee the distribution of the *Bust Book*, I volunteered.

I spent days at the Lawyers Guild Office helping Kathy, the lawyers, and other volunteers collate *Bust Books*. When they were all in piles, I took thousands of copies to my apartment in cartons. Then I spent hours calling SDS chapters all over the city. People would come and take as many *Bust Books* as they thought they could realistically distribute to their chapters before the year ended. Some charged a quarter a book; most were given away free.

The few times I had to approach Kathy concerning the distribution of the *Bust Book,* she had such an air of authority about her that I quivered inside. Women like Kathy and Bernardine could do things like write *Bust Books;* I could only distribute their work. They made up the theories, and I followed them.

Kathy affected me like Mark Rudd. She frightened me to death. She stirred the deepest of my insecurities by her aloof demeanor. How humiliated I always felt in her presence, because I was so inarticulate, my thoughts were so scattered, and I was prey to the demons of my body rather than the cool detachment of my intellect. Kathy seemed above sexual need, beyond the petty and childish fantasies I still secreted about falling in love and being loved. This is not to say that Kathy or Bernardine, or any of the forceful female leadership of SDS were anything like I saw them. They might have been as desperately insecure and lonely as I was, for all I know. But their commitment to the revolution seemed to grow from more profound and enduring roots than mine.

I understand, now, how deceiving appearances are. When I later became a leader in Seattle, other women feared and resented me as I feared and resented Kathy. To women and men who didn't know me, I was arrogant, impetuously strong and egotistical. Strange that I have never been able to see myself as others see me. Maybe it was the same with Kathy.

Just prior to the takeover of Math and Fayerweather, the Panther 21 were indicted for conspiracy to blow up Macy's Department Store and the Botanical Gardens in Brooklyn.[5] I would have choked with laughter over such charges, except that the government was serious about pressing them. I spent all that night at the Regional Office calling SDS chapters throughout New York to organize a demonstration outside 100 Centre Street, the courthouse, for the next day. Russ Neufeld, a New England Regional Organizer, flew in from Boston to aid in fund raising and to work with other organizers to build white support for the 21. Russ struck me as a serious and quiet person, quite different from the aggressive, charismatic style that characterized so many SDS men. His reputation as a hard and devoted organizer had earned him national respect, rather than a notorious reputation.

The next day there were several hundred people at 100 Centre Street. Considering that we had only one night to organize the demonstration, it was a pretty good turnout. We were nonviolent and we walked around in a picket line chanting "Free the Panther 21."

As I walked around the line I felt a presence at my side and looked up into the face of a friend of mine, Sam Melville. He looked drawn and exhausted. He wasn't smiling and he didn't have much to say. He seemed like a totally different person and it was obvious that his mind was not on the picket line.

We trudged around for maybe a half an hour, when Sam suddenly sighed and said drearily, "I'm living in hell, but it will soon be over," and then fell silent again. He plodded along, his head down, unaware of my presence. A few minutes later, he touched my arm, said good-by, and walked away.

I never saw Sam Melville again. Some months after that meeting on the picket line, when I was back in Seattle and in Weatherman, I read that Sam and the woman he lived with, Jane Alpert, and several others had been arrested for numerous bombings in New York. Jane and the rest were given bail; Jane jumped hers, and went underground. She didn't surface until November of 1974. The others did comparatively little time; one was a pig and he did no time. Sam was denied bail, and was eventually sent to Attica Prison in upstate New York. He was at Attica when the riots occurred during August of 1971. It was rumored at the time (but later denied by the official report) that Sam was specifically sought out by the pigs and shot down in cold blood because he was a revolutionary.

I still think of Sam Melville. At a time when the Movement seems to have died and there is a minimum of protest, at a time when I am writing a book about the revolution, a thing I would have scorned while participating in it, Sam is dead, and will never get the chance to begin again. All I can do is remember him, and his commitment to the struggle that he lived and died for and say, "Sam Melville, live like him."

4.
WEATHERMAN
JUNE 21—24, 1969

At the close of the sixties, SDS was like a big family spread across America. You could travel almost anywhere, and you would have an enclave of friends who would welcome you. You always had a place to crash, some food, some dope, and some sex. You visited your relatives, whom you might not have seen for a year, and exchanged all kinds of news; number of busts in your chapter or among your friends, best kind of acid, who fucked whom, growth of chapters, number of demonstrations, number of college dropouts. You got to know your family from coast to coast; you saw it grow by leaps and bounds. Your collection of buttons and banners grew with your war scars, and so did your stories. And so did your comrades. And so did your faith in the viability of the revolution. It was a time of hard work and growth, but one was rewarded by a sense of belonging. One knew one's place in life, whom to depend on, and that no matter where you were, you would be taken care of.

By the time of the Big Split in June 1969, there were over 500,000 SDSers in America. And when you hit their town, they opened their houses, iceboxes, and dope stashes to you, and you were among friends.

All that went with the Big Split. Not immediately. But inevitably. When SDS split, it sent a shock wave through the Movement which destroyed it as it had been during the latter part of the sixties. With increased militancy came increased security. Pig paranoia became a plague and doors which had been open for years to long-haired, bearded, pack-carrying strangers now were locked to all but tried and true friends. Joints which once had flowed freely at be-ins and parties and meetings were now hidden like concealed weapons; people were getting busted for passing joints to narcs. And the friendly long-hair next to you could be a narc.

The Movement was not only growing up, it was growing old. Some of us were over thirty. If you couldn't trust someone over thirty, and if you couldn't pass a joint or open your home to a stranger, then how were you different from everyone else in the country?

We had begun to feel many of these contradictions at Columbia, long before the June SDS National Convention. We expected drastic changes. The growing dissension in the NO, and in local chapters between PL and the rest of SDS had been building toward a confrontation. We expected a big fight at the June Convention, we anticipated chaos. Two completely separate personalities of one organization were prepared to duke it out until one side won; we never seriously thought about a split.

Then there was the Weatherman paper, *You Don't Need A Weatherman to Know Which Way the Wind Blows,* sitting formidably in the background, but never out of anyone's thoughts very long. Rudd had read it to us in the middle of April. Its call for more militant struggle frightened but intrigued almost everyone. It was a foregone conclusion that the paper would be a major issue at the Convention.

SDS meetings in the past had been helter-skelter affairs, requiring little procedure. At the door of the June Convention I met the first big change: I was frisked.

We had been very security-conscious at Columbia. A rising consciousness of pig infiltrators had required the posting of guards at every meeting. People with tape recorders or cameras had been repeatedly thrown out of meetings. Pig paranoia was not an illusion; unfortunately while we recognized the problem there was little we could do to keep pigs out, since we were an open organization which operated on a mass level. Somewhere in every mass lurked the pig.

To get frisked, I walked up to the female frisker, who patted me up and down the length of my body, around my crotch and under my arms with a professional air. She was fast and complete. I was asked to take off my boots, in case of a concealed weapon; my jacket and pocketbook were searched, but since I wasn't carrying dope or weapons, and didn't have a camera, nothing was confiscated. I didn't resent the frisking, although I was piqued because the process took so long. But you got used to long lines at Movement gatherings. And I understood, along with everyone else, that security was necessary for our survival.

Frisked and clean, I entered a cavernous room, reminiscent of a 1920s union hall. Totally barren, the walls arched up to a surrounding balcony, above which loomed a ceiling crisscrossed with exposed pipes and wires with bare light bulbs swaying at the ends. At the far end of the room was a small platform with a speaker's rostrum hidden beneath a tentaclelike mass of microphones. The entire floor of the room was covered with rows of benches; the balcony was covered with rows of bleachers.

SDS National Officers are elected at June conventions so the number of people attending is significantly larger than at other NC's. Over two thousand people were in the hall; about half of these favored PL. The remainder were SDS members and supporters, which included White Panthers, Motherfuckers, Women's Lib groups, among other Movement groups.[1] Within this body there were also political differences, which would grow more intense after the Convention but which were temporarily aligned against PL. These factions were divided between Klonsky's RYM 2 paper and the new Weatherman paper, which had grown out of the RYM paper.

Everybody had their mouths open and were shrilling slogans reflecting their politics. PL screamed, "You're anti-working class," at SDS, and SDS called PL racist. Mao books were brandished along with fists, as the two political factions squared off.

PL looked clean-shaven, neatly dressed, and grim. When they weren't sloganeering, they and their supporters sat in well-manicured rows on their side of the room. The other half of the room was a beehive of activity, dominated by the Michigan-Ohio region, who sat as a group, and would jump upon their chairs every few minutes and scream, "Dare to struggle, dare to win," and wave Mao's *Little Red Book* in the air.[2]

To keep order, we were all asked to remain seated. People sat in chapters, and in some cases chapters from the same regions sat together. To make sure no fights erupted, security forces patrolled the aisles, marked by yellow armbands. I got one from a friend, which gave me a lot of freedom to roam around.

From my vantage point in the aisle, it was easy to see that the place was berserk. At Columbia we had put on a big rush to get people to become national members, so that SDS would have more delegates at the Convention than PL, who had been busy getting people to become national members for the same reason. Now each delegate had a placard, like the type they have at football games in the cheering section. Whenever someone was voting, they would wave their cards high in the air, so that vote counters could see them. There were endless numbers of recounts concerning procedure.

There wasn't a moment of harmony throughout the whole damn thing. No matter what the subject, there were violent arguments between PL and SDS, which generally dissolved into fierce chanting, with each side standing on benches and stamping their feet in unison with their chants. Small fights continuously erupted and security guards would gallop to disperse them before they spread.

The people from Columbia spent a lot of time with Ayers and Rudd, who had both participated in writing the Weatherman paper. The Columbia chapter was strategic, since we had so many good organizers; so we received a lot of attention from heavies of all political persuasions.

We talked about the Weatherman paper for hours during the first two days of the Convention. I tried to read it one day over lunch, but it was too long and theoretical for me to assimilate. Instead of understanding it, I listened carefully to what others said about it, in order to parrot their remarks at future meetings.

The second night of the Convention, a small group of Black Panthers came to speak. SDS had been trying to build an alliance with the Panthers, who were contemptuous of all white radical groups. But Klonsky had worked very hard all year to lessen hostilities, and the Black Panthers' presence at the Convention was seen as an overture of friendship.

When the first Panther began to speak, I was standing toward the rear of the vast hall, not paying very much attention to what he was saying. Suddenly people from all over the room flew out of their seats furiously screaming "Fight male chauvinism." The Panther's speech, which had begun as an attack on PL had ended with an attack on Women's Liberation, which included a remark about "pussy power." Their line was that women should fuck anyone if necessary for the revolution.

The room erupted into a seething mass of women, embarrassed and defensive men, momentarily united against the Panthers in defense of Women's Liberation. I was angry along with all the other women. I moved closer to the stage, screaming "male chauvinism" without much heart, when suddenly the Panther speaker shouted into the mike, "Superman was a punk because he never even tried to fuck Lois Lane."

I saw red. The remark was stupid but infuriating. I stood under the stage screaming with hundreds of other women. In the background I could hear the roar of the men, yelling angrily. For a second my heart leaped in delight; the men were together, pulled together by the women; maybe there was a chance for SDS to stay together after all. Then the flush of happiness drained as I realized that we were all screaming at a black man; the white radical left united in defense of women against the Black Panthers.

If the June Convention was full of contradictions, that moment was the worst for me. In my dreams of revolution was a world where class and race had vanished, and only peace, love, and happiness remained. I looked forward to that day, believed in it, and I wanted to live to see it happen. But at moments such as that in Chicago, my dreams seemed ridiculous. SDS was put in the impossible position of attacking the Panthers while trying to cement political relations with them. And PL, ever opportunistic, was grinning from ear to ear, as though the fact that the Panthers were male chauvinists was a gigantic step forward in making the revolution.

On Friday, the third day of the Convention, I spent most of my time cruising around, saying hello to friends from other parts of the country. There were over thirty people from Seattle, among them

Robby. Everyone was discussing the Weatherman paper, and I was eager to find out what others thought about it.

Robby wasn't very favorable. "Who can relate to that thing!" he exploded. "It puts everybody down. You either have to be a genius or a madman to support it." Mike Justesen wasn't any more complimentary. Jean Shaffer, an old friend seated with the Independent Socialists was horrified that I liked the paper. "I hope that whatever happens with SDS won't interfere with our friendship," she said.

"Oh no, Jean, how could it," I said, and we hugged and made plans to sneak out together after the plenary.

Near the Seattle delegation, I ran into Roger Lippman. I had met Roger in Seattle just before I left the year before; he had come to New York several times during the winter and had crashed at my apartment. He was living with Robby in my old house on Woodlawn.

Roger seemed to have a handle on what was happening politically. He *knew* people. At least he was always talking about this person and that person from the NO. He was a theoretical genius, having read everything by Marx and Lenin and the rest of the boys, deciphered it all, and reorganized it in his head, so that at a moment's notice he was able to explain it very simply and clearly to others. Everything he said had a ring of authority and knowledge that made it very credible to me. His ability to make complicated theories understandable to the average person made Roger a very good organizer.

"What do you think of the Weatherman paper?" was his first question after he kissed me hello. It was on everyone's mind. I told him that I liked it, but I wasn't sure I really understood it. He smiled and offered to spend time with me during the Convention and explain the paper to me in detail. I was delighted.

Roger asked me what my plans were after the Convention. I shrugged my shoulders. He suggested that I return to Seattle. "Good people are needed there," he said, still peering around the room. His eyes never stopped moving. I told him I was thinking a lot about Seattle, and we said good-by.

Another group of Black Panthers arrived, and conferred with the NO people. I wandered up to the balcony where it was less noisy and crowded just as one of the Panthers took the mike to read a prepared statement urging SDS to expel PL. He hadn't finished reading when pandemonium broke out. People began racing up and down the aisles, security ran around the room trying to break up small fights, and knots of national leadership gathered around the speaker's platform arguing frantically as the Panthers left the hall. The room was filled with chanting, which bounced off the walls making one overwhelming, incomprehensible noise.

I hung over the balcony railing, fascinated, watching the room below as if it was a movie. SDS puffed to twice its size with rage. Then Fred Gordon, a PL leader and the NO educational secretary, grabbed the mike, but it was too noisy to hear what he said. Soon after, Rudd was at the mike, and the noise deadened slightly as he begged everyone to cool it and suggested a brief recess. Before he had finished, Bernardine came running across the platform, grabbed the mike furiously, and shouted something into it, then about-faced and stalked off the platform into a room next to the meeting hall.

There was a momentary hush. Falteringly, one by one, people around the room began to stand up, and slowly follow Bernardine into the other room. I watched in amazement for a few seconds, then ran downstairs feeling something big had just happened and I had missed it entirely.

Everything was in a bad state of confusion. Someone ran up to me excitedly screaming, "We're leaving, we're walking out," and went careening off. I wandered around the room in a daze, which was reflected on practically every face. Now that the split was upon us, nobody knew how to react.

I saw Robby and some of the Seattle delegation and frantically went up to them. "Well, what are you guys doing?" They all looked bewildered, standing between benches, arguing about it, as the group at the side of the room swelled with people waiting to go through the door to the next room. I wandered away from the Seattle group with a growing sense of alarm and isolation. Somehow the die had been cast, the split was on, but did I personally want it? It had nothing to do with me, really. I was just a plebeian; the leadership had made the decision, and now it was a fact. How was I related to this fact?

Around the entrance to the next room were perhaps fifty people, some looking as though they were about to break into tears, others looking as though they were about to commit murder. One SDS leader was trying to stop people from entering the room, shaking his head and saying over and over again, "This is wrong, we're killing SDS, this is insanity." He caught my arm as I slowly approached the door. "Susan, don't go in there. You know this is suicide." I really didn't understand what was happening but I did feel like Chicken Little.

I heard my name being called and saw Jean Shaffer coming toward me, tears in her eyes. I felt my own eyes begin to sting.

"What are you going to do, Jean?" I asked.

"I can't go in there, Susan. They're crazy. They're destroying SDS. I swear, it was prearranged."

"Oh, no, Jean, I saw the whole thing," and I pointed to the balcony, but Jean ignored me.

I was being jostled as people streamed around me and through the door into the next room, giving Indian war whoops, and striking the air with fists, or walking in contemplatively, or walking in looking back. I could see PL freaking out, nervously screaming, "No split," and running up and down the emptying aisles, their followers sitting there palely, looking around, scared stiff. In contrast, I could hear the bellowing excitement in the next room. I looked in and saw the NO staff in a cluster, talking intensely to each other. The pile in the bleachers was growing, but still only filled a small portion of the next room. In the bleachers, or milling around the huge, gymlike room were Jose, the Street Theater people, and all the other friends I'd made in New York. These were my people; there was no choice at all.

My eyes filled with tears as I backed into the room, leaving Jean on the other side of the door. Strange, I thought, that we're so close, and now a political decision will separate us. I felt very lonely.

"Don't worry, Jean, we'll still be friends," I called lamely. I didn't talk to Jean for a year and a half after that unless it was to call her a pig and an enemy of the people.

The last few stragglers around the door capitulated and reluctantly entered the room. Maybe a thousand of us sat huddled in one corner of it. Everyone looked confused. "What does it all mean?" kept buzzing around the room.

There were heavy speeches, one right after another by NO people, and leadership from chapters across the country. Most of the speakers were in favor of expelling PL, although a few thought it would finish SDS.

As midnight approached, people in the room relaxed more and began to feel better about the walkout. Many of the Columbia people began to breathe normally. Once everybody had time to think about it, it certainly did make sense to get rid of PL. There were political considerations, as well as questions of life styles. Their politics, their personalities, their dress was nothing like ours. They were racist. They didn't support the Panthers; they thought the Vietcong were sellouts. They were practically monks, almost Victorian. Feeling against PL began to rise, and by the time we left, although nothing definite had been decided, "off PL" seemed to be the feeling in the room.

That night I thought deeply about the split. I lay in bed all night and thought. I knew there would be a vote the next day, and I wanted to make a careful decision.

The next day we met again early in the morning, in the gym off the main hall. The speeches and discussion continued. It was a long, tedious day. Early Saturday night, no conclusion had been reached yet.

Then Bernardine got up to address us, standing in front of the bleachers. She gave an account of the history of the Movement, showing how SDS had become the primary white revolutionary group in the Movement, and how PL was in opposition to that development repeatedly. "Expulsion is the only answer, and directness the only means; we should simply go in there and tell PL that it is no longer a part of this organization. We're not a caucus. We are SDS!" she said. Her speech was so passionate, her explanation of the history and development of SDS so logical and complete, that it left no doubt in our minds that what she said was correct. We voted swiftly, and there was almost complete unanimity in deciding to expel PL.

The leadership drew up a statement for PL, and then, in formation, we walked out and took the speaker's platform. I felt a sense of history in the making. Bernardine was at the rostrum, with Rudd to the right of her, and me, by chance, standing to the left of her, and all the rest of SDS lined up across the stage, covering it in straight rows, standing at attention, alert and proud, scrutinizing the audience carefully for any would-be assassins or attackers.

Bernardine was talking, waving her arms, pointing into the audience. Her eyes flashed as she traced the counterrevolutionary positions of PL. It was one of the most exciting speeches I had ever heard. She finished it by saying, "SDS can no longer live with people who are objectively racist, anti-communist, and reactionary. PL members and all others who don't accept our principles are no longer members of SDS."

PL began to laugh. The sound fell pathetically after the passion of Bernardine's speech. Furious and impotent, PL began chanting, "Shame, shame, shame," as Bernardine shouted into the mike, "Long live the victory of people's war," the slogan which ends the Weatherman paper. Then she flung herself proudly off the platform, and we all followed her, jubilantly marching out, pumping the air with fists, chanting at the tops of our lungs, "Power to the people, power to the people."

Weatherman had been born, and SDS had died, taking with it a decade of valiant revolutionary struggle and burying the strongest white radical group since the Communist Party of the thirties. Now instead of a half-million members and supporters across the country, SDS Weatherman represented a few thousand at the very most.

On the night of the walkout, I didn't worry about this. After listening to Bernardine, I would have followed her into Dante's inferno. If it was energy and brilliance that enraptured me, rather than reality, I didn't care. I believed in the revolution with every quivering bone in my body. I was prepared to take on America, to do no less than save the world. I felt that I was a warrior of the people, and that I was fighting for freedom, that I had no choice, no matter what the odds. It was far better, I reflected against the rising mutterings of impending doom, to lose than not to have fought at all. Nor did I question the automatic assumption of leadership by the Weatherman faction. If I had any doubts, I repressed them; mine was a single-minded devotion that left no room for doubts.

I had not suddenly leaped to these conclusions. Although I was still somewhat confused, and although I may have missed the deeper significance of what was happening in Chicago, my course was clear. I had listened closely to people discussing the Weatherman paper for several days. I had listened closely to the speeches in the gym, especially to Bernardine's long explanation of SDS's position in history. I had lain awake the night before and many other nights reflecting on my politics, trying to strengthen them. My political orientation had been growing in the same direction for a year. Standing up on that platform, listening to Bernardine, I felt that I had finally connected with my own personal destiny; that I had a place, a function in life. That place was with the Weathermen, that function was to fight for the revolution to the best of my ability.

With the advent of the Big Split there was only one reality in my life. Weatherman. I fell in love with a concept. My white knight materialized into a vision of world-wide liberation. I ceased to think of Susan Stern as a woman; I saw myself as a revolutionary tool. Impetuously and compulsively, I flung myself at the feet of the revolution and debauched in its whirlwind for the next few years. PL, SDS, Jean Shaffer, Robby Stern, my family, my past all faded into dreary insignificance. For the first time in my life that I could remember, I was happy.

On Sunday, the final day of the Convention, what remained of SDS met in a church near the National Office; PL met somewhere else. Political debate continued all day, primarily around principles of unity, which seemed impossible to establish, since, with PL gone, the remaining factions had no basis for alliance. The only major proposal passed called for a National Action against the war to take place in Chicago later that fall.

I wandered around, bored with the debate. Everyone from Seattle was interested in my future plans; Roger Lippman was overjoyed when I told him I was heading west for the United Front Against Fascism (UFAF) conference in Oakland, which had been called by the Black Panthers.

I collided with Joe Kelly who was bopping around spreading good vibes and smiling from ear to ear. He gave me a smacking kiss of hello. Joe told me that he and Chip and some friends were moving to Seattle to set up shop sometime in August. Although I hadn't definitely decided to return to Seattle, we made plans to live together. I would rent a house for the Ithaca people and move in with them when they came in August. Joe gave me the phone number of Glad Day Press in Ithaca, where he could be located until the group left for Seattle. We promised to keep in touch and kissed good-by.

Meanwhile, selections for the new National Office staff were in progress. An all-Weatherman slate was elected. Mark Rudd became the new National Secretary, Bill Ayers the Educational Secretary, and Jeff Jones took the role of Inter-Organizational Secretary.

Jeff was stunning, with long blond hair and a beautiful face. J.J. and I had run with him at the Democratic Convention, and then I had known him at the Regional Office in New York. He was a charming man, whose good nature was his winning feature, rather than theoretical expertise or intellect. He was a dedicated SDS organizer.

I knew Bill Ayers only by sight. He was an impressive and charismatic speaker, and always had a flock of people about him. Like most of the SDS men, he was bright, good-looking, personable, and arrogant. Like Jeff, he was a longtime SDS organizer.

Many people at the Convention weren't pleased with the new slate. They thought it didn't really represent SDS. Robby was particularly opposed to Rudd, and both he and Justesen were pessimistic about an all-Weatherman National Office. At that time they both felt closer to Klonsky and the RYM 2 people than to Weatherman.

After the Convention, I drove to San Francisco. I danced topless for a week to earn some bread, and then took a train to Los Angeles to play for a week at the home of a famous photographer. My main reason for going to L.A. was to get my car, Zelda, which I had left there the year before. Then I drove to San Francisco for the Panther conference, which began on July 18.

During the conference Weatherman and RYM 2 people met in a church to discuss the fall National Action. The meeting was fraught with tension between the two factions. The threat of a PL attack hung over us constantly; I stood for hours on the church steps with a club in my hand, waiting for PL, but they never attacked the church.

Weatherman didn't like the conference, which was backed by the Communist Party. They also refused to support a Black Panther proposal for Community Control of Police. As the Panthers appeared to be stepping back from armed struggle and militancy, Weatherman was gearing to become urban guerrillas. Because of all these disagreements, an alliance between the Panthers and Weatherman was doomed. Shortly after UFAF, the Panthers began to denounce Weatherman as adventurist, and refused to work with any faction of SDS. This was a tremendous setback for Weatherman, which regarded the Panthers as the revolutionary vanguard in America and the black liberation struggle as the primary battle. It was hard to follow a vanguard who despised you.

During UFAF, and the week that followed, I began to understand Weatherman politics. I was interested in organizing for the National Action, which would be on October 8 in Chicago. Roger fed my enthusiasm. He was constantly talking to me about Weatherman, and repeatedly explained the paper to me. When UFAF ended, there were meetings of national leadership. At these meetings the positions of Weatherman and the RYM 2 people crystallized. I listened quietly during all these meetings, soaking in all the lines and memorizing them, so that I could repeat them during my organizing. By the time Roger and I left for Seattle, I was a connoisseur of the Weatherman line, and a rabid devotee.

I left San Francisco in Zelda with Roger and arrived in my beloved Seattle on July 26, the anniversary of Moncada, the Cuban Day of Liberation.

A young woman once asked Bernardine Dohrn how she would know when the time was right for her to become a Weatherman. Bernardine answered: "One morning you will wake up and look outside your window. And there, on your front lawn, will be a great flaming W and you will know the time has come." The discussion during UFAF, and following it had ignited a spark in my mind that was burning out of control. Now I was back in Seattle and I was going to spread the Weatherword. I couldn't wait to get started organizing around the National Action, which had been renamed Days of Rage by the Weatherman. I was sure we were on the brink of revolutionary war in America. I wanted to organize the white fighting army that would bring the war home to Seattle.

I crashed in a small gray house across the street from my old house on Woodlawn, where Robby still lived with his girl friend Ivy, and with Jay and his girl friend, Beverly, and with Roger Lippman and several others. Bill Ayers was in Seattle when I arrived, drumming up support for the Days of Rage. He was also crashing in the gray house. Roger arranged for him to meet with people at Reed College in Oregon the next day. When Ayers invited me along, I accepted, even though I had just arrived in Seattle.

The students at Reed who prepared for our arrival were waiting in the student lounge. I spewed out the Weatherman line like a cheerleader:

"We're all honky dogs. Because we were born with white skins, we have parents who can afford to send us to colleges where we are plied with art and literature and pampered and spoiled for four years, while the rest of the world starves. Our white skin gives us privileges that no one else has. While we sit here, the war in Vietnam rages. Women and children are dying, and what are you doing? Reading D. H. Lawrence and smoking dope?

"Now listen, there's a war going on. You're either on one side or the other. There will be no history to absolve you if you choose the wrong side. For if you choose the wrong side, then you're a pig, and the people's army will off you. So you have to choose, right now.

"Women have to learn that they are strong by themselves; men must be pushed into recognizing the necessity of strong female leadership. Living as couples will only hinder you in this development; monogamy is a tool of the system to oppress women. Leave your boy friends, your children, your parents, school—anything that comes between you and the revolution. Form collectives and relate to your revolutionary sisters and brothers. And remember that strength comes through struggle."

Most of the students objected violently to this ultimatum. The few who thought they agreed with it followed Ayers and me into another room, where we worked with them for hours, talking about Weatherman politics and the Days of Rage. We attempted to get the students really committed to the idea of the Weathernation, to life and death struggle in America, in Oregon. Most of the people who agreed with us were converted immediately and blindly.

Ayers left shortly after we returned to Seattle. Although I had been terribly attracted to him, I hadn't slept with him. I had decided not to fuck Bill Ayers almost as soon as I met him. There was a quality about him that I couldn't stand. It was almost as though he *expected* every woman in the world to want to fuck him. This was not true only of Ayers. It was common among SDS men, especially regional and national travelers. They would drop into small-town U.S.A. with their grinning good looks and their political palaver and just like any other superstar attract a bunch of shining little groupies. My pride eventually got in the way. Unlike the year before, I couldn't stand the thought of being just another piece of ass to SDS men; that summer, more than ever, I was anxious to prove my political strength.

Back in Seattle, I was insecure and defensive at first, feeling threatened by Robby. Everyone was very nice to me in spite of my paranoia, except for Jay, who was still hurt because I had been so unfriendly to him while he was in New York.

The house I was crashing in was rented by a shy, chubby woman of nineteen named Ruth. She shared the house with Hal—a pedantic ex-Marine who had an intense fascination with guns and weaponry, and a fanatical approach to security and protective measures—and Ray, an eighteen-year-old U of W art student who had been suspended because of his participation in a militant demonstration the year before. Terribly shy, gentle, and good-natured, Ray loved the action and excitement of demonstrations. His greatest love was his car, which he had practically handbuilt, and which could outdrag any car in Seattle. Another crasher in the house, Simon, had drifted in from Boston, and was living hand-to-mouth, waiting to see what Seattle had to offer. I slept on a couch in the living room, and lived out of my suitcase.

I wasn't very close to any of the people in my house; for the most part I ignored them. My interest was more with the people who lived across the street, but they avoided me. I was at least eight years older than most of the people in Ruth's house, and I had a stronger personality. Within a week, I was running the house. Although technically I was still crashing there, I saw the house as mine, and used it to suit my needs.

Although I was settled in the gray house, I looked for another one large enough for the Ithaca men and myself and found one immediately. Joe and Chip and several others did start out for Seattle sometime in August. They got as far as Chicago and the National Office, where Rudd and J.J. and several other Weathermen with whom they were friendly prevailed upon them to stay there and help with the Days of Rage. I phoned them several times after they left Ithaca, but I never knew what had happened to them until they finally made it to Seattle in December. Toward the end of August, the house I had found was rented to someone else.

As usual I had no money. So within a few days of my arrival in Seattle, I astounded everyone by taking a job as a go-go dancer at a foul little tavern in Ballard called the Dunes. The people in both houses on Woodlawn were appalled that I would go-go dance. Not at a time when the Movement was in a crisis over Women's Liberation.

I chose to ignore what everyone was saying and took an aggressive "who cares" attitude. Instead of hiding the fact that I worked at the Dunes, I flaunted it. Before work, I'd prance around the house in a minuscule G-string. Everyone in the house was too intimidated to stop my outrageous activity.

Weatherman had swung a pendulum in me. The vogue was to be tough and macho, and I was as overzealously aggressive and abandoned as a Weatherman as I had been timid and frightened prior to it. I was intent on being as outrageous as possible.

During the day I visited people and walked on the Ave. But the street scene was miserable, a ghoulish remnant of the sparkling flower generation. Now instead of bangles and laughter there was smack and burns, and police patrolling the area so heavily that it was impossible to hang out there. If I stopped walking for a minute, patrolmen, working in pairs, asked me not to loiter, and shoved me if I took too long in moving.

Still, the Ave was a meeting place for all kinds of young people, a worn-out symbol of our counterculture. There was constant tension between the youth and the police stirring beneath the surface calm, but flaring visibly each time someone was busted. Then small angry knots of people would gather and glare at the police, and there would be a few muttered cries of "Pig."

I found it very easy to meet people and make friends in Seattle. From these friends I pieced together the development of SDS in Seattle during the year I had been gone. In most ways, it mirrored the development of chapters across the country.

As the first hot, clear August days began, I lay in the sun in front of the house and tried to figure out what was happening politically in Seattle. It was a catastrophe. There was a small group of people loosely associated with the Weatherman paper, the new NO leadership and the Days of Rage. This group was led by Roger and included

Jay and Beverly, Ruth, and myself, among others. Then there was a group twice that large, representing many different tendencies, who were simply in opposition to Weatherman. Robby, Justesen, Ray, Hal, and Simon were in this group. They supported Klonsky and RYM 2. The Weathermen referred to them as Running Dogs.

Then there was a group of people represented by several notorious street hangers, hippies, dope dealers, doper types, who were mainly interested in clearing the pigs off the Ave so that the self-respecting hippies, freaks, street people, dope-blowing, pill-popping, mainlining population could have some turf and space. In this group was a handsome ex-jock turned freak named Garrity, and an alcoholic hippie named Indian. People like Simon, Justesen and Ray were friendly toward people in this group.

In August there were endless meetings and arguments between these three groups. Most of the meetings were consumed in frantic circular arguments between RYM 2 and Weatherman, with RYM 2 advocating serving the people with community programs like the Black Panther breakfast program, and the Weathermen arguing for immediate violent revolution in the streets. The street-people faction wanted to serve the people and have violent revolution as well, since both would benefit their constituency. They got really bored with the political arguments and the tedious but increasingly violent meetings, and finally left SDS to itself, and set up their own group, the International Werewolf Conspiracy (IWWC). This was the West Coast branch of the Motherfuckers. It was the heavy action, drunken, doping ribald style that this group most identified with.

As the first few summer meetings began, it became apparent that SDS women were still struggling with the problem of male chauvinism. All the women were brilliant and strong and through the year had developed concrete politics. Yet they were very much attached to SDS, and had decided to struggle within the chapter rather than form a separate, feminist organization. Later on in the summer, there were meetings limited to women only. The majority of SDS women supported Weatherman.

I had been in Seattle about a week when Sky River Rock festival occurred. Rock festivals were a bone of contention that year. Harmless in and of themselves, they were a potential threat to the Establishment if the energy vibrating throughout them was ever harnessed. Rock festivals were absolute anathema to the local communities in which they were held. Free dope, free love, nudity, lewdness, drug-mania, debauching, and all with the legal consent of the government. A cry resounded for the ending of rock festivals. But not in time to stop Sky River.

It was beautiful. A little slice of unreality in the middle of rank despair. We all took acid and took off our clothes and tripped under the August sun. SDS set up a candy concession and distributed flyers. We had a sign on our candy booth which said, "Free Huey Newton." Stoned, smiling kids came bounding up to the candy booth asking, "What's a Huey Newton Bar taste like? Is it really free?" I must have explained who Huey was a hundred times.

Next door to the SDS candy concession was The Werewolves concession—a kissing booth! The street people had an even lower awareness of the sins of male chauvinism than everybody else in the Movement. Having the kissing booth right next door to our candy booth outraged the SDS women. There were several clashes. At one time Indian, loaded on mescaline and drunk, came running up to the candy booth and called me a bitch. I tried to slug him, spewing out every curse word I could invent. People had to physically restrain us. After a while, I thought it was better to be friendly with those people; they were heavily action-oriented, and I wanted them to run in the Days of Rage.

I wandered over to the kissing booth camp. People were drunk and stoned; in every tent, people were fucking. I crawled into the back of a van, and a few minutes later, who should join me there but Indian, all smiles and apology. From the van we watched the festival go by.

There was an immense Harley-Davidson parked in back of the van. Garrity sauntered over to it and, getting on, posed in various positions. He looked beautiful with the sun pouring over his flexing muscles, his black hair long and gleaming. Indian told me that he and Garrity were homeless. I offered them the gray house as a crash pad. When we returned to Seattle, Garrity and Indian moved into Ruth's with me.

Indian was a heavy doper and Garrity was just heavy. They were both shooting any kind of dope that would dissolve in water; heroin, speed, acid, THC. Indian would come running up, his eyes glazed, slowly nod out in the middle of the living room, and then mumble to me, "Please, Susan, do up the cotton, it's so nice, baby." Instead of shooting the dope, I dropped it, mostly THC, generally at two in the morning when I came home from the Dunes. Then we'd stay up all night and make a mess in the living room, which Ruth or Ray invariably cleaned up the next day while we slept.

During the afternoons, I talked to Garrity. As the summer passed, I grew closer and closer to him. Although he was several years younger than me, he seemed older. By now he had a girl friend living with him occasionally, and I slept with Indian at night. I thought of Garrity as a dear friend. Then the Ave riots changed him into a revolutionary hero.

Earlier in August, the mayor and the police chief had announced a crackdown on drug traffic in the University District. The number of pigs on the Ave doubled. Any young person was fair play for police harassment. And any scene which young people gravitated to was potentially explosive.

On Sunday evening, August 10, pigs attacked a group of several hundred people quietly listening to a rock concert on Alki Beach in South Seattle. Without warning, they began gassing and then entered its midst with clubs flying. Not all the people on the beach were young; many of them were community people out for an evening stroll, who had just stopped to listen to the music briefly. There was no provocation for the attack, except that people were gathered.

All day Monday, people were infuriated about the unwarranted attack. By late afternoon, hundreds of people had collected in the University District, muttering darkly about pigs. That night the pigs attempted to arrest a young man; his girl friend intervened and was manhandled. Garrity tried to help free the young woman, who was screaming for help. In an effort to aid her, he took a heavy left jab into a pig's nose and broke it. When other pigs attempted to bust Garrity, a scuffle broke out. It quickly spread in the tense, infuriated crowd. Garbage pails were overturned and set on fire. Bricks were thrown through a pig car window. But there was no heavy trashing, and no damage was done. Garrity was hauled off to jail, and released the next day on bail. He was charged with assaulting a police officer. And the Ave riots began.

Tuesday night we all stood on the corner in front of the Coffee Corral, prepared to do battle. There was a noticeable increase of pigs in the area. There was a noticeable absence of dopers and freaks. The thousands or so kids lining the streets were not the usual inhabitants of the Ave. They were kids from Alki Beach and other parts of Seattle. They were of high school age. It was very calm Tuesday night; everybody was waiting for something to happen. As the evening wore on, blacks from the Central District began to arrive, sensing a confrontation. Still nothing happened. Around two o'clock in the morning everybody went home.

The next day, the Werewolves met with other Ave people, and formed a caucus to deal with potential riots. SDS also met that afternoon. The various factions stopped squabbling momentarily to cope with the Ave crisis; SDS agreed to take action. The RYM 2 people tended more to leaflet actively. The Weathermen talked about breaking windows, Molotov cocktails, burning pig cars. The women decided to work together, and in the event of a riot, to run together. Unlike the men, there seemed to be no discord about the type of action. The women were more interested in having an affinity group that could run smoothly, and attack swiftly, than in the exact mechanics of any action.

With a great eagerness the women waited for the coming riot to begin. We had agreed to divide into two groups which would stay close together. We wanted to fight. The women had waited for a chance to exert leadership all summer; the Ave riots provided the opportunity.

Dressed simply, with sneakers or boots for running, a dozen women met on the Ave, and waited in a group as it got darker. I was still not very well accepted among them. It was Robby's girl friend, Ivy, who had invited me to join the group. Unlike Robby, the

Weatherman militancy appealed to her. She liked street fighting, and thought it was politically correct.

The trashing began about eight o'clock that night. Kids trashed Captain Hook's, an overpriced mod shop on University Ave. Trashcans were overturned and set on fire. Windows were broken; rocks flew everywhere.

The pigs set up a howler siren on top of Bleaker's Funeral Parlor. They kept on telling everybody to go home, and the howler shrieked. When the trashing continued, the pigs started gassing. They would surround a square block and throw tear-gas canisters from all directions. The women ran through the gas and continued to break windows. I took a big rock and hurled it through the Coffee Corral window. Later that evening I would have coffee there, while resting from the riot. While some pigs threw gas, others went up and down the block beating people. When people ran, they were chased. And still the trashing continued.

Black kids arrived and looting began. Piles of clothes were taken from Captain Hook's and someone broke into a TV and stereo shop on the corner of University Way and hauled away TV sets and stereos.

I stood on the Ave with the women, and watched the black kids taking the clothes from Captain Hook's. "I want some of those clothes," I said, and started to cross the street, but the other women held me back. I got restless standing there watching the looting, and started to wander through the crowd. I was feeling so good. Everything was going well. Weatherman was so right on. The white street kids, the counterculture, freaks, hippies; this would be the white fighting force. Once people realized they could fight the pigs and win, they would go on fighting until they won.

Still sniffling from tear gas, I stopped near a big knot of people watching the looting. The kids were laughing and joking about the "niggers." One of them muttered that he didn't know whether to throw the rocks at the pigs or niggers. I stared at him aghast; unable to believe my ears, I asked the guy to repeat what he had just said. He looked at me and said, "I don't know who I hate more; the pigs or niggers. What right do they have to come here anyway, and steal from our stores?"

"Do you live on the Ave?" I asked.

"No, but I have a right to be here. Why don't they stay up in the C.D. where they belong."

My heart sank. The Ave freaks were my people; my politics were directed to youth. I was certain that the youth counterculture would be the core of the street fighting army. And here they were saying they didn't know if they wanted to throw rocks at the pigs or the niggers. I continued walking through the crowd and heard other kids saying the same thing. Many of them were so stoned they were just throwing rocks indiscriminately and laughing hysterically. I should have known right then and there that there was something wrong with the Weatherway of thinking, that basically there was very little difference between these kids and the people I served in the Dunes. But I didn't think about it that night or for many months to come, when the Movement had all but been destroyed, and the heads of some of the finest revolutionaries in this country had been blown to bits by homemade bombs and Weather-induced psychosis. I stood there paralyzed, fighting nausea, refusing to accept the fact that America's youth was so poisoned by racism and violence that no ideal, no amount of commitment could save them.

The Ave riots lasted for three days and included several thousand people at different times. We were severely gassed, and hundreds were beaten and injured. The newspapers declared it police war on youth. The community roared in protest. Many people had been gassed as they left the Neptune Theater and were returning to their cars on Wednesday night. The Ave merchants frothed; some had been looted and many had had windows broken.

It was hard to tell what was random violence on the part of the rioters, and what was selective trashing. Windows of the new Pacific National Bank were smashed. Pigs gassed the crowd there and were pelted with rocks and debris. That particular bank had some involvement with the war. The Navy-Marine Recruiting Station on the Ave had its windows shattered, and there were other political targets. But the mood of a great portion of the crowd was hilarious, not serious. As drunk and stoned as many people were, it was impossible to tell how much of the damage was accidental.

On Thursday night I began running with the women but got separated and ended up with Ray and Simon and a couple of other men. In a parking lot on the U of W campus, we were attacked by men who had blackjacks. One of them grabbed me, and when I began to kick and fight back, Ray ran to help me, followed by Simon. As they approached, the man holding me by the wrist, who was enormous, pulled a gun out of a holster under his armpit. One of his buddies growled, "C'mon, we'd better get out of here." Just at that moment I bit the man holding the gun deeply on the wrist. He loosened his grip on me, and Ray, Simon, and I ran like hell. Later we found out that off-duty pigs, acting as vigilantes, had been pistol-whipping people in the bushes bordering the campus.

Scores of people were arrested during the days of rioting, but all charges were subsequently dropped. Except for Garrity. He eventually did thirty days in County Jail for bashing the pig.

As a result of the Ave riots, the pigs did clean up their act on the Ave ever so slightly. They beat people more discreetly, in the patrol cars or downtown rather than on the streets of the U District. The University District Center was formed to help deal with the growing problem of transient dopers and penniless hippies. It was also supposed to serve as a liaison between the Ave merchants and the street people, and the pigs. What it actually was was a free freak service center, specializing in crashing, feeding, and finding rides for homeless, drifting youths.

SDS was flushed with the success of the riot, although they had nothing to do with it. There was no way they could have controlled the crowd. The affinity groups set an example for others to follow, and Weatherman presence probably generated more violence, as well as giving direction to selecting targets.

The riots were a real expression of frustration on behalf of most of the kids, although it had little to do with overthrowing the government. The rage that erupted into the days of rioting was more rebellious than revolutionary. The pigs represented an authority that was restrictive and one-sided. The kids responded from a gut level to the powerlessness of being white, middle-class, and adolescent at the close of the sixties.

The major thing that came out of the Ave riots was a heavy corps of street-fighting women. The nights of rioting and fighting together had made bonds among the women that years of talking had not done. We had a women's meeting after the riot, and it was full of electric energy. It was so high. The rush of women, long repressed, was suddenly and daringly undammed. Nothing but action, running in the streets, actually fighting with the pigs could have released such a pent-up force. We were tasting the macho strength that characterizes men, but we felt it keenly as women. Eyes glowing, we looked at each other warmly. Like a sweet perfume in the air we breathed in our first scent of sister-love. It was a precious, dazzling moment, and it turned the tide for the dozen women sitting in that room. Something was born that could not be forgotten. And like every newborn thing, it contained a revolutionary purity. I sensed my power not individually as a woman, but for the first time, as part of a group of women. Women from this group would form the core of the Seattle Weatherman collective barely a week later.

It was sometime in the afternoon. I was sitting in the middle of a mess Indian, Garrity, and I had made the night before, when Hal came stomping into the house, glaring. "Those motherfuckers have formed a Weatherman collective," he said, pointing to the house across the street.

"No," I said. "That's impossible. How could they form a Weatherman collective without me? They know I'm committed to Weatherman." And I laughed at the notion.

"Well, go see for yourself," Hal shrieked at me. "Ruth's there, and Roger, Jay, and Beverly—they won't let Robby or Ivy into the house because they're having a secret meeting. Well, go on," he roared when I didn't move. "Go see for yourself, Susan."

Hal's rage was volcanic; he continued to stamp around the living room shouting that they would never get away with it.

"A bunch of fucking fools. None of them even know how to use a gun, and they're yapping about armed struggle." He continued ranting, until it finally dawned on me that he was serious, that a collective had been formed. Well, they probably hadn't wanted to disturb me while I was sleeping, so they'd started the meeting without me.

Strange, though. Roger had talked to me repeatedly about forming a collective in Seattle up until about a week ago; I had heard nothing since, and had just assumed that there weren't enough people in support of Weatherman to do it. Kathy Boudin had flown in from the NO for a day or two; she had left yesterday. I never saw her. She spent all of her time in the house across the street. Ruth had been there frequently, but nothing had been said about forming a collective.

"Form a collective without me. Ridiculous," I said out loud to myself as I threw on some clothes and blitzed across the street.

I flung open the door of my old house and walked in, stood in the dining room, smiling. Seven unsmiling faces looked up at me blankly, and then hurriedly looked down. Nonplussed, I thought, "Boy, they must be discussing something terribly serious." I quietly walked in and sat down at the table, still smiling. Still everybody kept their eyes averted and no one said anything to me.

The awkward silence quivered for a second or two longer and then Ruth, gentle Ruth began to stutter.

"Um, Susan, I'm, um, sorry, but um, well . . ." and she looked helplessly at Beverly.

Beverly was a tall, slender woman, with shoulder-length, straight, light-brown hair, and an attractive but severe face. When she smiled she looked almost pretty and her face softened, but her main expression was one of solemnity. She appeared to be very aloof and cold. She had never been friendly to me. I had always assumed this was because she loved Jay so much, and that he had told her how terrible I had been in New York. Now she began to talk, swiftly and unemotionally, her voice tightly controlled, suggesting an underlying scorn.

"Susan, we have decided not to let you into the collective. We know that you are in agreement with Weatherman politics, and during the Ave riots you showed us that you are willing to fight and are not afraid of the pigs. But we are trying to forge a collective of people who can live and work together to make the revolution. To do this the individual has to subordinate herself to the group as a whole. While you fought well on the Ave, you fought as an individual. While the other women struggled to stay together as an affinity group, you ran all over the place, distracting everyone, and endangering everyone, because we couldn't depend on you to be where you were supposed to be.

"When the looting started, you wanted to go and loot. In the middle of a fight with the pigs, and you're talking about stealing clothes. Not to mention your machoness. It's one thing to fight pigs, and to defend yourself; it's quite another to go off shrieking and laughing to throw rocks in the Coffee Corral window. And then to compound all those mistakes by strutting around and telling everyone how you just smashed a window at the Coffee Corral."

All this came out in a gush, and then she paused to take a breath. Before she could continue, Roger leaned forward and in a wheedling voice said,

"I feel very badly, Susan, because I know I had a great deal to do with your coming back to Seattle. I also know that I encouraged you in your political decision to organize around Weatherman politics. But this is a new experience for all of us. We are entering a new stage. The revolution is no longer a game, when you can play at it when you want to. It's for real, now, life and death. What Beverly said was true; you endangered the entire affinity group by not staying with them, and then by bragging about your trashing."

"Well, how would you know, Roger—you weren't even at the riots," I blurted out before I could stop myself. My head was buzzing and my eyes were swimming with tears, which spilled over and slopped down my cheek. "Where were you when we were all doing the fighting?" I continued lamely.

Ignoring my question, Roger looked at me with exaggerated patience. "Look, Susan, what time is it? It's after two in the afternoon, and you just woke up. You stayed up all night taking drugs and keeping the entire house awake with that Indian, that paragon of male chauvinism . . ."

Georgia, another woman I had run with on the Ave, broke in, standing up, her fist clenched, eyes flashing darkly.

"Susan, Weatherman is supposed to set an example of revolutionary behavior to youth all around the country. To women especially. Now what kind of example do you think you set? Are you a good revolutionary woman for others to emulate? Are you the kind of woman appropriate to lead other women, and to show men the strength of women? Why you're living with two of the most notorious male chauvinists in Seattle."

"Not too notorious to bust a pig in the nose and start the Ave riots," I said furiously. "Garrity and Indian were all right by all you pompous, arrogant . . ." I couldn't finish what I was saying; I was crying too hard.

Roger continued in his flat and earnest voice.

"Susan, your life style is just not conducive to collective living. It won't hold up under the demand of Weatherman. A lot about Weatherman is fighting, but a great deal more about it is our ability to change ourselves, to get rid of the fucked-upness America has created in us. Individuality is one of those things. Male chauvinism is another. We must consciously choose who we are going to live and work with. Not everyone really wants to change.

"The revolution isn't fun. It's not supposed to be. We don't have time to play around. America is in her death throes; we have no time to lose organizing white kids to prepare for the oncoming struggle. The way you are right now, Susan, you'd hold back the entire collective. Ruth, come on, tell her what you said to us."

I looked at Ruth in astonishment. She had never shown the least sign of resentment to me, or anger. She had always smiled sweetly when I apologized to her for messing up the house and said, "Oh, that's okay." Now she was staring at her hands, and almost trembling.

"Well, come on, Ruth," I said. "Let's hear it. I mean, as long as this is shit on Susan day, you might as well get into the act too."

"Well," she started vaguely—and then, "Listen, Susan, it's disgraceful the way you've been acting. All those drugs, and shooting heroin in the house, and, well, it's true you cook, but you never help out around the house, and you make a mess of it. And that job of yours! How can you say you support Women's Liberation and then dance in a place like the Dunes?"

All I could do was stare at Ruth. She was looking at me with hatred.

"Don't you think there's a discrepancy between your stated position on women and your go-go job?" asked a woman named Katie energetically, with a little smile. She was the only person in the group who didn't look uncomfortable. She looked like she might even like me a little.

It must be Kathy Boudin, I thought bitterly, She must have organized this collective. She didn't like me in New York, and now she's got everyone to make up all these phony things about me and use them as a reason not to let me into the collective.

"Well, Susan," Beverly said.

Now everybody was looking at me, waiting. I looked around the table. Not a friendly face in the group. Seven of them. Seven motherfucking Weathermen out of the entire Seattle Movement, and they weren't letting me in. Because I had a job as a go-go dancer, because I took drugs, because my friends were rowdy street people? Furious, I sat there saying nothing, not knowing how to respond. Tears continued to drop out of my eyes and plop onto my cheek. And over and over again in my mind, like a dirge, "You're not good enough, you're not good enough, you're not good enough."

Roger began again, somewhat flustered by my silence.

"Susan, this isn't final, you know. If you change your life style, and begin to act more like a revolutionary woman should, then we will allow you, into the collective. We are all about changing people. But you must want to change first. You must prove to us that you want to change."

Prove to . . . prove to Roger, that little wimp? I looked at him, feeling deep hatred. Oh, I could see him so clearly now; that weasely little face, those sneaky eyes never looking straight at you, fumbling and fidgeting every time he ever talked to me. "He's so scared of me, it's pitiful," I thought behind my rising fury. And he's telling me I have to change? That little wimp?

I tried to talk, but couldn't. My head was hurting me from crying, and I felt numb all over. I began to see them all from the end of a long distance; their voices sounded muted. "Who cares," I thought, exhausted. "It doesn't matter what I do. I'm never going to please enough people."

Roger was still talking, but I couldn't hear him. I just got up, and started to walk out. Beverly suddenly looked concerned; Kate stared at me with innocent wide eyes; Ruth was shaking and Jay was cleaning his fingernails intently. The other two, Georgia and Mickey, a tall nineteen-year-old who hadn't said a word, stared at me silently as I walked to the door, and without turning to look back, walked out, leaving the door open behind me. I heard it slam resoundingly as I crossed the street.

I walked into the gray house. Many people, mostly men, were in the living room, talking agitatedly. It was suddenly dead quiet when I appeared. More faces staring at me. No one said anything. Then Garrity came up to me, and brushing a tear off my cheek murmured, "You don't need them. They need you, except they're too dumb to realize it. You're better off without them."

I had stopped while Garrity spoke. When he finished speaking, I continued walking. As I disappeared into the basement, to hide in the bedroom there, I could hear their voices again. I heard a lot of cursing, a lot of puffed-up male voices talking about "hacking those insufferable wimps into millions of pieces." Then I closed the door, crawled all the way under the covers, and went into gray.

As shattered as I was, I managed to suffer with dramatic finesse. For days I lay on different beds in the house, crying, and beating at the pillow with my fists, choking on the poison of rejection. My eyes were chronically red and swollen, my face puffy. I cried while I cooked dinner, and at the dinner table while I ate it. I cried as I washed dishes, and swept the living-room rug. I cried as I sat in the sun, surrounded by various people who came to sympathize with me.

One of these was Robby. His own life was disintegrating. Not only was Weatherman competing for his position of leadership but they were taking away his beloved Ivy. He and Ivy were having terrible arguments about politics. Ivy wanted to join the collective; Robby wanted to split for California and do working-class organizing. Women in the collective had told Robby that he was holding Ivy back; that it was only a matter of time before she would leave him for Weatherman. Why didn't he let her go now, and save them both the trouble and anguish? Monogamy was a deterrent to the revolution anyway.

Robby now saw me as an ally. He would come across the street and talk to me about the people in the collective. In a broken voice he told me one day that Jay had called him a pig.

"Susan, my best friend and he calls me a pig. Those people aren't human. Look how they treated you and you're one of them. What's so revolutionary about being cruel?" he'd ask over and over again.

I couldn't help Robby. He looked weak and insipid to me. I felt sorry for him, saw that he was losing ground, but felt too removed to offer any consolation. My own emotions boiled inside me, but I couldn't talk to anyone to let them out. I just festered.

Three days after the collective was formed, Ruth dropped out. She came home for the first time looking exhausted and drained. The first thing she did when she came into the house was to apologize to me for the things she had said about me. I apologized to her for acting so rudely, and told her that I had asked Garrity and Indian to find another place to live. When I asked Ruth why she had dropped out, she was very vague. Not looking at me, she finally told me that she just couldn't stand the pressure.

"You wouldn't believe what they're doing in that house," she said tearfully. "They have these criticism sessions, and everybody tells what's wrong with everybody else. It's supposed to help people change. Well, they told me again and again how weak I was, and how I had to get tougher. That I had to get tough to fight the pigs at the Days of Rage. Roger kept on saying some of us might die at the Days of Rage. I don't know. I got frightened. I couldn't stand it. I thought they were making demands of me that were impossible for me to meet. So I quit. They told me that I had no guts because I quit."

Hal interrupted savagely. "Well, I think it took more guts for you to quit. Goddam motherfuckers."

Simon muttered quietly, "Jesus. Those people are impossible."

Ruth said to me, "You're really lucky they didn't let you in, Susan."

None of it had any impact on me. I wanted to be in that Weatherman collective more than I had ever wanted anything in my life. More than I had wanted Robby Stern. It meant everything to me.

I thought that Weatherman was the only revolutionary group in the country. I believed their willingness to put their lives on the line put them in the vanguard. They took leadership even if no one was willing to follow. The vanguard did what had to be done even if they were the only ones doing it. J.J. had once said during the Columbia strikes, "If you think you're right politically, it's your obligation to continue what you're doing, no matter what the majority may feel." The majority in Seattle and across the country were violently opposed to Weatherman. Weatherman was the single biggest unifying factor in the Movement since the outbreak of the war. Ignoring opposition, Weatherman continued to form collectives, and to organize for the Days of Rage. It appeared sometimes that the Weatherpeople in Seattle were motivated because of the opposition to the collective rather than in spite of it.

I couldn't resist their appeal. Their flagrant arrogance, their contempt for everyone around them. I thought they were remarkable; I knew I belonged there. I had to be in the vanguard. Anything other than Weatherman was insignificant. I agreed with Jay that Robby was a pig if he didn't join the collective. I thought everybody was a pig who didn't want to be a Weatherman and go to Chicago for the Days of Rage.

It seemed so right. The politics were the only ones that remained after everything else had been tried and had failed. I had tried working in the Establishment, first as a teacher, then as a social worker. Then I had tried being a pacifist, first with the Civil Rights movement, then with the anti-war movement. I had joined SDS and demonstrated and marched for two years. And still the war continued. While the rich were getting richer, the poor were getting poorer. Since the government and the capitalists wouldn't listen to reason, then other means had to be employed.

Now it was time finally to attack. It was necessary. Black people were fighting regardless of whether white people helped or not. If people didn't want to die at the hands of blacks fighting for freedom, then they had to fight with them. There was no longer any middle ground. You were either part of the problem or part of the solution. With every pore of my body I wanted to be part of the solution.

About a week after the collective was formed, I was summoned to the Weatherman house at three o'clock in the morning. Putting on a bathrobe, I shambled across the street. Robby and Ivy were nowhere to be seen. Jay and Beverly, Georgia and Kate, Roger and Mickey sat around the dining-room table looking very serious and tired.

I stood waiting. Roger began speaking.

"We have decided to let you into the collective, Susan. We've been watching you this past week, and we can see some signs of change already. We are really impressed by how crushed you appeared when we would not let you into the collective. We still feel this was the wise decision. You seem much stronger as a result of it. You know there are only six of us; in a couple of days we may recruit one more person; but for the time being we are the only people in Seattle who will spend full time organizing for the Days of Rage. Although you are not completely ready to join the collective, we have decided to let you join. It's a functional decision; you're a good organizer and we need organizers. Well, what do you say?" And he leaned back, looking very pleased with himself.

"I don't want to join now." I heard myself say it, and I couldn't believe it. So I repeated it. "I don't want to join Weatherman now." There, I had said it again. And I realized I was telling the truth.

"You see, I believe in Weatherman, in everything we say; I am prepared to make a lifelong commitment to the revolutionary struggle, no matter how short my life may be as a result. But I don't think I am willing or able to change as much as necessary in the time allowed me. I agree with you all when you say I would be a detriment, if not a danger to the collective. I am too egocentric; too individualistic. I need some time to work these things out, and then I might be able to join the collective and be a genuine addition to it. For the present time, I would like to help organize around the Days of Rage, but continue living across the street."

Without any forethought, I had discovered a way to have my cake and eat it too. I could be a Weatherman, without having to undergo any of the rigorous transformation in my personality or life style that Weatherman demanded of its collective members.

Shocked silence greeted my statement. Roger started to speak, saying that wouldn't be good enough, but Beverly interrupted him with a commanding voice, and turning to me, smiled warmly and told me that would be all right for the time being. Perhaps I did need a little time to work things out. In the meantime, work around the Days of Rage was waiting. "Let's stop talking about Susan and start talking about bringing the war home.

"Now," she continued a previous discussion, "we are going to have to use Ty and Jean's printing press. That's going to be a problem since the entire house is corroding with Running Dogs. Kate, you used to live with them—maybe you could. . . ."

I had been allowed through the hallowed portals of Weatherland! Just like that, I had become one of several hundred scattered throughout America, the Weathernation. It was the happiest moment of my life. I felt like doing cartwheels. I was convinced that I had finally found my niche in life. I was so full of sparkling enthusiasm for the revolution, that I was sure it would vibrate out and capture dozens, hundreds, thousands, and eventually millions of other people.

I was a Weatherman cheerleader. I was a religious zealot. I was a crazy fool in love with the notion of revolution without any idea of its concept. I was thrilled with life, and felt I would now start living fully. My lips were parted for the revolution; my heart beating, my blood racing, and my tongue ready to pour out endless homage to it. And I didn't understand a damn thing about the revolution, and failed it miserably. But I couldn't have known that then, and even if I had, I would have ignored the truth.

The truth for me and too many other Weatherwomen and Weathermen in love with the revolution was that we weren't trying to build, but to destroy a country. That's the vital difference, the greatest single failure of Weatherman. We weren't too violent or exclusive. We simply represented no alternative to anyone. Once we tore down capitalism, who would empty the garbage, and teach the children and who would decide that? Would the world be Communist? Would the Third World control it? Would all whites die? Would all sex perverts die? Who would run the prisons—would there be prisons? Endless questions like these were raised by the Weathermen, but we didn't have the answers. And we were tired of trying to wait until we understood everything.

The next morning I woke up after only two or three hours of sleep, but I felt great. I ambled out into the living room; Robby and Hal abruptly broke off a conversation they were having.

Robby looked at me intently.

"Is it true? Have you joined the collective now?" he asked, looking as though it was a personal affront to him.

"Let's sit outside and talk, Robby," I said, walking out into the sunlight. "Yes, it's true. I'm now officially a Weatherman, whatever that means. But I don't have to move across the street. We all agreed that I still needed some time to develop more before I moved across the street."

"But, Susan," he began in desperation, "how can you agree with . . . *that?* It's wrong. It's terrifying. Susan, I'm frightened terribly by it."

"Why?" I asked curiously.

"Why? Because I'm afraid of dying. That's one of your lines, isn't it? Die if necessary? Not only is it foolish, but it's arrogant as hell. How can you tell other people they have to die for the revolution? Dying now would be suicide. The revolution isn't going to happen in two months, or even two years. Besides, it has nothing to do with people, real people, Susan. It has only to do with a bunch of macho, upper-class kids who are acting so irresponsibly that they are threatening the entire Movement . . ."

"Listen, Robby, you go to California and get a job in some factory and just try organizing the workers. They won't listen to you. They don't want to listen to you. They hate black people; and they have all been in the military and their children will be the ones to fight in Vietnam. They don't want to change, and you will not be able to organize them any more than PL or any of those groups.

"It's just a copout on your part. It's easier to go off and organize workers than it is to go out and face the real issues. Either we have to fight or we will die as enemies of the people. It's much easier to hide in some factory and say you're doing your part, while the Black Panthers go on getting creamed, and the ghettos are like concentration camps. The revolution is already in progress. You know that. You can see it all around the world. And here in the United States, black people are fighting too. Well it's time for white people to join that fight.

"You're afraid of dying, and you're also afraid of changing. You're still basically a white, middle-class, Jewish boy who will grow up to be a lawyer and a staunch pillar of liberal . . ."

Pale and trembling, Robby towered above me.

"Well, just who is going to make the revolution, Susie? Are you going to fight everyone who doesn't agree with you? Are you going to kill every white person in this country? Are you and a few thousand other people the only revolutionaries in the entire fucking country? Well, sister, I feel sorry for you. Do you really think all people with white skins should die, Susie, do you really?" He was practically screaming at me.

"If they're not going to do shit, well . . . yes, I do. If people won't join us, then they are against us. It's as simple as that. That includes the working class, and kids, if necessary."

"Everybody has to die."

"Everybody has to die."

"Good for you, Susie. That's the kind of dogmatism I like to hear."

"I wasn't being cryptic, Robby. I don't see any way out of it. If nobody wants to do anything, then they might as well all die."

"Well, you know, that's the way you view the world. You didn't start seeing things that way when you became a revolutionary. You have always done these numbers behind suicide."

"Suicide is just taking my own life."

"Now Weatherman can give you some kind of social basis for doing it as opposed to a personal basis."

"Do you think that's why I'm a Weatherman?"

"To a certain extent. A lot of the Weatherpeople come from rich backgrounds, and I think that's the reason why a lot . . ."

"Roger and Jay don't."

"No, Bernardine didn't either. But most of you do. Weatherman is composed of a lot of intellectuals, many people who were very unhappy, who had a neurotic upbringing, and also some people who have some very decent visions about what they want the world to be."

"That's true of me, Robby, about the neurosis, but it's certainly not true of all Weathermen. Lots of them are vibrant, healthy, brilliant people who just can't stand how fucked up this country is and how it's destroying the rest of the world. They are people who think this country is worth saving, and who are willing to sacrifice their lives to do so. What's sick about that? No, you're just trying to attach a sickness to something beautiful and rare, because you aren't strong enough to cope with it. You're so afraid to deal with dying, so unable to give up your old way of life, that you castigate people who do. But it's too feeble, Robby. Weatherman is right, good, and strong, and we're going to win. Thousands of people are going to come to the Days of Rage. Kids, lots of them working class, all around the country are going to see us win militarily against the pigs, and they will realize they can do it too."

Looking dejected, Robby sighed.

"I'm going to leave for California. I only hope Ivy is with me. It's unbearable in that house." He laughed bitterly.

"I'm being kicked out of my own house. When they have collective meetings, Ivy and I are told to leave. Even if I didn't go to California, I would have to find another place to live. It's almost unbelievable. I've lived with Jay for two years, and with Roger for over a year; I was largely responsible for bringing Mickey and Beverly into the Movement. Now they all act as if I were an enemy of the people."

I didn't say anything. God, the worm had turned. Now I was the one who felt strong and solid, who knew who my friends were, who knew what my place in life was. Arrogant in my position, I felt little pity for Robby, torn by indecision and circumstances which were sweeping him along, oblivious to his needs or fears.

The last week in August, tensions between the people in the Weatherman collective, and the Running Dogs grew intolerable for everyone but the Weathermen. People who had been friends for years became enemies almost overnight. Jay and Robby couldn't talk without erupting into violent disagreement about the role of the working class, or whether community programs which served the people were a better revolutionary tool than the gun.

The Running Dogs were by no means a coherent group; their only common bond was their hatred for Weatherman. For a while there was a secret group which existed primarily to subvert Weatherman. Then there was a group of men, mostly street people and friends, who met together on a social basis. This group fluctuated between wanting to "off" collective people, with the exception of Jay, and wanting to talk some sense into them. Mike Justesen had been with this group until the middle of August. Then he had left for Japan, a trip which had been arranged for him through the National Office, and especially Bill Ayers. Although Mike was in disagreement with the Weathermen by that time, the NO still wanted him to make the trip. It turned out to be wise planning on their part.

With Mike gone, the theoretical level of the group deteriorated, and what was left was dominated by the vindictive Stalinism of Hal. Ray, Simon, Garrity, and, when he was around, Indian, and several other men were in this group.

The women, with one or two exceptions, refused to be categorized because they were constantly in contact with non-Weatherwomen through a women's caucus. Furthermore, the Weatherwomen seemed to have less difficulty in maintaining friendships despite the increasing schism in their politics. Georgia and Kate had lived with Ty and Jean Baxter in a large Running Dog house; Jean, Kate, and Georgia had remained close throughout the summer, and through the fall. Jean, as a result of this friendship, never developed the violent hatred of the collective that consumed most of the men. Either because of her discussion with him, or because of his own political consciousness, her husband, Ty, also remained ambivalent toward the collective throughout the fall.

Ivy, Robby's girl friend, was not ambivalent. She wanted to join the collective, but found it impossible to choose between Robby and Weatherman. The Weatherwomen talked with her a great deal about smashing her monogamous relationship. Intellectually she realized they were right, that Robby was holding her back. Emotionally, she was not yet strong enough to deal with the thought of being without him. Miserable, she continued to make plans to leave for California with Robby.

Ruth, although no longer in the collective, was still committed to Weatherman politics. In her gentle way she would try to argue with Hal when he harangued about the collective; but she found him impossible to talk with.

While all the people opposed to Weatherman ran around frenetically trying to develop some alternative to it, the collective itself concentrated only on itself. Every time I entered the Weatherman house, it was like crossing the threshold to a new world. Politics and change; transformation and commitment, individual and collective: this was all we thought about and talked about.

The key to the hours of criticism was struggle. Struggle was the only way to produce change; change was growth. To purge ourselves of the taint of some twenty-odd years of American indoctrination, we had to tear ourselves apart mentally.

With an enthusiasm born of total commitment, we began the impossible task of overhauling our brains. Out all the garbage our parents and schools taught us—in all the wisdom of Mao, Ho Chi Minh, and Che Guevara—OVERHAUL![1] That's what we attempted to do in a few short weeks. Turn ourselves inside out and start all over again. Fearless and unmindful of the dangers involved, we plunged into the process.

DARE TO STRUGGLE,

DARE TO WIN.

That was our credo. We began to teach ourselves how to live it.

All of our money was given to Beverly. She was chosen by the group as the most responsible person. She then opened a bank account under her name, but which belonged to the Handle-Vandals.

My car, Roger's, and Mickey's became collective property which was used by the collective when work needed to be done. Thinking only a few months ahead, upkeep was not considered: Zelda and the other cars were literally run into the ground.

Everyone quit work. There was no time, since we were in criticism sessions almost twenty hours a day. Besides, there was money around at that time, and living was cheap. We collected food stamps as a house, which took care of our food. For gas, we had credit cards. For electricity we had Ray hook up a special electrical outlet which didn't register with Seattle City Light. We never considered paying our telephone bill; when the present phone was turned off, we planned to get a new one.

Then there were material possessions, all of which had become worthless to us. Most of us came from middle-class backgrounds; all had little things that we could sell and get enough money to operate on. Puss and Books, a used-book and antiques store on the Ave, began to support us.

I will never forget the day I sold my library. Almost fifteen years of reading. Each book a precious friend. In my room, I leafed through book after book, piled them in giant cartons, and took them across the street. Beverly had her pile; Georgia had hers. Maybe we got a hundred dollars for all those books.

Next went the records. Jay's Mose Allison, my Nina Simone; stacked neatly, tied in bundles, sold at Puss and Books for maybe another hundred dollars.

Then Beverly and I collected all the jewelry. A precious little set of pearls from Georgia; a pin from Kate; Mickey's wedding ring; a pile of jewelry my father had given me through the years. Sold for maybe a couple of hundred at Puss and Books.

And the antiques. In tears, Georgia handed me a little Chinese jade statue; I got over thirty dollars for it. With it went eight delicately carved miniature ivory horses my father had given me; over twenty for them. And so on. Stripping ourselves of possessions we would no longer need, we lived off our past, while in the very process of stripping ourselves of our past.

Our aim was to make ourselves equal, men and women, practically interchangeable. We had no guidelines, no scruples; we simply started. Some of us suffered more than others, all of us were tortured to some degree. But no amount of anguish was intolerable when one considered the end result: a revolutionary warrior, worthy to fight in the world-wide struggle for liberation. Our ideal was nothing less than the Vietcong. All eight of us were committed to the notion of transforming ourselves into Americong. The process of criticism, self-criticism, transformation was the tool by which we would forge ourselves into new human beings.

We were all very different people.

Georgia's family moved a lot when she was growing up. Although she was straight, she was always different from the rest of them. She became something of a scapegoat after she became political. She rarely talked about her past.

In 1968–69 Georgia was a terribly shy, extremely nervous student in the School of Social Work at the U of W. She became involved in politics through Black and White Concern, a white liberal group studying black problems. There she met Ty and Jean Baxter and Kate, and moved in with them in the spring.

Apparently Georgia made a complete turnabout in personality when, at the age of twenty-three, she joined Weatherman. Lonely, neurotic, and in terrible need of love and understanding, she threw herself into Weatherman totally. With a tremendous effort she repressed her fears and timidity, and became a study of the tough, masculine woman that characterized so many Weatherwomen. Wearing heavy men's boots, jeans, and an army jacket, her hair uncombed, no make-up, chain-smoking with trembling hands and drinking either tea or wine constantly, she learned the Weatherman line and stuck to it. By the time I entered the collective she was a drawn, thin nervous wreck. Through sheer force of will she managed to function under the tremendous pressure of the collective. Her mind was kept together with safety pins; I always expected them to come open at any moment.

Beverly appeared rather aloof and cold. She seemed to be frightened of nothing, until suddenly I'd discover she had a bunch of really peculiar little fears. One of these concerned driving. She would rarely drive a car above thirty-five miles an hour even on the freeway. She panicked when someone else was driving.

Beverly had led a straight, middle-class life. Twenty-six when she entered the collective, she had been married to a very mild, professorial-type man for several years. They led a quiet life, built around their relationship and their home. Beverly loved to cook delicious little meals for them; the house was decorated with dozens of plants and crafts that she made—little table mats that she had woven, old furniture that she had redone. She was very much the young housewife. She had been an airline stewardess for two years, and when she quit school in 1969, she was just short of obtaining a doctorate degree.

Beverly had a strong sense of herself. Everybody, including me, looked to her for direction. That's why she had the money; she kept the thing together.

In 1968 Beverly did work with the Peace and Freedom Party in Seattle; she then went into Black and White Concern, and eventually into SDS. In the spring of 1969 she met Jay, who had just returned from New York, immediately fell in love with him, and in a matter of weeks left her brokenhearted husband, left school and her sweetly decorated little house, and moved with Jay into the Woodlawn house. For Beverly this was an important political as well as personal step in her life. It was characteristic of her strength of purpose that she did it cleanly, and with little hesitation.

Beverly was perfect to direct the collective. Bright and articulate, exuding strength and confidence, she was everything a strong woman leader should be. Soft spoken, proud, attractive, her eyes blazed at you as she spoke; many people were intimidated by her, especially after she became a Weatherman. I loved and admired her, and felt honored when she allowed me to become her closest friend in the collective after Jay.

Kate Saddler was probably the only person in the collective to whom revolution was not at all artificial. Her parents had been very liberal both in their political views and in the rearing of their daughter. Falling in love with a quiet, studious man when she was barely seventeen, Kate left home and went to live with him, ignoring all the social conventions of her high school peer group. She eventually married him.

A small, pixielike woman of twenty, with frizzy black hair and vibrant eyes, Kate bounded with healthy energy and the gusto of life. To her life was revolution; politics meant the way she walked, breathed, talked and smiled. Having figured out the contradictions in her life at an early age, she was revolutionary in a totally natural way. She loved politics as enthusiastically as she loved everything she did. Her conversion was rapid. She quickly became disenchanted with Black and White Concern and moved swiftly toward the more militant factions of SDS. She was committed enough to Weatherman to leave her bewildered husband and join the collective when it was formed.

Weatherman changed Kate least of anybody. Although she left the collective soon after it was formed to work at the NO, she never lost her sense of herself. Smiling and bobbing, Kate was not broken by her revolutionary dreams. Perhaps she was strengthened by them. She was an invaluable asset to a collective that inundated itself by taking itself far too seriously.

Carol was recruited to the collective about a week after I joined it. About twenty at the time, she had been a college student in a small college in Washington. Robby had gone there to organize and spent some time with her while he was there. She was something of a leader in the SDS chapter on her campus. Inclining toward Weatherman politics, and being more advanced than anyone else in her chapter, she came to Seattle, and became a part of the collective.

Carol seemed to have boomeranged straight from a strict upbringing and the Catholic church right into Weatherman. Her role in the collective was logically derived from her background. She appeared unemotional and totally repressed. She disapproved of drugs and drinking, of sex and sheer fun. Serious to the point of absurdity, she was the toughest person in the collective. She had absolutely no use for anybody outside of the collective, unless she thought they were organizable. If you weren't a Weatherman you were a pig. Period. Exclamation point.

I never liked Carol, although I never gave her a chance to be other than what she appeared to be. In a world where we were all trying to live up to impossible standards, Carol's Stalinism was just another frustrated form of expression. I attributed to her the very worst aspects of Weatherman; the lack of love and lovingness; the lack of emotion, the singlemindedness which refused to accept human difference and human error; an inability to enjoy life and people. I saw her relentless determination to adhere to the very last letter of the Weatherman line as a weakness, rather than a strength. When Carol laughed, she didn't smile.

Mickey had been in SDS the previous year. At the age of twenty, he had a wife and infant to support. He was himself more an adolescent than a man. Tall, gangly, shy, and not very bright, he followed stronger personalities, no matter where they led him. Perhaps he had been confused when Roger and Robby began to argue and the SDS chapter factionalized; I don't know how he ended up in Weatherman. But whether out of pressure, honest commitment, or plain relief, he abruptly left his wife and child, and came to live in the collective house. Since smashing monogamy was one of Weatherman's greatest points of emphasis, this was seen as a great strength in Mickey, rather than as irresponsibility.

Mickey rarely ventured to do any thinking on his own. Generally he parroted what Roger or Beverly said, attributing to them the theoretical expertise in the collective. I didn't like him very much. To this day I don't know, as with Carol, how wrong or right I was.

Jay was a source of light and warmth to me, and to the collective generally. Although his politics became more defined when he became a Weatherman, his personality changed very little. There were two things that meant everything to him: Beverly and the revolution. He needed both to survive. After those basics, he liked plenty of beer and wine, lots of marijuana, Mose Allison, and a kitchen to cook in.

At a time when everybody disagreed about everything, Jay was universally loved. Inside and outside the collective, he was our image of the Communist man. Sincere, honest, cheerful, loyal, roaring to tear into life, he was one of the finest people I ever knew, and one of the countless unsung revolutionaries of our time. Looking at Jay made me smile, made me feel good, and I would think, "Well maybe, just maybe, there is a chance for humanity."

From the time the collective was formed and I was not allowed into it, I didn't like Roger. I always thought of him as a snake, slipping around under cover of night, or in disguise. I never saw him express any real emotion. Unobtrusive, soft-spoken, hovering in the background, Roger was the Great Manipulator. It's still not clear to me how such an innocuous person could have wielded so much power. But whatever way the wind was blowing, Roger was headed in that direction.

There was no doubt that he was a brilliant theoretician. There was no doubt that he was a fine organizer; he had organized me into Weatherman. And in some way, he must have been committed to the revolution. But I think he used it more than he was ever committed to it. As much as Roger talked about the people of the world, I don't think he ever let them inside of him. His mind was filled with strong ideas, but his heart was empty. He addressed people, saw their faces, but was never able to love them. That was tragic for Roger, because that love for people was our strength.

Roger had the main ties with the NO and to the Weatherbureau, which is what the leadership collective in Chicago was eventually called. He would telephone them several times a week, get directions, and carry them out. In a collective where everybody was supposed to be equal, Roger made it clear that he would hold onto his leadership at any cost.

The oldest of four boys, he was like the older son who misses out on everything. His younger brothers were all more personable and less insecure than Roger. The brothers seem very close, and all the younger ones are political. Presumably they followed in their older brother's footsteps.

No matter how pathetically I saw Roger, I never trusted him, and I felt he was a destructive force in the collective.

I differed little in background from the others in my collective, except that my father was very wealthy. My parents divorced when I was three, and at the age of nine, after years of brutal courtroom battles, I went to live with my father and brother in New Jersey. My father, unstable and insensitive, loved me compulsively. In his frustrated attempts to prove his love, he bought me everything in the world: all kinds of lessons, expensive clothes, Caribbean cruises and vacations with him at the most exclusive resorts in the Catskills. My mother, beautiful and childlike, remarried when I went to live with my father, and devoted the next ten years of her life to the dashing, tumultuous man she could not live without. She loved my brother and myself, but she loved her husband more.

I grew up terribly shy and introverted and convinced of my inferiority to everyone around me. By the time I entered Syracuse University at the age of eighteen, I was a slight, sallow girl with sad dark eyes, short, unstyled hair, and large black-rimmed glasses. I always half-dreamed of suicide as an alternative to a drab, meaningless, and miserable existence.

In 1964, my last year as an undergraduate at Syracuse, I met Robby Stern and within a few weeks moved out of my dormitory and into an apartment with him. We were married six months later. I became pregnant and had an abortion, and dropped out of graduate study in English literature. I became involved in CORE and the Civil Rights movement, and worked for five months as a teacher in a ghetto grade school while earning teaching credentials. I was thrown out of the teaching program because my methods of teaching were too radical.

Next I set up a library for a Peruvian Peace Corps Program. Through my research, I began to learn about American imperialism. Robby's friends were talking more about the war in Vietnam; they supported the Vietcong, and when one of them, whom I knew and liked, burned his draft card and went to prison, I swung sharply left.

Robby and I were never happily married. Neurotic, depressed, insecure, and totally dependent on Robby, I demanded constant attention. Comparing myself to him endlessly, and always finding him superior, I hated and resented him for the very qualities that made me love him: his charm, brilliance, robust handsomeness, and charismatic appeal. Our move to Seattle was an attempt to leave our old life behind and start out fresh. But by the time I entered the School of Social Work in September of 1966, the scars of my childhood stood between me and the ability to simply slide soundlessly into the niche the system had provided for me. It was not until the spring of 1967, when I separated briefly from Robby and immersed myself in the hippie counterculture, that I began to rip myself away from my past, and focus with an awakening sense of urgency on the future.

During the last week of August, as the days shortened, Weatherman became my world. Everything I did, I did as a Weatherman. The way I dressed, the manner in which I talked, what I said, my friends, whom I slept with, my eating, my sleeping, my reading, my feelings about my past, all were open to the closest scrutiny. There was no part of me left unexposed and unchanged by Weatherman.

With the others in the collective I found my identity as an outlaw, living beyond the pale, hating and fearing the pig, surviving by my wits, proud and uncompromising as an Indian in battle, fiercely loyal to my comrades, ready to die every moment for the struggle to which I was devoting my life.

I had anticipated changing, I had expected differences, but not in my wildest dreams could I have projected the Weatherman experience until it happened to me. I struggled in the collective with Weatherman as I had never struggled in my life. I grappled desperately with my past in an effort to change, hoping to set an example for other women and men to follow. No matter how much I suffered, I never lost sight of the goal. There could be no life if there was no goal. I saw America as so destructive, its people so damned that I had no choice but to struggle on, until we either won or died.

While our friends outside the collective alternately raged and laughed at us, we geared ourselves for total subjugation to Weatherman discipline and our vision of the revolutionary life.

At the end of August, Georgia was sent to Cleveland, to an NIC meeting to discuss the Days of Rage. But the rupture in SDS was so deep that RYM 2 people stayed away from the conference. Only Weathermen showed up for the three-day meeting. On September 2, SDS in Seattle met to hear Georgia's report. I chaired the meeting.

Georgia was radiant. Her eyes sparkling, her cheeks deeply flushed, she looked like a woman who had seen a vision. "It was mystical," was all she could say. She smiled, almost to herself, looking around the room, separated by the invisible barrier of her unique experience. "I don't have the words . . . the openness, the closeness . . . the love . . . it . . . it . . . was just mystical." And in a dreamy voice, not at all characteristic of Georgia's frenetic speech, she went on to tell us that the Days of Rage could never fail.

"There's something new here, different, something people in this country haven't experienced before. When they begin to see the strength of Weatherman, they will want to be a part of it."

She went on to tell us that one of the strongest concepts of Weatherman was the smashing of monogamy.

"You could see the women getting stronger as the relationships between the men and women began to change in Cleveland. Lots of women were criticized heavily for not really struggling with male chauvinism. Some couples broke up right there, and the women, who had been real quiet before, you know, like women generally are, well, suddenly they were different. They looked different, talked different. They began to talk up more at meetings, and many of the men were surprised; the women had their own ideas and opinions." If Georgia was any example of the amazing growth and change of women so swiftly, then it must have been startling. Having gone to Cleveland a nervous, agonized wreck, she had returned supercharged, but under control. Full of confidence in her role, looking forward to winning, she bore the unmistakable mark of a woman in the process of discovering herself.

Georgia told us about Bill Ayers's speech, to the boos and groans of the Running Dogs in the meeting.

"We have been attacked," Ayers had said, "for fighting the people instead of serving the people. The more I think about that thing— fight the people—there's something to it. What's true about it is that we've never been in a struggle where we don't have to fight some of the people . . .

"There's a lot in white Americans that we do have to fight, and beat out of them, and beat out of ourselves. We have to be willing to fight people and fight things in ourselves, and fight things in all white Americans—white privilege, racism, male supremacy—in order to build a revolutionary movement.

"What we have to communicate to people is our overwhelming strength. . . That's the image of Vietnam—strength, confidence— that's what we have to bring to our own constituency. You join the Movement because you want to be part of the world-wide struggle that's obviously winning and you win people over by being honest to them about the risks, about struggle, by telling them they're getting into a fight. It's not a comfortable life! It's not just a dollar more an hour. It's standing up in the face of the enemy, risking your life and everything for the struggle. But it's also being on the side of victory; that's the essential thing we have to show people . . ."

As Georgia spoke, I felt goosebumps. "It's really true, then, there is a war going on, and I'm part of it," I thought, close to tears.

As Georgia finished speaking, the room erupted in emotional outbursts. The Weathermen cheered exultingly; jumping up and down on the desks, screaming, "Bring the war home." Some of the Running Dogs, livid with fury, began screaming that we were left-wing adventurists, irresponsible, and that everybody thought we were ridiculous. Hal, Ray, and several others shouted that Weathermen were such wimps, they would probably run the minute pigs appeared on the streets of Chicago. Robby, Ty, and Jean looked confused. And in the far left corner of the room, quietly nodding out, were Indian and Garrity, having copped some smack on the way to the meeting.

I was a rather laissez-faire chairwoman. Slouched in my chair, my feet on the desk, I had managed to keep fairly good order until the conclusion of Georgia's presentation. Then, enthralled like all the other Weathermen, I did my share of screaming and jumping. Then I tried to get the meeting back to order.

"Listen," I shouted over the bedlam, "nobody in this room agrees with anybody on anything. But please, let's try. If this is the way we handle the first SDS meeting in September, then we'll turn off everyone who comes. Now when someone wants to speak, raise your hand."

A Running Dog raised her hand and, glowering at the Weathermen, who were laughing and talking among themselves, she explained that there would be another National Action in Chicago during the Days of Rage. "This," she said, "would be an alternative to the suicide squad organized by the Weathermen."

Roger wanted to speak next. He, Georgia, and Kate had a fall program proposal prepared; it suggested work on campus, building for the Days of Rage; it also suggested the first September SDS meeting end with an action on campus.

Beverly suggested that the women should form a caucus and meet together more frequently and organize for an action at the beginning of the school year. The Running Dogs said this was Weatherman manipulation since the majority of SDS women were Weathermen. In spite of objections, a caucus of women was formed.

That meeting was a turning point for Weatherman. Georgia and her vague but thrilling description of the Cleveland Conference had imbued us with something akin to divine inspiration. We decided to begin organizing around the Days of Rage immediately. It was only five weeks away.

The main leaflet we handed out describing the Days of Rage said that it would happen on October 8–11, would be in Chicago, and that there would be a series of actions aimed at exposing the real nature of the pig power structure, that there would be a memorial rally for Che Guevara, who had been murdered by the CIA on October 8; that there would be actions at high schools all over Chicago; a women's action; a march on the courts, demanding freedom for all political prisoners; a youth rock festival, and a mass march demanding that U.S. troops get out of Vietnam, Latin America, and all foreign countries, out of the schools and out of the streets. Thousands of white youth would come to Chicago, and we would bring the war home. That was how I saw the Days of Rage; that's what the Weathermen in Seattle organized for. The month of September and the first week of October were consumed in building for the action.

I would get up at six in the morning, skip breakfast, quaff coffee, and launch into final plans and instructions for the attack on a high school planned for eleven that morning. Usually all eight of us went on these attacks. It took something like twenty to thirty hours to plan for one good attack that lasted for two minutes.

The normal attack ran something like this: two people would stand guard, one just inside the door of the classroom, the other just by the phone in the class, so that the horrified and petrified teacher could not call over the phone to the principal's office or to the pigs. Two people would hand out *Bring the War Home* leaflets, with information on it pertaining to racism and the war, as well as the Days of Rage. Two people would spray-paint on the blackboard things like OFF THE PIGS, END THE WAR IN VIETNAM, FREE HUEY NEWTON, and other demands. Usually one person would be there just to lead the attack in general, and he or she had to control unruly teachers and students. The last Weatherman stood on the teacher's desk, orating a prepared one-minute speech. The speech was much like the leaflets and notes on the blackboard—usually exhortations for the kids to drop out of their boring hellish schools, leave their dehumanizing parents and empty home lives, and come with us to Chicago for the biggest party-brawl of their lives.

As soon as the speech ended, we'd bolt like mad from the school-room, flee a hundred miles per hour down the academic hallways and out into the sunlight and down the block to eight different escape routes, planned so that all eight people would not be caught in case the police were following us.

After following our escape routes, we would hastily get into Zelda, which was parked conveniently nearby. Usually an action ended by eleven-thirty, and we were on our way to leaflet at another school for the noon hour. This ended at one-fifteen, at which point we'd go home and begin a criticism session about the action. At two-thirty we returned to another high school to leaflet the kids as they left school. By three or three-thirty, we had returned home to continue the criticism sessions, clean the house, do grocery shopping, plan a new action or work on another leaflet.

Our high school attacks were largely unsuccessful as far as recruiting went. But the level of political consciousness was raised unbeliev-ably among the kids. Wherever we went, we stimulated energy and emotions. Pushing them to the furthest extent, we confronted high school kids with their racism, the war, male chauvinism, and their ever-diminishing power in society. Angry and defensive, they would fight back bitterly and sometimes violently in response. We never got discouraged, no matter how poorly they responded. We knew it took time for people to admit their lives were fucked up.

I loved the high school organizing, and thought we were doing the right things no matter how the kids reacted. Dressed in tight jeans, a tight sweater, a great purple hat, a long purple scarf, a black leather jacket, black high-heeled boots, and long dangling earrings, I would bop onto the school grounds, and station myself near the school building. Pretty soon people would come by to read that day's leaflet and rap. Lots of times they'd shake their head at me and tell me I was a fool when I talked very earnestly about fighting the pigs in Chicago. But they never got too angry; I generally switched the subject matter to music or dope before they exploded. We'd talk about Jimi Hendrix for a while and then I'd start in again about the war.

Day after day we went back to the same schools. Day after day we got nowhere. Our spirit undaunted, we figured it was only a matter of time before the kids would see the light and come around.

One of the major ideas behind Weatherman was that everyone should be totally self-sufficient, like a guerrilla fighter. This applied especially to women, since, as a rule, they had been denied the general development of various skills taken for granted among men. Everyone in the collective had to learn how to do everything.

We all had to be automobile mechanics. Roger, who was a skilled mechanic, spent time teaching the women about the different parts of a car. At that time I was pretty skilled in changing tires, replacing fanbelts, and putting oil in cars. I wasn't afraid of grease.

There was an old A. B. Dick offset printing press at Ty and Jean's house. Although they resented the intrusion, especially since they were not wholly sympathetic to Weatherman, they allowed us to use the press. It had several parts missing, among them the feeder, and one of the "sucking" mechanisms, so you had to push one of the feeder rollers into the ink manually, then run to the other end, and lift out the newly printed sheet. In time we all learned how to run the press, how to load it, ink it, fix it, where to buy supplies for it, and how to find used, inexpensive parts for it. The press was our lifeline; we used it day and night to produce the endless flow of leaflets necessary for our high school organizing.

We all learned how to lay out leaflets, how to type them up fast. No matter how timid or shy we were, we all gave speeches, either during high school attacks or on the campus, where we began to make our presence known toward the end of September. It wasn't very difficult to make a speech, since we all said the same thing— there's a war going on. You're either on one side or the other. And if you're on our side you'll be in Chicago October 8 through 11.

It was impossible to argue with us when we were giving speeches, even though many people of all ages, political persuasions, and in every kind of situation imaginable tried to. We spoke so harshly, and so contemptuously of anyone who would dare to argue with us, that people either walked away or simply had to listen. Some people looked terrified when we talked about the disintegration of America and the impending battles to be waged in the streets of Seattle and all other cities. Others looked confused when we explained how America was on the brink of collapse. The majority were overwhelmingly hostile. Many times I had things thrown at me while I spoke. In reaction, I would shriek that the man, or woman, was a racist, honky pig, and that the armies of the people of the world would smash them if they didn't join us.

We all took turns cooking and cleaning the house. That is, we took turns in those rare instances when we cooked or ate or cleaned either ourselves or the house. Our lives were run on such a tight schedule that a bath or shower, or a meal where you actually cooked and then sat down and ate from a washed plate was an almost unthinkable luxury.

Dishes piled like mountains in the sink and on the counters; molds and funguses grew on them, and if you got a chance to eat, you scraped the whole glop off and whizzed some water over it and golumped on the new mess you were going to eat. The dust gathered in drifts where the floors met the walls, and suddenly we would get a free half hour and a mop and broom would appear and we would clean frenetically. For half a day there would be no dust, and no oily layer of dirt anywhere. Then it would accumulate all over again, and two days later the house looked like a trashcan.

There was never any time to make a home out of what had once been a beautiful house. Extra leaflets were piled in heaps along with old Seattle *Times*, old *New Left Notes, Guardians, Movements,* and newer underground newspapers, since we felt it necessary to be on top of all the revolutionary news happening over the entire country. If there was ever a moment when we weren't involved in some activity, or deep in criticism–self-criticism, then we had the responsibility to read and study. We had to know what we were talking about in order to explain it to other people. Behind the seemingly simplistic Weatherman line was a complex series of political equations; each of us tried to understand them.

During the month of September I averaged three hours' sleep in twenty-four. I frequently stayed up all night working at the press, and then caught a couple of hours' sleep during the following afternoon. Since Beverly had the money, and I frequently kept her company, I did a lot of the grocery shopping, and running around getting ink, parts, and paper for the press. I was always exhausted, along with everyone else in the collective.

Just when increasing hostility at the high schools would begin to subvert our enthusiasm, or when exhaustion would threaten our commitment, Roger would casually mention at a criticism session that he had received a letter from the Weatherbureau—they were broke, they couldn't raise enough money to get out the Weatherman newspaper *Fire Next Time,* they were being busted right and left, pig harassment was heavier than ever, but they were getting courage from all the collectives pushing so hard for the Days of Rage around the country. Please send money; keep on pushing. Remember, Chicago is less than a month away. And newly inspired by the heroic example being set in Chicago, the collective would plunge on.

These missives from the Bureau would warn the collectives that we were on our own financially. As a result of Weatherman politics—more clearly revolutionary—the old, liberal sources were drying up. Parents, convinced that their children had gone insane, or, at the least, unable to relate to them as criminals and violent revolutionaries, started to cut them off by the thousands. With bail beginning to escalate, and anticipating extensive arrests in Chicago, the collective began to cut down severely on living expenses so that we would have bail money for the Days of Rage.

According to instructions, much of this money was collected by Roger and sent to the Bureau. If we heard rumors that the Weatherbureau was eating steak and flying first class while we in Seattle were eating rice and spaghetti and hitchhiking, we ignored them. Our leadership was infallible. Our leadership was our source of inspiration. They were the creators of Weatherman. They took the most chances and thought the most seriously. If they had steak every now and then, didn't they deserve it? There was nothing our leadership could do that they could not justify.

Meanwhile, we pushed ourselves harder, criticized ourselves more vehemently, pummeled away at our bourgeois hangups until we were groggy. Most of our criticism–self-criticism centered around fighting, and how we fought, and how we reacted to violence.

All of us had weaknesses that were constantly being called out. All of us were lacking in a billion ways for the task of building for the revolution. If the task was impossible, none of us was aware of it. We continued to attack high schools and to organize them. We increased our criticism sessions. We doubled our efforts to be prepared for the Days of Rage. As we grew internally, we became more and more isolated from everyone outside of the collective, no matter what our relationship to them had been previously. Outside of organizing for the Days of Rage, we had nothing to say to anybody.

Mike Justesen returned from Japan early in the second week of September. Robby went to pick him up at the airport, and told him about the collective. Then he gave him a copy of Bill Ayers's Cleveland speech to read, the one in which Ayers stressed fighting the people. Mike was very upset.

"Oh no, man, what is this shit? This is political suicide," was his reaction.

With Mike back, the RYM 2 people had a leader with some strength, and some new experiences. His stay in Japan had been overwhelming to his political development. He couldn't adjust to being back in Seattle with "all this political shit flying."

Mike made many visits to the Weatherman house. He would come in and sit down at the head of the dining-room table and slouching in his seat, glare at all of us.

"You pompous assholes," he'd shout. "You motherfuckers. Who the hell do you think you are? You think you're going up against the pigs? With what, your sheer stupidity? You think you got all the answers? Well, who's listening to you? Everybody fucking hates you. All the high school kids think you're ridiculous. The Panthers won't have anything to do with you; they're afraid of getting fucked by the pigs because of you. You don't know the first thing about security. Go around telling everyone how to make Molotovs, and why they should pick up the gun. How many of you know how to shoot a gun?" He would rant on and on, getting more and more infuriated until he'd start pounding the table with frustration.

All of us would calmly sit there, and tell him he couldn't ignore us for long, because he knew we were right, and that's why he was getting so upset. He must have learned something in Japan. He must see how the international struggle is being waged. He must see that the working class has chosen to take the crumbs big business offers it, and to remain opposed to the black race. He must see that the only way women will get stronger is to fight actively around racism and imperialism. He must see that the Days of Rage were going to be the greatest action in the history of America, and that it was just the start. He must see that Weatherman had to go on in spite of what anyone would say, because we were right. And he would realize we were right. And he would join us eventually.

"There's no one who has dedicated his life to the destruction of the capitalistic system of the United States and can avoid being a Weatherman. Don't let your Running Dog friends hold you back, Mike," Roger said softly.

With that, red in the face, Mike jumped up. He was so furious he could barely talk.

"God damn it," he shouted. "You all deserve to get killed in Chicago, you idiots." And trembling with rage, he ran out the door, and across the street where he was crashing.

Late that night in the gray house, Mike got very drunk with Simon and some of the other Running Dogs, and told them about his experiences in Japan. I sat quietly on the couch listening.

"When I was in Japan," Mike said, "there was a big struggle over an airport there. Peasant farmers were living on the land, and the government was evicting them to build this huge military airport. So the Movement, which was mostly students, got together with the peasants. They did a snake dance. The Japanese invented it, you know. Everybody links into a line. The people at the end of the line have big poles. The energy keeps on building up and so does the anger of the people against the military. Then in a gigantic burst of energy, screaming, the line broke through the rows of pigs lined up with shields in front of us. The next thing I knew I was in this dancing snake of energy. People were just whipping through and knocking pigs down.

"We won. We fought the pigs and won. That's how the people fight the state. That's how to win. Not that . . . that . . . those wimps over there," he shook his head in the direction of the Weatherman house. "Now can you see Mickey or Georgia with a gun? I mean, with the exception of Jay, can you seriously imagine any of those people fighting anybody? Fucking Roger's scared of spray-painting!"

"People change, you know," I said, feeling obligated to defend the collective. But everyone ignored me. Feeling I didn't belong there, I went to bed.

Mike was quiet for a time. He kept on drinking out of the bottle of sake. Then he said very quietly,

"I just don't understand them. I don't understand them at all."

One of the other men in the room, Alex, said, "It's like they're all possessed. If you don't agree with them right now, you're fucked. They're crazy, man, it's almost as if they want to die."

"But there's something in it," Mike said musingly. "Something that no one else has. They're willing to do something. No matter how fucked up they may be, no matter how off the wall, they are willing to do anything, put their lives on the line to bring about the revolution. Now can that be said of us? Maybe the real reason we resent them so is that they show us how weak we really are. I mean, there they are, and they got absolutely nothing, you know, a bunch of women and wimpy men, and they can't shoot, and probably couldn't fight if their lives depended on it and it doesn't seem to matter to them. They just keep on organizing for those fucking Days of Rage."

"Yeah," said Alex softly, very drunk, looking deep into his own motivations, frightened by the reality of death. "It's like they're children. Not afraid of anything. As if they had somehow missed all the fear mechanisms this country drums into you. Like a children's crusade," and he laughed drunkenly. "The innocents going up against the serpents." He looked at Mike, who was looking out the window at the dark house across the street.

"But to go up against serpents, you have to have the wisdom of serpents," Mike said. "They don't have any wisdom. They don't have shit. It's a weirdness. I have to understand it—I don't think we can just ignore it."

Mike was a genius from Seattle. He grew up in Seattle, never leaving it until he joined SDS. As a kid he got into cars and drinking; that's all there was for him to do. Building, rebuilding, and dragging cars was his life, and drinking made up for the fact that this was not enough.

Mike's father died while Mike was still young. Mike never spoke much about him. His mother, a tired, overworked, timid, and simple woman worked for the Jesuit priests. Mike worshiped his mother. He was always concerned about hurting her, always wanted her to approve of him. Watching her become an old woman before her time working for pennies, was probably responsible for a lot of his hatred for the system and its institutions. He first got involved politically with draft resistance as a freshman at the U of W along with Alex, Ray, and a number of other men who were in his class. Then he went into SDS. Quite suddenly in 1968 he realized that he couldn't continue as a student; that he wanted to devote all his time to the revolution.

When the RYM 2–Weatherman split happened, all of Mike's friends and political mentors went with RYM 2, with the exception of Jay who went with Weatherman. Unable to act unless he understood completely what he was doing, Mike was at first stunned by the Weatherman collective. Our utter uniformity infuriated him. But more important, our implacable insistence that the revolution was already in progress, and that we had to deal with it today, not tomorrow, at once challenged him and terrified him. Torn between his Running Dog friends and Weatherman, in which he sensed the first real attempt to consciously mold middle-class people into guerrillas, he spent several weeks prior to the Days of Rage agonizing about his politics.

As time moved on and it got closer to the Days of Rage, tension mounted and so did criticism–self-criticism. The major topic was the smashing of monogamy. The rest of the country had been smashing monogamy all summer; married couples had separated, and gone to live in different collectives. Longtime lovers had parted, in some instances to organize in different parts of the country. Yet in Seattle, in our collective, there was a flagrant monogamy—Jay and Beverly.

The Weatherbureau began to call Roger more frequently with the command: smash that relationship before the Days of Rage.

The ending of monogamy had some real advantages. If two people were monogamous, then they paid more attention to each other than they did to any other person they came in contact with. This was a deterrent to collectivity. If monogamy was smashed, the theory went, everyone would love each other equally, and not love some people more than others. If everyone loved each other equally, then they could trust everyone more completely.

Suppose Beverly and Jay were running with the collective on an action, and one of them got hurt; the other would stop, thus losing the protection of the collective and also weakening the collective through the loss of another person. In criticism sessions, it was felt that Beverly never criticized Jay and vice versa; they couldn't because they weren't objective enough about each other.

Endless criticism sessions were called to deal with the problem but Beverly and Jay were adamant; they refused to be separated. The collective, realizing that they were two of our strongest people, refused to throw them out of the collective as other Weathermen across the country had done with rebellious monogamies.

My friendship with Garrity had intensified so that I saw him every day, in spite of the rigorous demands of the collective. But we hadn't slept together, although I really wanted to. Initially the problem of smashing monogamy didn't apply to me, since I was sleeping with no one. But I was horrified at the thought of Beverly and Jay being forced to separate. It was true that they excluded other people because of the intensity of their relationship, but I thought their total commitment to each other a precious and rare thing.

What was supposed to replace the antiquated monogamous relationships? Group gropes, homosexuality, autosexuality, or asexuality. The last seemed to predominate prior to the Days of Rage. In an effort to encourage collective members to sleep with each other if they had to have sex, a sleeping schedule was set up. According to it, you were to have a different bed partner every night, regardless of sex. The schedule was never enforced in our collective, but its very presence testified to the seriousness with which we approached the problem of smashing monogamy.

Although the Bureau continued to send, through Roger, instructions for us to smash our monogamy, little was done about it prior to the Days of Rage. We were too swept up in constant actions to deal with Beverly and Jay.

In the month before the Days of Rage, a lot of criticism was leveled against me for my consumption of dope. I understood the reasons for it. Dope made people too relaxed, unprepared for emergencies, for sudden actions. Dope added danger to lives already under constant strain; it would be hell for a Weatherman, or any political person to be busted buying or selling dope. Dope was expensive; the money was necessary for food and rent—essentials. Most important, dope was a detriment to rigorous discipline.

As much as I understood the reasoning behind Weatherman discipline about dope, I refused to give it up. I thought the politics concerning monogamy were right; the state says the norm is monogamy, an institutional form of control, so we say, smash monogamy. But in spite of discipline, I saw dope as a political weapon. Dope made a criminal out of every kid who used it. It seemed to be helping the state out not to use dope, since that's what they were trying to tell kids as well. Besides, what kid in his right mind would want to join a revolution that banned dope?

No dope? No gentle on my mind cannabissssssss, no slippery, eerie startling Day-Glo acid vibes, no sultry, jittery mescaline, no embalming, quivering, friendly cocaine, no strung out get it on high intensity speed, and no darkness darkness be my pillow, take me to the endless deep reds and other barblike pills and potions? No dope? To me that was just so much jive. What would a freak like me do without dope?

Beverly and Jay defended my dope taking, the same way I protected their monogamy. It was advantageous to the three of us to maintain this special relationship. Because they defended me, I could do practically anything I pleased in the collective. As much as I loved Weatherman, I loved my individuality more.

In some ways the relationship between Beverly, Jay and myself was healthy since it allowed us to reach beyond the collective environment. As it got closer to the Days of Rage, the collective became even more isolated. Roger, Carol, and Mickey never talked to anyone but collective people unless they were in the act of organizing. And ordinary conversation was impossible. Once they decided a person didn't want to be a Weatherman or go to Chicago, they simply ignored them. There were no second chances.

Perhaps it was because we refused to subjugate ourselves entirely to the Weatherbureau, or maybe it was just the way we were, but Beverly, Jay and I didn't become Stalinoids, and we refused to become Mansonites and support violence just for the sake of violence. We never became automatons, unthinking tools parroting the Weatherman line, with no opinions of our own, and we always tried, even if we didn't always succeed, to be human beings while we were becoming revolutionaries.

Two weeks before the Days of Rage, sleep became a thing of the past. We stepped up our work to twenty-five hours a day. Now we not only went to high schools and community colleges, junior colleges and the university, but in preparation for Chicago we had training classes in tear-gas protection, mace protection, the correct clothes and shoes to wear for street fighting—which would give the most protection while offering the most mobility. We had classes in which we were taught how to put together medical kits, and everyone learned how to use their contents to administer basic first aid for cuts, burns, abrasions, mace, or gas burns. We had classes in karate for self-protection against clubs. We exercised and ran so that people would be in shape for all the running that we would have to do. The collective had been running around the block four times every night through September. We had trained volunteer personnel to teach these classes. Doctors, gym teachers, and Marines helped to make us into the best-prepared group of Weathermen and sympathizers in the country. No one came near Seattle when it came to being prepared and having courage.

The group of recruits we were working with was small and motley. They'd been dredged out of high schools and community colleges, or had come in off the street as a result of our leafleting. There were about thirty people attending these training sessions; about fifteen of them would actually go to Chicago.

It's hard to say what attracted these particular people to Weatherman; probably like me and many other Weathermen, they felt they had nothing to lose. Most of them were young. A few were barely sixteen. Over half were women. The majority were students, high school or early college. They were all bored and alienated. Now they would have some excitement and maybe do something decent as well. And if they died in the process, well, it was better to go down fighting heroically, than to live meaningless lives.

I should not project this suicidal tendency on all early Weathermen, but it certainly was a tendency on my part, and it was reflected in the attitudes of my collective. A large number of the pre–Days of Rage recruits, outside of collective cadre, were wide-eyed idealists, who were languishing in America for want of something pure, good and creative to do. The flower children had given way to the Days of Rage.

Out of sheer necessity the collective began to interact with the rest of SDS. People would be needed to arrange for bail for Weathermen from Seattle; those who remained behind would have to take control of communications. Seattle would have to be told about what was happening in Chicago. We turned to non-Weathermen for these tasks. If people didn't go to the Days of Rage, the least they could do was stay safely in Seattle and send us bail money and talk about the Days of Rage. A surprising number of people agreed to help us. Among these were Mike Justesen, still snorting vehemently about "those wimpy assholes." He volunteered to co-ordinate bail.

Ty and Jean Baxter were in a quandary as the Days of Rage neared. Throughout the fall they had been ambivalent about the action; most of their closest friends were Weathermen. They themselves had been doing work at the Shelter Half, a GI coffeehouse located in the small industrial city of Tacoma, thirty miles north of Seattle. I had gone to the Shelter Half with Ty and Jean to try and organize GIs around the Days of Rage. Although no GIs came to Chicago, I was impressed with the painstaking work they had done in raising GI consciousness about the war.

Jean and Ty vacillated about the Days of Rage. Ty finally decided to go and "check it out"; Jean would stay in Seattle and work on bail and other legal matters.

The street people, including Garrity, were against the Days of Rage until the time we actually left for Chicago. They saw the collective as a suicide squad on a doomed mission. "If you want to be a kamikaze," Garrity once told me, grinning, "go ahead. But as for me, well, I'm too young to die, especially for a bunch of nuts like the Weathermen." The feeling seemed to be universal. No one in their right minds would go to Chicago on October 8. Everyone who went was going to die.

Events happened so rapidly I had no time to think. I had never felt better in my life. My friendship with Garrity had grown deep and beautiful. Although he hated Weatherman, he respected my commitment to the struggle. Quiet, thoughtful, strong and loving, he gave me all the support I needed to keep up with the superhuman activity of the collective. He never understood my desperate commitment to Weatherman, and always insisted that my attempts to change myself were misguided.

I would tell him of long criticism sessions of me, in which my continued drug taking was examined, and my persistent protection of Beverly and Jay's monogamy was dissected. I would tell him how Carol would tell me with a stony face that I laughed too much when I was talking to kids at the high schools, and that I looked too attractive; that I was a sex symbol to many of the high school boys and to people like Simon, Ray, and Alex. Garrity would shake his head while I poured out all the criticisms of me, and he'd tell me that it was because of all those things that kids actually listened to me, otherwise they would ignore me as they ignored all the other Weathermen. He never had anything good to say about the collective or our way of doing things.

"They all look like their faces would crack if they smiled," he'd say. "If those are the people who're going to lead the revolution, then it ain't my revolution."

We'd walk across the campus together while I leafleted about the first SDS meeting for the quarter. I listened to what he said, but I had no doubts in my mind. The news in *Fire Next Time* was all good. Across the country people were mobilized for the Days of Rage. There would be thousands of people there, and we would defeat the pigs militarily.

On September 27 we attempted to train our small band of followers in street action. About twenty of us marched up the Ave, spray-painting and carrying a Vietcong flag. Nothing but incredulous stares greeted us on our way up the Ave, but on our way from the march, Kate was arrested for damaging property. Without any struggle on her part or ours, she was led away to jail. A couple of hours later she was released on a hundred dollars' bail. The newspapers described the marchers as "members of SDS."

The march told us two things. The first was that no one knew who Weatherman was. Although the schisms that had rocked SDS seemed gargantuan to those involved, to the world outside the Movement, SDS was still just SDS. To our amazement we still had the protection of anonymity. Our spirits soared; just think what we had done so far, and they're so dumb they still don't know who we are!

The second thing the march showed us was how unprepared we were for Chicago. In spite of all our talk about how we were going to fight the pigs, defend our people, we had just let them walk up and haul Kate off.

"We should have attacked those pigs and fought with them at least until Kate was free," argued Carol fiercely.

Beverly looked skeptical. "If we had, we might all have gone to jail, and not have been able to go to the Days of Rage. I don't think that was the time or the place—right there on the Ave."

The argument was never settled, although it went on for hours. We realized that we still had a long way to go. We decided to have a number of actions before Chicago, which was a week and a half away. This would prime us for fighting with the pigs, as well as allow us to publicize the Days of Rage. We turned our attention to the campus, and the first SDS meeting.

The next day the women's caucus met. The collective women suggested that the women organize and lead an action to end the first SDS meeting. The other women wanted an action but were afraid of the negative reaction of the men. Someone suggested having an action of our own before the SDS meeting. The idea took hold.

"We can disguise ourselves as men . . . and attack one of the ROTC buildings."

"We can get that little one . . . what's its name," I said, "Air Force ROTC. Since it's so small we can just run in one end, do our shit, and run out the other end."

Laughing excitedly we divided up the labor. We decided not to tell anybody about the action. Jean and Beverly were especially asked not to tell Ty and Jay. We wanted to have the action early in the afternoon on September 30, which gave us only one day to prepare. Every woman there, no matter where she stood politically, decided to carry something with which to protect herself. Using the arrest of Kate as an example, we were prepared to fight if any one of us was caught—to fight until we were all free.

Having made our plans, agreed to them, we were silent. Some of the women present had only been peripherally involved in the Movement, had never been in SDS. Ruth was so gentle it was almost impossible to think of her fighting physically. But we were taking a vanguard action; it was our responsibility to be exemplary.

The next day the Weatherwomen told Roger, Mickey, and Jay that we were having a long women's meeting, and to please leave the house. By nine o'clock we were all busy at work, some of us making stink bombs, others pouring paint into bottles to spill on desks and files, still others making clubs out of tightly rolled-up newspapers. These had the power to knock someone out, but were not considered deadly weapons in case of arrest.

In the midst of our preparations the pigs came up the steps. Beverly, calm and composed, met them at the door. The rest of us sat around the dining-room table not breathing.

The pigs were asking for me. There were warrants out for my arrest because of unpaid tickets for Zelda. Beverly told them that I lived across the street, but that she didn't think I was home, and offered to pay for the tickets then and there. The pigs said that was fine, took the money, and left. The minute they drove away we continued our work.

Around twelve forty-five we were driven to the edge of campus; then we walked to the ROTC building. Rushing inside, we told the horrified secretaries to stand away from their desks so they wouldn't get covered with paint. Two of us dumped paint on all the papers covering the desks, then overturned the desks; four of us dumped out all the contents of the filing cabinet, and smeared them with paint; two women were spray-painting "SMASH ROTC" on the walls. When one ROTC officer tried to stop a woman from throwing paint on the files, two other women threw gobs of paint on him.

In two minutes we had demolished the place and, setting off the stink bombs, ran out at a gallop. The Weatherwomen, who had been running around the block every night ran effortlessly now, and could easily have outdistanced the others. But we stuck together, the safety of the group being more important than flight.

We hadn't gone a hundred yards when the ROTC men caught up with us. They grabbed one of the women, who was far behind the rest of us; she screamed, and we all stopped dead in our tracks. Without stopping to think, but shrieking at the top of our lungs, we ran back toward her, and began smashing at the ROTC trainees. Because they were caught completely off guard by the violence of our attack, and by the fact that women would fight a group of men, it took just a second for us to get free, run off again, reach the car, climb in, and barrel away.

Jubilant, roaring, exulting in our successful action, we were nevertheless very careful. We went straight home, threw away our paint-covered clothes, carefully washed off all the paint, cleaned up our cuts and bruises, and returned to our separate homes with plans to meet later in the night to criticize the action.

Our action had been a complete success. The press played down the amount of damage we did but stressed the fact that we were attacking ROTC because it trained officers to fight in Vietnam. The FBI was totally baffled. "There were no pictures taken, and the witnesses are vague. We have no positive identification; we don't even know who these people are."

SDS men of all factions were flabbergasted. They had known nothing about the action. The women, keyed up by success, were restrained in their attitudes but firm; we wanted to end the first SDS meeting with an action. Women would organize it. I was asked to lead it.

Over three hundred people showed up on October 2 for the first SDS meeting of the year, drawn there by the demonstrations which had ended the previous school year. The meeting had been well organized in advance; it ran like an overly long, boring, well-rehearsed play. No one at the meeting knew about the RYM 2–Weatherman split except for the thirty people who had met together all summer.

Jay began a series of speeches with a heavy Weatherman rap, talking about Chicago, urging people to go to the Days of Rage. Then he distributed leaflets about the actions to the crowd. Next one of the Running Dog leaders gave a long, incredibly boring speech about the SDS split and explained that there would be a RYM 2 National Action as an alternative to the Days of Rage. Ty followed, speaking briefly about the Shelter Half and the work he and Jean had done with GIs. Then Alex gave a two-minute freakout rap about how we were all mobilizing to tear down the Pacific Northwest—out in the streets. Almost everyone had followed a Weatherman line.

As Alex sat down, I jumped up to replace him. I had on my purple hat and scarf, and my black leathers and miniskirt. Inside me a rocket was slowly taking off, gathering momentum. The rush of adrenalin flowing through my body staggered me so that I felt dizzy for a second. I plunged into my speech. Stalking up and down in front of them, shaking my fist at them, reaching my open hands out to them, begging for them to join me, crouching, bending, twisting and pacing, I urged them to action.

"I'm a Weatherwoman! I'm fighting with the Vietnamese and with black people and with all Third World people for my freedom. I'm fighting for my freedom as a woman. The road to my freedom leads me to fight for the liberation of all people.

"I'm no longer content to nurture children, or to give a husband support and strength. I need all my strength for the Movement, to fight imperialism, to create a world in which people can live with dignity and without fear and starvation and war.

"As the years have passed I've seen my efforts fail along with thousands of others in the Civil Rights and anti-war movements.

"The time has come not merely to protest but to fight for what we believe in. The war is going on—we must join it now. I know you don't want to wait any longer. And in fighting, women will discover strengths they never knew they had. They will take leadership and, along with men, create a new world on the ashes of the old.

"Fighting is the key not only to the liberation of women, but to the liberation of all human beings."

My voice rising with my urgency, I strained myself into a frenzy, compelling people to listen to me. I felt possessed. My enthusiasm roared within me; at times I felt it was almost too much for my body to take.

"Now we're going to smash an ROTC building. I'm not saying which one, because we want to get there before the pigs. You'll just have to trust us; we have this very well planned. Leadership is important, and revolutionary leadership is the most important kind of leadership to follow. In the front of the room are Vietcong flags, and cans of spray paint. Those of you who want to can take them.

"If anyone interferes with us—if any of us get caught by those ROTC people, it's our obligation to fight to free them. No one can be arrested or hurt if we stick together. Like a fist!"

And I threw my fists clenched up into the air. And screaming, I finished.

"Now we're all going to go, and we're going to fight, and we're going to win. LET'S GO!"

Before the words were even out of my mouth, people were leaping out of their chairs. Everybody seemed hot to go. I couldn't believe it. Chairs scraped as people rushed to get spray cans and flags, and lined up in front of the room. I was pushed to the front of the line, and as we walked out of the building I began screaming, "Ho, Ho, Ho Chi Minh, Vietnam is gonna win," and behind me, tumultuous, bursting out over the quiet campus like a sudden spurt of life, was the chanting of the students who had attended their first SDS meeting just out of curiosity and were now on their way to smash an ROTC building.

We never saw a pig on the way to Clark Hall. I led the crowd almost past it, stopped suddenly and yelled,

"Let's take Clark Hall!" and with a surge, the crowd was in the building, galloping up the twin staircases. People spray-painted in huge letters all over the wall, "SMASH ROTC," "OFF THE PIG," and all our other slogans.

In seconds the ROTC cadets were out in the hall. They were so startled at first they stared at us as we spray-painted. Then they began hitting people with spray cans, trying to get the cans away. One of them grabbed Georgia. To his astonishment, she began kicking and punching at him immediately. More cadets came to aid him. Two had Georgia by her legs, and were dragging her down the hall. With a war whoop, we followed, and a couple of people grabbed Georgia's arms. We then had a tug of war while Georgia was yelling in agony.

Someone finally landed a smashing hook into a cadet's nose, and, bellowing in agony, he let go of Georgia and put his hands to his face. His buddy stopped dragging Georgia to help him, and we carried her away.

A cadet grabbed me by the wrist. I kicked at him but missed; I felt something heavy smash into my stomach and I heard my breath whoosh out, and then I couldn't breathe, the pain was so intense. Panic flooded through me and I began to struggle wildly, unable to scream for help because I couldn't breathe. I still had the paint can clutched in my hand. I aimed it about three inches from the cadet's eyes and squeezed; red paint sprayed into his eyes which slammed shut, and clawing at his eyes with his hands, he stumbled away, crying.

I fell to my knees; people picked me up and helped me down the stairs. Around us the fighting continued until all the SDS people had left the building. No one was arrested that day. The campus security pigs showed up about five minutes after the demonstration had ended.

Injuries for the enemy: one broken nose, one severely lacerated face, one bad case of red-eye.

The newspaper headlines read, "Young Animals Attack ROTC." The Weatherman spirit was careening. Finally we'd been effective.

That night my car, which was parked in front of my house, was shot up by plainclothes pigs. Ray saw the pig car drive away. Zelda received a bullet through her venerable windshield, and two through her stately ass, one of which penetrated her lusty engine. As a result of this horrible shooting, Garrity, Hal, Ray, Simon, Ruth, and I in my house, and the collective in the house across the street, stayed up all night with arsenal ready. We had collected a lot of arms and we were ready to use them.

Now get the drift of the scene. Here were two houses facing each other with one miserable car in the middle. Both houses were filled with macho males and females with loaded shotguns and bad aim and paranoid temperaments. Now if someone had gotten smart, and thrown a firecracker out into the street, the two houses would probably have gone berserk and, shooting at each other, killed off some of the finest revolutionaries in the city. Fortunately, that didn't happen, and both houses finally went to sleep around dawn.

Garrity and I didn't go to sleep with the rest of the house. We finally made love, tenderly and exquisitely, while the new day dawned. Around eight o'clock, as Garrity fell asleep, I ran across the street in time for the morning's high school leafleting.

On October 5, late at night, I went to rent a Ford microbus. I told the rental man that I was taking a trip to the Olympic Mountains, two hours away. The fact that driving the bus to Chicago might be considered theft never occurred to me. I was told I could have the bus for a week.

Around ten o'clock that night the collective, plus Ty Baxter, our sleeping bags, medical kits and street fighting clothes, all crammed sardinelike into that bus and we were on our way to the Days of Rage—to Chi-town, 2,500 miles across America, to take our hands and put them around the scrawny neck of American imperialism and squeeze until the head of capitalism was severed from its neck and, eyes bulging, fell kerplop all over the cement of the Gold Coast, and Chicago's richest and finest, in testimony that there were some people in the motherfucking country who were ready to kill and die for their freedom and for the freedom and dignity of those the world over. Yippie—we were on our way to freedomland!

Finally we were on our way, after many days of anger and frustration, sleepwalking, heavy talking and pigs oinking after us, high school kids throwing our leaflets in our faces, college kids throwing Marx in our faces, parents laughing and tear-jerking and earthquaking at us, and everybody conceivable just hot-hating us eight Weathermen who had undertaken to organize the entire city of Seattle to serve the people's army. In some ways we had done a very good job. For instance, everybody knew about us. All the high school principals, all the schoolteachers, all the white-hating black kids, the honky, racist white kids, all the academic Marxist types, and certainly now, the entire police force of Seattle.

In one month's time we had handed out almost a million leaflets in at least two hundred different places swarming with potential revolutionary youth. We had learned how to use guns, carrying pieces that we could shoot, in some fashion or another. I had carried a .22-caliber revolver tucked into the waistband of my jeans, plus a whammie slingshot stuck into my back pocket. We had all learned how to make Molotov cocktails, but to my knowledge we had never used any. We could all recite verbatim the ABCs of racism in America, the history of the Vietnam war, and sundry other political raps.

As I lay squished in the microbus, which, incidentally, had no heater, I was thinking keenly about the past month, not knowing if it would be my last. Certainly that was possible. I thought about Garrity, who had whizzed me along Lake Washington just that morning; my favorite quiet road in Seattle, my favorite man and me on a gigantic motorcycle, serenely gliding along with the October sun warm on our backs, the little kisses of Lake Washington on the shore as gentle and ticklish as the wispy ends of Garrity's mustache as it brushed my lips. The soft, murmuring nearness of sweet love. I had clutched at all that just a few hours ago, and now, like some screwball, I was wedged into a microbus crammed with eight other idiots, speeding toward Chicago, the nighttown James Joyce death scene, and farther and farther away from Garrity.

I was scared shitless. Suicide. Suicidal. That's what all my friends had said—it's suicide. That's what Garrity had said when he definitely, and for the last time, refused to leave with me. "Oh my sweet red ass; how did I ever get my funky self into this mess. This is no place for a good Jewish girl."

Thinking Jewish made me think about my father and my childhood. I suddenly understood that I resented my father not only because he had tormented me for the first twenty years of my life, but because he was a capitalist, and he was very prejudiced. I don't know what he really learned from the massacre of six million Jewish human beings in Germany. He hated any color, but even if you passed the color test, he certainly hated all other religions. He has somewhat repented in the latter years of his life by marrying out of his religion, which was his most progressive act since I've known him.

Thinking about my father as we stumbled along in the night helped me get a grip on my terror, because it once again made me think about the goals of the Days of Rage. We weren't just a bunch of superviolent kids out to destroy Chicago because we enjoyed vandalism. Nor were we adolescents rebelling against our parents or adult authority. We were serious revolutionaries, who felt the necessity of doing something so earth-shattering in America that the American masses would finally take notice. Mr. and Mrs. America would really look at the news on television—would see our young bodies being blasted by shotguns, our terrified faces as we marched trembling but proud, to attack the armed might of this Nazi state of ours. Running blood, young, white human blood spilling and splattering all over the streets of Chicago for NBC and CBS to pick up in gory Technicolor, panning in close the gouged faces on TV for racist parents to see, for the parents of all the helpless GIs killed in Vietnam to see, for the parents of all the lynched black sons in the Deep South to see, and for America's children to see and hear and perhaps empathize with. But in order to make America really look and see, we had to do something so unholy, so strong, and so deadly, that they would have no other recourse. And that is what we were about.

"The whole world is watching," is what they had chanted at the Democratic Convention in August of 1968. We would chant it again. By taking the offensive in Chicago, by the force of our attack and numbers, we hoped to enable dying America to give itself one last appraisal while there was still time—before the ultimate doomsday battle came, and millions more would be piled in maggoty mountains.

Most of us in the bus machoed our way to Chicago, but many hours passed quietly when I would look at the reflective faces of the others and think, "They're probably thinking the same things I am. No matter what they say, they must be trying to figure it all out." I knew I was right, when, out of the clear blue sky, Georgia muttered, "Jesus Christ," and looked around at all of us palefaced. Then she laughed tightly, and we all laughed—a short, nervous twitter. We began to talk about our fears, and criticize each other. It was brief, but I felt so close to everyone in that bus.

As we trucked through the blackness, little by little, everybody in that crowded, smelly microbus began to feel better. Then, on the night of the seventh, we heard over the car radio that the statue of a pig had been blown up in Haymarket Square in Chicago. The pigs said, "This is a declaration of war. It's kill or be killed."

At the news of the bombing, a cheer went up in the bus. We started singing, first low and slow, then louder and faster, until we finally forgot the image of death and just felt the power in our vocal cords.

Chicago was a scary city when we first arrived. Pigs everywhere. The police force must have multiplied the traffic of Chicago by the thousands. Trying to bolster ourselves up, we continued singing as we drove along.

The pigs tailed us all the way from Cicero. We wandered all over the city trying to lose them. When we realized we couldn't, we finally drove to one of the buildings where the Weathermen would be congregating and sleeping during the Days of Rage. Then we unloaded our stiff and weary bodies, and mobile war equipment, our medical kits, and went to check in at a building which looked like a college dormitory but was a religious seminary.

The big question on everybody's mind was, how many of us would there be? For weeks now I had been living on the grand theory of instant revolution. Rudd, Dohrn, J.J., and all the big wheels who knew about such things had promised us truly that at least 25,000 people were coming to the Days of Rage. They were coming from everywhere, any way they could get there. Seattle was as far away from Chicago as you could get, and we had brought twenty people. Fifteen people had come from Oregon; now that wasn't bad for the Pacific Northwest region.

There was supposed to be a train coming from Michigan, and on it would be roaring thousands, just craving to run in the streets, slicing pigs. And there would be at least ten thousand from the Chicago area alone. I had lived so long with the idea that thousands would be here that the doubt and anxiety raised by those from other cities was intolerable to me. No it just can't be, no, no, no, no, no it just can't be now. We began a criticism–self-criticism session about how we need never doubt the word of our inviolate leaders. They had said 25,000 people would be here, and that meant 25,000 would indeed be here. That was all there was to that.

At some point early in the evening we left the big room and went to another building on the same campus and entered a gym. Here we had a war council, until the appointed time came to move out into Chicago. There were about two hundred people in the gym, all with street fighting clothes on.

A typical man or woman wore dark clothing, generally jeans, and dark, long-sleeved, and high-neck shirts, so as much of the skin as possible would be covered and protected from mace. There had been an argument about boots as opposed to sneakers. You could kick just great with boots, but they were heavy and more difficult for sustained running. On the other hand, you couldn't kick at all with sneakers; in fact, you would probably break your toes. But in sneakers you could run like a motherfucker. I chose sneakers, figuring with all those pigs with guns and clubs, I would have a better chance if I ran for it. Besides, you had to be down on your back if you were my size and wanted to kick anything important on a six-foot-three pig.

Everyone wore gloves, to protect the hands from mace, to keep from getting burned if they retrieved a tear-gas canister and threw it back into the pig forces. Gloves were also worn to protect the hands from the broken glass that would soon be flying and shattering as the Gold Coast windows began to fall.

No jewelry of any kind could be worn. It could only strangle or entangle you, or fly in your face. People with long hair were to wear it in pony tails, or long, single braids tied down their backs, and tucked under their collars, so that the pigs couldn't grab them by their curly locks and tug them off. For similar reasons earrings and scarves were taboo. You could wear a belt, if you felt it might be useful as a weapon.

Everyone from Seattle had a little army surplus medical kit which hung on their belts. Nearly everyone had a wooden stick made from rungs of ladders in the gym, an iron pipe, or rolled-up newspaper, painted to look like piping. Everyone had either an army surplus helmet or a motorcycle helmet for protective headwear. Finally, everyone had a little piece of damp cloth, wrapped in a plastic bag to keep it damp. This was very helpful with tear gas; you could press the damp cloth against your nose, or wipe your eyes with it.

We all prepared, some silently, some noisily, some alone, others in twos, threes, and fours. Everyone was tensing for the great battle. We almost all thought we might die. We took it very seriously when the pigs said it was kill or be killed.

Foremost on everybody's mind was the big question: "How many of us were there?" But we really had little time to think about this. We were busy trying to memorize the route from the seminary gym to Lincoln Park, and then from Lincoln Park to the Gold Coast, and from there to the Drake Hotel on Michigan Avenue, where Judge Julius Hoffman of the conspiracy trial was staying. We were trying to remember all the orders; cities should remain together, divided into affinity groups, and walk quietly from the seminary to Lincoln

Park by twos, on the sidewalk, stopping at corners for lights. We would rally in Lincoln Park while the thousands collected, then, running very swiftly, we would follow the route we were in the process of memorizing.

Around seven o'clock we left the gym and with helmets on, clubs carried low, marched silently in two lines by city to Lincoln Park. Before we left the gym we'd divided into affinity groups of four to eight people. Those of us who had been in previous street actions were familiar with affinity groups, but some of the new recruits had never been on the streets before.

The Pacific Northwest stayed together as a unit, numbering around thirty-five people. Our collective formed one affinity group, minus Kate, who had left for Chicago the day after her arrest to work at the Bureau. My affinity group was considered the "command" group, since we were the only collective. The remaining people were loosely divided into four smaller affinity groups. Several of the people in the other groups were very young; some were only fifteen years old. Of course we had not bothered to think carefully about what that meant at the time. Now we were here and it certainly mattered. But it was too late to do anything about it.

Jay and Beverly in the lead, Georgia and myself next, Carol, Roger, and Mickey taking up the rear, we marched to Lincoln Park. We formed silently around a roaring bonfire. And we stood. And we stood. And we twiddled our thumbs. And we waited. We glanced around nervously, and there were still only three or four hundred of us.

We waited and stood quietly, barely whispering among ourselves. Then like a rising wave, the murmuring started around me, cresting with fear.

This is all there is, there are no more coming, no train from Michigan, no band of ten thousand whooping Indians from everywhere, no others, just us, us only. My stomach rolled like a rotten pit and little streams of itchy sweat rolled tickling down my back and from under my arms. Tears formed in my eyes and slid down my cheeks. Beverly muttered in a voice choked from between clenched teeth, "All that work, our lives almost destroyed and nothing . . . nothing."

I stood there dripping sweat and tears, feeling queasy and headachy, contemplating the truth of the matter, not yet daring to wonder what it meant for the battle. In the midst of this, one of the tiny teen-agers we had coerced to Chicago came tripping up to us and with a tearful expression informed us that one of her high school buddies was an epileptic and was about to have a *grand mal* seizure. Beverly and I, snuffling back our tears, went to attend to the freaking-out kid. Just in time I stuck a hanky in his mouth, so he wouldn't choke on his tongue or worse, bite it off. Several of us held him so he wouldn't bash his head on the hard ground, or kick anybody around him.

The seizure lasted for several minutes. Beverly told the high school kids to take him to a hospital; I yelled at them to change his clothes and theirs too.

I never saw any of those kids again, never knew what happened to them, if they lived or died, if they ever made it back to Seattle. I never even remembered those kids until I started writing about all this. Some great revolutionary I am—great revolutionary. FUCK!

Once again we waited, the fire roaring as brightly as ever. A couple of hundred people marched in and joined the crowd, but there were still only five or six hundred.

Finally some of the leadership, camouflaged by battle fatigue, started making speeches. The speeches said: I know this isn't what you expected, but you must make allowances. They talked on and on about courage, and how we were the only white people in the country who realized what it undertook to make the revolution. They said we were the revolutionary vanguard of America—just think of it; only five hundred people in this country were good, strong, and brilliant enough to come to Chicago.

I thought about the revolution as the Weatherbureau rapped, but I didn't think of it exactly in that light. I thought that somehow I had been misled, that what I had anticipated had not come to be. Where were the thousands? Where were the troops? Sure I wanted to fight, but I didn't want to lose. How could you hope not to lose if there was such a small number of you? All right, so the masses wouldn't rally. But this! This was sheer insanity!

I know my feelings were shared by others. I could see pools of eyes reflected against the fire glow. I could still feel the silent shaking of Beverly beside me. I really didn't mind dying, but only if I had to. But this really was suicide. We were all going to die, and fast— probably as soon as we hit the streets.

Yet the leadership continued to tell us how brave, lovely, and revolutionary we were. We were the Americong.

It took an hour of rapping, until the odds finally didn't matter to most of us. I don't know why. Maybe it was mass hypnosis. Maybe it was just that the notion of us being the only non-racists, and the only Americong in the country appealed to our egos, and spurred on our revolutionary lust. I don't know why I didn't run—in the other direction, to home, to Garrity, to my bed, to safety. Maybe I actually believed that I was part of the real revolutionary vanguard. I don't really think so, but I have no other answer. For some reason I stood rooted to the spot. So did Beverly and Jay and the rest of the collective. So did several hundred other people. And I don't know if anybody but the leadership quite knew why. Sometimes you do what you feel you have to do, because you think there is nothing else to do—and you don't ask why.

Around ten-thirty someone calling himself Marion Delgado told us we were going to "get Judge Hoffman." That was the signal we'd all been waiting for. We moved out. Running in cities, divided into affinity groups, we swarmed across the streets leading to Chicago's stylish Gold Coast. Even though I'd been running around my block four times a night for weeks, my breath was exhausted by the time we left the park. I kept running. My side began to pain me, a piercing, staccato pain that became intolerable as the minutes passed. I was a mass of itchy sweat; I burned all over. My clothes felt like dead weight on my body, from head to toe. The helmet was smothering me. Still I kept running. My chest felt as though it was going to explode into a million pieces. My breath came in heavy pants, forcing itself out. I clenched my teeth and kept running.

We were at the Gold Coast now. I could see the richies sitting in the fashionable restaurants and bars, and strolling down the streets. I hated them. They looked so cool, clean, and comfortable. I passed one man in a restaurant with a luscious piece of steak on the end of his fork. My taste buds erupted. I started galloping like mad. I wanted steak.

I looked up from the steak and there was an army of pigs—some standing, some kneeling, others running. Simultaneously, I swung at the restaurant window with my iron pipe; if I couldn't have steak, neither could that lousy man. The window shattered, and I felt high as a motherfucker. Boy, did that feel great. It just shattered, and glass flew in on the man, as I looked back, and the people in the restaurant all got up screaming and jumping around and pointing at us.

Things were really cooking now. Pipes and clubs were ramming against windows, rocks were flying. I ran down the block as fast as I could, chopping at every window, watching them shatter and fall like glaciers falling over mountains. A literal rain of glass. I loved it. I was running and swinging so fast and furiously, that I forgot about my affinity group. So when the shooting started, and I awoke from my window-shattering orgy, I was separated from them . . . And the pigs were shooting.

Someone screamed, "Hit the ground," and then I flew around the corner and galloped on. I ran and ran down block after block. I ran faster than I have ever run in my life. I didn't think about my affinity group, I didn't think about anything except getting away from those bullets. I could see my shadow silhouetted against the side of the buildings, going as fast as some of the cars in the street.

I ran all the way back to Lincoln Park. By the time I got there I couldn't see straight. I fell in a panting, exhausted heap under some bushes and lay there gagging and crying. I was so tired I didn't think I could ever move again. But finally I needed to know what had happened more than I wanted not to move. I got up and walked out of the park.

Now dig the scene. I still had on all of my battle fatigues, including Garrity's motorcycle helmet. I still carried my lead pipe. I also had a blouse full of bricks which I had never gotten to use. In this condition I had run from the Gold Coast to Lincoln Park, and in this condition I walked back to the Gold Coast. No one bothered me. No pig ever stopped to question me. No elderly couple even gaped at me. I became convinced after thinking about this for a while that I was invisible, and smiling a dreaming smile, walked safely onward to the Drake Hotel. In and out and among the pigs. Back and forth, twiddling my iron pipe, humming a jaunty little tune, calling out in a pathetic little voice, "Seattle, Seattle," but no one from Seattle answered my call. No one even resembling a street fighter appeared on the streets. Just lots of richies, standing around in minks, and lots of pigs, milling, rapping, shoving each other.

I must have walked around Michigan Avenue for an hour, until finally, in a stupor, I was convinced that everyone, all four hundred, had either been offed or arrested, and that the Days of Rage had ended. I was crushed beyond belief. Now all I wanted to do was go home.

I wandered around for another half hour, until I found a bus stop. At the bus stop, I dumped my bricks, took my helmet off my head, and put my lead pipe in my blouse. A bus came and I got on. Before I realized the bus was going to Evanston, Illinois, I was miles away from the seminary. I was really tired. I stank from dried perspiration. I was streaked with tears and grime. I was lonely, in pain, miserable and lost. And penniless.

The bus dropped me in a strange part of Chicago. To this day I don't know where I was. I walked for perhaps an hour, but I didn't know what direction I was going in. Then on a dark, empty street, I saw a man trying to start up a motorcycle. I went running in that direction. As I approached, the man looked up and I realized it was a woman. She smiled at me. I smiled at her.

"What 'r' y'doin'?" she asked.

"Running from the pigs," I said.

"Need help?" she asked.

I nodded yes, almost nodding out. She told me to get on the bike in back of her. I climbed on and held onto her tightly. She grabbed my hand and turned around, and asked in a real low voice, "Are you straight, or do you get it on with women?"

I told her I'm straight, and super tired, and sorry that I'm straight, will she please take me to the fucking McCormick Theological Seminary (that really got a rise out of her) and God will bless her for the rest of her life.

She took me, stopping only long enough to get me the most delicious hot sausage sandwich my hungry lips had ever tasted. She never made any more overtures to me, she never questioned me again. Somewhere in this friggin' country that woman may still be wandering around, and believe me, I love her to this day. Because she is one of the few people in my life who did exactly as I asked them to in a minute of need. And who the hell can ever get anyone to do that!

I couldn't believe that it was only one-thirty when I entered the seminary. I had been on the streets for three hours and it seemed like three years. To my profound amazement and relief, there were sixty or seventy people strewn across the gym floor. Some had bloody bandages on their heads; others were limping around, using sticks as canes. After a while I spotted Mickey, and he told me what had happened to the Seattle collective.

Kate, who had run with the Weatherbureau, had been trampled by the pigs. She was in jail. Roger, Georgia, Carol, and Jay all had been beaten and arrested. So had ninety per cent of the other people from Seattle and Oregon. A street person named Jim Bryant, who didn't like Weatherman but liked action, had come on his own to Chicago, having been convinced at several of the Weatherman meetings in Seattle that the Days of Rage would be the riot to end all riots. He had joined a loose affinity group with other men who had come to Chicago alone. The group ran into a band of pigs, and instead of retreating, attacked, as many Weathermen had done that night. The attack was quickly repulsed and as they turned to run away, a pig whipped out a pistol and standing just a few feet from Bryant, shot him in the neck. The bullet churned down his left arm, severing most of his tendons and nerves.

Bryant continued running briefly with his affinity group, then stopped, telling them he was shot and couldn't run. Someone from the group wanted to stay with him, but Bryant, macho to the end, insisted that they all go on without him. He was left standing there, the pain in his arm flaring.

Bryant was taken to a hospital by the pigs, but the doctors didn't see fit to operate and remove the bullet. As a result his arm was paralyzed. Today his arm is stiff and lacks co-ordination, but with a great deal of rehabilitative treatment in Seattle, he did manage to recover partial use of it.

Then Mickey told me Beverly had been shot. Like me, Beverly had run into an army of pigs. But I had been close to the windows, on the sidewalk; she had been running out on the street. When the shooting started, she was in the direct line of fire. The collective didn't run. They and a hundred other people fought with the pigs. The burly, hulking Chicago pigs, known for their ex-Marine status, their excessive racism, and their Neanderthal stupidity, went berserk, and pulled out shotguns. Beverly got it in the arm—two diagonal, penetrating buckshot holes. Those holes were so deep and so wide, that I once stuck most of a ball-point pen down them before they healed. The rest of the collective stuck by her, and dragged her into an alley, where they waited until the shoot-out moved elsewhere, and then called an ambulance. The ambulance came and took her to a hospital. The rest of the collective, including Jay, continued fighting. Everyone in the collective was busted, except Mickey, who managed to escape.

When people began to return to the seminary, Mickey discovered that all the victims of gunfire had been brought to the same hospital. He called the hospital and inquired about Beverly. She had been treated, and a guard had been stationed outside her door. There was a police hold on her.

Mickey, the squeamish man-child, had gone to the hospital, sneaked in past the guards, grabbed Beverly out of her room, and somehow had gotten her past all the doctors, nurses, and pigs and out of the hospital. Then he had taken her to a private residence where she stayed until she was well enough to travel back to Seattle. Mickey had then returned to the seminary, where he had been criticizing the few tired people from the Pacific Northwest who had not been arrested.

By the time Mickey finished the story it was after two o'clock. But we were called together for a mass criticism session. The gist of the session was that we had fought hard but not hard enough. We had run from the pigs, not attacked them. At the crucial moment, we had faltered and retreated from the pigs when the shooting had started.

Many of the exhausted people sitting around me were infuriated. They blamed the leadership for having misled them about the number of people who would be there. Many people said they were afraid to go back out into the streets, that the pigs had shot enough people, they didn't want to be used for cannon fodder. Again the criticism session went on for hours. And the leadership and cadre battled it out, both knowing that lives were at stake. But the fact remained that Weatherman politics were right, if a person really believed that the time to pick up the gun had arrived, if one believed that the revolution was already in progress. By dawn, the remaining people had decided that the actions should be continued. The next thing scheduled was the Women's Action.

All through the criticism session I sat like a corpse, numb from my nose to my toes. The fact that all my collective had stayed and fought and had been beaten, shot, and jailed made me sick with guilt. I had run.

"Tomorrow," I thought, "I will not run away no matter what happens. I'll be right up there with all the female leadership; I will fight if it kills me." Even as I sat there thinking about how brave I was going to be on the Women's Action, I half wondered if it was commitment or gut-checking that was egging me on. "Gut-check" was when you did something foolhardy just to make sure you weren't afraid of doing it.

But my questions about my motives were beginning to dissolve, along with the shape of the room, into the drowsiness that was creeping over me. I lay down on the cold, hard gym floor, curling up fetuslike around my iron pipe.

Someone shook me awake. "Time to get up. Women's Action. All women are to gather in far corner of the room. Hurry—we have to move out." It was Kathy Boudin, looking fresh as a daisy. "God, how does she do it? She hasn't slept in two days. How come I'm falling apart and she looks like she's been on a vacation? I guess she must want to win much more than I do. I just want to sleep," and I shut my eyes again. Then I remembered last night, and that my collective was in jail, and Beverly was shot, and I jumped up and ran over to the group of women.

What a Women's Militia! About sixty women huddled in the corner of the gym, looking too exhausted to move, blood-spattered and smeared with grime and sweat, eyes swollen from tear gas and lack of sleep, hair gummy and hanging limply. One woman had a bandage over her eye, where she had been cut with glass. Another had a bandage covering her scalp, where she had been clubbed, and had had stitches. Still another had bandages up and down her leg, and could walk only very slowly with the help of a cane. Others insisted that she couldn't come on the Women's Action; she pleaded to come. "I want to fight, please. I want to go on the action." The woman with the bandage over her scalp, and the woman with the patch on her eye, stood by her. "We'll run together, so we won't hold anybody else back." Grimly they stood there, an inspiration to the rest of us.

We were told to organize our affinity groups according to cities. I joined an affinity group of four other women who, like myself, had lost the rest of their collectives.

One of the four women was a rosy-cheeked eighteen-year-old named Barbara Beam. Barbara did not want to go on the Women's Action. She was quaking. She wasn't ready, she said, for such a serious commitment. In tears she wailed, "I don't want to die, I don't want to die."

I was something less than sympathetic. Going whole hog to make up for my miserable showing the night before, I was utterly contemptuous of Barbara's fears. The only thing I was afraid of was not getting a chance to show how courageous I could be.

I tried talking practically to Barbara for a few minutes, but she was adamant; she did not want to go. As the others began to put on their helmets I whipped around and shrieked at Barbara that I would massacre her if she didn't come. Christ, it was like leading a fucking baby to slaughter. She was so stupefied with fright, that she would have jumped off a bridge if I had told her to.

We took a subway to Grant Park, and at eight o'clock we assembled under a statue of a horse and rider, to wait for the women from Michigan—the train had still not arrived. An hour later, they came marching and chanting, about ten of them—one one-hundredth of what we had been promised. Oh hell.

There we were in the chilly morning, about seventy-five women, helmeted, and replete with clubs or pipes, in two-by-two formation, in our affinity groups. We had been told that our tactical objective was a draft board, on Michigan Avenue, two blocks down from Grant Park.

About nine o'clock, Bernardine, hidden by a Vietnamese flag, gave a rousing speech in which she said that though the odds were against us (meaning that there were about five pigs to each woman) we nevertheless had the obligation to ram that draft board—were we up for it? YES we all nodded our heads. Yeah, we all mumbled.

In five minutes we were off, walking fast toward the bridge that borders Grant Park just down from the statue of the horse and rider. Even from where I stood, toward the back of the line, I could see the endless rows of pigs, standing alert, holding their black clubs in one leather-gloved hand and tap-tap-tapping it steadily against the other, preparing for the prodigious head bust which was soon to take place.

With a galvanizing shrill, we all began running directly toward the pigs. That's the last I saw of Beam. Around me women were fighting with pigs; I could hear the clubs smashing down on them. I stood there for a second, turning in time to see the majority of the women running away from the pigs. As I turned, I saw a woman from my affinity group wedged up against a park grounds shack. Two pigs were working her over with their clubs as she lay there, her arms wrapped around her head. Something in me clicked at the sight, something stronger than the danger all around me.

I galloped like one possessed right toward the pigs, who were smearing the woman with her own blood. One of them was bent over administering his pounding.

I stood behind him for a split second, and then I carefully lifted my pipe and brought it down with all the strength I had right at the base of that motherfucker's neck, right where it was exposed beneath his helmet. He fell forward. I turned to find another pig towering over me. He rammed me across the chest with his club, staring at me as I fell backward to the ground. Then he grabbed his club with both his hands, like a baseball bat, and he raised it as high as he could in the air, as I had just done, and he smiled, and I saw the scar on his nose wiggle—then he brought that club down on my face. My glasses shattered; then I was spun around as another pig kicked me hard in the shoulder.

"They're killing me," I thought. "Funny, I can hear what they're doing, but I can't feel it. All that beating and I can't feel a thing."

Three pigs dragged me to a waiting paddy wagon, already filled with Militia women. I was still struggling, and fighting, biting every arm in reach, and screaming at the top of my lungs. In my heart was a wild little song—you can't touch me, you pigs—you can't hurt me. Three of them hauled me still thrashing into the paddy wagon, then lifted me up and bashed me against the floor. As I lay there kicking, they closed the metal door. One of the women bent down and pulled my helmet off. That was the end of the Days of Rage for me.

In the paddy wagon we were all chained together. There were twelve of us. The wagon was lined with two rows of benches on which we all sat, not talking. After about a half an hour of driving, we jerked to a halt at 2600 S. California Street—Cook County Jail. I was more curious than frightened, this being my first arrest. I couldn't really relate to being arrested; to me, it was all still a wild adventure. Jail was just another part of that adventure.

We were led out of the wagon, and into an elevator, still chained together. In the elevator was all the female Weatherman leadership, with the exception of myself and the girl I had attempted to aid. I could see Bernardine in her black leather jacket, with her head inclined against the elevator wall, her eyes staring at the ceiling, contempt for her surroundings on her face and in her posture.

From the elevator we were led into a room divided into rows of single cells, with only a short iron bench in them. We were each put in a cell. After a while a matron came by and gave me a bologna sandwich and sweetened coffee in a tin cup. Then nothing happened for several hours. I tried to nap on the iron bench; it was freezing in the cell. I was awakened once, and taken to a large room for my mug shot, which was not very different from taking a photo for a passport. Then my hand was pushed into a pad smeared with thick black grease, and my fingers, one at a time, were carefully printed. While

I was being fingerprinted, I saw Kate and Georgia being led through another room. They saw me and smiled, and gave me the fist. I raised my fist in answer; the matron slapped at my hand.

Sometime in the afternoon we were herded into the big, square drunk tank off the courtroom. Several more hours dragged by, during which we conferred with our lawyers. These lawyers were from the People's Law Office. They were very political, and devoted to political defendants. Besides having good politics, they were fine lawyers.

One after another, the eleven women I was arrested with were called out of the tank and and bail was set. When I was called, my lawyer reeled off to the judge my educational diplomas: B.A. English, M.A. Urban Education, M.S.W., Master of Social Work. He also explained very clearly and patiently to the judge, who was looking at me intently with his lips pursed, that this was my first bust. I stood quietly staring back at the judge, wondering what kind of father he was, what kind of husband, lover, what events in his life had put him on the bench and why he wanted to be an enemy of the people.

The judge didn't buy my lawyer's story. He claimed that I had brutally assaulted an officer of the law and clapped three thousand dollars' bail on me. Bails for the other women I was arrested with ran from two thousand five hundred dollars to ten thousand dollars for Bernardine.

I was charged with three counts of aggravated assault and battery, and one count of assault with a deadly weapon. Each charge was a felony, punishable by up to ten years' imprisonment. Still enthralled by the adventure and excitement of my first bust, I was not very staggered by the thought of forty years in prison. I didn't believe that it could ever happen to me.

While bails were being set, I sat by myself in the drunk tank and looked at the women around me. Bernardine had hurt her leg, and was limping slightly. Other than the limp, there was no discernible reminder that she had just been through a violent battle with Chicago's finest. She looked like a fashion model. Short black leather jacket, nice slacks, neat purple blouse, the boots—everything just so. She was reclining on an iron bench with one arm supporting her head, the other dangling to the floor, staring at the ceiling. Although she didn't move, didn't talk, hardly seemed aware of the other women in the room, everyone else was quite aware of her. I just plainly stared at her, unable to fathom the source of her charisma. She possessed a splendor all of her own. Like a queen, her nobility set her apart from the other women. Fascinated, I watched the secondary leadership sit themselves around her, while the third-ranking leadership talked together in another group, looking covertly at Bernardine and her intimates.

There was a clearly defined pecking order in which people like me didn't even get crumbs. As the day passed, it became obvious to me that you didn't get to be leadership just by following the example set by leaders. It wasn't enough to be in the vanguard. There was something else, a type of authority, a sense of self that one had to have before one could lead other people, before they would follow.

I had seen Bernardine fighting with the pigs; I had seen her fighting with genuine rage. I had watched the women about her fighting just as hard. But she was still the high priestess. Whatever quality she possessed, I wanted it. I wanted to be cherished and respected as Bernardine was. More than that, I wanted to know Bernardine. I wanted to be an aristocrat too. I wanted to be part of that special, select group permitted to know her as a human being, rather than a mythological silhouette. All day I sat in the drunk tank, watching the female leadership talk among themselves animatedly, as I mooned in the shadows.

Finally we were taken up to the prison. One floor in Cook County is reserved for women; the floor is divided into two tiers of cells: A and B. After an interminable wait, in which everything but our clothes was taken from us, we were divided up among both tiers.

The women in my tier were very inquisitive about the action; they had met the women who had been arrested the day before. They were mostly black, and many of them were in Cook County waiting trial. Some had been waiting over a year. Most of them had already done time and expected to do more time.

They thought we Weatherwomen were nuts, but they admired our spunk. They could relate to our talk about racism, and how we hated the pigs. What amazed them more than anything is that we had actually attempted to fight with the pigs. "That takes balls," they'd say. Impressed as they were by our courage, we got the deluxe treatment: candy from their commissary, fresh fruit, cigarettes, coffee, hand lotion, and toothpaste. For the first time in days I showered and washed my hair.

I spent three days in Cook County. My time was taken up in endless, steaming hot showers and long meals. For breakfast we actually got bacon and eggs; dinner was meat and potatoes and vegetables and good, strong coffee. I had heard how terrible Cook County food was; it didn't seem so bad to me. Only later would I find out that the state provided special food for us white children of the upper classes. The black women liked having us there, because they benefited from our privileged treatment. How they must have laughed at us, being carefully coddled in Cook County.

The Weatherwomen did calisthenics, read, watched TV, and spent a lot of time among themselves in criticism–self-criticism. Cathy Wilkerson was in my tier. Tall and slender, the beautiful young woman listened critically but intently as I told her about my life, and the progression of events that had led me to Weatherman. But Cathy wasn't there very long. All the leadership was bailed out the next day. The rest of us sat in Tier A, wondering when we would get bailed out and by whom. I knew my father had been contacted. But I was pretty sure he would not go my bail.

Saturday morning I borrowed some clothes from my cellmate and began to wash my filthy street clothes. I was in suds up to my elbows when the matron came lumbering in—"Stern, get your things. You've been bailed out."

Waiting for me downstairs was a well-dressed lawyer hired by my father. What did I want to do? I wanted to find the rest of the Weathermen and finish out the action.

He drove me to the seminary. It was deserted. A hippie lounging in the area told me that it had been raided and everything taken from it. All the people had been busted. Leaving the lawyer in his car, I phoned a number that we had been made to memorize on the first night of the action. The person on the other end of the line informed me that the last part of the action had just ended, and everybody who had been bailed out of jail was being requested to leave Chicago, that it was dangerous to hang around. The lawyer drove me to O'Hare Airport, and got me a ticket to New York. I boarded the plane, and slept all the way to New York.

My mother met me at the airport. Her jaw dropped open when she saw me, and then tears started streaming down her face. "My baby, my baby girl," she sobbed while everybody in the airport stared at us. "You look like you've been through a war," she said to me, dabbing at my face with a perfumed hankie.

I looked at my mother, all made up and expensively dressed and thought, "How nice that I can fight one day in the streets of Chicago, and then fly to New York the next and have my mother pamper me." Then I thought about the black women I had left behind in prison, the victims of junk, of poverty, of racism. I thought about how I must have looked to them, big, bad, Weatherwoman. I suddenly felt sad and stupid. All my macho dribbling away like dirty dishwater. There was no way I could explain it to my mother, no way that she would understand how much I hated my white skin.

"Why you're emaciated," she was babbling. "Didn't they feed you in that awful jail?" Black eyes in black faces stared at me with quiet dignity, as the barred prison doors swung behind me, and I was led away by my lawyer. I turned back once and gave them the fist. Unsmiling, they returned the salute.

Docilely, I allowed my mother to lead me into the dining room, where she ordered me a sirloin steak.

"And a shrimp cocktail, too, please," I added, and began to reassure my mother that I was fine, just fine.

I stayed at my mother's house my first night in New York, allowing her to take care of me, but feeling very removed from it all. It was as if a body named Susan Stern was being bathed in sweet oils, and eating steaks and lying down between clean, fresh-smelling sheets. The mind was still raging with the Weathermen on the streets of Chicago, and imprinted on it indelibly were endless rows of bars and the clanging of iron doors. My mother and I were breathing the same air, but living in two different worlds.

The next day I went to my father's office. He greeted me tight-lipped, barely able to suppress his fury in front of the office people.

"You're a disgrace to the family," he whispered to me.

I cut him off sharply.

"I just came to thank you for putting up my bail, and for hiring the lawyer. But I think I want to use the lawyers all the other Weathermen are using—you won't have to pay for that."

"Do what you want—I'm disgusted with you already. But remember, Susan, I helped you this time. I didn't want to, either. If it hadn't been for your brother and some of the other people in this office you'd still be sitting in that stinking jail. Maybe it would have knocked some sense into your head."

I thanked my father, kissed my brother hello and good-by, and fled from the office. The only thing I felt for anybody in my family was hostility.

I spent a week in New York, crashing at my old apartment on 102nd Street, which had been taken over by other friends. I concentrated on being tough. I wore my jeans tucked into my boots, and I strutted around in my leathers carrying a stick. I passed some of my old friends who were now in RYM 2 on the street one day. "Well, Susan," one of them said jocularly, "you look like a lion tamer," and they all laughed. I sneered at them. Intellectual punks! Armchair radicals!

I got plenty of flack on that trip to New York, but I was right. No matter what anyone said or did, nothing could change that fact. The reports from Chicago were good. We had done hundreds of thousands of dollars' worth of damage. We had injured hundreds of pigs. Greatest of all, one of Richard Daley's chief counsels, Richard Elrod, was paralyzed from the waist down. I had a right to walk with my head high; I had done my share while all these motherfuckers sitting in New York were criticizing us for going out and fighting for them.

On October 18 my distraught mother drove me to the airport. "Please, Susan, please don't get into any more trouble," she begged. "Stop all this before it's too late." I didn't even bother trying to explain. I tolerated a kiss and ran onto the airplane. From the window I saw her standing there, a pathetic figure, putting on sunglasses to hide her tears. If I felt anything, it was disgust.

I flew to Chicago where I had the first of several hearings before my trial, which was postponed. After the hearing, there was a meeting with the Weatherbureau during which we were urged not to let up now that the Days of Rage were over, but to push harder to build Weatherman collectives in Seattle. I was then given the job of driving the Ford microbus back to Seattle with Don Sick, a Weatherman who hid his eyes every time I drove, because he was terrified of driving over thirty miles an hour. I insisted on driving most of the way so we would get there quickly.

I discovered I was something of a people's hero when I finally got home. The Days of Rage were the biggest thing that had happened in recent American radical history. I noticed the change in people's attitudes immediately. Even the Running Dogs were conciliatory.

Everybody wanted to hear about them in real life—no one could believe they had actually happened.

Beverly was the first collective member to return to Seattle; she had arrived the day before. The fact that she had bullet wounds gave her an awesome status. Calm and aloof, she had little to say about Chicago. Staying alone, resting, she had to spend several hours a day with a fluorescent light shining on her bullet wounds to dry them out. She seemed relieved when I arrived; I had been there, I had experienced it too, I understood. I too needed time to digest the Days of Rage.

We spent quiet hours alone in the little gray house. We knew we had changed somehow—it was intangible, but we were different from the people who had not gone.

"Do you think it's because you got shot?" I asked, looking at the gaping holes.

"No. It hardly hurt. No—I think it's more because there were so few of us. I couldn't believe it when we were standing around that fire. I was so afraid, and I kept on thinking how crazy it was. I'm not so sure any more that we're right. There must be some reason why nobody came."

White-skin privilege. It loomed like a great blank wall between us and the people who hadn't gone to Chicago, who were now so eager to hear about the Days of Rage, hoping some of our unique experience would sink in by osmosis.

Garrity came by the first night. He didn't say much—just kept shaking his head when I described Chicago to him. He couldn't believe that even after such a sparse showing, I was still as rabidly devoted to Weatherman as I had ever been. But I noticed that he wasn't referring to Weathermen as wimps any more.

Two days after I returned to Seattle, we got the news that Georgia had driven off the road somewhere in Montana. Roger, Mickey, and Jay had been in the car. Roger was in a hospital for whiplash, Georgia had minor injuries; Jay and Mickey were being held for questioning. Beverly didn't hesitate a second. As frightened as she was of driving, she hopped into her car, bullet wounds and all, and drove by herself deep into Montana to retrieve Jay. She had asked me to come along, but I had not wanted to leave Garrity.

Late the next day, Beverly returned with Georgia, Mickey, and Jay. Slowly the collective was returning to Seattle. Roger had to stay in the hospital another week and Carol was still in jail in Chicago; there was no money to bail her out.

I spent most of my time across the street, or at Ty and Jean's house. Ty had gone to Chicago as an observer, and had been inspired by the Weathermen. Bored at the RYM 2 demonstrations, he had gone with the Weathermen the first night, and been totally astonished when they galloped right into the pigs. Now he and Jean spent hours talking in their bedroom. Like everyone else who went to the Days of Rage, Ty was changed.

Mike Justesen hadn't gone to Chicago, probably out of stubbornness. But as the reports filtered back, he became visibly excited. By the time we arrived home, it was impossible to tell that Mike had never been a Weatherman. He was eager to hear everything about the action; avidly he hung on every word as Jay, arms flying all over the place, launched into a vivid account of Beverly's shooting, Mickey's daring rescue of her from the hospital, what it felt like to assault a pig, what jail was like. We were all so high. Our excitement grew as we fed off each other's stories. Our enthusiasm buzzed out to everyone. The doubts that Beverly and I had shared faded away now that the collective was back. Alone we were insecure and unsure. Together we grew strong and sure of success.

I had been back for a week. Beverly, Georgia, and I were visiting Jean, trying to convince her to join the collective. Ty was already convinced, but he didn't want to join without Jean. Somehow we avoided the question of monogamy; both of them were better than neither of them. Our arguments with Jean went on for hours. They were much more patient, and less dogmatic than they had been before the action. We didn't need to act so tough now; we had proven ourselves. Chicago spoke for us. Jean resisted. She was frightened. She was an artist. She wasn't sure she was ready to give up her artwork.

"But Ty is a poet," we pointed out. "He isn't going to give up writing poetry. All he's giving up is his bourgeois standard for writing. The revolution needs artists and poets. You know all the leaflets we put out."

She would talk with us for several hours, and then disappear into the bedroom to confer with Ty. It went on for days.

That particular afternoon when Jean locked herself in the bedroom with Ty, Georgia and Beverly broached the subject of my moving into the collective house.

"There's no reason for you not to, Susan. You're a Weatherman, just like the rest of us. You spend most of your time there. It would be easier if you actually lived there."

I knew they were right. But I resisted. At first I said no, I wasn't ready. But they weren't buying it.

"You'll get readier faster if you struggle with it."

I searched frantically for some excuse, anything, while they bore down on me gently but relentlessly.

"Tell us why. What are the real reasons."

Suddenly it all spilled out in a rush.

"I have it pretty easy in that gray house—you know, I practically run it there, everybody does what I tell them to do. And I don't have to bow constantly to collective discipline. I mean, in some ways, I can be a Weatherman when I want to be, but I don't have to be one constantly. And then there's Garrity. He just hates Weatherman. And you know, with the line on monogamy, well, if I couldn't see Garrity, I would really suffer. I love him. I want to be with him. I want to make the revolution, but I need love too. I need to sleep with people. I can't hand out leaflets and criticize people twenty-four hours a day. I'll go crazy. And I still take dope. And I like to wear make up. I was ugly all my life—I want to be pretty. I don't want to dress and act like a man, and I don't want to wear army boots. I like high heels."

I stopped, out of breath, looking at them, waiting for their wrath to descend upon me. But something had happened in Chicago. We had changed more than we realized. Beverly and Georgia responded quietly and with great love and support.

"It's easy to take the easy way out. The choice is yours. You can stay in the gray house, and play mama to all those younger kids, and pretend you're a big deal, or you can come to live across the street, and struggle with your revolutionary sisters and brothers, and grow strong because of it."

Across the street. It could have been Mars. The move to the collective house meant totally giving up my freedom. It meant finally, that I was for real. I looked at Beverly and Georgia. They knew all along that I had been holding out. Couldn't fool them. Now was the time to decide. Which side was I really on?

"Will I be allowed to see Garrity?"

"Of course. What do you think that house is—a prison?" asked Beverly.

"Well, you know, no one outside the collective is allowed in there. I just want to make sure he will be allowed to visit, and spend the night. I won't let it interfere with my work. But I want to make sure I will be free to see him. And I don't want to be forced to adhere to some sleeping schedule. Garrity is the only person I want to fuck."

"Susan," Beverly said softly, "do you think I'd ever let anyone but Jay touch me?"

Feeling reassured, I waited a second longer, and then, tears in my eyes, I said yes, yes I will.

The three of us were silent. I looked at the two women through my tears. I loved them, respected them so much. But I was full of fear about moving across the street. I thought it must be like entering a nunnery.

"Let's move you over today," Beverly said, jumping up.

"Today! Well . . . yeah, I guess so."

As we went downstairs, Jean and Ty came out of the bedroom. Jean's eyes were red, but there was a radiant smile on her face.

"Ty and I want to join the collective. Do you think we'll be able to?" she asked.

The three of us laughed. I told Ty and Jean I was moving my stuff in. Beverly told them we'd have to wait until Roger and Carol came back to make a decision about expanding the collective.

I was moved across the street that day. There wasn't much left to move; most of my belongings had already been sold. It was strange to move back into my old house. If the walls could talk, what would they say?

My room was very small, almost like a jail cell. It was really half of a larger room, separated by a partition that did not extend all the way to the ceiling. Georgia had the other half of the room. I fixed my cubbyhole up as best as I could. I put my few remaining books on a crate, and stuffed all my clothes into a carton, leaving only jeans, a few blue workshirts, and sneakers in another wooden crate. Mickey's eyebrows knit together, but he said nothing when we dragged in my double mattress, and when I proceeded to put sheets on it. Everyone else, except Beverly and Jay, had a single mattress and a sleeping bag.

Garrity helped me move, and stayed for dinner. Jay did most of the cooking, and Beverly did most of the grocery shopping, just as they had done before the Days of Rage. The house was still a wreck, but no one seemed to mind. That night it was almost cozy. We drank a lot of wine, smoked some dope, laughed a lot, and joked about Richard Elrod—we had hoped he would die. After dinner, Garrity and I retired to my little room, and Beverly and Jay went to theirs. Georgia sat looking forlorn and lonely in the living room, drinking glass after glass of wine.

"I guess it will be all right," I said to Garrity as we snuggled under the covers.

Roger returned the next day. He wore a collar brace; it kept his head tilted to one side. He looked absurd, but was obviously uncomfortable, so I tried not to laugh. Several times I caught Jay limping around the house with his head cranked to one side, and he, Beverly and I would crack up. Poor Roger, we weren't very sympathetic.

Roger's arrival changed the atmosphere in the house. Mickey, Jay, Georgia, Beverly, and I had formed a tight group, and Roger didn't fit into it very well. He refused to relax and have fun. He insisted that we had to have a criticism session. The rest of us wanted to avoid it as long as possible. We didn't think a little relaxation could hurt us.

Then Carol came home. She had been in jail for over two weeks, and then had spent a few days with the Weatherbureau. She had changed too—into a tyrant. She was all business as she issued Bureau commands: no dope, end monogamy, collectives must engage in group sex. In her monotone voice she kept coming on with the Bureau tirade: tighten up, more criticism—that will help fight demoralization; work—that will answer all questions; organize—there's a war going on. She was like Scrooge—bah on laughter, bah on drinking wine and smoking dope together. She wiped out all the collective mirth and vitality we'd felt for a week. SMASH MONOGAMY! NO LOVE! NO LIFE! An hour after Carol arrived home, we were all around the dining-room table deep in criticism–self-criticism.

We shut ourselves away from all the people who had been flocking to Weatherman. When they came to the door, Carol answered it, severely telling them we were engaged in criticism—to leave us alone. Beverly complained that it wasn't fair to people who really desired to join the collective, like Ty and Jean and Mike; Carol and Roger insisted that we had to criticize ourselves first, and develop the correct attitudes before we could think of expanding the collective. It seemed backward to me. I wanted everyone to be in Weatherman.

We were locked in criticism for five days straight, taking time out only to sleep. The second day, out of sheer desperation, I went back to my job at the Dunes. It seemed the lesser of two evils to work at the Dunes than to sit through the endless criticism sessions. No one objected to my taking the job; the collective was almost broke, and I would only be away six hours a night.

Most of our criticism was about the Days of Rage and our feelings about it. Carol said the Weatherbureau was aware of discontent among the cadre; that many people blamed leadership for being unprepared, for misleading us. We discussed, unnecessarily, the reasons so few people had come to Chicago. Everyone in the collective knew it was white-skin privilege—we didn't blame the leadership. No one had tried harder than they; they had failed because no one was interested.

Carol wouldn't drop the subject. She was obsessed with it. The more she attempted to convince us we were demoralized, the more demoralized we became, trying to convince her we weren't.

Then Beverly brought up the '57 Chevy. I looked at her blankly. There had been a '57 Chevrolet parked on one of the streets we'd rampaged on. The Chevy had been demolished. Beverly maintained that no ruling-class person would be caught dead in a '57 Chevy, that it probably belonged to one of their maids—a poor, working person, perhaps black. And we had demolished it. Now what about that?

We speculated for a while that it might have belonged to the teen-age son or daughter of the ruling class; but Beverly continued to insist that it belonged to someone poor, perhaps Third World.

Although the argument went on for two days, we never came to any real conclusions about what it meant when a '57 Chevy got destroyed during a riot. Roger's answer was that the car and the owner were war casualties—that's just the way it was in war. Occasionally you make a mistake and hit the wrong target. Beverly said that sounded remarkably like what the American military said about hitting civilians. Roger said it wasn't that important—it was just one '57 Chevy. Beverly said it probably happened a lot, only no one ever stopped to examine how it could be prevented, and that if we didn't deal with such questions, we were no different from any-body else in the country.

Like so many questions that we discussed in the collective, this one was very important—we simply didn't know how to answer it. After endless hours of arguing, we would get very tired and depressed. There were always so many questions and we had so few answers. It seemed far easier to discuss actions. If the state didn't come smashing down after an action, at least it was a definitive statement.

Differences in the collective emerged as the days wore on. Carol and Roger represented the Weatherbureau line; every time they spoke, they would always mention someone from the Bureau. Bev-erly, Jay, and myself still thought that leadership was very important but refused to agree with Carol that it was everything and that we should stop thinking and just wait for Chicago to issue orders to us.

"After all, they don't know what Seattle is like—they're not here," Beverly would say. "Everything that might work in Chicago or Cleveland might not be good in Seattle, and we're the best judges of that."

Georgia would vacillate; she needed the authority of the Bureau, since she was so insecure. But she could think very clearly at times, and when she was thinking well she would struggle with Carol and

Roger for more autonomy for the Seattle collective. Mickey never committed himself to any particular line; he would listen closely to all the arguments, and then parrot what either Roger or Beverly said. As it became clear that Beverly was the leader of a dissenting faction opposed to the ever increasing Bureau dogma, he tended to parrot Roger more frequently.

These arguments had begun even before the Days of Rage. Two men had come from the Bureau a week prior to the action, with a very heavy line about shooting soldiers and GIs just like "any other pig." I had incurred their wrath one night when I said I thought soldiers should be treated differently than pigs; I thought we should attempt to organize them, talk to them, rather than to shoot them. I pointed out that the Vietcong didn't consider soldiers the enemy—they were just lackeys of American imperialism.[1] I was heavily criticized for my position, and told that the reason I took it was because I really didn't want to go to Chicago at all—that I was frightened. This was ridiculous, and I hooted at the idea. It was a moot point anyway, since we were subsequently told not to bring guns to the Days of Rage.

Halloween Day, tensions had built to exploding proportions. We started the criticism at eight o'clock in the morning. Carol had a set look on her face as we congregated around the dining-room table—before my butt had even touched the chair she was screaming at Beverly, Jay, and me about monogamy. She had called the Bureau yesterday . . . she had told them about me and Garrity; she had said that Beverly and Jay were making no noticeable attempts to smash their monogamy. She also warned them that Ty and Jean, another "couple," were interested in joining the collective. They had laid down a mandate—SMASH MONOGAMY—immediately.

The argument raged all day. At times Carol and Jay, or Carol and Beverly, or Carol and I were screaming at each other. I was utterly contemptuous of her. "You just want us to give up our relationships because you don't have anyone to fuck."

The argument continued through dinner and was still going on at nine o'clock when I left for the Dunes. By that time everyone was in the living room. Roger had been falling asleep off and on for hours; Jay and Georgia were drunk, having had me sneak a gallon of Chianti in through the kitchen door—only Carol was still into it, still going on and on about monogamy. I left the house feeling very low. This was not the collective that had worked together so smoothly prior to the Days of Rage.

Before leaving the house Beverly gave me a hit of acid—"to celebrate Halloween," she said ironically. She and Jay were going to take theirs in just a little while. They were going to try and get everyone in the house to trip together. Apparently collective "trips" were permitted by the Bureau.

I got morbid at the Dunes. The job was becoming increasingly intolerable to me. The hopelessness of the other women, my own depression from the five days of criticism, an increasing desire on my part to be with Garrity constantly, while he was much more blasé about it, all combined to make me miserable that night.

To make things worse, I was asked frequently to table-dance. It was precarious dancing on those tiny round tables, and beneath me, eyes glowing, tongues licking, hands reaching and prodding, were the men, going bananas at the sight of pubic hair. Around eleven o'clock, I'd had it. I swallowed the tab of acid, went into the dressing room, changed my clothes, and told the infuriated bartender I was quitting. I didn't worry about finding work. It had never been a problem for me before.

When I got home, I found Roger sitting in a rocking chair in the kitchen, his head craned to one side, and a blanket across his knees. He told me the whole house with the exception of himself was on acid. I went upstairs and opened Beverly and Jay's door. The room looked as though a cyclone had struck it. They were nude and giggling like children, wrestling around on the floor. Beverly showed me where they had peed into her flower pots. They told me that several times during the evening Carol had come in, sometimes with Georgia; they wanted to have a serious talk about the collective, about relationships, about monogamy. Beverly and Jay would chase them out, and return to their fucking and laughing. They told me Georgia was on a bummer—Carol and Mickey had taken her for a walk trying to calm her down.

The acid was making me horny, but it was obvious by now that Garrity was not going to show. I realized how hard it must be on everybody else in the house having Beverly and Jay upstairs—they really did exist just for each other, and even in this depressing situation, they had each other for support.

"That," I thought wryly, "was what the collective was supposed to do for everybody."

When Georgia, Mickey, and Carol came back from their walk, they tried to talk to me about collective conditions, but I concentrated on a TV horror movie and refused to talk with them. Georgia was obviously upset; Carol, who was enjoying the acid, spent her entire evening trying to calm Georgia down. She wanted to go across the street to be with Mike Justesen. They had some kind of strange relationship that had been going on and off for months. Georgia really loved Mike and she suffered constantly because he rarely responded.

I stayed up all night watching the tube, flopping around the house, getting more and more morose. By dawn all I could think of was escaping. I had conned the collective into letting me buy a Vespa, on the pretext that it would save gas; I was trying it out for a week. Coming down from the acid, nervous and sleepless, I decided to split for San Francisco. Throwing some clothes into a knapsack, I mounted the Vespa and took off. I had a helmet, but no license. I stopped for gas, but at the gas station, I couldn't find the gas-tank opening, and neither could the station attendant.

Almost in tears, I went to Hippie Hill instead of San Francisco, and fell asleep in the pale sun. When I woke up, Garrity was looking down at me. He asked if he could come over later on. I immediately felt happier. I wondered how I could have been so depressed the night before.

That night we had a brief collective meeting to discuss the Moratorium Peace March scheduled for November 15.[2] We decided that the Weathermen would attempt to take over the peaceful march and make it into a riot.

Work began on the Moratorium march. We churned out two leaflets each day, and distributed them at Seattle Community College, the U of W, at the twelve high schools, on the Ave, in the parks, downtown at the Pike Street Market Place, and at the old World's Fair site.

In some ways work was easier because we had more people helping us. Nothing concrete had been established about expanding the collective. Roger continually told us that someone was coming from the Bureau, but the days passed, and no one came. Meanwhile a half a dozen Weathermen from out of state had arrived, including Barbara Beam, and were crashing at the gray house across the street. So there were another half-dozen people who had gone to Chicago, survived, and were still committed to Weatherman. Along with Ruth, Mike, Ty, Jean, Ray, and Don Sick, they were considered part of a very loose, secondary collective. My collective was the command collective.

That gray house was amazing. Over a dozen people were living there; eight people slept in the big back room, which was wall-to-wall mattresses and sleeping bags. The house reeked! But no one who lived there had time to clean; we kept them moving. Sometimes they would grumble about all the work—Mike especially—and we'd tell them it was part of collective discipline. However, discipline was less rigorous when applied to Beverly, Jay, and myself.

The look on Carol's face got grimmer. She barely talked to me or Beverly any more. She and Roger spent more time across the street with the new Weathermen. Soon Mickey was spending most of his time there too. I'd laugh and say, "Well, all those nurds belong together." I thought most of the people in the house across the street were an absurd joke. I thought Roger, Carol, and Mickey were ridiculous too.

"They're all so ugly," I would say to Beverly. "That's what they all have in common." I thought they were stupid as well, with the exception of Mike and Roger. I hardly ever spoke to any of them, except to tell them where to leaflet. They had been living there for almost a month before I finally learned the names of the people from out of state.

I was constantly preoccupied about Garrity. I was afraid he would come to the house while I was gone, or visit during a criticism session. He made jokes about the people across the street, which fed my own contempt for them. Instead of going across the street at night and trying to get to know them, I found it much more exciting to go with Garrity to El Roach Tavern, which Indian was managing, and take THC, get drunk, dance, and listen to the local musicians.

I loved the Roach. It was my one escape from the collective. Every Friday and Saturday night under the pretext of working there, I could drink, dope, and dance to my heart's content. No one in the collective could object, even if they never saw my money. Beverly controlled the collective funds, and she never brought up the fact that I never gave her my nonexistent pay. She liked Garrity, and she thought our relationship healthy for me. And she needed another monogamy—to deflect some of the collective's increasing antagonism away from her relationship with Jay.

In spite of my ever growing anxiety about Garrity, my participation in organizing for the coming Moratorium march never flagged. I got up at seven o'clock in the morning with everyone else, and went out leafleting even if I hadn't gone to sleep until five o'clock. Whether I was hung over or still high on drugs, sick from constant dissipation or lack of sleep, I was always one of the first dressed. Throwing on a coat, I'd dash across the street and start screaming to awaken the sleeping people in the little gray house. It was just more proof to me that they were absolute morons—only absolute morons needed so much sleep. How very American my attitudes were! I only respected very aggressive people with lots of energy and initiative.

By eight o'clock we were at the high schools and Seattle Community College with our leaflets. Our leaflets reflected our ever changing line. Now we were trying to loosen up a bit, and not be as serious. Most of our leaflets had comics on them, taken from ZAP Comix. But the line was essentially the same: "America is the cop of the world!" On every leaflet, a cartoon character would say, "N when yer smashin' the state kids . . . don't ferget t' keep a smile on yer lips an' a song in yer heart!"

I took the little slogan quite seriously. No matter how I felt, I wanted to present the revolution as something appealing, something fun, something anyone would want to do, especially if the only other alternatives were school, boring jobs, or Vietnam. Smiling, laughing and joking, I bantered with the high school students.

I didn't always talk about the war. Sometimes I talked about music with the kids. I liked music—they liked music. Or we'd discuss dope, buying and selling, the increasing burns, the accelerating use of hard stuff. We'd all agree that the pigs sucked, that parents were nowhere, that school was a drag, the army sure suicide, and America, in general, a lousy place. That was my approach—lots of jiving, lots of laughing, but always I would get in something about racism and imperialism. I always left a high school exhilarated. And I was always impatient to return the next day.

While the new recruits made our organizing easier in some ways, and while people in our immediate community of friends were more sympathetic to us, the remainder of Seattle, running the gamut from far left to far right, just thought we were an abomination. The Panthers despised us; they were convinced that we'd pull some jerk-off action in the Central District and that the black community would catch shit for it. They were scornful of our talk about arming ourselves. Generally, they'd call us only when they wanted to borrow a car or use our press.

Political groups on campus didn't appreciate us either. The Black Student Union wanted nothing to do with us, and most white groups on campus had been sucked in by the pacifist Vietnam Mobilization Committee. Jean Shaffer worked with the Mobe.[3] When I encountered Jean on campus, she'd avert her head, and walk determinedly in the opposite direction. I kept on saying what a pig she was even after I heard that she'd quit her job as a professor of economics and was working at some menial job in the post office.

There was one group of kids that was invaluable to us. They lived in the heart of the Central District, but they were white. There were about thirty of them. They were known throughout left Seattle circles as the Anarchists. These kids, ranging in age from thirteen to twenty-one, might have looked like any other hoodlum gang to the rest of Seattle. To Weatherman, they were a dream come true. They would attack anything, steal from anywhere, fight like the dickens, and run like the wind. All of them had dropped out of school, and lived in two or three derelict communal homes. They were entirely contemptuous of Weatherman, but they loved to riot and would eventually come around to talk to us when we were brewing one.

Four days prior to the action, the command collective met to discuss conditions in the house across the street. We decided that it was impossible for so many people to continue living there and that we'd have to rent another house. We decided to rent it in Ballard, since we did a lot of organizing at Ballard High School, and since there were a lot of hangouts for kids there. That afternoon a couple of collective people were dispatched to Ballard—by evening, a third Weatherman house had been rented.

Once again sleep was forgotten. We organized around the clock, and some of the tensions that had plagued the collective since the Days of Rage seemed to abate as momentum built for the Mobe action. On the night of November 13, the collective met at a house we were sure was not bugged. Criticism about monogamy was shunted aside for the more immediate questions of strategy and tactics for the march. It was decided that I would lead it. We would scope out downtown, and choose one block as a target. We'd break from the main body of the march, breaking windows as we ran and fighting with anyone, Mobe marshals or pigs, who attempted to restrain us.

The next day, with some of the Anarchists, we chose our rampage block, and staked out escape routes. On the block we chose, the sidewalks were lined with trees planted in gigantic pots. We decided to store rocks in those pots. That afternoon I went rock gathering with Beverly. We filled up burlap sack after sack full of fist-sized rocks, and loaded them into Zelda's trunk. Bubbling with enthusiasm for tomorrow's demonstration, we drove home and went roaring up the stairs and into the house.

There, sitting on a lawn chair, was Mark Rudd, surrounded by the rest of the collective sitting on the floor. His head was resting on the back of the chair, his legs crossed. I got the impression of a king holding court with a roomful of humble serfs.

"Well, come in," he said, looking at Beverly. "We were just discussing monogamy."

Jay's head was hanging to his knees. Carol was openly gloating. Roger's eyes were flitting from Rudd to Beverly. Georgia had a cigarette lit in the ashtray, one in her hand, and was trying to drink her cup of tea with another palsied hand. And Mickey was staring at Rudd with something akin to a hypnotic trance.

"Listen, Rudd, we got a demo tomorrow . . ." I began, but he answered me, not taking his eyes off Beverly.

"Yeah, tomorrow, but today we're going to talk about monogamy. Aren't we, Beverly?"

We talked about monogamy all that afternoon. It was clear from the get-go what Rudd's tactic was. Weaken Jay by attacking his masculinity. All day long Rudd needled.

"Poor pussy-whipped Jay. Run around for Beverly like a good boy."

The criticism went on and on. Beverly said very little, except to explode occasionally when Rudd looked at Jay patronizingly and called him a poor little pussy. Only Beverly mentioned the utter male chauvinism of the entire discussion. She pointed out with undeniable logic that if Weatherman really was serious about altering male-female relationships, then the fact that she might dominate in her relationship with Jay meant nothing. That they complemented and supported each other was the most important thing. She intimated that Rudd could never understand anything like that, since his only relationships with women depended upon his domination.

When Beverly said that there was stunned silence. Georgia's teacup was shaking violently—even Carol was speechless. But Rudd took it in stride. Unperturbed and smiling, he looked back at Beverly and continued with his original arguments, as if she had never said anything at all. It was like talking to a wall. Nothing anyone said made any difference. After several hours, Beverly finally shut up and just kept on agreeing with Rudd. Jay looked agonized the entire time. It must have been unspeakable torture for him to watch Beverly humble herself, and to contemplate losing her. By dinner, I felt sick. But there was more to come. The collective from across the street would be joining us after dinner.

We all went into the kitchen to prepare dinner. The fare was a cut above the usual rice and spaghetti because of Rudd's presence. I was leaning against the counter, somewhat separated from the cluster of people around Rudd and the kitchen table, thinking about tomorrow's demonstration. "This is shit," I was thinking. "Instead of discussing the fucking demonstration, Rudd comes, and we discuss monogamy." I was leading the action tomorrow. If it didn't go well, all the busted heads and arrests would be on my conscience.

My dog, Reddog, was lying at my feet. I looked down at him absently as he scratched a flea. Out of the clear blue sky, Mickey, who had been standing quietly near the table said, "I hate that fucking dog. I'd like to kill him." I thought he was joking at first.

Before I could say anything, Rudd said, leveling me with a gaze from his steely blues, "It's not the dog you hate, Mickey, it's Susan. Wouldn't you really like to kill her? You just say it's the dog because you're afraid of her," and he stared at me with such mockery and contempt that my skin crawled.

Everyone in the kitchen was frozen, as if a movie had suddenly stopped at an interesting frame. Someone stood with a fork rigidly suspended in the air; Beverly's eyes were wide with amazement, and Mickey was green with terror.

"Well," persisted Rudd, "isn't it really Susan you'd like to tear apart? Look at her standing there looking so cool. She's got all the answers; she's just too much, isn't she?"

If I looked cool it was sheer luck; I felt like collapsing. The tension in the kitchen was so thick it was smothering all of us, and still Rudd just sat there, tilting the chair back on its rear legs, gazing at me unblinkingly.

"You're so fucking sick it's disgusting," I said, as I flounced out of the kitchen.

Before I reached the door, Mickey, leaped across the kitchen and kicked Reddog in the guts. The dog went howling into the living room. Mickey stood there grinning stupidly. I stared at him, realizing that Rudd was right, that Mickey hated me. That hardly bothered me, since Mickey was insignificant to me. I didn't like him and barely acknowledged him. There was no doubt that I treasured Reddog much more than Mickey.

I looked at Rudd, who was smiling openly now. He had proved his point. So what. I didn't like Mickey; he didn't like me. I couldn't be expected to like someone automatically because they were in the collective. Rudd was not going to pop in from the Bureau and tell me whom to like. I finally turned and sat down on the living-room couch, curling with rage. I sat there all through dinner, petting Reddog. I was still sitting there when the people from across the street, and Ty and Jean, began to filter in for the evening's criticism session.

Twenty-five Weathermen were gathered in the living room. Rudd took his position on the lawn chair, and I moved toward the center of the room, to sit on a wooden crate that we used to keep logs in. Ty and Jean and Beverly and Jay weren't the only monogamies present. Two new couples had been recruited, one from Seattle, the other from Oregon. I just assumed the discussion of monogamy would continue, but when we were all settled, Rudd turned to me and matter-of-factly told me that he wasn't sure I belonged in Weatherman.

I was stunned! It was the last thing on earth I expected. Before I could recover my wits to ask why, he looked around the room and asked if anybody would give a reason why I belonged in Weatherman. Heavy silence for a minute, and then Ty spoke.

"Susan is the best high school organizer we have. She's the only one that the kids really like. You should see—whenever we go to a school, she knows all the kids, and they crowd around her, and they laugh and get all excited. You can tell she loves the organizing— she's always smiling, even when it's pouring rain." Ty was smiling at Rudd; it seemed so clear to him.

"I'll bet all the kids like Susan," Rudd said. "Why not? It's easy to like someone who doesn't put you up against the wall, who doesn't make you face your own racism, your white-skin privilege. It's easy to like someone who's always got a joint, or who's more interested in singing rock-and-roll songs than in talking about U.S. imperialism. Sure they like her. She goes down to those fucking high schools, dressed like a whore, gives out joints, giggles like an idiot—why wouldn't they like her? But is she really organizing them? Is their level of consciousness raised at all? Or do they just go away thinking, 'Boy, is Susan Stern groovy.' Look at her now, seated in the middle of the room like a queen or something. You think you're a queen, Susan? How come, no matter what's happening, you always have to be the center of attention? Is your need for admiration that over-whelming that you got to simper in front of high school kids to turn them on? Who are you really organizing for—Weatherman or Susan Stern?" And with that, Rudd, who had been leaning forward, sank back into his chair, and closed his eyes. I watched his hands drumming softly on the arm of the chair.

Ty tried again.

"That may all be true, but Susan works harder than just about anybody in the collective. She's the first one up, and one of the last to sleep. And she fights harder than anybody else; she's always at the head of the attack, and she never leaves until it's all over. Maybe she does try to get some glory for herself, but, well . . . I think she deserves it. She demands more of herself."

"BULLSHIT!" It sounded like the retort of a gun. "She doesn't demand anything of herself—she thinks it's all a game." And he turned to me, glowering.

"You've been laughing and jumping around all day, Susan. How come you're so goddam happy? What the fuck have you got to be happy about? Have the Vietnamese won? Have the pigs left the ghet-tos? Is the revolution won? How can you be so happy when people are struggling and dying all over the world? Or are you above all that?"

I was dumfounded. "Sure, I'm happy. Why shouldn't I be? I love what I'm doing . . . I love Weatherman. I . . . going to the high schools everyday, talking to those kids—that's all I want to do. I'm fighting the revolution the best way I can, and that makes me happy."

Beverly spoke up wrathfully. "How do you know what Susan does or doesn't do? You're not here every day. Why should she be miserable? She's so successful precisely because she enjoys herself so much. It's the same way at rallies. Everybody keeps on walking by or stands there looking dead until Susan starts speaking, and then they all listen because she . . ."

"Puts on such a good show?" Rudd prodded.

"No, man," Jay said. "It isn't a show. She throws herself into it totally. No one can mobilize a crowd like she can. You should have seen the first SDS meeting here . . . she got three hundred new students to tear Clark Hall apart . . . man you're so off the wall," he said, looking disgustedly at Rudd.

"Susan this, Susan that, Susan, Susan, Susan. Ain't it too much, I mean, some far-out coincidence that all the people who have defended Susan need her to protect them. She does a good job for you, doesn't she, Beverly? Makes sure you can keep Jay here bouncing like a puppet on a string. And, Ty . . . your heart goes out to her, cute, isn't she, little and exciting, turning on all those high school kids, throwing herself into speeches. Well, what do the rest of you think about Susan?"

I looked around the room. Everybody was fidgeting nervously. Then Don Sick spoke.

"She . . . I can't stand her. She makes me feel like I'm, um . . . dumb or something."

Then a woman who'd come with us to the Days of Rage: "She only talks to us to give us commands. She doesn't ask anybody to do something . . . she tells them. Take these leaflets. Put up these posters. I hate her. All she does is try and get every man around her sexually attracted to her. She can control everything that way."

Then Justesen, who had been ominously silent up until that point: "She's hungry for power. We all know it, but I doubt that Susan realizes it. And she's ruthless, in a rare way; she's unconscious of the way she manipulates people. But when Susan wants something, she gets it. The collective exists only as a vehicle through which she operates, and she operates only for Susan Stern. Outside of Beverly and Jay, I doubt that she respects any of us; she's openly disdainful of many of us."

And then Carol . . . on and on about my relationship with Garrity. About how I refused to run off leaflets. About how I stopped the rest of the collective from dealing with Beverly and Jay.

One after the other, the new recruits all said their piece, and, with the exception of Ty and Jean, it was bad down the line. I was individualistic, egotistical, self-centered, power-hungry, manipulative, monogamous, dope-crazed, sexually perverted, dishonest, counter-revolutionary and arrogant. When everybody got through, the list of my sins was a mile long. The overwhelming impression I got was that practically everyone hated me.

I had a pounding headache and I felt numb all over. My mind was an absolute blank. I felt so alone, so isolated, so wrecked, that I was afraid to look up. Around me people were moving, getting up, stretching, talking, laughing, the criticism session apparently forgotten. It was incredible—how could they forget all that? I looked up finally to see Rudd staring at me, something vaguely resembling sympathy on his face. "How can I lead that demonstration tomorrow?" I asked him, almost in tears. "I'm in no condition to. A leader is supposed to have strength and confidence. Couldn't you have waited until after the demonstration to tell me what a pig I was? Now I'm useless."

"You'll do a better job now," he said. "You'll lead with more humility. A true leader has to have humility."

"Look who's telling me I have to have humility," I thought vaguely. I looked at the clock. The session had lasted five hours. We had to be up early for the demonstration tomorrow. It was already past midnight and there was so much left to do.

I started to tell Beverly that we should go somewhere and discuss the action, but Rudd interrupted me. He said that everybody should get together, get to know each other, have some revolutionary fun— that was more important than tomorrow's action. Rudd thought it would be a good idea for us to go to El Roach as a group. Since I worked there everybody could get in and drink for free. I was furious. This was no way to prepare for an important action. People needed to rehash the plans, get the timing correct. The newer collective members had to be bolstered against defeatism, their anxieties about fighting with the pigs. But Rudd insisted on revolutionary fun.

We all thronged into the Roach—Garrity was behind the bar. I asked him if the group could have some free pitchers. He gave me a dirty look, but complied. Everyone began drinking the beer and dancing in a big circle, whooping and yowling, Rudd the loudest of all. It was so contrived that I was mortified, and sat hunched at the bar, hiding under my purple hat, tears slipping down my cheeks, as I lamented to Garrity about the criticism session that had taken place. Maybe a dozen times he begged me to let him smash Rudd. Rudd never knew how close he came to being laid out by Garrity that night.

At one point Rudd careened up to me and asked me how I felt. I told him how miserable I was. He looked at me tenderly and said, "I know how hard that first real criticism is—it's the toughest thing in the world to face how fucked up we are. But you'll be much stronger for it, Susan." Then he unexpectedly grabbed my face and tried to kiss me. I tore away from him, revolted. Immediately his face froze into that imperturbable mask, and, whirling about, he began whooping and howling, dancing round and round with the drunk new recruits.

The ride home was a nightmare. Fostering good will and getting to know everyone, Rudd was grabbing and kissing everybody within reach. First he necked with Georgia, then Carol. Then he shocked the shit out of Don Sick by grabbing him and firmly planting a hard kiss on his lips. Sick giggled, and turned and kissed some other man. I sat scrunched under a pile of people thinking it must be the most fucked-up, phony thing I'd ever seen.

Once in the house, everyone fell silent. It was after two o'clock. The Mobe action was only a few hours away. Rudd slid an arm around Carol and they wandered off toward her bedroom. Georgia and I silently walked upstairs and got undressed without talking.

I was pulled out of a deep sleep by a voice crying out, "No, please, no." I opened my eyes in the dark, and heard a man's voice ask, "Why not?" It was Rudd on the other side of the partitioned room, with Georgia, having just come upstairs from Carol's bed.

Georgia pleaded with Rudd. I heard him whisper that she and Carol had to assume command of the collective, that Georgia had to strengthen herself to fight the reactionary tendencies within the collective.

The bed creaked.

"No, no, no, Please don't." Georgia's voice was choked with emotion.

Rudd whispered again about leadership, building strength, and then his mumbling was drowned in a muffled sob which shredded the night.

"I don't want to. All I can think about is Justesen. I love him. I don't want you, I want Mike. I can't help it, I love him. I love him."

Rudd whispered, "You have to put the demands of your collective above your love. Nothing comes before the collective . . ."

I jammed my fingers into my ears, and started rocking from side to side, trying to drown out the voices on the other side of the partition.

A thought streaked darkly through my mind; I felt it like a twinge of pain through my body. "Perhaps Weatherman is wrong."

Georgia's cries were killing me. How far could she be pushed before she cracked. How far could any of us go? What was the limit of human endurance? Where did building strength end and torture begin?

The questions pounded on my brain. I forced myself to think of the Vietnamese people, of their endless strength and dignity. They had endured a thousand years of war fighting for their freedom— what a pittance my life was compared to that. Rudd's leadership might be wrong, but the politics had to be right.

"We'll see how the action goes tomorrow," I thought. "If it's nothing more than a last-ditch effort, then well have to revise, reconsider, find some new ways of bringing our politics to the people. But we can't stop now. If we stop now there's nothing. Nothing to fall back on, nothing to look forward to."

I lay there thinking until six o'clock, when I sneaked out of the room to dress before I awakened the rest of the collective.

November 15 dawned gray and raw, but it wasn't raining. At seven o'clock the collective finally met to discuss final plans for the march. Rudd didn't attend the meeting or the march.

Around noon, the command collective, plus Justesen and Ray, piled into Ray's car and headed downtown. The news over the car radio informed us that the Moratoriums across the country had been peaceful. Someone in our car muttered, "Wait till we get there." We were all very excited, energy mounting for the action.

No one but the command collective knew the target. At the appropriate time I would wave my Vietcong flag, and shrill in my special way, "Let's tear this place apart." Hopefully, hundreds of people would follow.

There were over three thousand people congregated for the peace march. At the appointed time, they began walking in a very orderly way, surrounded by Mobe marshals and Seattle police. Our group of Weathermen was located in the middle of the march. Without sympathizers, we had about one hundred people. Most of those were the Anarchists. Three thousand people chanted, "End the war in Vietnam," and we chanted, "Bring the war home," and waved our Vietcong flags.

When we reached the target block, I threw my flag in the air and roared, "Let's tear this place apart," and without looking back to see who was following, ran toward an airlines agency and smashed a rock through the window. I heard other rocks flying into windows around me. In the melee, I saw that the Moratorium march had stopped—the next instant, the pigs were on us. The forty or fifty people who had followed me were summarily beaten and swept away. I saw the pigs clubbing Ty as he lay on the sidewalk. I watched them pound at Jean as she bent over him, trying to protect him. Rage engulfed me. I turned around and right in front of me was a pig, with his back to me. I had a wooden stick, and swung it at the pig with all my might across his back—he pitched forward. Before I could move an inch, another pig was upon me; I felt a sharp blow on my left shoulder, and then something hit me on the base of my skull. I felt nauseated and everything around me whirled and then I saw a patch of cement . . . and then black.

A million weights were attached to my eyelids, pulling them down. In a distant roar I heard screams and groans and glass shattering. The pain at the base of my skull was unbearable. I thought I heard myself screaming. I forced my eyes open. All around me were men in white suits, pushing men in blue suits . . . I couldn't remember where I was, what was happening.

A white-suited man materialized into the friendly concerned face of Dr. John Greene, who slowly turned me over and asked me if I could talk. I nodded yes. Then he pulled me to my feet. Immediately the nausea and dizziness returned—the world looked weird, out of proportion. When I tried to walk, my knees buckled.

"Susan, you've had a severe concussion," John Greene said to me. "You must go home to bed, and I'll see you later. Please lie down immediately. It's dangerous for you to be walking around until we find out how serious it is."

I looked at him blankly. By the time he had finished the sentence, I couldn't remember what he had said.

I felt someone tugging at me. It was Beverly, her face desperate, pleading with me to help her.

"They've got Jay . . . they're killing him!" she screamed and pointed.

Crushed between the sidewalk and the façade of a building, Jay lay on his back. A monster pig had his foot on his neck, choking him; the pig's face was all screwed up with sadistic delight as Jay gagged, turned blue, and his eyes began to bulge. Another pig was working him over with a club. I saw Jay's hand convulsively covering his genital area. I watched the club pound methodically . . . I saw the foot press deeper . . . I heard Beverly screaming hysterically . . . I heard more screaming and I felt myself in motion and Beverly and I were kicking and clawing and biting at the pigs. There must have been twenty of them now surrounding Jay, slapping Beverly and me away with their clubs as if we were a couple of noisome flies. Then Ray grabbed me from behind and dragged me away, yelling at me,

"It's time to stop, you're hurt, you can't help him any more."

I screamed and struggled with Ray who had my arms pinned behind me until John Greene helped him drag me away. I refused to leave the area until I was sure everyone else in both collectives had either left or been arrested. Ray followed me as I staggered around for about fifteen minutes, and then I couldn't walk any more. I couldn't see clearly. Everything was hazy. Ray finally threw me into a taxi and we went home. That was the last-ditch effort of the Seattle Weatherman collective to save itself.

There was something wrong with my mind. It wouldn't work. I would start to say something, and then, before the words were out of my mouth, I would forget what I had started to say.

I looked over at the ruggedly handsome blond boy driving the car, but I couldn't think of his name. I didn't know where we were driving to. I had a staggering headache, and a throbbing pain in my left shoulder. And my eyes weren't focusing well. I would look at something, and then it would disappear. "Have I gone insane?" I wondered dully.

With immense relief, I recognized Garrity when we arrived at the little gray house. I tried to explain to him how strange I felt, but I forgot how to say the words. I heard the blond boy telling him that I had been clubbed by a pig, and that Dr. Greene said I had a serious concussion. Garrity threw a blanket around my shoulders, and took me to Dr. Greene's house.

Dr. Greene asked me questions about my symptoms, shined lights in my eyes, and attempted to get me to focus on his moving finger. He banged on my knee with a hammer, and stuck pins in my hands. Then he gravely taped my arm against my chest, and told me not to take the tape off for a week—my shoulder was dislocated. About the concussion—it seemed pretty bad, but only time would tell how severe it was. I should expect loss of memory, occasional loss of sight, nausea, states of depression, general confusion, and an inability to connect events logically.

If the loss of eyesight and memory persisted, then he would take X rays. For the time being I was to get into bed and not move. Of the utmost importance was that I should not be upset or excited in any way. The less I moved about, the better for my head.

"Oh, and let me tell you something, young lady," Dr. Greene said very kindly, and with a heavy sigh. "You may have been lucky this time—you'll most likely recover full use of your brain capacity. But there can be no next time. Another blow to your brain, however slight, and you'll live out your days like a vegetable. Do you understand me?"

I heard the words, but they didn't register. Every word melted and was forgotten. The doctor gave me a box with ten little red capsules in it. "Seconals," he said. "They will put you to sleep. The thing you need most is sleep."

Garrity drove me back to the Woodlawn house. He followed me inside. Beverly, her eyes swollen, her face ashen, turned even whiter when she saw me. I tried to talk, but it came out as a gurgle. I dimly heard her telling me that Ty, Jean, and Jay had been arrested and charged with assault. They had all been beaten but were basically all right. Scores of other people had been beaten. I stood there dumbly, still unable to speak.

Rudd came down the stairs, and took a look at me and grunted. Then Garrity told Beverly he was taking me to his apartment, because I needed total quiet and sleep. No one said anything, and Garrity pulled me out the door. Once we were at his house, he gave me one of the Seconals. I swallowed the pill and lay on the couch. In a few minutes I sank down down down into sleep.

I woke up the next morning with a terrible headache. I couldn't remember anything. When I tried to move my left arm, I found it taped to my chest. I panicked! Then Garrity came in and kissed me gently. I tried to talk, but I couldn't put words together to form a sentence. It was terrifying.

Garrity helped me to dress and took me home. I heard him telling Beverly that I needed total rest and quiet, and that I shouldn't be allowed to get excited or upset. He told her he would come back for me later in the day.

No sooner had he walked out the door, than I was bundled into Zelda, and Rudd and the rest of the collective drove to the Ballard house, where all the new recruits had been since the action. Apparently my criticism session the other night had been a warming-up exercise—it was to be continued now in earnest.

I tried to tell Rudd that I needed rest, that I couldn't think too clearly, but it seemed to have no impact, I was seated in a chair, and the criticism was begun. I was attacked once again because of my attitude toward others in the collective and toward the new recruits, because of my monogamous relationship with Garrity and my persistent defense of other monogamies. My motives for being in Weatherman were questioned, as was the extent of my commitment. Was I really ready to die, or was I just hoping to slide by while the Third World took the brunt of U.S. oppression?

On and on it went. The hours were a blur marked only by the agony in my head and shoulder and by the terror of not being able to answer. As time went on, people around me began to look like monsters. Noses getting bigger and eyes narrowing into slits . . . teeth growing into fangs, and red lips dripping saliva. In my chest there was a weight so heavy, I thought it would crush me.

While I was being criticized, the new recruits were in the basement taking group showers, fucking and engaging in tentative wargasms—the Weatherword for gang-bangs. When they weren't playing, they too were deeply involved in criticism–self-criticism largely led by Carol or Roger. They were also being organized into collectives.

After a long time the criticism of me seemed about to end. Everyone got up and was shambling around. I sat still, trying to remember where I was, what had just happened. In a distance I heard my tremulous voice saying, "Mark Rudd, you'll never force me to say I'm a bad Communist, or that my heart and life doesn't belong to the revolution. Fuck you! It's not true."

I felt the flush of fury within me and then my head hurt so fiercely that I grabbed it, and began to moan with pain. Just at that minute, Garrity and Indian walked in. Garrity grabbed me, threw his coat around my shoulders, and took me back to his apartment.

The next day was a continuation of the previous day. Once again I was driven to the Ballard house and subjected to a punishing criticism session. The new recruits were present part of the time. As muddled as I was, I was cognizant of the undisguised pleasure with which some of them undertook criticism–self-criticism. Don Sick seemed to evince insidious delight in pummeling away at me, and when the criticism eventually switched to monogamy, he was just as grueling with Beverly.

Barbara Beam also appeared to derive a great deal of joy out of criticizing people. Once she ferreted out a fault, she refused to drop the subject until Rudd, Roger, or Carol stopped her.

Rudd sat quietly in a corner most of the time. I thought back to the first time I'd met him at that farm in Indiana, throwing rocks at trees. What enemies were those rocks hitting? Who was I really fighting? My father? Myself? Who were any of us fighting? What made us fight? Was it Fate, genes, or happenstance?

There had to be a reason why we were all in Weatherman, in this room struggling to change ourselves into true revolutionaries. There had to be a difference between us and all the people who were on the other side, who didn't care. Our motives had to be real—discernible, just like our flesh and blood. We had to be more reality than appearance.

I looked hazily around the room, and saw Beverly sitting, her normally straight back sagging slightly, her face severe with sorrowful eyes. She caught me staring at her, and moved to sit beside me, squeezing my hand. Then Georgia sat down near us, and, her hand shaking violently, lit a cigarette for me.

We sat there like the Three Fates, skeletons of the new womanhood we were so desperately trying to create; Weird Sisters corrupted by a destiny that had never really been ours to control. We sat as close as three women could be, each lost and lonely, and each still convinced that Weatherman was the only source of American Salvation.

Rudd left that night, leaving behind a legacy which assured the disintegration of the Seattle Weatherman collective. Our collective would have withered away without Rudd's visit, but certainly after he left, there was no way we could save ourselves. Just as Russia crushed the American Communist Party of the thirties by refusing to recognize their need for autonomy, so did Rudd crush our Weatherman collective by securing its commitment to the Weatherbureau in Chicago, rather than to the people of Seattle.

To the Movement world outside Weatherman, the changes were primarily structural. The new recruits were now organized into two collectives. The first was considered hard-core cadre, or secondary leadership. Included in this group were Ruth, Ty, and Jean when they got out of jail, Don Sick, a woman named Melanie, a couple, Sara and Bill, and Karen, the woman who had come with us to the Days of Rage. This secondary leadership would continue to live in the gray house.

The second new collective was composed of Weathermen who were not considered strong enough to be cadre. In a sense they were upwardly mobile, needing only to prove themselves sufficiently to become part of the secondary leadership. This group included three new people from out of state; Tim and Toddy, a young couple just beginning to become interested in Weatherman; a sixteen-year-old dope-dealer from Queen Anne High School named Lenny Wood; a pathetically shy friend of Ruth's named Korrine, and Jim Bryant when he got out of the hospital. Until we found a house on Capitol Hill, this group would remain in the Ballard house—out of the way, as it were.

One person was moved into the leadership collective—Mike Justesen. Not only was he a theoretical genius, a spectacular fighter, a patient and tireless organizer, and a brilliant tactician, but his commitment to Weatherman and to the revolution was unquestionable. A longtime favorite of Ayers and others in the Bureau, he had been considered something of a prodigal son. Now he was assuming his long-awaited role. Everyone in the leadership collective agreed that he belonged there. The addition of Mike into the collective was perhaps our last unanimous decision. Including him, there were now twenty-four official Seattle Weathermen.

Outside of the twenty-four actual collective members, there was a group of very close sympathizers who could be counted on to appear for actions, to help with leafleting, and who would hopefully join a collective someday. These people included Simon and Ray. They were now living with Hal in an apartment on Capitol Hill which became known as the Fortress because of Hal's outlandish concern with security. Alex, Garrity, Indian, and a few other Werewolves, while no longer regarded as a political group, would always show up at actions. But they never had anything good to say about Weatherman.

Finally, the thirty-odd Anarchists, while persistent in their contempt for Weatherman, were always ripe for rioting, and were spending more time around the leadership house. It was hoped that eventually several of them would see the light and join a collective.

Along with the reorganization into three collectives on a clear hierarchical scale, Rudd's visit perpetuated a reorganization of leadership within the leadership collective itself. Leadership was no longer undertaken by those most capable either because of past experience or force of personality, or because other people thought of them as leadership. Leadership was designated by the Weatherbureau. Rudd informed us that Carol and Roger were leadership within the command collective, and that if Georgia could ever get her shit together, she was a strong runner-up.

Carol and Roger were chosen because they adhered most closely to the Bureau line. Not only did they not question it—they followed it religiously. To Carol, the smashing of monogamy was no longer a question of collective survival and security. It was tantamount to smashing imperialism. Somehow in her mind the destruction of one paved the way to the destruction of the other. To Roger, the smashing of monogamy meant more free men to aid him in his battle to retain his dwindling supremacy over the naturally strong female leadership within the collective.

The natural leadership—Beverly, Jay and myself, were formally shunted aside by Rudd, although everyone in all the collectives still followed Beverly and me; Jay was still in jail. Leadership was not something Rudd could grant to any individual. It was either taken, or it didn't exist. But Carol, having been given the mandate, took the reins. And like any other titular head, she became increasingly mired in her own impotence. And Roger, shrewd manipulator that he was, waited with his head craned to one side for the collective to choke itself to death.

Georgia, overwrought and strained almost beyond endurance, tried valiantly to keep some perspective on her commitment to the revolution. Drinking voluminously, chain-smoking, she fluctuated between her natural tendencies toward compassion and love and her attempts to batter the collective into shape.

Day by day she deteriorated. It was a slow and tragic process to watch. When she spoke, her words smashed out like a waterfall. She grew startlingly thin and was so continuously on edge that she appeared almost insane at times. Her teeth began to rot, and her complexion took on a greenish hue. Toward the end of November she developed a hacking cough. Her coughing would awaken me at night and I would rush into her room to find her sitting and holding her chest, gasping from pain, or spitting thick globs of phlegm into a bowl she kept beside her bed. The sicker she got, the harder she drove herself. It was almost as if she thought she would die, or perhaps kill herself, if she stopped to think about what she was doing.

Beverly continued to hold her head high, but beneath the strong façade was a crumbling foundation. She missed Jay desperately. She was distracted—Beverly went through the motions of living, but there was no soul in anything she did.

She clung to me in desperation, and we became inseparable. We went everywhere together. Around the time Jay went to jail, Garrity did his month for assaulting the pig during the Ave riots. So we even went down to City Jail together to visit our boy friends. And each Sunday, as we left City Jail together, I would be in tears, but I never once saw Beverly cry. As the collective began to disintegrate, she became even more aloof, but her commitment to the politics was as firm as it had been that day just a couple of months before when Georgia so vividly described the Cleveland meeting as "mystical."

The days that followed Rudd's visit are still a blur to me. The loss of memory and eyesight continued, and I was X-rayed and given a series of tests by Dr. Greene. I was terrified that my memory wouldn't return. There were words missing from my vocabulary— common adjectives and nouns that I had used all my life, and I couldn't remember them. I forgot the names of people in my collective. And then there were the patches of time, gone somewhere, just simply not there. "It will go away in time," Dr. Greene told me gently. There was nothing he could do. No operation, no therapy, nothing but time and plenty of rest.

"You must start taking care of yourself—your life style will take its toll not only on your brain but on your body. You must slow down, Susan," Dr. Greene said.

Out of the blur come fragments of memory, disconnected, unrelated, happening sometime before J.J.'s visit.

Things got worse in the collective, instead of better. Beverly got more withdrawn, Georgia sicker. Carol's neurotic Stalinism penetrated every moment of our lives. One morning she came storming into my bedroom at six-thirty and started screaming at Garrity and me to get up. I asked her why—was there something I had to do? There was nothing in particular for me to do. She woke us up because you weren't allowed to sleep late and cuddle if you were a revolutionary. Shit. I think Garrity threw something at her. That was just before he went to jail.

Roger, who still had his head in that ridiculous collar, sat around the house most of the time. He hadn't gone on the Moratorium march because of his injury; for some reason, he found it impossible to leaflet. He spent a lot of time with Carol in confidential conversation, and he put through numerous private calls to the Bureau. He wrote up endless leaflets and engineered an uncountable number of criticism sessions.

Monogamy was still the number one topic. SMASH SMASH SMASH! The illness was growing like a cancer. Jay was in jail—safe there for the time being, so Beverly was off the hook. Instead, the collective settled like vultures on Ty and Jean. Then there was Sara and Bill—they seemed to sleep together exclusively—was this not the case? Don Sick insisted it was. They were all there in that back room together. He knew who fucked whom and who didn't fuck whomever.

Then Tim and Toddy. They were A Couple. They came into Weatherman a couple, and they clung to each other like glue. If ever two people needed to get rid of each other, it was Tim and Toddy.

And last of all, Garrity and me. The worst of them all, because Garrity wasn't even in Weatherman. Of course, he was in jail too.

And besides, he was finding it harder and harder to compete with Weatherman for my attentions. Even before he had gone to jail, he had begun to disentangle himself from his relationship with me.

Justesen was not the best of Weathermen, it proved, once he had moved into the house. For one thing, he didn't like to get up in the morning, and was prone to throw things at people, or sock them if they entered his room. Everybody in the house was scared of his violent reactions, except for me. Somehow, I could never imagine Justesen really hurting any one of his comrades physically. But then, I never knew him very well.

One day no one could get him out of bed—he was armed and ready to do battle with one of his immense boots. First Carol tried, then Georgia, then Mickey, but no go. I was outraged—how dare he sleep late if I had to get up?

I flew upstairs and into his room. There he was crouched in his bed, his teeth bared, with his boot raised in the air, his myopic eyes narrowed into a squint which screwed up his entire face, his hair popping out in a billion different directions. He looked so funny that I burst out laughing. I leaned against the door, unable to stop. Mike got beet red, slammed the boot on the floor, and leaped out of bed and threw on his clothes. Everybody was wonderstruck that I had gotten him out of bed so easily. It was impossible to reason or argue with Justesen—but if you laughed at him . . .

I remember one beautiful, happy night. I was with Garrity, and Georgia was with Mike. We were all in the kitchen, and I was trimming Garrity's hair. Garrity and I watched as Mike and Georgia danced and kissed and laughed. Mike was drunk and funny in his wry way. Georgia had a lovely smile on her face; her eyes were sparkling, and she looked so pretty . . . Her smiling face is burned into my memory. It's the only time I realized what she could have been like if we weren't all so fucked up. Garrity and I listened to them fucking that night like proud parents. It's so much nicer to be happy when your friends are happy too.

Violence by itself is neither good, bad, right or wrong. The thing to get a handle on is what's necessary to build a revolution in the world. We've got to see the connection between the sabotage of the imperialist's office buildings in New York, the SDS riot in Chicago, and the violent motion that came off of Washington.[1] We know that the only way the fat cats who run this country are going to give up anything—the Vietnam war or their whole power to suck off everyone else—is when the people take it back from them.

(from *Fire Next Time* November 1969, Page 1)

The Stones always close with Street Fighting Man. What they're saying to us is—Revolt! Tear it down! Rip it up! Chicago, Washington, and Your Town USA. The time is right for violent revolution. The time is right for fighting in the streets!

(from *Fire Next Time* November 1969, Page 2)

"OUR SONG WILL RING LOUDER THAN THE SOUND OF ALL AMERICA'S BOMBS."

(Vietnamese chant from *Fire Next Time* November 3, 1969, Page 3)

"NEW YORK: Three simultaneous explosions rocked the offices of three of America's major imperialist corporations on the morning of November 12 . . . Chase Manhattan, Standard Oil and General Motors. These bombings are the latest in a series of terrorist activities that have been increasing and will continue to do so.

(from *Fire Next Time* November 1969, Page 8)

During the 1960's the Amerikan government was on trial for crimes against the people of the world.

We now find the government guilty and sentence it to death in the streets.

(from *Fire Next Time* Vol. I, No. 3, December 6, 1969, Page 1)

In times of revolution, just wars and wars of liberation, I love the angels of destruction and disorder as opposed to the devils of conservation and law and order.

> In order to stop the slaughter of the people, we must accelerate
> the slaughter of the pigs.
>
> (from *On Weathermen* by Eldridge Cleaver; used on a Seattle
> Weatherman high school leaflet December 1969)

On December first, Seattle Weathermen attacked Army ROTC on the U of W campus. The attack was led by Justesen and Roger, who had been forced out of his collar and into action. I argued furiously to go, but because of my concussion, I was not allowed. I took care of bail, and felt humiliated.

The action was a fiasco. Barbara Beam got her club caught in a door, and was busted in the process of prying it loose. Ray told me that some sucker from the crowd named Horace (Red) Parker came along on the action. He was busted too. Apparently he caused the only excitement during the action by putting up a fight with the ROTC officers before he was dragged off. Red Parker, as it turned out, was an undercover pig.

> We know that with all the bullshit out there, you can come to
> consider yourself on the mountain top. I may even consider myself
> one day on the mountain top. I may have already. But I know that
> in the valley there are people like me and people like Huey P.
> Newton and Bobby Seale. And that below the valley are people like
> Bobby Hutton, people like Eldridge Cleaver. We know that going
> into the valley is a dangerous thing. We know that when you go out
> into the valley you got to make a commitment.
>
> (Fred Hampton, Chicago Black Panther Party)
> FRED HAMPTON
> MURDERED BY THE PIG
> December 4, 1969

"Oh my fucking God," I thought, when I heard about Fred Hampton's death over the news. "What next?" The motherfuckers sneaked up on him like rats in the night and murdered him while he was asleep in his bed. I started crying. I'm crying now as I write this.

I hope someone murders me when I stop crying over Fred Hampton and Mark Clark and all the others they killed.

I wanted to go down and bomb the Wallingford pig station. I wanted to take the shotgun and snipe at the Ave pigs from the roof of the U bookstore. I wanted to do something, anything, but everyone looked paralyzed, horror ground like mud into their faces, unable to react against such a wanton act of repression. And on their faces fear. Mingling with the horror was the unnamed fear—it could happen to me too. Revolution is not a game.

I didn't bomb the Wallingford station or shoot pigs—I drove blindly to El Roach and got fucked up on as many drugs as I could squeeze down my throat or inhale into my lungs. I raged to all the blank-faced bikers that Fred Hampton was dead. "Oh, yeah," they said dully, "some nigga got offed." I tried to tell the people in the band about it—they played a song they had composed called "Today's Pig Is Tomorrow's Bacon," and they commented over the mike on Fred's death. None of the long-haired freaks in the bar paid very much attention.

The drugs didn't kill the pain—in my heart or in my head. They aggravated them until I couldn't see straight, and I couldn't talk or walk, and somebody scooped me up and drove me home and somebody else put me to bed. The house was as silent as a tomb.

For days we screamed, "Avenge Fred." But we didn't do shit. Black people in Chicago put off some bombs, rallied, grumbled. But compared to the holocaust that exploded in the wake of Martin Luther King's death, the reaction to Fred Hampton's death was like a thin reed in the wind. It fell with a dry whisper.

We criticized ourselves about being defeatist. We were. We and everyone else. But I am mostly concerned with myself—when the crunch came, I copped out. All my talk, so many words, a bag of wind. Susan Stern Sham.

> Oh lost, and by the wind grieved, ghost, come back again.
> (Thomas Wolfe from *Look Homeward, Angel*)

> . . . I believe in armed struggle as the only solution for those peoples who fight to free themselves, and I am consistent with my beliefs.

Many will call me an adventurer, and that I am—only one of a
different sort, one of those who risks his skin to prove his truths.
(From *Che Guevara Speaks*; Farewell letter to his parents April
1965)

I could not face my dying dreams. I worked at the Roach, visited
Garrity in jail, took a lot of drugs, continued to leaflet high schools
and on the Ave about Fred Hampton's death, the war, about racism,
the pigs, about life in general.

Around the world, the revolutionary peoples were moving. The
Palestine Liberation Front, the Tupamaros, the French students,
Italian and Mexican students, in South Africa, and Vietnam, the
voices of the people were raised, screaming for freedom.[2]

In the United States, the Movement swung sharply left, following
the tradition set by the Weatherman Days of Rage. Radicals now
thought of themselves as revolutionaries. Talking was not enough—
action was everything.

A spate of terrorist bombings began that would last for two years.
Anti-war groups appeared by the thousands. On campuses all over
the country, ROTC buildings were attacked, went up in flames, and
sank into cinders. J. Edgar Hoover began to develop a special ulcer
labeled SDS Weatherman, and put out a secret list with everybody's
name on it who even looked to the left before crossing the street. As
the decade of the sixties ended, it looked like Weatherman had
called it right—we were inept, but we were the white vanguard.
The world was ripe for revolution, the Third World was ready, it
was time to seize the time.

Sometime in the second week of December, Garrity was released
from jail. That night in the Roach, he told me he loved me for the
first time. That same night I was approached by a repugnant
smacker named John Dung, who asked me if I wanted some dynamite or a .357 magnum pistol. I had seen him hanging around the
Roach before, copping smack, and I had always steered clear of him.
Something about him put me uptight. I told Dung I would have no
use for dynamite or a gun. A few months later, when it was too late,
we found out Dung was an undercover pig.

J.J. arrived around the eleventh of December, barely a month after Rudd's visit. He had proven himself as a theoretical genius—to J.J. has been attributed much of the theory behind the Weatherman paper. He and Bernardine had shared a long and tempestuous relationship, which made him something of a Richard Burton to the incessantly gossiping Movement voyeurs. He still looked like a street punk—tough but not very dangerous. Pugnacious, arrogant, sneering and stalking around like Mack the Knife, J.J. aroused in me a love and hatred that were almost indistinguishable. I didn't know him very deeply, but I believe he must have suffered greatly because of the insensitivity of the few people he really loved.

I also believed J.J. was one of the sincerest of the Weatherman leadership. Maybe because he seemed more human than any of the others; maybe because I saw magnified in him the best and worst in my own nature.

J.J. ignored me completely when he first arrived. He had a number of missions, and I was far down on the list of important things he had to do during his three days in Seattle.

He spent most of his time with Georgia, bolstering her as leadership. When he wasn't with Georgia, he was with Carol, commending her for her heroic efforts to smash the flourishing Seattle monogamies. In the very first criticism session, J.J. informed the collective that the Bureau thought Carol was the strongest person in the collective—this was quite in contradiction with the majority of the collective, who thought she was the weakest. Even Roger was surprised; he wanted to be the strongest.

J.J. leaned on Georgia heavily. Maybe be didn't notice how her hands shook, how pale she was, and how constantly she coughed. Perhaps he noticed and just ignored it. Like a bulldozer, he swept through the leadership collective with his list of lines, leaving no alternatives. Rudd had lined us all up for the kill—J.J. was shooting us down, one by one. Ty and Jean were massacred—end your monogamy, or split the collective. Sara and Bill were told they must live in separate houses or split the collective. Tim and Toddy were told they had to live in separate houses or split the collective. He never mentioned either me or Beverly. We sat through the entire day waiting for our turn, and it never came. We looked at each other fearfully—what was happening?

That night, J.J. said he was tired of criticism, that he wanted to just relax. He turned to Beverly.

"You know some bar we can go to and just talk?" He was so charming, so sweet, his smile so soft, his eyes gentle, his hand tenderly pulling at a little strand of Beverly's straight hair.

Beverly looked at him intently for a minute and then coolly told him that we could go to the Roach, we could get in free, drink free, drive there in my car, and she would only go if I came. J.J. looked irritated, but relented. The three of us left for the Roach.

In the Roach it was very quiet. Garrity was not there. The three of us sat at a round table, with J.J. in the middle, his back turned to me, talking urgently to Beverly, then dancing with Beverly, stroking Beverly's hair, whispering in her ear, his strong, brown arms wrapped firmly around her, his lean body swaying closer to hers as they danced. When the song ended, she went to the women's room, and he returned to the table.

"Many ways to skin a cat, eh, J.J.," I said, admiring his utter balls. It was obvious now that J.J. had been sent to Seattle to seduce Beverly. Super Stud! And it looked as though it was working. At his best J.J. was impossible to resist. What he couldn't do through sheer charm, he got by dogged persistence. I would have placed ten-to-one odds that Beverly would sleep with J.J. that night.

But I didn't know my friend well enough. In her exquisite way, she rebuffed him. Thanks but no thanks, and she turned haughtily and walked upstairs to her bedroom. Much later on, I sneaked in to see her, and we giggled on her bed with the cats and dog.

"Did you really think I was going to fall for that?" she asked scornfully. I loved her so much. How could we lose with people like Jay and Beverly on our side?

J.J. spent most of the day reorganizing the collectives, making it impossible for the monogamies to stay together. The Capitol Hill house had been rented a few days ago; it was across the street from the Fortress. We now had four Weatherman houses, with from four to six people living in each house. The people from out of state had some money which was divided among the houses and helped support us for a while. All the houses got food stamps each month; we all stole a lot of food and other necessities.

J.J. completely dispensed with the striated collectives Rudd had set up. Our collectives were heterogeneous now: leadership, secondary leadership, and rank-and-filers would all live together based on organizing needs and abilities.

Beverly and I groaned. I especially put up strong resistance to living with anybody but the leadership collective: I barely knew the out-of-state people, and I didn't like most of the other Seattle Weathermen. In my mind, everybody outside of my collective was a nurd, and I wanted to stay right where I was, isolated and on top.

I guess my protest about moving was the straw that broke the camel's back. J.J. turned on me ferociously and informed me that I was being demoted. It didn't matter a flying fuck where I lived—I was no longer part of the leadership.

Very carefully, barely controlling his rage, he went through my list of sins. Then he opened it up to the rest of the collective. Carol, Roger, Mickey, and Justesen responded as usual. And then, Chicken Little! Like a piece of steel, cold as ice, my dear friend Georgia started screaming at me. Anti-Communist this, defeatist that, counterrevolutionary this and that. I could take it from Rudd, Roger, J.J., Carol, and the people in the other collectives, but not from Georgia. I could take it from people I hated, but not from people I loved.

I collapsed visibly. I was the wounded wolf in the pack—the others, sensing my weakness, closed in, fangs bared. Rudd and J.J. had come to smash monogamy and to burn out all resistance to their total leadership. To do this, errant egos had to be broken. I was the exemplary egotistical whipping post. The wolves howled, and I smelled my blood on their breath.

They smashed and shattered and splintered and choked and beat and punched and knifed and torpedoed and tore and maimed my ego for so many hours, for so many days, in so many ways that I barely recovered. Rudd had sanctioned their hatred; J.J. encouraged them to destroy me. Long after he left, the collectives maintained their strangle hold on my jugular vein. I was in my death throes, but I had to be devastated before I could die.

After the collective assault, J.J. and Roger took me to the Dirty Shame, a bar up the street. There, J.J. continued the criticism. At first it was subdued, because I was completely passive and we were in public. Then J.J. hit me with his ultimate weapon.

"You know what, Susie, I think you're a pig."

He said it so nonchalantly, that it didn't mean anything to me at first. Slowly the words sank in.

I was so astonished that I couldn't say anything. Then J.J. leaned across the table and rasped in his most repellent manner.

"Did you hear what I said, Susie? I said," and he raised his voice an octave, "I THINK YOU'RE A PIG!"

He had betrayed me. I had thought he was basically good and he had betrayed me. Phony. He was worse than Rudd. Rudd at least made no pretensions about being anything but a viper. J.J. was a phony, acting as though he really cared and then pulling the rug out from under my feet.

I began to fight back, bitterly, loudly, goaded by months of eating Bureau shit. I told J.J. exactly what I thought of him. Hatred and frustration poured like poison from my mouth. Unlike Rudd, J.J. didn't just sit there and look at me. He shouted right back. At one point we were both standing; his finger was jabbing the air at me— I flashed back to the first time I had seen him at the Chicago Democratic Convention, so very long ago. I hated him. I just wanted to tear him to bits; wipe that punk sneer off his fucking face.

We stood screaming at each other in the tavern, but not even my loudest screams could hide my growing realization that J.J. was right, just as Rudd had been. I understood the reasoning behind Weatherman theory; I agreed with it. Ignoring what I knew to be basically correct was dangerous not only for the collective, and the revolution, but also to myself. How could I possibly be trusted?

It wasn't the theory that I fought against. It was the manner in which the theory was put into practice.

I tried to tell all this to J.J. but he was contemptuous of most of it. In spite of his calling me a pig, in spite of the hatred of most of the Seattle Weathermen for me, my commitment remained the same.

MY COMMITMENT! It wasn't worth a spit in the wind. J.J. knew it; Georgia knew it. How little I knew, how little I have always known.

I came home from the bar, and lunged up the stairs and into Georgia's room. She was coughing uncontrollably; tears were streaming down her face.

"I hate you, you fucking bitch, you . . . I hate you."

"Please, Susan, please, let's talk about it, please, I had to do it. You're destroying the collective. You have to give other people a chance, people who aren't as strong or pretty or powerful as you. You can't ignore people, can't pretend they don't exist, you can't . . ." She was interrupted by a spasm of coughing.

"I despise you. I'll prove it to you yet. I'll make you all see what a good Communist I am. If it's the last thing I do, I'll do it."

"Please, Susan, please," and she moved weakly toward me, her face soaked in tears, coughing, pleading, and I pushed her away and walked out. Her cries followed me down the stairs, and out of the house. I hear them now; I will hear them always.

J.J. stayed home with Georgia that night, but the rest of the group had an orgy, of all places, in Garrity and Indian's apartment. It was the only one I ever saw, and frankly, it disgusted me, and I refused to participate. Everyone was fucking everyone else, in a wiggly, ugly pile, and yet during the day they could hardly stand to talk and look at each other, let alone touch each other in a nice, human way. It was obscene to me, and I was heavily criticized for refusing to have anything to do with it. It added to the already overwhelming resentment almost everyone in all the collectives felt for me.

J.J. also encouraged the women to fuck and the men to fuck. Breaking down the old relationships. The next day I told everybody I didn't think you could force homosexuality; for which I was heavily criticized for having bourgeois sexual hangups. I admitted that I was sexually hung up again and again.

I really felt I was. I really wanted to be sexually attracted to other women. But every time I closed my myopic eyes and leaned to kiss another woman, I froze up. The collective really made me feel fine about this. They almost convinced me that I was an utter pervert because I couldn't get into other women. They never understood how much I really wanted to, how much it would have meant to me if I could have depended upon women for sexual as well as emotional release. But except for Beverly, my explanations fell on deaf ears.

It was interesting to note whom Rudd, and then J.J. when he came, slept with, because it was all part of positioning for power.

Rudd left Beverly alone, and both he and J.J. totally ignored me sexually. J.J. made a special effort to seduce Beverly, who ignored him. Both Rudd and J.J. slept with both Carol and Georgia, for they were the chosen Bureau leadership. They slept first with one and then with the other. They traded them off, putting them in competition for Bureau approval, and for position as primary leadership. Although both Carol and Georgia loved Justesen, and neither particularly liked Rudd or J.J., they both submitted to sleeping with them. Georgia put up resistance to Rudd, but she liked J.J. and enjoyed her relationship with him; Carol never talked about it.

The rationale behind the breaking down of old forms of relationships was good enough, but the way collective members were forced into their new sexual roles was brutal, unnatural, and impossible. Still, it was primarily because of the example set by Weatherman that many Movement women became lesbians, allowing thousands of American women to love each other honestly and openly, freeing them completely from any dependency on men at all.

When J.J. left, he tried to kiss me good-by. I averted my face. I had refused to talk to him since that night at the Dirty Shame. I tried not to listen but I heard him say to me, "I hope you understand. I know you'll forgive me then."

I refused to look at him. There was an awkward silence as he waited for a response, and then, warmly embraced by everyone except Beverly, he left.

I moved to the Ballard house the next morning. Beverly stayed in the Woodlawn house, and Georgia went to the Capitol Hill house.

Ty and Jean, refusing to separate, moved into a tiny one-room apartment near the Capitol Hill house.

That night, December 14, Beverly came rushing into the Ballard house, her face radiant. Jay was going to be temporarily released.

Jay got out the next day. He and Beverly stayed in bed all day. Later that night they came to pick me up at the Ballard house in Beverly's car, and we went to the Roach. And there, very quietly, they told me they were leaving that night. They were all packed and ready to go. They had stopped only to say good-by to me. No one else knew; I was to tell no one.

We sat there in silence. What was there to say? After a while, they drove me back to the Ballard house. They each kissed me good-by. Then they got into the car and drove off. I walked into the house, into my room, crept under the blankets, and went deep into gray.

> . . . I'm going to show you baby, that a woman can be tough,
> come on, come on, come on and take it, take another little piece of
> my heart now baby, break it, break another little bit of my heart
> now baby . . .

I listened to Janis Joplin and lay in bed staring at the ceiling, so sick, so crumbled, unable, for once in my life, to act at all. Janis' voice called through the void, sharing my anguish. Her torture, her pain, her shredded voice repeating itself again and again, burned on my brain.

I lay there for three days, talking to no one. They all came, asking about Jay and Beverly, and sat on the edge of my bed looking scared. Georgia, white as a ghost, quivering there, crying, finally collapsed, and called her father to come and take her home. She had had pneumonia for months.

At the end of three days Roger and Carol told me that I had to move back into the little gray house; the collectives were reorganizing, filling the gap left by Beverly and Jay. I moved into the front room of the gray house. I didn't even unpack. I just lay on the bed.

The collectives were buzzing like busy little bees. High school organizing every day, going to Seattle Community College, and haranguing at the U. Every day they would prepare to leave the house and insist that I go with them. I just stared at the wall.

A week passed. Finally Ty and Jean got me up. They came over one day and wouldn't leave until I got up, bathed, and ate something. The strain they were under was showing in their eyes. With Jay and Beverly gone, they were the number one monogamy. While I had passed a week in torpor they had been under criticism constantly.

The days of December droned on. I couldn't think, couldn't feel, couldn't function, I went to a high school one day, but the words froze in my throat. I was beaten, bent, and broken, and still, I was committed to Weatherman. There was still no alternative. I would cling to my symbol of hope until the last bitter dregs had been drunk. I would never quit, I resolved; they would have to throw me out.

On December 22, I flew to Chicago for a second hearing for the Days of Rage. Again the trial was postponed. I steered clear of the Weatherbureau, and as soon as I could, flew to New York. Garrity would meet me there for Christmas, and then we would go to the Weatherman War Council in Flint, Michigan, together.

I crashed at my old apartment again and gratefully relaxed and began to look at my time in New York as a vacation. I may have seen my mother once or twice; I doubt if I visited my father. There was no room for them in my world now—I who had been making speeches encouraging kids to "kill their parents" in the past few weeks. I hated mine along with the rest of white America.

When Garrity arrived, I played with him for one day. I made up for months of deprivation. I fucked and sucked and drank and ate and doped and laughed and swaggered and loved and was thrilled and happy. I didn't think of Weatherman at all, I forgot the people of the world. I repressed the war and poverty.

Then it was December 26 and the bus was leaving for Flint, Michigan, and the War Council. Garrity wanted to go, which amazed me, but then, we didn't know what to expect. The War Council had been billed as anything but a War Council; it was supposed to be one big orgy-party-trip, a gathering of the freak counterculture clan—White Panthers, Motherfucker types, Weatherpeople, and your average hippie high school dropout, alienated youth, plus various other Movement people.

It was Weatherman's attempt to give the Movement and the youthful counterculture another chance, before we gave up on white-skinned Americans altogether.

In the last two months, Bureau policy had shifted several times. Things had loosened up briefly just after the Days of Rage; people had begun to mingle with old Movement associates and friends, smoke dope, party, and generally relax their unbending militant posture. Then once again the Weatherbureau stomped down on its collectives across the country, and any kind of frivolity was out of the question. Now there was still another shift toward the freak counterculture; drugs, music, and fucking were not only in style, they were now considered necessary elements to the revolution. Freak culture types like the White Panthers, and the Motherfuckers were an important link to the broader freak masses.

I took the line shift with a grain of salt. I had always considered dope, sex, and music part of my life, and I couldn't view it as a "political tactic." I also didn't think the attempts to renew old associations with counterculture leadership meant anything; no matter how we writhed around trying to make Weatherman alluring to youth, they weren't biting the bait. They simply weren't interested. Down the line—freaks, Movement people, students, hippies, dopers—they just plain-assed were not going to get involved. Weatherman may have eased up their "up against the wall" attitude, but the politics were unchanged. We still believed in the necessity for full scale urban guerrilla warfare, and white kids, no matter how hip, were not ready or willing to put their lives on the line.

I went to the War Council with very few expectations. I went, thinking back to the June National Convention, when SDS had split, and my expectations then.

What happens to a dream deferred?
Does it wrinkle
Like a raisin in the sun
Or does it explode?*

I had taught that poem to my class at Croton School; we had never really answered the question.

*The Panther and the Lash by Langston Hughes © 1967 Alfred A. Knopf, Inc., reprinted by permission.

The War Council was scheduled to last for five days, from December 27 through December 31. We arrived late on the first day, because our bus had gotten stuck in the snow. After signing in, we were thoroughly searched, men by men, women by women, just like when you go to jail. But it had to be done.

I could see immediately that it was not going to be a very big turnout. Maybe three or four hundred people were there; most of them were Weatherman cadre, but there were many new faces, some of them looking exceedingly young.

A great deal of the earlier zest and spirit had evaporated, although there was a lot of chanting and forced enthusiasm, mixed in with general Movement bantering—giving five, boasting about busts, showing and telling of battles and battle wounds, holding dear friends closely, not knowing if they would make it through the next months. Mixed in with the roaring chants, and feverish macho, and deep emotion, was a feeling of pride, a strange resonating sensation singing in the spirit; we have suffered, fought, and loved. We have not won or lost, but we haven't given up. Our pride was unique to our experience, growing out of our commitment and strength of purpose, giving a richness and meaning to our lives that we could share together.

The War Council was held for the most part in a vast room which had no seats. Blankets, sleeping bags, pillows, garbage, bodies and food—the usual convention scene—were strewn all over the floor. There was a little concession where you could buy foul hotdogs and other shit food for highway-robbery prices. The walls of the room were covered with posters of our revolutionary heroes.

To my surprise, I was genuinely happy to see the Seattle people. They all looked eager and excited, and there were over thirty of them. I couldn't believe it; we always brought so many people with us. It was amazing. No matter how I felt about some of my collective comrades, I had to give them credit; they sure kept trucking.

Ty and Jean were especially glad to see me; they each embraced me warmly. They looked awful. While I had been in New York, they had been criticized constantly about their marriage. They had been forced by the collectives to take acid and engage in a criticism session about their monogamy; it was their first acid trip. Jean had almost freaked out several times. Apparently it had gone on for two days. Though they were haggard, exhausted, and drained, their spirit seemed as high as ever.

Justesen was also in good shape. It was obvious that he had taken more of a leadership position in my old collective. People in the other two collectives tended to look toward him for direction, as they had once looked to Beverly, Jay, and myself. Unfortunately, Mike's leadership took the form of domination; the strength of his personality overwhelmed everyone around him. Arrogant, aggressive, brilliant, and perpetually convinced that he was right, he was impossible to argue with. If someone dared to disagree with him, he would turn on them violently, and shout,

"Oh go fuck yourself," or "You're a dumb asshole," and then look as though he was going to murder whoever had aroused his ire. Most of the people in all the collectives were intimidated by him, with the exception of Carol and myself. Georgia almost shrank visibly when he would turn on her during a criticism session and rave about how ridiculous and stupid she was.

I thought I understood him, and I was very fond of him. I was astounded by the depth of his theoretical understanding, and intrigued by the complexity of his personality. At times I felt a great affinity with him; lonely, insecure, and unable to communicate, but also vain and convinced of his own superiority. I believed he was shrewdly biding his time, taking power, making the most of Weatherman, but ready to bail out when it exhausted its possibilities. I didn't believe that he was ever going to place the revolution above Mike Justesen.

I was amazed at the new people the Seattle Weathermen had brought to Flint. There were about fifteen kids I didn't know, most of them of high school age. Some of them were only fifteen and had run away from home to come to Flint. They were so very excited and gung ho. Looking at them, I felt some of my old enthusiasm reviving—maybe we would make it after all.

The first night of the War Council almost reminded me of earlier SDS conventions; except that no one spoke but Weathermen. The Bureau people gave some of the most beautiful and moving speeches

I have ever heard. They concentrated on explanations of Weatherman's insistence on violent revolution, the historic rationales behind our political theories, and pleas to youth culture to wake up and join us before it was too late.

There was a new direction to the speeches: the notion of forcing the disintegration of society by creating strategic armed chaos to replace pig order. The threat to pig America that wherever they were, we would be making their lives impossible to live. There would be no peace in America as long as one Weatherman was left breathing.

The speeches, especially Bernardine's and J.J.'s stirred the people from Seattle. Garrity was rapt, and when J.J. finished, he stood up and cheered and clapped along with everybody else.

J.J. had said, "We're against everything that's good and decent in honky America. We will loot and burn and destroy. We are the incubation of your mother's nightmare."

J.J. was not speaking just for himself. He had said exactly what I felt about white America.

J.J.'s speech was the last that night. When he finished, I went racing up to him and threw my arms around him. He held me closely for a second. I whispered to him that I forgave him. I couldn't put it into words then, but he had helped me tremendously with his speech. He had made it all clear again; he had made me believe in my own commitment once more.

After that speech, excitement and emotion permeated the room. I had totally forgotten the miserable month of December. All I knew was that Weatherman seemed together again, that we would struggle on, and that we would win.

Garrity and I took some mescaline and joined in the snake dancing. Then we returned to our sleeping quarters. The Seattle collectives were staying in a nunnery. There was a tiny room reserved for monogamous couples—the nunnery library.

There were three couples. Tim and Toddy, Ty and Jean, and Garrity and I. The room was so small that we were scrunched together; it also had no window, so we were broiling. Soon Garrity and I, vibrating on mescaline, lost all restraint and began to ball, and the

others gladly followed suit. There was no group grope. Just a pile of
people pleasantly making love under crowded but sensational conditions. I'm sure they had to do it that way in Vietnam!

The second day of the War Council, Seattle began a criticism session that lasted the next two days. It was generally overseen either by
Rudd or J.J. It was the old routine, only more severe than ever.

The prime target of the criticism, the real reason it had been
called, was Mike Justesen. He was pronounced a pig early in the
War Council, and for two days, the Seattle collectives spent their
time smashing Mike. To my everlasting disgrace, I got right into it!
Finally someone I could attack with outrage. A tyrant if I ever met
one; a sneaky, ratty, manipulative, power-hungry, ruthless, sexist
pig. I threw all Mike's criticisms of me back at him. I had a ball eating him up alive.

But it wasn't mere vengeance—I thought I was correct. I believed
Mike was all those things, just as I was convinced he thought his criticisms of me were just. Only through total smashing of his defenses
could he really see himself and his role in the revolution, and begin
to change. We were exorcising Devil America out of Mike Justesen.

I had always appreciated the intrinsic value of criticism—self-
criticism; I had just not approved of the pleasure some people
derived from it. Now that I felt justified in criticizing Mike, I could
understand to some degree the self-righteousness inherent in the
process. Not hating Mike—on the contrary, feeling very fond of
him—it became very important to me that he not be a pig, that he
realize the error of his ways and begin to turn himself into the revolutionary leader he could be.

Hour after hour we screamed and shouted at Mike. Not only did
we carefully explain to him why he was such a pig, exactly how he
manipulated and undermined people, but we made sure that all his
rationales for why he acted as he did were smashed. We put Mike on
the rack, and pulled, until he was stretched to the breaking point,
and then we pulled some more, until we could see him begin to snap.

Using Mike as the example for us all, we delved into the question of
why we were in the revolution, in Weatherman. Were we involved
because of the power of ideas, or because of ideas for power? Were we

in it for something completely different than our vision of communism—reasons that got in the way of visions that respected the integrity we had for each other, and wanted for all humanity?

With X-ray eyes we penetrated Mike's consciousness. We didn't have the answers to our questions, but we knew Mike had to change. All of us had to change. History had not taught us how. Our parents had failed us; in some cases, they had perverted us. Our educations had left us hopelessly enmeshed in endless lies. There was nothing left but total overhaul.

Criticism! Self-criticism! Transformation! Change!

We assaulted all of Mike's faults thoroughly. Carol, as much as she may have loved him, was as unrelenting as everyone else. But I brought out the killer—I tore off his nails at the quick. I brought up his relationship with Georgia. Haltingly, tearfully, uncertain, thinking that I might be driving a man and a woman insane, I spilled out their story—his almost sadistic treatment of her, his ugly sexuality, staggering over to fuck her only when he was so blind drunk that it didn't matter whom he fucked, the way he terrified her at meetings, undermining any strengths she might have had, and making her afraid to say what she thought, making her afraid to think at all.

When I trailed off, others picked up the theme. Georgia suffered through it all, as much for Mike as for herself. She said nothing; she barely breathed.

At the end of the second day, we had finally finished with Mike. He sat blankly in a chair, looking the way I had felt at the end of each rough session. Looking like a man who has just had his brains mashed, and can't quite figure out why he can't think any more.

He was isolated from everyone—the first in the caste of untouchables. No one would look at him or talk to him. When I attempted to speak to him, he looked at me, or rather through me and then grinned weirdly. Then he got up and walked out.

We didn't know if Mike would ever come back. We didn't know if we had pushed him over the brink. We didn't know if it was worth it to him. I felt, along with Carol and Georgia and everybody else, that we had done what had to be done. Whether he came back or not, went insane or not, the criticism session had been necessary.

That night, very quietly, her eyes glowing, Jean asked me if she and Ty could sleep with me. All three of us together. There was such profundity in the offer, that I was staggered and humbled. I flashed upon the correctness of Weatherman politics still again. The breaking down of old relationships. The shedding of old values. I saw my two friends looking at me not with lust, or depravity, but with love. I felt their love radiating about me, a glimpse of the beauty, the bounty in humanity. And I felt my own repressed, stagnant inability to respond.

Susan Stern Sham.

I shook my head no, I'm sorry, I can't. And they understood and didn't pressure. Maybe they thought that in time I would grow, and I would want to share their love with them. Or that I would be able to. How I wish I had been able to accept their offer. How I wish that my values were based on the new foundations we were trying to create, rather than on those we were attempting to destroy.

My inability to say yes to the stirring offer made by Ty and Jean was a reflection of my inability to change, to grow strong enough to be really worthy of my revolutionary rhetoric. People around me were really changing; Ty and Jean were trying to deal with their monogamy. How had I changed?

I could fall back on my white skin any time I wanted to, go to New York, and be Susan Stern, well-educated college girl from wealthy background. My involvement in the revolution was superfluous; I was a hoax. Rudd, J.J., Carol, had been right. I had been in it for Susan, and not for real; me and Justesen. Oh, Mike, where the fuck are you. I want so bad to tell you that you're really not alone; I'm a rat too.

While the Seattle Weathermen were holed up in the nunnery, the rest of the War Council continued. The Weatherbureau tried desperately to revitalize its old way of doing things. In their willingness to admit that they had made a mistake by being totally strict and tight, they swung toward love and laughter, song and dance, marijuana and acid, intertwined with a great emphasis on criticism–self-criticism. They were still absolutely committed to the smashing of monogamy.

After a day and a half of frenzied appeal to the youth/freak culture, the Bureau suddenly disappeared without explanation into a back room, and when they came out a day later, the emphasis had changed, and we were going under, deep, deep underground.

The startled cadre was told that there was no longer any hope for white youth. American defeatism had conquered; they were not willing to struggle for themselves, let alone the peoples of the world. Weatherman, with a clear vision of what had to be done, could wait no longer. To hold back now would be to fail the Vietnamese, the blacks, and the revolution.

The rest of the War Council concentrated on war. We divided into small groups, and discussed terrorism, its roots in revolutionary history, and what would be required for us to go underground. It was all very vague and frightening. Some of us would have to change our names, create whole new identities for ourselves, estrange ourselves from friends and families, disappear. We would move to other cities, take up normal residence, divide into cells of three or four people, instead of collectives. Only the very strong among us would be able to stand the strain of leading dual lives; those who lacked strength or commitment would stay aboveground and communicate to the rest of the Movement and the world the politics which had led to this serious decision.

The mood of the remainder of the War Council was one of dissimulation. For those of us who agreed with the necessity of going underground, and who had transformed themselves enough to do so, life would never be the same again.

My reaction was one of total stupefaction. The new line had emerged so suddenly, that I had no time to analyze or react to it. I listened to the words, but I couldn't relate their implications to my own life.

All I understood was that things would not go on as they had, that soon, all the Weathermen would disappear like moles into the vast reaches of some netherworld, never more to be seen by human eyes. In my mind I saw a whole scheme of interlocking, dank, slimy and dripping tunnels, spread throughout the cities of this lousy country, underground, in cellars, beneath mountains and seas and lakes and rivers, with thousands of busy bomb makers working away earnestly at their trade, and then,. when the clockwork struck orange, in a great holocaust, all the prisons, banks, and pig-inhabited homes and offices would go up in violent flames, and the freed prisoners would pour out into the streets and, with the rest of the masses, form the people's government . . .

I was frightened by the prospect. But most of the others seemed thrilled—even the youngest, newest recruits. To be a criminal at large in the United States; a tapeworm in the belly of the monster, eating it up alive from the inside out.

To make bombs. See big buildings topple. IBM got it last week—how about AT&T next? Who owns Standard Oil anyway? Let's get his kids, his wife. Get a racetrack, like they did in the battle of Algiers. Pour acid into the water supply of Shaker Heights, Ohio. Go out on sniping raid and kill pigs. Bomb a pig station—avenge Fred Hampton. Get your local draft board, your nearest military installation, your campus ROTC building, your high school principal's office. The possibilities were inexhaustible.

There was a history for us to follow. The Algerian guerrilla terrorists did play a big role in freeing Algeria from French tyranny; VC terrorists, the Huks in the Philippines, the Tupamaros in Uruguay, the Boston Tea Party in the American Revolutionary War, the Palestinian Liberation Front.[1] The topic was not approached lightly; it was a deadly serious meeting. Everyone knew the implications for even talking about terrorism. And we were discussing what would be necessary to actually *do it!*

The theme of violence dominated the convention in other ways which disturbed me, because it seemed more the product of insanity and depravity than revolution. The major thing which horrified me was the interest in, admiration for and concentration on Charlie Manson and his Family. Almost everybody in the Bureau ran around saluting people with the fork sign. This is like a peace sign, except that you hold up three fingers instead of two. And what is the fork sign?

When the Manson Family maniacally murdered the LaBiancas in Hollywood, they slashed Robert LaBianca's throat and left a knife stuck in it, and then jabbed him in his rotund belly with a long, slim three-pronged serving fork, and left it sticking there like a hardon. Then, the story goes, the killers raided the refrigerator, scribbled PIG all over the walls in their victim's blood, and all went home and fucked Charlie.

The entire Charlie Manson thing outraged and disgusted me. There was a picture of Sharon Tate up on the wall, in tribute to Manson's murder of the star in her eighth month of pregnancy. I didn't agree that all white babies should die; I had been a white baby once, and now I was trying to be a revolutionary. And I didn't think Sharon Tate was more worthy of slaughter than Marilyn Monroe, or Janis Joplin, or Jimi Hendrix, or the Stones, or the Beatles or Ike and Tina Turner. They were all pretty rich and privileged.

I believe the Mansonite trip was born out of despair and frustration. It in no way corresponded to the quality of the rest of Weatherman politics. It was the last putrid drop of American poison still flowing in the blood of those people who most wanted to bring about revolutionary change. Embittered by the refusal of white American youth to join in the international struggle, they went to impossible extremes expressing the worst tendencies in Weatherman politics. Anything that had a modicum of left politics in it became elevated to superlative heights in those last few weeks. Anything was applauded as long as it was against the American system, as long as it outraged middle-class morality, as long as it terrified the bourgeoisie, made them think they were next.

Charlie Manson was the death rattle of the children of the old Movement, the decade of SDS. Sharon Tate's white baby would be reborn underground, and it would live to become a symbol of revolutionary spirit and integrity to a confused and dispirited American youth.

Three sixteen-year-old women refused to return to Seattle with us. They were going to work in the Bureau. Some of us argued furiously with Rudd, but he just laughed and told us youth would make the revolution. The young women set their lips in contemptuous lines and told us to get fucked.

For those three women-children, for the Seattle collectives, for all us Weathermen, there was no time for reflection, for careful perusal of our astrological charts, for a glimpse of the Tarot, for consultation with loving parents, teachers, or gurus. There was only the fight, there was only today and NOW.

As I was climbing into a car to leave Flint and return to Seattle, the Ithaca Individualists were also climbing into a car they called the People's Chevy, and were also headed toward Seattle. Crammed into the People's Chevy were Joe Kelly and Chip Marshall, and Jeff Dowd, a frenetic genius from Westchester, New York; a dropout freshman from Cornell named Mike Abeles, Bé-Bé, a beer-drinking high school friend of Chip's, and one woman—Anne Anderson, a Boston debutante who liked to hang out in poolrooms, banter with bikers, who adored mountains of sex and dope and food and alcoholic beverages, and who was a natural-born, dyed-in-the-wool hedonist with a heart as big as the Grand Canyon, a mind as sharp as a clear Seattle day, a smile as vivid as sunlight, and the soul of a revolutionary.

The five men and one woman had fashioned themselves into a collective they called Sundance, after the Sundance Kid.[2] Chip also had with him a rickety female puppy named Etta, after the woman in the Sundance clan. Departing from their destined route only long enough to find Hole in the Wall, the hideout of the original Sundance gang, the People's Chevy roared its way toward Seattle.

12.
KICKED OUT
JANUARY 1—FEBRUARY 2, 1970

It was New Year's Eve. There was snow everywhere when we left the War Council and headed toward a house an hour or so outside of Flint. I was still in shellshock from the War Council, but I felt more spirit than I had since Jay and Beverly had left. I caught myself thinking frequently, "What would they think about this?" Then I'd remember that they were already underground.

I brought the New Year in on my back, in bed with a seventeen-year-old boy from Seattle who kept on telling me about his wife to be, and how he thought the Weathermen were crazy.

Back in Seattle, things were bleak. My misery returned, settling on me like a damp blanket. Winter rains, no money, illness, dissatisfaction. The light drained from the hopeful faces of Ty and Jean as we entered the gray house, the scene of their forty-eight hour criticism session on acid. Almost immediately we found ourselves in criticism, all very subdued and weary once again.

Mike returned from somewhere, more serious and slovenly than ever. He had come to the realization that the criticism of him was justified; he was a pig but he wanted to change; Weatherman was his life. He was still in the caste of the untouchables. He moved into the Fortress with Hal, Simon, and Ray.

The house in Ballard was abandoned, as was our organizing there: Ty and Jean kept their small apartment, and a group continued living in the Capitol Hill house. The rest of the Weathermen were divided between the two Woodlawn houses.

All the houses were falling apart. Although we were not very active, no one had the inspiration to clean at all. There was a look of dejection and dreariness about everything. Lights were out and remained out. Windows were broken, and boarded over with cardboard. Everything was hanging, waiting for the big move underground. Our work in Seattle was at a standstill; all we could do now was push ourselves into shape, be ready when the time came.

There was little singing, dancing, fucking, doping, or jiving. People looked wan and broken, at the end of things. The criticism–self-criticism continued, and the staggering participants creaked under the load. Each was like a punching bag which has been punched so many times that it was deflated and now thudded dully and flipped around a little when it was hit, instead of bounding back. We had all been hit too often. We were tired. The revolution seemed old. We were hungry. We were about to kick out, and it wasn't the jams.

The weight of the underground loomed over us with devastating certainty. There was no escape. No heroism, no splendor, no glorious revolution, no marching bands and banners. We were just on the verge of learning that revolution is more than hard, and greater than human; that it is a lifelong experience and a lifelong burden; that its rewards are rarely visited to the recipient like any other reward, but only received in the vague and out-of-reach concept of history. We were just beginning to recognize that revolution is the one unchanging truth, the one real guiding staff, but that accepting its cloak meant giving up oneself entirely. The pain and heaviness of that knowledge, just barely discernible, was breaking us.

We were alone and isolated. We constituted a fraction of a fraction of the population at large. Everyone was disgusted with the Weathermen. The dream had turned into a nightmare. Liberals considered us at best adult vandals, at worst such things as Stalinist butchers, narodniks, hebephrenic schizophrenics, murderers and criminals.[1] Other radicals considered us to be the victims of infantile paralysis. And the political freaks, like the Motherfuckers, White Panthers, and the Anarchists in Seattle thought we were ridiculous.

We were finished, but we didn't know it yet. The end was coming swiftly, but no one warned us. Ignoring the reality, we filled our minds with visions of the new underground. I was still seeing a race of molelike creatures inhabiting caves, with feelers for eyes, automatized to do nothing but build bombs which would eventually kill off all the bad people, freeing all the captive humans left aboveground. I was living science fiction.

It was the loneliest, most morbid time of my life. I literally lost my will to live. Every day I was criticized for something, and I smiled vaguely and agreed. And believe me, I agreed. I had been convinced, over a period of months, that I was the most racist anti-Communist, the worst sexual deviate, the most blighted egotistical wretch, the greatest anti-Women's Liberationist, the most exulting warmonger, and the weakest, most selfish, least desirable person that had ever lived. I was warped and unfit for Weatherman. I was dirty and like the rotten apple in the barrel, spoiled everyone I came in contact with. People were told, as we had just been told with Justesen, not to touch me, not to talk to me. I was in the caste of the untouchables, and no one recognized my existence, let alone my needs. I tottered on the edge of total despair and loaded myself with downers, until I couldn't walk, couldn't think.

Bleak images of Beverly and Jay were continually torturing me; I missed them intolerably. I still worked at the Roach, still saw Garrity, but the music seemed tinny now, the laughter tarnished, and his tender kisses and strong arms could not squeeze out the terror in my heart. And no amount of dope could stop the pain.

I came home one night still shaking from a massive dose of speed that I had taken to relieve my depression. I still had the front room of the gray house to myself, even though everyone else shared the large back room. The thought of sleeping in the same room with Don Sick was repulsive to me.

It was freezing in my bedroom. The window was broken because the pigs, or some right-winger, had thrown a rock through it one night while I was sleeping. I had awakened to the noise of glass shattering all over me. It was the third window that had been broken that month. Now I usually slept in the living room on the couch because of the cold, and because I was afraid that the next thing to come through the window would be a bullet.

The window had never been fixed. Ray had helped me put a piece of plastic across the gaping hole but every time the wind blew, the jagged glass ripped the thick plastic so that it hung in tatters. Also the light was out in the room, and I had no money to buy a light bulb. When I stole one, it was generally taken to the kitchen.

It was freezing in the house when I came home so late that night because the heat had been turned off. We had no money to pay the bill. It was colder in the house than it was outside, a dead cold that crept through my jacket and started me shivering. I couldn't seem to move. Where was I to go? This was my home.

The living room looked like a garbage pail. Dirty plates, cups, beer and wine bottles were strewn all over the place. Plates serving as ashtrays were overflowing, so that surrounding each plate was a pile of ashes and butts and empty matchbooks and used matches. Dirty clothes lay scattered in piles everywhere, and a dozen shoes were left lying where their owners had walked out of them before going to bed. Damp towels were thrown in with the dirty clothes; they smelled foul. The room was permeated with a rank odor, as if it was decaying around me. The posters on the wall were falling down. Where they had come loose, they were flapping from the rush of cold air which blew in from my broken bedroom window. Leaflets were scattered about in crumpled heaps, thrown in disgust or rage when they had been rejected at the high schools we still sporadically tried to organize.

I moved into the dining room. The table was covered with a layout for a new leaflet. I glanced at it briefly: MAXWELL SILVERHAMMER—LIVE LIKE HIM; FRANK ZAPPA—LIVE LIKE HIS HEAD THINKS. And then the leaflet had verses from the Beatles song about a kid who kills his teacher.

Over the table was the poster of the little Vietnamese girl running and shrieking in agony as napalm flames blazed into her frail body, burning her alive. I wanted to avenge her, and Fred Hampton, Bobby Seale, and myself.

I kept trucking, kept trying. Every day I woke up exhausted and hungry and lugged myself out of bed, took a pile of leaflets to the corner of Forty-fifth and University and stood in the rain passing them out to the stream of students who blandly walked by, making a wide detour around me. Nobody wanted to know, nobody wanted to listen. All honkies, all deserve to die.

I watched the Jesus Freak on the opposite corner handing out his propaganda, just as determined to win people to God as I was to win them to the revolution. Only in America could a commie and a religious zealot leaflet on opposite sides of a street. And only in America could both of them be ignored.

I watched the students go into Captain Hook's and Jay Jacobs and come out with their new blue jeans and dresses neatly folded in crisp paper bags. I had been just like them only a couple of years ago. Prancing primly down the Ave, buying this and that, worrying only about my next exam, or the grade on my last one, and which dress would turn Robby on the most.

As I held out leaflets to the people passing by averting their heads or staring doggedly at the ground, the rain spattered the paper, and it went limp in my hand. Finally the rain soaked the whole pile so thoroughly that it stuck together, and I turned around and walked home thinking about my dreams for humanity. Soggy dreams running together like so many wet pieces of paper, the words painstakingly written on them, indistinguishable.

I began to cry and my tears spattered on the layout spread before me, until the ink began to run. I still had not recovered from my concussion. Could that be the reason for this numbing depression, for my lapses of memory, for my absolute weariness with everything?

I turned back toward the living room and saw the gaping hole in the wall where Justesen had accidentally pulled the trigger on the shotgun one night when he was drunk. The plaster was peeling around the edges of the hole. I walked to it and began to pull pieces of plaster, stripping them one after the other, dropping them on the couch, where I would eventually sleep. I began pulling damp towels and clothes from the couch, dropping them on the floor. Under the clothes was a pile of yesterday's leaflets. I picked one up and began to read it. "The armies of the people of the world are winning. In Vietnam, in Laos, in the Middle East . . ." Winning. What were they winning? Who was winning? "In revolution one wins or dies," Che had said. No one was winning. Everyone was dying. The Vietnamese would never lose; if they didn't win they would die. The bombing was heavier than ever. The American military was like a great white shark viciously tearing up everything in its path; rice paddies, villages, cities, hospitals, schools, homes, and little girls with flames that dropped from invisible silver birds roaring through the clouds.

Che had won, but then he too had died. Trapped in the jungle, choking with asthma, without food or medication. Because it wasn't enough just to win. The revolution demanded that you keep on fighting, even after you won, because the process of losing began again almost immediately. You can't win, I thought desperately. You just have to keep on fighting until you die. There will always be an enemy to be fought. There will always be someone who hates so bitterly, who is so warped that they will want the ultimate thrill of killing and starving and enslaving the helpless.

I suddenly felt enraged. Why wouldn't anyone listen? There was truth in what we said, our theories did mean something. Weatherman wasn't some idiot's dream. It was real, just like napalm and war and starvation was real. But somehow, when we put our theories into practice, they disintegrated, just like the leaflets in the rain.

I stood there helplessly, shivering, crying, looking at the peeling hole in the wall. I wanted someone to come and tell me everything would be all right, that the dream was not destroyed, that Weatherman had not existed in a vacuum, that we could, somehow, win.

Do you understand, has it become clear, how much I wanted to change, what the revolution meant to me? How much I loved and believed in Weatherman? There had been a time when if I had been told to walk barefoot on broken glass I would gladly have done so. I was willing to do anything human, but we were expected to be superhuman. And we had to be.

More downers, more depression. I was dying. I wanted to die. And then the final blows, in the space of ten days, put out all the lights in my life.

On January 10, the Sundance gang hit Seattle and, bumming a dime, called some Running Dog house, and begged to crash there.

They knew I was in Seattle but were doing their best to avoid me because I was a Weatherman and they had already been through Weatherman and had had enough. Joe Kelly had stopped in Colorado to visit an old girl friend. The next morning Anne Anderson, having been Macho Mama for the Sundance boys too long, split for San Francisco. Bé-Bé followed just to hang out. All that remained of Sundance in Seattle was Chip, Abeles, and Jeff Dowd (Dude), and their puppy Etta, who was dying a slow death.

I got wind of the arrival of Sundance and gave them a phone call. Reluctantly they came over to the gray Weatherman house. Abeles had a cast on one of his legs, having broken it when he stepped off a precipice loaded on acid. Dude stalked the room drooling, grumbling to himself, and shaking his head as if he couldn't believe what he saw. Chip looked pained and uncomfortable . . . so I took them all to the Roach.

I had put on my mind for the occasion, and my black boots and jacket, purple scarf and hat. They were mighty impressed with the bullet holes in Zelda. They were mighty impressed with the Roach, with Garrity, with all the dope I gave them and with the endless flow of free wine and beer. They were still more impressed when Indian closed up early and we had a private party.

"This is party city," they said, giving me five.

"Yeah, and I'm the party queen."

Chip looked like Che Guevara, if you stretched your imagination. He talked to me very earnestly about Weatherman, and how bad the entire scene was, how the Bureau people were crazy, and how I should leave the collective and join Sundance. He told me his plans for organizing a city-wide movement; all kinds of people; kids, students, working class, welfare, old and young. He talked and Dude and Abeles echoed. I thought their enthusiasm was wonderful, and I liked them all. But I couldn't leave Weatherman. I laughed with them and joked with them until late in the morning. Then they went their way, and I went mine.

On Saturday, January 17, 1970, Jerry Rubin, of Chicago 8 fame, came to the University of Washington campus to speak in the Hub Ballroom, at the invitation of Michael P. Lerner, who had been teaching philosophy at the U since the fall, and had once been a roommate of Rubin at Berkeley.[2] Rubin gave an interesting enough speech about how we had to DO IT! He was exciting enough to arouse me slightly, but I was too loaded on downers to really respond. I wandered out of the ballroom just in time to miss bellowing Barbara Beam, that new acolyte of revolutionary zeal, take the stage from Lerner and extort everyone to "take an ROTC building." Then she started chanting piggy-wiggy, piggy-wiggy, and the Weathermen in the huge room joined her, trying to build up enthusiasm and momentum.

To the amazement and horror of everyone present, no one moved an inch. There were a few titters, some smirks, and a low undertone of embarrassment. Not even those who hated us most said anything; they were embarrassed into silence. Beam withered, and slithered off the stage. Then Georgia followed her, and put in a few dramatic, frenzied cents, and about thirty Weathermen quickly left their seats. They slid out the front door and sidled back in the back door. When they returned, Lerner was talking again; it was almost as if they hadn't been there at all.

By this time, I had moved to the Capitol Hill house; ostensibly I was going to organize at Seattle Community College. Back there, a few hours after the Beam debacle, all was silent, morose, and down, very heavily down. We were all sitting around the kitchen table, and everybody was so exhausted, no one could even talk. No one had the energy to fix dinner. It was so depressing that I had to get out or freak out.

I called Garrity at the Roach and he came and got me. I was so foggy from reds that I can't remember anything else about that night except that very late, about three in the morning, when he returned me to the house, he told me that he loved me. It made me genuinely happy, and feeling warm and calm and peaceful and happy all over, I walked into the house and into the kitchen. And there, slumped in a pool of weak, greenish-yellow light was Georgia, looking like a gone whore from a Degás painting; tears streaking her puffy face, looking pale and sick, as though she were in the last stage of terminal something.

"Georgia, what the hell has happened? You look awful." I tentatively put a hand on her shoulder. She crumbled.

"Susan," she managed to sob out, "Ty and Jean were just arrested for trying to bomb the ROTC building at the U."

The world stopped, and then I was slumped under the sick light. Tears were streaming down my face nonstop, and my fucking heart broke in a torrent. First Beverly and Jay; now Ty and Jean, out to prove that they could bomb a building and be monogamous, and now in jail with fifty thousand dollars' worth of bail between them and freedom, and the court saying no bondsman, and a ten- to twenty-year sentence if they should be found guilty.

It was just too much for me. I couldn't stand it. I couldn't stand anything. I slipped into my room, took enough reds to kill a horse, and fell into a drug-deadened stupor.

You think that was the end? That was only the beginning of the fucking end. Tim and Toddy, noticing what had happened to two of the other monogamous couples in Weatherman decided they'd better quit while they were still alive and unarrested. 'By, fair Weather-friends!

Then there was the Lenny Wood incident. Lenny was the sixteen-year-old dope dealer who had dropped out of Queen Anne High School to come and live in the gray house. I had done a few dope deals with him. There was a time back during the War Council when six hundred dollars' worth of marijuana that I paid for had been replaced with typing paper by the time it reached its destination. But I was too charmed by Lenny's golden locks to really believe he had burned me, so we struck up a close friendship. The collectives were outraged by this heterosexual perversion, since I was ten years older than Lenny. Later, they claimed that I had totally destroyed the boy when, in the middle of January, he whimpered that he wanted out of Weatherman. I personally thought his request was most sensible for him, and didn't argue much when he presented his feelings to the group at a criticism session. For hours the collectives tried to convince Lenny to remain in Weatherman, but he refused to change his mind. Finally they agreed with him that he wasn't ready to go underground, and he was allowed to pack up and leave that day.

I met Lenny about a year ago; he was working in an International House of Pancakes, clearing tables. His youthful good looks had matured into a rather innocuous paleness, and he didn't have much of the old verve left. Shit, maybe I did destroy him, or maybe Weatherman did, or maybe he would have ended up in the International House of Pancakes looking like a pancake if he had never had the experience. You know, for every person broken by Weatherman, there were at least a hundred enriched by it in some way.

I was meeting with Ty's parents every day. They had come to Seattle to do everything possible to help Ty and Jean. Not one other person in all the Weatherman collectives tried to help them. Not one. Not even Georgia, who had lived with them and had been closest to them. I was outraged beyond expression.

The parents finally hired a prominent Seattle lawyer who arranged for Ty and Jean to be bailed out to the custody of their parents. Fifty thousand dollars in cool cash was put up for their bond, and eventually they were released, and flew back home. At no time did they have any contact with anyone from Weatherman except me. And Roger Lippman, who sneaked in the back door of their hotel one night, to explain to them that Weatherman would not be able to take responsibility for helping their children.

The days between January 17 and January 25 are a blur to me. Amid the general depression, and sullen attempt to leaflet, little happened. With one exception.

There penetrated into my blur talk of a new political organization on campus, organized and led by the philosophical prof, Michael Lerner. He had wiled away dissident youths from an insipid campus organization called Radical Organizing Committee, which had been started that fall by Jean Shaffer and some of my old SDS friends. Now these same dissident youth, under the dictatorship and inspiration of Lerner, had formed a new group called the Seattle Liberation Front (SLF), inspired by the Berkeley Liberation Front, in which Lerner had been active.

A first meeting was called on January 19 to lure in more new recruits. The SLF was based on premises exactly *opposite* to Weatherman, and we were not invited to the first meeting, or to any others for that matter. Our adventurism, our suicidal tendencies, our "up against the wall" tactics, our disdain for the working class and our isolation from absolutely everyone were Lerner's reasons for building an organization excluding Weatherman.

Trying to exclude us was like slapping a knight in the face with a glove. It was a challenge, so of course we went to the meeting. Chip, Abeles, and Dude were also at the meeting. I went with Roger and Mike. All too soon, along with Joe Kelly and Lerner, we would all become partners in a conspiracy plot. Barely a month from that first SLF meeting, some assholes in a back room in the White House would sit down with cigars and coffee, and under a clandestine pale light, behind heavily guarded, locked, four-inch-thick maplewood doors, would add Joe's name to the list of people in that room and would concoct a conspiracy out of those names. And this SLF meeting was our First Overt Act.

I was there, an almost twenty-seven-year-old divorcee, loaded but not lurching on reds, with miles of Weatherman rhetoric to go before I slept. And Michael P. Lerner, a radical from Berkeley, obsessed with free speech, as long as it's not mine. And on my right, Roger the Dodger, a male chauvinist pig whom I can barely stand to look at, even though we exist in baleful toleration at the same falling-apart collective. And on my left, Mike Justesen, a shrewd and devastating man, a loyal friend and a frightening enemy. And there in the left front corner of the room were the three musketeers, Chip, Abeles, and Dude, who had crossed state lines in the pursuance of sunny weather from Ithaca to Seattle. Here we were all together, calling each other every name we could think of, and attacking each other as scathingly as we could, screaming at each other at the tops of our lungs, and this the government claimed was the First Overt Act of a Conspiracy.

The argument that night stemmed from historical roots. Lerner wanted to break down into discussion groups and talk. The Weathermen and various sympathizers wanted to have a demonstration the next day, when a Marine recruiter would be on campus. The three musketeers wanted both, and thus stood out as the arbiters. Well there was hemming, and there was hawing, and there were quiet little meetings in corners, and not so quiet eruptions between Lerner and myself. At one point Lerner got so incensed by my repeated inflammatory statements to his meeting that he lost his patience and his cool, and made the mistake of calling me a "bitch." Immediately every person in that room was on the defensive; the three musketeers, Hal and his gang, the Weathermen, and some of the SLF people all protested. Lerner was forced to shut up, and I was allowed to speak.

I toned down my speech, but it was still provocative. I explained why it was important to demonstrate militantly against the Marine recruiter, how ROTC had direct links to the war in Vietnam. After a long speech, and some more discussion, we broke down into discussion groups. About half of the people there discussed forming more SLF collectives. The other half discussed how to take over the peaceful picket line already called by the Mobe for the following day.

The next day dawned drizzly. Many of the Weathermen came to the demonstration in disguise, as well as Garrity, Ray, Simon, and Hal and Alex, none of whom considered himself a Weatherman but who ran with us on actions. A number of the Anarchists showed up as well. And Chip, Abeles, and Dude were there, along with Lerner, most of the new SLF, plus about a hundred peaceful anti-war students organized by the Student Mobilization.

Chip was supposed to make the speech that would send the Mobe's peaceful picket into a frenzy of hatred for the Marine recruiter, and have everyone bounding up the stairs of the ROTC building and at the bastard's throat. Chip gave a mild little speech, which did nothing for the nodding bunch trudging around the small square in front of the Administration building. Some frantic woman came bounding up to me and gushed that only I could say the words which would send the mannequins into war. "DO IT," she crooned, and how could I resist?

A veritable fury, I charged through the pickets, took hold of the bullhorn and bellowed, "Let's go get the motherfucker."

The change was instantaneous, and magnificent. As if they had all been shot with powerful doses of speed and adrenalin, the group flew into activity, and howling, braying and snorting, kicking up dust with their heels, flourishing the fist and the finger, charged up three flights of stairs to the Marine recruiter's office.

It all happened so fast and furiously that the people working in the office had no time to prepare. SMACK. BAM. ZIP. ZAP. Paper started flying. And fists started flying, and bookshelves started toppling, and in no time flat there was quite a battle going on. At one point I picked up a chair and sent it hurtling across the room. It hit one of the campus pigs squarely in the face, and he staggered and fell backward. I stepped back into the fringes of the crowd.

When some of the fighting lessened, it was possible to see the brilliant red hair of one of my young Anarchist friends grasped in a formidable pig's hand, which was smashing the head under the red hair against a counter top. Most of the people in the room were staring as the pig banged his head up and down very hard, again and again.

I couldn't stand to watch it. I flung my 100-pound body at the pigs, and began to apply lethal bruises to the creases in their uniforms, at which point someone shouted, "Arrest that woman, she threw a chair at an officer," and before I could say "Hit the road, Jack," I was struggling and squirming and handcuffed, along with my Anarchist friend, and two other people, and shoved into a back room. The demonstrators ran outside, tore up a portion of the pavement, and sent a pig car careening into a stone wall. I got to spend three days in City Jail.

My bail was a hundred dollars, and the charge was assaulting an officer. Now I was charged with assault in two states: Illinois and Washington. This was only the first of perhaps a dozen visits I made to Seattle City Jail. In the next two years I would meet many matrons, and many Seattle whores. But so much was still to happen.

When I was released from jail, things were worse than ever in the collectives. Now everyone was depressed. Surprisingly Georgia, always the most overwrought among us, was almost single-handedly keeping the entire thing together.

I moved back into the Woodlawn house the day I got out of jail; it was decided that I would do better work on the campus, since I had started such a good action.

On January 25, two days after my release, Russ Neufeld arrived with Cathy Wilkerson.[3] I rarely saw Cathy, who stayed at the Capitol Hill house, working mostly with the women up there. Russ and

Cathy came from the Bureau; they were sent to separate the wheat from the chaff, as it were. After they left, only people who would go underground would still be calling themselves Weathermen. Russ was very polite, unlike J.J. and Rudd, and didn't seem very interested in any of the women sexually. He stayed at our house while he was in Seattle. During the first day of his visit, he ignored me totally. Very quiet and exhausted, serious and sensitive, Russ was going to be the one to deal me the mortal blow.

For some reason, I didn't think I would be kicked out, probably because I had led such a good action and just gotten out of jail. But that apparently cut no ice. I should have known something was brewing when I heard Russ talking to the Bureau on the phone, and he said,

"I have gotten rid of problem number one and two, and I'll take care of number three at tonight's meeting." Problem number one and two were both from out of state. They had already packed their bags and gone somewhere else.

The criticism session that night started innocently enough, until suddenly Russ interrupted it and, turning to me, informed me that I was going to be the topic of discussion. I felt an icy dread immediately. I clearly remembered his phone conversation—"Don't worry, I'll get rid of problem number three tonight . . . get rid of . . . get rid of."

I think I experienced a mild seizure in the few seconds that Russ continued his unperturbed rap, not cruelly, but firmly, like an executioner who has no real interest in the condemned, but intends to do his job carefully and completely. I knew it didn't matter how much I appealed; the issue was already settled. But I was expected to follow the procedure, and so, with my heart flapping like a dying fish, I emotionally reeled off for perhaps the twentieth time my list of sins: yes, I still loved Garrity. I was afraid of going underground and never seeing my parents or friends again. I liked oodles of sex, mountains of dope, make-up and earrings and other female artifacts, that I considered myself pretty and was glad I was pretty, that I had aspirations to fame and glory, that I didn't want to die, that I wanted to be loved and appreciated, that I was scared of being useless, that my ego was malshaped and deformed and ran me ragged, that I was a gross failure as a revolutionary because I really didn't love the people but kept on being beaten and going to jail because it gratified my ego; that I didn't love my revolutionary brothers and sisters as much as Garrity, who was not a Weatherman; that I did not like some Weathermen at all, like Roger, Carol, or Don Sick, that I liked books and other material things, spent good money on movies and other vices, that I wanted to live, live, live, live, live, live.

I bore up well enough under the criticism, but I caved in when Russ told me in his most diplomatic way that I could not do anything more for Ty and Jean, because what they had done might reflect badly on Weatherman, and Weatherman didn't want to be connected with it. He asked me please not to have anything to do with the case *after I left the collective.* There they were, the deadly words, after you have left the collective.

My eyes began to fill with tears. I wanted to be strong and tough, but I couldn't help it. I looked around me at all the loving revolutionaries, all too anxiously licking their chops over the killing of one of their leaders. I was a reject! I had not been good enough. Once again I had failed. I was not good enough for the revolution, for Weatherman, for going underground, for the Vietcong. They didn't love me, want me, approve of me. I was alone.

In a hysterical flurry I darted up to my little room and quivered on the bed. No one came to touch me and murmur a friendly word. No one came to say they liked me. No one tried to say they were sorry. No one cared at the crucial minute when I was screaming silently, "Please, help me someone, I can't do this alone."

I must have lain there for an hour when some dragging footsteps approached. It was Russ, who in a gentle enough voice told me that he and Roger wanted to talk with me some more, but not in the house. Back to the Dirty Shame, and there Russ laid it on me.

"You can still be in a Weatherman collective if you really want to work hard for it," he told me, looking at me kindly, intently, studying me. "But, you can't remain in Seattle."

"You mean, if I want to be a Weatherman, I have to leave Seattle?" I asked, amazed.

That's exactly what he meant, and Roger explained to me the crystal logic of this decision. I had to be in a collective with stronger women, women who could control me, and not be held back or intimidated by me. I had to be in a collective where I could really struggle, and not run things as I had done, in Seattle. I had messed things up in Seattle; it was impossible for me to stay here. I had to give up my relationship with Garrity, I had to give up the Ave, the dog, the house I loved, the streets, the city.

"You see," said Russ, "we are giving you a second chance, because we realize how valuable you could be under the correct conditions. Away from Seattle we feel you will be able to advance more, and eventually be prepared to go underground. After all," and he smiled, "the Vietcong can't just stay in any little village they like. Their war of liberation necessitates that they sever all ties, swim like fish in the sea. You too must sever all ties."

I was offered my choice of four cities. And that was that! Take it or leave it, and decide by tomorrow. I was also told that since I was no longer in the collective, I could not sleep in the house that night; I could return for my clothes in the morning.

Reddog was sitting on the stoop when we returned to the house. I went into the gray house to call Garrity and ask him to pick me up. He came from the Roach in a few minutes, and we walked out just as Russ walked in. As we drove away, I turned to look at the gray house, and I could see Russ standing at the window, looking at us thoughtfully. Russ, what were you thinking?

Several months later, when they were in Cook County Jail together, Joe Kelly told Russ that I thought he had treated me kindly that night. I still do. Compared to the real abuse I had gotten from others, I saw Russ as trying to be fair and merciful. Even then I saw him as a victim too, not of the Weathermachine, but of the whole friggin', shitass America, and a culture that would make decent young people like Russ and myself almost destroy each other in an attempt to bring some positive change for humanity. No, I wasn't angry at Russ, or even Rudd, or J.J. I was just tired beyond expression, and hopeless in the face of our adversary.

Garrity took me for a drive along Lake Washington, as he sometimes did when I was upset about things, as we had done the day I had left for the Days of Rage, just a few months ago. We talked quietly about many things that night, and that is the way I like to remember him; quiet, strong, gentle and tender. I realize how much I did love him; I realize how good a friend he was to stand beside me through such unique times of stress.

I hadn't been this upset since I had left Robby, and then at least I had had something to look forward to. Now that something had come and gone. My dream. Shriveled like a raisin in the sun. And what was I to do now? What becomes of a dream deferred? What would become of me? I was getting older, I was almost twenty-seven years old. I had given up all my youth. And they didn't want me. No one wanted me.

"Oh Christ, they must be right," I thought, "they must be right about me, if I can get this emotional and blubber all over the place. Yes they must be right. I'm a worm, disgusting, foul, unworthy of living, unworthy of the Vietnamese, I'm just awful, the utter world's worst," and so on, until I had worked myself into a frenzy.

Garrity had never seen me have a real tragedy before and he was beginning to get upset and stopped the car and attempted to put his arms around me. But I was too far gone for any mere mortal to help, so as in other crises, I dropped a couple of tabs of the great THC that was out at that time, and Garrity drove to the Roach. I nodded out on the THC, and when I awoke a couple of hours later, Garrity was kissing me and holding me in one of the dark corners of the tavern, and I felt like a fluff of cotton, so soft and airy and light, and I loved Garrity so much, and quietly and without tears, nestled in his big arms, and he took me out to Indian's farm with him, and we made strong and tender love and I fell asleep fulfilled.

But when I woke up the next morning, the terror was there just the same, building in me wave after wave until I wanted to screech it hurt so. Terror, more terror, and the suffocating load of failure.

Garrity dropped me off at the Weatherman house to pack my things. He had said I could move onto the farm with him and Indian.

That made me happy, but did not solve my basic problem. He left, and I began to pack my clothes. Boxes here, there, all the mess of packing. And with each article I packed there flooded back a memory, and tears kept springing into my eyes and running down my cheeks, and I just couldn't stand it. I was so tired. I just wanted some peace.

And then I got the idea. Suicide! Why not, I had tried it before, when I was thirteen and my father slapped me because he thought he had seen me driving in a car with my lovely mother, and I told him I hadn't seen her for months, but he wouldn't believe me, and at thirteen it's a long time to go until you're free from that much oppression, like not being allowed to see your own goddam mother when you want to. And so I had swallowed several bottles of pills, and puked until I almost did die. And here I was at the age of twenty-seven, still as emotionally unequipped to deal with myself as I was at thirteen. Shit. Sure the Weathermen were right. I didn't deserve to live. Anyway, I didn't want to.

I had a pile of forty Seconals—a lethal dose. It was my intention to take them all, and out would go the lights, and I would serenely drift to my death. I could almost see them finding my body. . . . In grandstand style I took three reds, and got hung up in a daydream. The reds took effect while I was lying there daydreaming, and I fell into a downer sleep. I woke to Garrity shaking me, and when I raised my hand to touch his face, all the reds I hadn't taken fell on the floor. Garrity looked at the reds, and then at me, and got very upset. He told me again that he loved me, helped me pack, and off we went to Indian's ranch.

I stayed on the farm for one beautiful week, working at the Roach at nights, and then coming home with Garrity and Indian at four in the morning, sleeping till noon or one, having Indian's girl friend fix a great lovely breakfast every day, making love morning and night. I was really into Garrity, into love, into being someone's "old lady," and into living on a farm with horses, with millions of great records, good food, plenty of dope, no worries, a tailormade job—I mean, what more could you want out of life?

In this peaceful way I had my twenty-seventh birthday on January 31.

Two days later the itch hit. I got restless and cranky. I got bored. I resented the way Indian treated his girl friend. I had lost my attraction for the quiet country life. I loved Garrity, but I needed something more. Love was not enough.

Garrity told me about a meeting between the University District Center, the Ave pigs, the Ave merchants, and some street people. He wanted to go and check it out; I went with him, even though I thought such a meeting absurd. As I walked into Arabesque Fabric Store, who should be standing there stoned out of their gourds but Chip and Dude. They smiled at me. I smiled at them.

"How'd you boys like to let me into Sundance? I've been kicked out of Weatherman, you know? Yeah, last week. And I need to have some base to organize from. Let me into Sundance. You need women, and you know I'm a good organizer. There must be something for me to do."

Chip and Duke were really stoned and quite taken by surprise. They didn't have much time to think about it; they just sort of nodded yes.

"Great," I said, "I'll move into the house tomorrow."

Weatherman had won. I was giving up Garrity for my politics. In another month I would be ready to give up all my possessions and leave Seattle. The Bureau had kicked me out of Weatherman, but they couldn't kick Weatherman out of me. Once I got into Sundance, I felt I could easily work my way up to some position of power. Then I would begin to combat some of the right-wing elements, such as Lerner, and bring Weatherman politics to the newborn SLF. SLF meant nothing to me. The Sundance people, their politics and plans meant nothing to me. Sundance was merely my ticket to ride . . . Weatherman was still charting my course.

The Sundance house was set on a hill off the road. There were houses on either side, both rented by Sundance, a kind of package deal. There were no other houses around. The middle house was considered the command house and in it lived the top leadership of the Sundance gang; the people from Ithaca—Chip, Abeles, Bé-Bé, Dude, and Joe, when he arrived. Other people would live in that house, following Chip or Joe out from Ithaca, drawn initially by their energy and political creativity, and then falling in love with Seattle and putting down roots of their own. I like all the others followed the source of energy to the Sundance house. Morbid and suicidal, I was seeking an alternative. It was hard for me to realize that I had only been in Weatherman for five months. It seemed to characterize my entire life.

Those first few days in the Sundance house I was in a stupor, sitting in the living room taking reds, never leaving the house, morosely comparing the Sundance people to my friends in Weatherman and finding them seriously lacking politically.

I watched the Sundance men paint the living room black from top to bottom. And over the fireplace, Bé-Bé painted a brilliant sunburst, and the word SUNDANCE. The living room looked like a perpetual party. Beer cans, wine bottles, roaches, joints, and scraps of food lay everywhere. Everybody was getting stoned and drunk while they painted. They were laughing and screaming "Smash the state!" and "Fuck America!" slugging down beer and toking away.

Amid this sunny frivolity I sat like an ice cube, unwilling or unable to melt.

There were at least twenty people visiting the house every day. They'd wander in and out in droves. Cars and motorcycles were always parking in the winding driveway, and people would sit outside in the warm February sun, rapping with the men from the house. Discussion was dominated by The Day After demonstration (TDA), that was being organized nationally to protest contempt citations for the Chicago 8. Some people would, come just to get stoned or joke with Bé-Bé, who spent most of his time amiably getting drunk with anyone who wanted a beer. Abeles and a bunch of the Anarchists were working on stickers for high school kids to put on the back of their jackets which said TDA, with a picture of Bobby Seale bound and gagged. Two newly recruited women talked about forming a women's caucus within SLF. Chip and Dude discussed possible organizing tactics and strategy for actions with the other collective members who constantly visited.

People got their identities from their collectives. "Susan, this is so and so from Red Avengers," or "Meet so and so from Guerrilla," or from Tupamaros, or from Paisano, taken from the wine they drank by the gallon. There were half a dozen collectives and more were forming every day. Each collective was organized around a specific political task. One collective worked on welfare rights, another distributed food at the unemployment office, another was building a free medical clinic, one was organizing day care, and still another worked on a tax initiative. They all worked autonomously, except for building for the TDA demonstration. The people from Ithaca were taking the major responsibility for this. The Sundance collective co-ordinated all the other collectives very loosely. Not having a specific function, except to direct, its members floated around giving advice and participating in the work of the other collectives. Wherever they went they were inspirational and energizing. They waltzed through a room and left it careening, throbbing with energy and excitement. They were cataclysmic, Chaplinesque, hedonistic and brilliant, young and impetuous, strong, fearless, prudent, and irresponsible.

Instead of putting people up against the wall, they gave parties and drowned people in beer and dope. They danced them into a frenzy of political upheaval, laughed them into new collectives, and brought them back to the people and to the luxury of feeling alive. Life was in the bars and on the streets, not on the campuses. Life was on the welfare lines and in the unemployment offices, and on the docks, not in the classroom. Life was a wild, reckless bacchanalia, a festival of joy.

Eating on food stamps, living was cheap. There were no worries. Life was fucking lots of beautiful women and handsome men, and no heavy ties except to the men from Ithaca. Life was a party, humming and throbbing out into Seattle, seeing your picture on the front page of the *Post Intelligencer* every day, getting stoned while you watched yourself on television each night, hearing the word Sundance on the lips of people all over Seattle. The men from Ithaca hit stagnant Seattle like a cultural bombshell, and in weeks the Seattle Liberation Front was a reality and not a myth.[1]

I agonized from my chair in the living room about the paltry politics of Sundance.

"Chip," I would say in deadly earnest, "how can you let all these people in the house? Isn't it bad for security?"

He'd snort contemptuously, "Fuck security. How can you build a mass movement if you shut everybody off? Security is important, but the people are more important. The house is open so that people can come here and rap with us. We want people to come here, we want them to feel free to come here. We're trying to break down some of that elitist, stratified leadership bullshit Weatherman thrived on."

"But, Chip, the politics are awful. Practically nothing about racism, an emphasis on reform and education and you make the idea of armed revolution sound ridiculous."

"Well, it is ridiculous right now, Susan," he would patiently tell me. "We already tried those tactics, and they didn't work. Those Weatherpeople were crazy. I was close to some of them; J.J. and Rudd were great, but they were foolish, and I don't really think they cared at all about the people. The revolution is not going to happen tomorrow. It's going to take a long time. Rather than driving ourselves insane and alienating everyone in the process of making it, we are trying to build it from the ground up. Old people, women, Third World, students, workers, everybody. And programs organized by all of us to sustain us while we are doing it. You can't fight a revolution without the people. Weatherman tried to do that and it can't be done. If the leadership is too far ahead of the people, it's the same as being too far behind. Good leadership has to start where the people are."

I listened to Chip with a mixture of confusion and contempt. I respected him greatly, but what he was saying was heresy to me. I decided to keep my feelings to myself, and to do the best I could to bring some politics to TDA. It would be hard, because everyone in Sundance was really antagonistic to any Weatherman theory. They made it very clear to me that they didn't want any cadre, they didn't want any exemplary action. They wanted a mass, city-wide movement, and they were willing to take years to build it. Although I was very grateful that the Sundance gang had taken me in at a low point in my life, I resolved to fight what I clearly saw as their right-wing tendencies.

I began by going with Abeles and Bé-Bé to the high schools. We would meet at seven-thirty in front of the Id Bookstore, and wait while other collectives arrived. Then we would divide up into several groups and each group would take a car and go to a school. Once there, we would urge the kids to come to TDA, give them stickers to put on their jackets, and posters to paste up in their spare time. We encouraged them to spray-paint. The organizing style was just like my own; ribald, high energy, enthusiastic, full of laughing and joking, dope smoking and jive. But the content was not at all alike. Many of the collective people were very close to Lerner, and were very conservative in organizing about TDA. They would describe it as educational and peaceful. They would discourage any idea of violence. Abeles and I were in complete agreement; destroy the Federal Courthouse, off the pigs. The high school kids loved Abeles, and he was one of them. His Afro flying, his impish eyes glowing, he would wave his fists in the air and advocate total mayhem. I tried to add some political theory while I assured the kids that "anything would go during TDA."

Within a few days the college kids from the collectives began to assume I was in charge of high school organizing. I would make all the announcements about it at the growing meetings during which the entire SLF would gather together to discuss The Day After demonstration. I began to develop my own constituency within SLF, and frequently, I would see Chip and Bé-Bé looking haggard as I got up and spieled off my invective against the state. Less and less could they control me. Abeles always agreed with me, and Dude part of the time; the Anarchists came to many of the meetings and they agreed with my violent tactics. Mike Justesen, who had also been purged from Weatherman, would come to those meetings with Garrity, Ray, Simon, and Hal. They generally agreed with what I said; several times Justesen spoke to defend or support points I had made.

Those meetings were being carefully documented by undercover FBI agents, and would eventually become overt acts of conspiracy indictments.

To the SLF and Sundance I was in my prime; flashy and vulgar, hard and funny, aggressive and dramatic. I got the Sundance boys hordes of dope, I forged checks and got them boots; I fucked them all methodically, one by one, whether they wanted me to or not. It was part of my act, part of being the Macho Mama. So was taking downers and sitting mournfully in the living room at night unable to sleep, even after an exhausting day of high school organizing and endless meetings. Night after night I sat with Etta, who was dying of distemper, and looked at the black walls of the Sundance house, and wondered what it was like for my friends who were preparing to go underground, wondered about Beverly and Jay, Ty and Jean. I tortured myself endlessly with the thought that I was copping out by not leaving Seattle and going underground in some other city. I yearned for Garrity, and wondered what women he was with, wondered why I couldn't just settle down and be somebody's old lady.

As the days raced toward TDA, I grew more frozen inside, more animated outside. Everyone in Sundance knew I was unhappy, but no one knew the extent of my misery. I was obsessed with death and dying. I began to think about bombing the police station again, making sure I perished in the explosion. I fantasized about shootouts with a dozen pigs, killing some of them, and finally getting killed myself. I daydreamed of setting an ROTC building on fire, and burning to death in the blaze. My death had to count for something. I couldn't just die any more; I had to die with meaning. My life couldn't be wasted by a wasted death. In those last days before TDA, I was consumed with murder and suicide and violence.

The day before TDA I had to fly to Chicago for another pretrial hearing. It was not clear if my case would be postponed, or if I would go directly to jail. So I said good-by to everyone as if I was going to jail.

My trial was postponed again, and I left Chicago on the next plane, arriving back in Seattle that same night, February 16. I couldn't get anyone from the Sundance house on the phone, so I called Garrity. He picked me up at the airport, and I returned to the Fortress, where he had been staying.

There the final plans were being made for TDA. Justesen, Garrity, Ray, Simon, and myself decided to run in an affinity group together; we decided to carry iron pipes with us. Ray was sent to get the pipes; he came back with a dozen of them, each twelve inches long. We decided not to wear helmets, because we wanted to blend in with the rest of the crowd. I was excited and on edge, prickling with energy as I always was before a demonstration. The impression that Justesen and Garrity gave me was that the Sundance people were fucked; they were not interested in a militant demonstration. It was up to us to up the ante. For that reason, I didn't bother calling the Sundance house. I had given them a chance; now I was back with my people. Now we would fight. Now we would show them how it is done.

There were over two thousand people gathered on the broad lawn in front of Seattle Federal Courthouse and spilling over onto the sidewalks. About a thousand of these were high school kids, college students, and freaks who were there for a demonstration that could possibly provide action and excitement. The remainder were older people, with anti-war sentiments, who resented Judge Hoffman's punitive response to the Chicago 8, and had come to the demonstration cautiously: to demonstrate peacefully, or to observe.

It is possible that many of these people believed Lerner when he had said that all we wanted to do by demonstrating was to provide an educational experience, by going into the courthouse and peacefully talking about the inequities of America's legal system. A letter to this effect had been sent to U.S. Attorney Stan Pitkin and to Mayor Wes Ullman in advance.

Surrounding the milling crowds were rows of pigs standing at attention, ready for trouble. Pigs were hidden in the library across the street from the Federal Courthouse, and inside the courthouse as well. No one but a few hundred other people expected a peaceful demonstration, although few people came prepared with sticks or rocks to throw.

Someone threw some paint up against the side of the building; someone else lobbed a tear-gas grenade inside a window; I saw a man at the glass doors, kicking with his feet, breaking in the glass, and then the pigs gassed the areas liberally and the crowd scattered. I was immediately nauseated, gagging and sneezing, my eyes burning. Within a few minutes the gas cleared, and the crowd, infuriated, swelled across the lawn, and ran toward the building, as if to tear it down with their bare hands, and once again they were gassed. The pigs lining the streets tensed and strained forward; the roar of the crowd rose to a howl, as they stampeded away, frustrated by the gas.

A chant started from within the crowd. "Downtown, downtown." It was repeated over and over again. The crowd seemed confused. Every once in a while it would turn downtown and take a few steps, but the majority meandered in front of the courthouse.

Then Chip jumped on top of a car, and began to urge the crowd downtown. He looked beautiful standing there, alone, his hair whipping around his face in the wind, his fist cutting the air, his voice, full of strength and rage, carrying to a small crowd around him all his anti-Weatherman rhetoric, his working-class theories, forgotten in his excitement.

Just as Chip began to speak, the pigs attacked. They suddenly reached a point where they could no longer restrain themselves and went wild. They rammed into the crowd and attacked viciously using their clubs indiscriminately upon old people and street kids, men and women, against curious onlookers and passers-by caught in the mob, against people standing dumfounded or blinded by tear gas. People trying hysterically to escape the smashing clubs were thrown against others on the crowded streets, fell, and were trampled as the mob grew more frenzied. People on the periphery, seeing what was happening to those in the center, began to run toward the downtown area. In seconds a thousand people were galloping furiously down the hill to the business district of Seattle. The police, so intent upon massacring those who couldn't escape, didn't realize there was no one left until everyone had reached downtown.

There followed a riot unprecedented in Seattle. Many people who would never have considered throwing rocks were angered by the senseless beating and by being gassed. The mob surged out of control and proceeded to destroy downtown Seattle. Bank windows, restaurants, hotels, expensive shops, airline offices, travel agencies, every window within sight, within reach, was smashed. When occasional pedestrians attempted to interfere, they were fought back. Some people within the crowd kept on screaming out not to break windows belonging to small shop owners, but the people would not listen to anybody.

I ran for several blocks smashing windows, feeling that elation once again as the glass gave beneath my blows. In one glorious instant I saw Garrity throw a pipe right through the windshield of a lone pig car; the windshield shattered, and the car careened crazily. For almost a half an hour we ravaged the streets, and left before the pigs even arrived. After we left, those who remained fought bitterly with the pigs, throwing rocks and attacking them. The whole thing lasted four hours.

Eighty-nine people were arrested that day; hundreds were injured. Damages were over $75,000. Dozens of pigs were hurt, and pig cars had been destroyed. By all criteria, TDA in Seattle had been an outstanding success. It was by far the most stunning of all The Day After demonstrations across the country. News of it flooded underground newspapers, and put Seattle on the political map. News of it hit J. Edgar Hoover in his SDS ulcer and enraged him; it made John Mitchell look like an idiot and incensed him; it made

Richard Nixon look like a dolt, and he ordered the other two to do something about it, to make some kind of example out of those upstarts in Seattle.[2] "They can't do this during my administration," he declared, drooling. "Law and order, respect, decency, our American heritage, etc. . ."

The next day I left Garrity once again. I had to take several hits of mescaline to do it, and by the time he dropped me off at the Sundance house, I was high as a kite. The boys were in the midst of "cleaning." Chip was grabbing ten, twelve beer cans at a time and shoving them into an immense sack. Bé-Bé was on his knees, picking endless cigarette butts and particles of rotting food off the floor. Abeles and Dude were oiling the guns and ruminating about the demonstration. Dozens of people were wandering in and out recalling their particular experiences. I sat in my chair facing the fireplace and strobed, while the room moved about me.

That evening I was still very loaded, too loaded to go with the boys to a legal meeting they had set up just in case conspiracy indictments were handed down. They were afraid the pigs would attack the house, and rather than leave me alone, took me to a friend's house in the U District.

There I sat incoherent. Half the time I was dreaming; the other half of the time I listened as three men plotted to dynamite a construction site on the campus. One was John Dung, the scuzzy smacker who had offered me guns and dynamite in the Roach. I was so stoned that I was never sure I had heard them correctly, not until a few weeks later when they had attempted to bomb the post office. Dung had turned out to be an informer whose reward was a fix right in a Seattle jail cell, with heroin procured and administered by a Seattle pig. The others went to prison for two years.

Three days after TDA, Sundance had a retreat during which I was kicked out of the collective. It came as a complete shock to me; I knew I was suspect because of my past ties to Weatherman, but I had thought I was safe enough, even though Lerner hated me. There was nothing personal, they tried to assure me. But they just didn't trust me.

"If you're a Weatherman, you're a Weatherman," Chip told me gently. "That's it, that's where you're at. In a certain sense you can't be trusted. That's the highest thing in your life, and anything else comes second. And I can't trust something that comes second best."

They were all very nice about it, but definite. I would endanger everyone. Perhaps I already had. My speeches during the organizing for the TDA had been inflammatory; the content of my high school organizing excessively violent. And my conduct during the demonstration, kamikaze.

"You're still too much of a Weatherman," Lerner told me in his philosophical way, after two days of trying to figure out exactly what my politics were.

"I shudder every time you get up to speak," Bé-Bé told me amiably, sipping a beer. And so on.

I looked at them all from someplace behind my eyes. I couldn't quite understand that it was happening all over again, that in less than a month I was being kicked out of still another political organization. First I hadn't been enough of a Weatherman; now I was too much of one. Weatherman seemed to be my private demon, like bad breath. It came spewing out whenever I opened my mouth.

I left Sundance and returned to the Fortress, to Garrity, to Justesen, to Ray, the other rejects. I tried not to feel bad, but I felt hopelessly that there was nothing left for me. The Fortress was like a military enclave; people were constantly cleaning guns, and kneeling at the lead barriers protecting the windows. There were double doors with triple locks. Everyone looked nervous and frightened as if the armed might of the state would single out our house and attack immediately if not sooner. Most of the paranoia came from Hal, but it was harrowing to live constantly on the verge of annihilation.

I flopped around doing nothing for two weeks, sunk in melancholy. I continued taking downers. I drank—anything to relieve my misery, to allow me to sleep. I no longer cared about looking flashy. Everything seemed dull and unimportant. Although Garrity lived in the same apartment, we didn't sleep together every night and I was in a constant state of nervous tension over him.

Sometime during that period Robby returned to Seattle briefly. He was a very different Robby. His story was tragic, and I pitied him greatly, although I felt for the first time that I no longer loved him. He was so woebegone, so hopeless; those huge shoulders slumped, that broad, rosy face with its expansive smile crushed, an apprehensive question in that voice once emitting authority. One night he told me the gruesome details.

The Weathermen had been concentrating for some months on his collective in Los Angeles, California. The women had been especially pressured to leave the men and children and form a Weatherman collective of their own. One of these women was Ivy, who had always been sympathetic to Weatherman. Soon after Bernardine paid a visit to L.A., the women threw the men out of the house, and locked themselves in intense criticism–self-criticism. When they emerged a few days later, they were Weatherwomen; looks, line, dress and emotions had altered seemingly overnight; they were willing to give up their children and their men. The men could either form a collective of their own or split; but the past was past. It was unalterable.

Robby, who loved Ivy passionately, was destroyed. Not only was the woman he loved leaving him, but she was leaving him for a political group that he was totally opposed to, that terrified him, that made him feel weak and impotent. Tortured, he began to search his soul for answers. What was there about his relationship with women that made them leave him to throw themselves so violently, so completely into destruction? First me, then Ivy. What was wrong with him that he could not see the light?

In agony, he wandered around aimlessly for a few days, and then flew to Seattle. He hated Weatherman, they were inhuman, he said. I felt deeply for him, and the story revolted me. But in a way, I applauded Ivy, although she dropped out of the collective a few weeks later. Robby was finally facing himself, finally seeing a reality that most people lived with all their lives; there is a price for everything. Not a money price, but a life price. Weatherman was changing life. Some people in America would never be the same after the experience. Robby would have to change too, or he would be left behind. There were women who were stronger than he was now, who had higher priorities than Robby Stern.

I slept with Robby once during that time. He came into my room and asked me if I wanted to sleep with him. It was cold, automatic, and disgusting. Sitting on top of him, going through the gestures of love making, I wondered how he could have dominated my life so totally for so many years.

One night early in March, I was lying on my bed. I had been lying there for hours in a stupor, drugged. Suddenly there was a great commotion from the living room and someone came in with a horrible look on his face.

"The town house . . . there's been an explosion in New York . . . some Weathermen were killed, maybe Mark Rudd . . ."

I stumbled out of the bed. On the screen was the wreck of a Greenwich Village town house, home of Cathy Wilkerson's parents, a house right next door to actor Dustin Hoffman. They flashed on a picture of the house as it had looked prior to the explosion; it was the house where I had visited Kathy Boudin less than a year ago.

Blandly, the newscaster was speculating about what had occurred; young revolutionaries making bombs . . . headed irrevocably down the road toward violence and terrorism . . . at least three dead, maybe more . . . only one body identified at this time, that of Ted Gold . . . police have found a finger and hope to make another identification . . .

Ted Gold. I had known him briefly while I lived in New York. Quiet, shy, and intellectual, he made up many of those crazy songs we sang at the Days of Rage and at the War Council. He had been a teacher of retarded children. The Columbia People's Street Theater had gone to do a play for his class. He hadn't liked Weatherman at first, but then slowly had been drawn to us, drawn by history, by his unavoidable reflections about the hopelessness of life in America. Later when the finger was identified as belonging to Diana Oughton, I felt the same sense of betrayal. A vague image of a smiling, thin, blond woman with a serious face, not exactly shy and not very gregarious, just pleasant, walking with Jose and me to have breakfast. Diana, a woman who always said hello to me, who always had a smile for me, who had passed through my life like a sweet shadow, seeming to be what I aspired to be. She and Ted always seemed so alive, and now they were dead. Blown themselves to smithereens. A finger. They found her fucking finger. Those were people who were real. Their lives had been as positive as their deaths. I was horrified that they had blown themselves up, that they had not known enough, that they had made a mistake when a mistake was deadly. But their deaths were instructive to me. You had to know all the time what you were doing. No mistakes. No more children's crusade. To go up against serpents, you have to have the knowledge of serpents. You must be a serpent yourself.

My life looked rank to me. I hated my flesh, my breath, my nose, my feet. I despised the tenacity with which I clung to it. My thoughts swung even more morbidly. If one could not live meaningfully, one at least could die meaningfully. That much control one had over one's life.

Diana Oughton and Ted Gold turned like a tiny nail in my brain, excruciating, unforgettable.

A few days after the town house explosion, Mike told me he had seen Jay and Beverly, and that they wanted to see me. We were sitting outside in front of the Fortress, in the pale sun when he told me. I looked at him wonderingly. It was almost as if he had seen Lazarus. He was very quiet, very serious, so typically Mike, so hurt, repressed, so brilliant.

"I think I'm going underground, Susan. I've thought it over very carefully and I don't see any alternative. The above-ground Movement is eating itself up alive and the best you get are second-rate groups like the SLF which are contaminated by the likes of Lerner. I want to do something that will have meaning. There must be some way and it's no longer around here." He fell silent. Then he turned to me, and very slowly, carefully, as if he was measuring each word because each one might be the winning or the losing straw, he said,

"Maybe it would be the best thing for you too, Susan. We've both burned our bridges pretty fast behind us. We've swept through the past two years not thinking very much or very well about the future, pulled along by the necessity of the present, by the emptiness of the past. We've learned about ourselves through our politics; they've defined us to a great extent. I don't-see anything left to do. I just see doing the same, impotent things over and over again. Not to go on, not to attempt the only alternative left, would be to deny your own nature, not to be crazy and visionary, not to want to pry your way out of the mire. That means not being afraid to say good-by to some things. But those things aren't going anywhere. You're holding onto your present life like a prized possession and it's nothing. You're miserable, hopeless, dying."

We sat silently together. How could I answer something like that? I was amazed at the utter clarity of his understanding. His message was clear; I would have to be part of the revolution or part of Babylon collapsing, in chaos, the end of the Western world for the rest of my life.

"Do you know where you're going?" I finally asked.

"Yes."

And that's all we said. We sat there a while longer, and then we got up and went our separate ways.

I took to my bed again; this time I denied myself my embalming downers. For two days I lay on my mattress on the floor not eating, not sleeping, just thinking. And at the end of two days I had decided to go underground. My plan was to find Beverly and Jay and see if they were interested in going with me. If not, I would find other people, perhaps go to one of the cities Russ Neufeld had suggested to me.

Going underground was not just a wild gambit for me. It was all that was left before death. All my fears, my anxieties about going underground paled beside the specter of living out my life untrue to my revolutionary visions, simply for the sake of living. Life was not that appealing to me. It never had been. Its loss could mean little, if in the process something better for humanity could be born. Besides, I was facing forty years in Chicago and ten years for assault in Seattle; the chances were that I would end up doing at least a year or two in prison and that thought was terrible.

I left to find Jay and Beverly a few days later. We had a wild reunion, and I was happier and more excited than I had been for months. They had been living a quiet, secluded life, hadn't done anything political, surviving frugally off odd jobs Jay would take, and off the handcrafts which Beverly made. They were as power-fully in love as ever, but they were dissatisfied. They felt the lack of politics in their life, knew that they wanted to resume their work on a higher level. After hearing about the town house explosion, they had contacted Mike, and he had visited them. During his visit he had stressed the necessity of moving underground, the politics of utter alienation, the logic of sabotage. They had resisted at first, say-ing that they refused to be separated, and that if returning to Weath-erman meant separation, then they would rather stay where they were. Mike told them they had to decide, and left, telling them he would send me.

Finding Beverly and Jay was like finding myself. Finally a focus. Finally people who understood my cravings, my isolation. Finally others who were not content with a half-life.

Ty and Jean were living with relatives in the Midwest, awaiting trial. We decided to contact them, and if they were at all interested, I would fly there and make arrangements for us all to get together. We called Ty and Jean almost immediately; they were thrilled to hear from us. Arrangements were made for me to visit with them, to discuss the possibilities of forming an underground collective.

Jay, Beverly, and I talked far into the night. All of us would of necessity have to change our identities, since everyone but Beverly was facing charges. We decided that two weeks would be enough time for the three of us to split with our past. For Beverly and Jay it meant giving up their precious, handcrafted love nest, their pets, their privacy, their possessions, their peace. For me it meant letting go of my clothes, scrapbooks, poetry, and other relics from my past, my dog, Garrity, and most of all Seattle. Everything to be reduced to one suitcase.

We were strangers about to journey into a strange land, with only our wits, our courage, our dreams and commitment to guide us. Yet that night as I lay awake listening to Beverly and Jay fucking in the next room, I felt my aloneness press upon me more than ever. It didn't seem to me that Jay and Beverly were giving up that much, since they would be together no matter what they did. But I was giv-ing up the chance to find what they had; I was facing the unknown alone. I recoiled at the idea of shutting myself up in a forsaken room in some raunchy city and making bombs for years; never being free to get drunk or stoned, to fuck just anybody for fear that they might be a pig, that I might talk in my sleep, that too relaxed and stoned, I might give a clue. I felt all these misgivings, but I swallowed them. I was resigned. It was a fait accompli.

I flew to Chicago for my fourth pretrial hearing; once again the trial was postponed. Then I took a bus to still another joyous reunion, this time with Ty and Jean. They had already decided not to appear at their trial, and were more than excited at the prospect of forming a collective with Jay, Beverly, and myself. The three of us phoned Jay and Beverly, and set a date for our meeting. We decided to have it in New York.

I returned to Seattle and, finding out that Joe Kelly had finally arrived, I went straight to the Sundance house and informed them I was splitting Seattle. Chip immediately looked suspicious and anxious, but I said nothing more. I asked instead if I could please stay at the Sundance house for the two weeks before I left. Joe wanted me to, so Chip assented. In my absence people had had second thoughts about asking me to leave Sundance. Joe told me that if he had been in Seattle it never would have happened. Chip and Dude told me that I didn't really have to leave; they wanted me to stay.

But I was adamant. I was leaving. "Where are you going?" they'd ask repeatedly in the next two weeks. "With whom?" I would just shake my head. I never told them. But they knew and were concerned. Chip would come up to me and shake his head and say, "I hope you're not going to do anything foolish, Susan. Like go off and try to find the Weathermen. The Movement isn't dead, you know. There's plenty of work for you to do around here with us." I just shook my head and refused to talk about it. Even Garrity was upset. He moved back into Sundance with me, was very attentive, told me how much he loved me, asked me again and again not to leave.

It amazed me that now that I had made the decision, set the wheels in motion, my life should suddenly open like a flower.

Robby had left Seattle for a week or two, but had returned again, now obsessed with aspects of Weatherman politics. Everything was counterrevolutionary, bourgeois, defeatist, individualistic, and uncollective. As violently as he had railed against Weatherman just a few weeks before, that's how staunchly he harped away at everyone he met, until it was impossible to be near him. He muttered constantly about doom and destruction, about white-skin privilege. Nervous, paranoid, insecure, yet driven by his despair, he seized upon Weatherman as an opiate for his heartbreak. Nothing could kill such a pain; it only drove him deeper into a pit.

His pet issue was male chauvinism. He would talk about it making a martyr of himself in the process. He thought he was the utter world's worst male chauvinist. He was evil, malicious, and brutal when it came to women. All he wanted to see in the world was for women to get stronger, learn to love each other, and leave rotten men like himself to ponder their atrocities against women. Robby was holier than thou. He was fanatical to the point of absurdity. Frightened by the changes in him, I had as little to do with him as possible.

I stayed out at the Sundance house and had fun. I woke up one beautiful, spring morning and taking a box full of acid, I proceeded to distribute it to everyone in the house. At that time there were about twenty people living at Sundance. Everyone had a ball tripping that day, and in the afternoon I cooked a great chicken pilaf, and we had a small party, going to the Roach that night.

I left the Roach about eleven o'clock, still loaded on acid, with another woman from Sundance. The house was empty when we arrived. We sat there strobing at the black walls of the living room. I noticed some oil paints and paintbrushes scattered on a table, and decided that what that living room needed was a symbol of liberated womanhood. Together, the other woman and I painted an eight-foot-tall nude woman with flowing green-blond hair, and a burning American flag coming out of her cunt! One graceful arm was raised in a fist; the other held a shotgun. Her breast was crisscrossed with a bandoleer. A caption beneath her said LONG LICKS OF LUST!

It was the first thing you saw when you entered the Sundance house. It dumfounded the Ithaca men, and infuriated all the radical women. No one could understand exactly what I had tried to represent. Perhaps in my acid frenzy I had painted what I wanted to be somewhere deep in my mind; tall and blond, nude and armed, consuming—or discharging—a burning America.

During those two weeks the Black Student Union held a series of demonstrations closely co-ordinated with the SLF. The strategy was amazingly effective. Several hundred people would rally, seize a building, run through it telling everyone to leave, and then once the building was effectively closed down, run out, and seize another building and do the same thing again. The thing that thrilled me most about it was that black and white radicals were finally working together. I had practically nothing to do with the organizing of it, although Sundance was considered the white leadership. I just ran along, taking building after building, until we'd effectively shut down the entire campus for several days.

On March 11, I left the demonstrations just long enough to sign divorce papers that Robby had drawn up. Although I had considered myself divorced for two years, it was nice to have it legal. We celebrated our divorce by drinking an Orange Julius.

One bright day a week later, I sat out in front of Sundance and tore up my life. All the photos of my youth taken out of my album, one by one, torn up and into a big garbage can. Then my scrapbooks. Then all the poetry I'd written, notebooks filled with the odyssey of my adolescence, with the panic scribbles of those endless, sleepless nights of my youth. Short stories written, wrenched onto the paper, torn up and thrown into the garbage. The precious compositions from the kids I had taught saved all these years, so stark, so heartrending; rip and into the garbage. Love trinkets, old letters, all traces of Susan Harris Stern shredded and into a foul garbage can.

Joe sat beside me the entire time, begging me to save some of it, telling me there would come a time that I would want it all. But he didn't know that I was about to jump off, make a clean break, split. Soon there would be no more Susan Stern. She would be dead, and the person she had been would have another face, another color hair, another name, another past. She would invent it, build it, engineer it to be exactly what she wanted it to be, what she had never been. She would make jobs, homes, towns and parents. A past of fiction, a life of science fiction. Susan Stern Sham would end finally, finally she would end.

That day I gave away all my clothes, all the things accrued by an upper-class girl from a father who measured love by such things as clothes. Five coats, one of them suede. A dozen pairs of shoes. Dresses, skirts—all the paraphernalia of middle-class society. Gone to a couple of hippie women, gone somewhere. Leaving only one dress, a couple of pairs of pants in the bottom of a blue valise.

The next day I went to meet a man who knew how to get phony identity. I met him in a bar, and I paid him one hundred dollars and he gave me a blank Social Security card, a voter's registration card, and a birth certificate of a woman who would have been my age, had she lived. I stared at the name on the birth certificate. Stella Smith.

"It's so anonymous," I said to the man dumbly. He shrugged. What was in a name?

That afternoon I took my Martin guitar, which an AWOL soldier had given me back in 1967, and I sold it to a person on the Ave for fifty dollars. That same day I sold my car Zelda to Hal for fifty dollars. Then I took the rest of my money, about a hundred dollars, and went to meet a man who dealt in unregistered firearms. He sold me an Ithaca model double-barrel shotgun and a .38 caliber handgun. I went to the sporting goods store and bought a supply of bullets. Late that night, when everybody was asleep, I sneaked the guns into the house, and packed them into my valise. The man had shown me how to disassemble the shotgun.

That was it. I was ready. I called Beverly and Jay, and made arrangements to meet them.

The next day I went to a knitting shop and bought four skeins of wool. I had never knitted a thing in my life, but had an urge to leave something of myself with Garrity. That day there was a long meeting of Sundance. There was great concern that the leadership was getting separated from the rest of the collectives, and there were charges of elitism among leadership. I participated frequently in the meeting, as I would on any other day. I outlined what I thought would be necessary to keep the SLF from falling apart, what Weatherman had not done. My suggestion was that Sundance disband, and that each of its members move in with one of the other collectives, and give leadership by example instead of by command. Everyone was taken aback by this suggestion; it was so much fun, so easy living up at Sundance, up on that hill, away from all the trivia, the chaos, the involvements down there. My idea was dismissed, but the seeds had been planted. I sat knitting through the meeting; I finished the scarf around eight o'clock, gave it to Garrity and asked him to drive me to the bus station. The people in the living room fell silent. Everyone looked at me as if I were a ghost. Joe came to take me in his arms, pleading, "Please don't do this." He squeezed me so tightly, and he was so upset, that I almost gave up the idea. But it was too late. I had to see it through.

Good-bys were said. I felt strangely removed, aloof. I didn't regret leaving, but I didn't look forward to it either. I was simply going.

At the last minute I ran into the kitchen for my electric coffeepot. I guess that shows how unprepared I was for my future. Somehow I thought, where I would be going they wouldn't have coffeepots. And I had to have my morning coffee. I knew Beverly and Jay would be irritated because I couldn't fit it into my valise, but that coffeepot was necessary to my well-being.

Garrity drove me to the bus depot, pleading with me not to go. I felt how much I loved him, but it was already fading. I had to find out. I had to try.

Jay, Beverly, and I made the three-day drive across the country, and met Ty and Jean in New York as we had planned. Our happy reunion was shortlived, because we were in a rush to find a place where we could make our plans unobserved.

There then followed one of the most ridiculous fiascoes of my life. We drove to the Lower East Side, to St. Mark's Place, thinking it was scuzzy and crowded enough so that we could swim there like fish in the sea. I went to the Valencia Hotel, but they wouldn't rent me a room; they told me they didn't allow prostitution. The same at the other hotels. There didn't seem to be a place where we could meet to discuss how to go about going under. When we finally did find a place, the meeting was incredibly short, and intolerably excruciating, for me. I could not help but notice that our collective would contain two couples and myself. That fact concerned me.

"What am I going to do every night, after we have finished making bombs for the day, and the four of you retire into your separate bedrooms, lay whispering and fucking, and I roll around sexually frustrated all by myself?" I asked. "How will I get to meet people? Will I just be able to trot down to the corner bar, and pick somebody up? No. I won't be able to bring them back to our apartment, and I won't be able to go with them, because soon they will want to know something about me, and I will have nothing to tell them. I'll just be alone, month after month."

My very real concern was met by disdain on the part of my best friends. Ty and Jean had the sensible, easy answer.

"We'll all trade off. It won't be contrived or forced like it was in the old Weatherman collective; it will be nice because we're all so close." Beverly and Jay agreed to this willingly, to my surprise. All four of them sat there grinning at me. I felt sick. Once again, I would have to admit to that awful perversity of mine. I simply was not sexually attracted to any of them, as much as I loved them. I had no desire at all to sleep with any of them. My sexual desires came from a different part of me than my revolutionary ideals, from a baser, more primitive part. Many times I grimaced the morning after sleeping with some sleazy wreck of a man. But I had long ago given up trying to understand my sexual whimsy. It drove me relentlessly, out of control, sick and unsatiable, and all I could do was feed it. For my cunt I preferred muscles to brains, good looks to good nature, facile wit to understanding. My friends were too good for me to desire sexually.

"No, that won't work. I can't do it," I said, and they looked horror-struck.

Then started my last criticism session, the worst I had ever been through. For these were the people who loved me most, and from their mouths poured all the venom I had heard so many times before. Humbled, and disgusted with myself, I could finally see how unready I was for Weatherman, how weak I was, how shallow, how defeated. I looked at them through my tears and envied their love, envied them the position of having their decision already made for them. For Ty and Jean, for Beverly and Jay there was no turning back. But for me, the doors had not yet swung closed.

The criticism session came and went. I saw the contempt on their faces; most keenly I saw the disappointment in Jean's eyes. Of all of them, she loved me most. She felt my failure was partially her fault; she could not understand such a dead despair as mine.

I left them, not looking back, knowing how angry they were, knowing it was over for me.

I went to the apartment of an old boy friend; the door swung open and Georgia stood there, thin, pale, nervous, and with a cigarette dangling from her shaking hand. I almost fainted with surprise.

"I thought you were underground?" I said questioningly.

She told me the terrible story of her past month and a half since leaving Seattle.

"I was working in a New York collective. It was horrible. Pure torture. We worked twenty-four hours a day, lived on soup and beans, slept on the floor. No one listened to us; the criticism sessions were brutal. Then one day I was taking a bath and the pigs knocked down the front door. They burst into the bathroom and hauled me out of the tub. They made all of us line up in the living room. They were searching for Weathermen. Then they told us about the town house explosion; it had happened that day. They questioned us for a long time, and then tore the place apart looking for explosives, but they found nothing. They told us we had to clear out of the apartment.

"I had no money, no clothes, no place to stay. A Movement person told me about this place, and I came here about a week ago. Before that I roamed the streets at night, sleeping on park benches, picking cigarette butts off the streets. I don't know anyone here. I've never been so miserable, so lonely.

"Now I'm a go-go dancer." She looked down while she said this, embarrassed. How amazing that Georgia was still basically so straight that she could be mortified by being a go-go dancer.

I told her that Ty, Jean, Jay and Beverly were in town, that we had come here initially to form a collective together, but that I had decided not to stay with them because they were all monogamous. She got very excited and wanted to see them. I felt it would be good for her. Maybe she would form the collective with them. She left and

254 WITH THE WEATHERMEN

I didn't see her for several days. When I did see her briefly, she told me they had not been able to organize a satisfactory collective and Beverly and Jay had left abruptly, disenchanted with Weatherman, the underground, and the Movement in general. She had no idea where Ty and Jean were going or what they intended to do. Georgia herself was more bitter than ever.

I was terribly shaken by what Georgia had told me. What I had feared seemed to be true: life in the underground amounted to nothing but terror, police harassment, self-torture, loneliness, and bitter frustration. Compared to that my life in Seattle with Sundance had been like Paradise.

For three weeks I stayed in New York, finding out what I thought it was like to be underground. I didn't contact my parents or any of my friends. I stayed alone in the apartment, doing little, going out only at night. New York is the loneliest place if you don't know anybody. People passing by me would appear to avoid my gaze. I didn't know how to start conversations with strangers. In restaurants, if somebody looked at me too long, I would think he was a pig, and leave. Eyes were everywhere, boring into my head, glancing swiftly away, intently fastening on my face, peering through the skin to see what was hiding in my mind.

One day I talked to myself in a mirror; I hadn't spoken a word for a week. One week I went to see *Midnight Cowboy* three times; there were two people who knew how I felt. The terror of helplessness. The helplessness of hopelessness. The hopelessness of loneliness.

Finally I couldn't stand it any more. I phoned Sundance. Chip answered the phone.

"Chip, Chip, it's me, Susan. I want to come home. Please, may I come back to Sundance?"

"Of course you can, come whenever you want."

The next day I visited the Columbia campus. Someone there told me that I was an unindicted co-conspirator in the Chicago Weatherman indictments for the Days of Rage. Somehow I was flattered. Well, at least to J. Edgar I was threatening. Someone was taking me seriously. But I also suddenly realized that the odds were mounting up against me. Pretty soon I would have no choice about going underground. An unindicted co-conspirator could be indicted at any time; I was already facing fifty years in jail; any more time added to that would be disastrous for me.

I took a late flight out of New York the night of April 15, arriving in Seattle about three o'clock in the morning of April 16. When I let myself into the Sundance house, I discovered an attractive young man sleeping in my bed in the living room. Not having fucked in three weeks, I was more than ready. I gently shoved the man over, waking him up in the process. He smiled at me, and wordlessly, not knowing each other, we made love.

Joe woke me early that morning, hugged and squeezed me and we sat out on the porch in the warm sun. I asked a million questions about what had happened while I was gone. He never asked about my experiences and I never volunteered the information. In less than two weeks Ty and Jean would not have reported for their trial in Seattle. It was imperative that no one know that I had seen them, that no one have a clue to their whereabouts.

Things had changed drastically at Sundance. After I left, the collective had partially split up; Chip and Lisa, the woman he had lived with on and off for years, had moved to Ballard to resume organizing there. Abeles had gotten a house on Capitol Hill and moved in with several of the Anarchists; it was euphemistically called the Rebel House. The women who had considered themselves part of Sundance had become increasingly incensed over the male chauvinism of the men from Ithaca, and had moved en masse into the red house to the left of Sundance, and formed an all-woman collective called Fanshen. In the Sundance house remained the new Sundance collective: Joe, Bé-Bé, and several new men from Ithaca. The Dude had moved into a newly formed collective with some serious hardworking SLFers. Lerner had his own collective built around his tax initiative proposal to shift the tax burden from workers to the wealthy. The Weatherman rejects—those people who had been purged before the group went underground—were still scrounging around, living in the Fortress. Joe had heard that they were continually besieged with crabs and clap, and were doing nothing politically. Mike Justesen and Roger Lippman had not been seen. Robby had also disappeared.

Joe and I decided together to pull Sundance into shape, and we made plans to call a collective meeting that night to try and establish some kind of project that the collective could work on as a whole. Joe felt that the SLF was in danger of collapse, as its goals had become obscured; people did not seem to understand the necessity for long-range planning and in-depth work.

Around eleven o'clock we prepared to go to a high school rally that would hopefully prelude a high school strike. I discovered Zelda in a corner of the driveway. Hal had returned her; he didn't like riding around in Susan Stern's car; all the pigs tailed him and that made him paranoid as hell. Zelda was much the worse for the wear. Abeles had driven her one day and accidentally shifted into reverse and accelerated before the right door was closed. The open door hit a telephone pole and had been ripped completely off. Now it was fastened by a seatbelt to the rest of the car. There were also a half-dozen dents that hadn't been there when I had left.

On our way to the rally we got very stoned. The top was down, and I lay back and looked at the clear blue sky. Up front, I heard Joey muttering.

"Jesus, this is a setup. Look at all these pigs." I sat up and looked around, but I didn't see any pig cars.

"Joey, you're so paranoid. There are probably just a couple of pigs here in case of any violence."

"No, the place stinks with pigs. I can see them at all the corners."

I thought he was ridiculous, and got out of the car and sat down on the grass, plucking a long blade from the school lawn, and chewing on it. It was such a beautiful day, and I was soooooooooo-stooooooooned. And so glad to be back in Seattle.

The rally turned out not to be a rally at all, but a rather antagonistic football game between black and white high school students. There was more tackling than anything else, and it was sad to see the racism on both sides of the two teams.

Joey suddenly couldn't stand it any more. He kept muttering, "Where's Abeles, this is his thing, why ain't he here," and pacing around, seeing pigs lurking behind all the trees. "Let's leave," he said, so firmly that I decided it was easier to leave than to argue with him. We got into the car; Joe driving, Bé-Bé sitting next to him, and the man I had shared my bed with and I sitting in the back seat. I was still chewing on my blade of grass, thanking my lucky stars that I was not cursed with paranoia.

We started down the street slowly.

"There's a pig following us," Joe said tensely. I knew enough not to look around; you never look around if you think a pig is following you; that will alert him that you are uneasy. Instead I glanced in the rear-view; there was a white car tailing us closely.

We stopped at a stop sign. From nowhere, five white cars surrounded us, and before I could take the blade of grass out of my mouth, twenty FBI agents with guns drawn were around the car; one muttered, "This must be Stern," and yanked me out, pulled my arms behind my back and I felt the tight cold click of handcuffs; they had me jammed up against the car. I saw them pull Joey out, and handcuff him. I couldn't repress this awful urge to giggle; it all seemed so ludicrous.

"What are we being arrested for?" I heard Joey ask.

"Yeah, you're supposed to repeat our charges," I said, the blade of grass sticking to the corner of my mouth.

This puny FBI agent with a Jewish beak told me to shut up, they'd inform me of the charges on the way downtown.

I looked at Joey and laughed. He laughed. It seemed so funny. When was somebody going to scream, cut, retake, and let us out of those fucking handcuffs?

On the way downtown, the punk with the Jewish nose, who introduced himself as Sidney, told me I was indicted for conspiracy to destroy federal property; the property was the Federal Courthouse, and that I was further indicted for crossing state lines to incite a riot. "That's the H. Rap Brown Act," he told me with great satisfaction.[3]

There were four pigs and I in the car. I was sitting in the back seat between Sidney and another FBI. They all appeared to be extremely nervous; Sidney kept reaching behind my back to check the cuffs. One of the men in front kept his hand on his gun inside his jacket the entire time. They all looked at me as if I would suddenly metamorphose into

Superwoman, break the cuffs, slay them all with my cyanide fingernails, and fly away to Istanbul.

I laughed all the way to jail! It was all so absurd. Conspiracy. That
was a good one. Sidney fidgeted and told me he was sorry he had to
do this. "It's nothing personal, you know," and he tried to smile, but
he was too nervous. I wisecracked about good Germans and looked
at him in amazement; he was petrified of me; they all were. The one
sitting in front, who had turned around to face the back seat, paled
as I stared at him. Sidney was sweating profusely. Frightened? Of
me?

Downtown, at the entrance to the Federal Courthouse, there was
a large crowd, mostly of reporters, TV men, photographers. How
the hell had they known? A bunch of fucking bloodhounds, sniffing
out everybody's personal business. I machoed it out. My hair short,
my dark glasses hiding my eyes, a man's shirt covered by a V-neck
sweater, tight jeans, and a scarf tied around my neck, I looked like a
butch in the newspaper pictures. But I was smiling, and I gave the
fist and chanted with Joe close behind me. Ho, Ho, Ho Chi Minh,
Vietnam is gonna win.

They took me into a large room filled with a dozen desks. They
made me sit at one desk, and Joey at another. I leaned back against
the swivel chair and put my feet on the desk. Joe had his feet on his
desk. FBI men came in and studied us intently. One wandered over
to me, sat on the desk, smiled, offered me a cigarette which I
accepted and then said,

"Where's Bernardine Dohrn?"

I began laughing uncontrollably. So did Joe. The man shifted
uncomfortably on the desk, the smile was replaced with a deep
frown, and he swung around and walked out of the room.

A few minutes later Abeles was led in. We all cheered, and gave
each other the fist. He called a lawyer, the same one Joey and I had
called. Then, swigging on a Coke, Abeles related to us the story of
his arrest. Pure Abeles. He had been arrested for speeding, taken to
jail for not having a license, then held, and finally rearrested for conspiracy. His mind blown, he nevertheless was treating the situation
with the same disdain Joey and I were affecting.

We had been there about an hour when the Dude was brought in, spitting and raving that he would sue the government. "This is really serious, you guys," he said angrily when he saw our flippant attitudes. But even the ultra-paranoid Dude couldn't keep a serious perspective for long. "These guys are ridiculous. We can't even agree on the time of day," he said, and joined in the banter.

His arrest was hilarious. Hearing the news, he first thought of protecting Chip, who was out of town. So he deployed a car to intercept Chip. The car waited on the freeway, and after several hours, Chip drove by, was duly intercepted and taken to a friend's house to hide. Then the Dude, ever cautious about security, began to clear the guns out of the house. He was caught with a shotgun and a rifle, trying to escape through a bedroom window.

Bé-Bé was in the house when the FBI came for the Dude, having driven Zelda back to Sundance after Joe and I were arrested, stopping long enough to get two cases of beer to sustain him through the ordeal. Just as he entered the house the phone rang; it was Anne Anderson.

"Annie, everyone's been busted," Bé-Bé told her excitedly. Anne told him she was coming immediately. As Bé-Bé hung up, he looked out the window and saw five cars careening up the hill. Then twenty FBI agents jumped out of the cars, guns drawn. Bé-Bé walked out to the porch and asked,

"What do you want; what's going on here?"

"Who's in charge here?" they asked.

"Nobody's in charge here. We're all just kind of hanging out. Do you have a search warrant?"

They said yes. By this time they had handcuffed Dude and were taking him away. The search warrant, they said, was for "approximately forty-seven sticks of dynamite. . ."

Bé-Bé told the stunned people sitting in the living room to each grab an FBI and make sure he didn't plant anything. So each agent was followed by an SLFer as they tore the house apart, looking for dynamite.

They found our sawed-off shotgun. Bé-Bé, a little drunk at the time, told them it was his duck-hunting gun, but they confiscated it anyway. The people in the house hassled and fucked with the FBI agents as they raked though the rooms. They found a bunch of booby traps. Bé-Bé tried to tell them you could catch a whole lot of ducks with booby traps.

Finally the FBI left. As they were getting into their cars, someone threw a beer bottle at them. When the bottle smashed on the ground, they whirled around, pulling out their guns. One FBI said, "If anyone throws anything else, I'll plug them." Bé-Bé then began calling lawyers and SLF collectives to make sure they knew about the bust.

Lerner was brought in a few minutes after Dude. Chip was not captured for two days, when he made a speech at a rally, then went to the Century Tavern for a drink, where the FBI arrested him. Roger Lippman was in jail in Berkeley at the time of the bust. Mike Justesen was the eighth conspiracy member; he was never found.

We laughed and joked, until they took us and put us all in jail without bail. Then we became a conspiracy case. We became a symbol of fascist repression. We became a cause. We would thereafter be known as the Seattle 7.

Suddenly I was someone. I knew I was someone because there were so many people hanging around me, asking me questions, looking to me for answers, or just looking at me, offering to do things for me, to get some of the glow from the limelight. Half a dozen lawyers came to visit me in jail, asking if they could take the case. Newspapers across the country carried my pictures along with those of the other defendants. Reporters came to the jail to interview me. A priest came to comfort me; law students attempted to get credentials to visit me. My cellmates gave me their commissary, telling the other inmates, "I'm in the cell with Susan Stern. You know, from that conspiracy thing, the Seattle 7."

When they came to let me out on personal recognizance after five days, the steps in front of the Federal Courthouse were jammed with newspapermen, TV cameramen, FBI agents, undercover investigators, and our supporters. They descended upon us like vultures, pulling at us, cawing, "Please, a statement, what does it feel like, what will this mean for the SLF, are you guilty?"

"Shit no, I'm not guilty," I screamed into a mike. "Nixon's the real conspirator—him and all the other capitalists—Rockefeller, Mitchell; they conspire against the people of the world."

"We're going to ignore this whole ridiculous thing," Chip told them. "The SLF is not finished; our work will go on. The government is trying to harass us with this farcical conspiracy charge—it's not going to stop us."

"We're going to keep on trucking, shucking, and jiving with the people, hanging out, getting stoned and organizing," Joey said, smiling and dimpling, his furry head bobbing up and down as he trucked a little for the fans.

Abeles, his hair spiraling, shouted, "TDA was only a warmup—the next one will be even bigger."

Lerner turned green when Abeles said that, grabbed the mike, and began very lucidly, as if he was addressing a class,

"We're going to fight this indictment by building a popular base for the SLF's politics in Seattle's working class. The government is afraid of us because they know that when people hear about our tax initiative, they'll get the message that the left is really on their side and not just a bunch of window trashers."

The Dude grabbed the mike from him. "We're going to fight this thing tooth and nail. The people won't let us go down."

Joey was asking people for joints, and smiling at the young women clustered in the crowd; Abeles was vying with Dude for the mike. Chip wanted to go to the Century Tavern and get drunk; Joey, Abeles, and Dude concurred. I wanted desperately to find someone to fuck. Lerner was sizzling to start shopping for lawyers. "This is our lives," he repeated plaintively. "Don't you understand. We're facing twenty years in prison. Don't you understand. We have to find a lawyer. Now I suggest we all go to my house and begin to discuss . . ."

"We'll meet you at your house in a half an hour, Lerner," Chip told him casually; and he, Dude, and Joey ambled off together, Abeles trailing desperately behind them, asking, "Hey, where are you guys going? I want to go too." Just as they were about to get into the car, Joey whirled around.

"Where's Susan, come on, Susan." I began to move toward the car. Joey grabbed my hand and squeezed it, and pulled me in on his lap. "Don't worry," he whispered in my ear. "If your ship goes down, I'll be right there with you." I snuggled down against him, profoundly grateful that he realized how confused and lonely I was.

I was in with the boys. Being part of the same trial, living in the same house, I was with them constantly. I was privy to many of their "backroom" sessions; hours they spent together smoking dope and telling stories from the good old days at Cornell, each outshouting the other until it was impossible to understand anything at all. They loved to tell those stories to a select audience, who would sit captivated and watch them perform, unable to stop laughing with them, yet unable to become really a part of them. Chip and Joe, Joe and Chip. They argued constantly over who was Butch Cassidy and who was the Sundance Kid.

That ended with the conspiracy bust. Chip became much more serious, and tended to ally himself with Lerner, and anti-Weatherman sentiments. Joey and I became inseparable; there must be hundreds of newspaper clippings and photos taken during those first few months after the arrest; on all of them Joey and I are side by side. Dude and Abeles were the two youngest, but Dude, being more articulate, commanded more respect; Abeles was regarded as something of a pest by everyone except Joey, who found it hard to dislike anybody. Roger Lippman was barely tolerated by almost everyone. He and Lerner did a lot of research during the trial. Mike Justesen was never found; we got two tape recordings from him which we played at fund-raising events. In them he gave us his love and support and strength; in them he told us he was alive and well in America. In them he told us he would never change his position for ours. My role among the defendants was unique, since I was the only woman. The "lone woman defendant" they would call me a hundred times in the newspapers.

We were on a merry-go-round from the time of our arrest until the time we finally went to prison. It never stopped once. It whirled very fast until the trial began, and then slowed during the year and a half of appeal; but there was no way to end the dizzy ride. My position as the only woman made the entire experience harder for me than any of the men. Chip, Joey, Abeles, and Dude had each other, in prison and out; their friendships were strained terribly by the trial, but it was more sustaining than debilitating. Lerner had Chip for all intents and purposes; the two intellectuals discussed things in realms none of the rest of us could understand or were interested in. I had no one. No other woman to go through that experience with me. No one to whom I could turn and be afraid with, no one with whom I could discuss strategy from a female point of view. And finally, no one but me to undertake the tremendous responsibility of being the female voice which would be carried to other women across the country. All the heavy Weatherwomen were underground since the town house explosion; it was my voice which would be heard at rallies, mine in classrooms, mine in newspaper interviews, radio talk shows, and over the news. I had to know something, since I had been singled out by the government; other women wanted to know what I knew.

Joey helped as much as a man possibly could. He was the only one of all the defendants who really understood how difficult my situation was. Throughout the whole experience, he included me in everything; he was my entry into the realm of the boys. But he was not enough. As strong as our friendship was, he was limited to understanding my needs, my frailties, my strengths from a man's dimension; I hungered from the beginning for a woman.

Anne Anderson arrived on the day I got out of jail. I eyed her from a distance for those first few days. I saw a plump woman of twenty-two with a wide-open face and electric hair. I saw a woman very much in love with Joe Kelly, hurt and puzzled that he would ignore her for a dozen other women who barely knew him. I saw a woman who very capably and efficiently began to work with Chip on organizing law students to begin research, and who began to hunt down potential lawyers. I saw a woman whose smile lit up every room she entered, and whose energy filled it like a rose, sweet and sensual; whose laughter pounded out, making me want to giggle too, who never seemed to be too tired or too bored to listen; who made sense whenever she spoke. The more I watched her, the more she intrigued me. When I finally heard that she had worked at the Weatherbureau and had just come from Chicago, I decided to try to get to know her.

I loved Anne immediately. She became my friend. She gave me the greatest gift one person can give to another. She taught me how to love. She helped me flower, petal by precious petal; she watered and nurtured and lit my soul with her sunny smile until I bloomed.

Weatherman brought us together. We felt we were a little Weather oasis in a political desert.

"All these guys have shitty politics," was about the first thing Anne ever said to me.

"Maybe together we can do something about it," was my overture, and on that basis we formed a partnership. Anne and Susan. Susan and Anne. We immediately billed ourselves as the Macho Mamas, and were seen by our friends as a couple. We never did anything alone; we were partners. I only left Anne after that to go to make speeches or to go to jail.

We struggled to bring Weatherman politics into everything. It wasn't hard. The spring and summer of 1970 was the high point of the Movement; the response to Kent State in the beginning of May superseded any previous political activity on the part of white America. Anne and I stirred up Weatherman support and politics wherever we went. We became a thorn in the side of Sundance, the SLF and the conspiracy. We were so loud, obnoxious, militant, unruly, drugged that no one could stand to be around us; no one could keep up with us, at any rate.

From the moment we got out of prison a bonafide conspiracy trial, the Seattle 7 could agree on nothing. Lerner wanted a big-shot lawyer like Michael Kennedy or Bill Kunstler: he arranged for Kennedy to come to Seattle, but Kennedy wasn't interested in the trial. The rest of us more or less agreed that we wanted local lawyers, not star types, but those we could develop politically. Chip vacillated, although it was less important to him since he knew from the beginning that he would go pro se—he would defend himself. I wanted a female lawyer; none were available.

We finally settled on four lawyers. Jeff Steinborn was a twenty-six-year-old attorney with a very prestigious Seattle firm; a Yale graduate, he was considered something of a prodigy. When he met us, he had made his reputation defending draft cases; so his politics were considered sympathetic. Anne latched onto him immediately, took him out to the Sundance house, and the boys finished the job by telling him so many funny stories that he knew he had to stay with us no matter what it cost him; we were an alternative to his increasingly stagnating life.

Lee Holly was about thirty-five and had a great deal of experience in legal research. He did most of the research for the case. Anne spent weeks compiling it with him. Out of his research he wrote dozens of magnificent legal motions for our case.

Carl Maxey was the compromise between Lerner and the rest of us. He was running against Scoop Jackson for senator when he became our lawyer; he was the most respected lawyer in the state of Washington, and he was black. In his early fifties, he was older, which made him venerable in the judge's eyes. He also had a good rapport with judges, and since he was admittedly liberal, and a staunch Democrat, it was thought that he would offset the youthful enthusiasm of Jeff and Lee.

Our final lawyer was for Lerner's sake, although he was indispensable to the case. Lerner wanted flash and name; he got it in Mike Tigar. His major claim to fame was some work he had done on the Chicago 8 trial. He was a young genius who could remember whole sections from lawbooks he hadn't read since law school. Mike was a veritable almanac of legal technicality. He was handsome, liberal, and a very good lawyer. He, along with all the other lawyers, believed in the legal system; he believed in American justice; he thought we could win the case legally, that justice would win out against an unfair and unconstitutional law.

Getting lawyers was just the beginning. Let me tell you, running a conspiracy trial is like running a Broadway play; you need stars, secondary characters, and then stagehands. The legal assistants were the major stagehands; they were mostly law students. I first became aware of them at Mike Abeles' birthday party; they came to it to interview witnesses to TDA. With their yellow lined legal pads, they trotted around among the drunk and stoned SLFers, who were doing everything in their power to maintain life as usual in spite of the conspiracy. Sundance roared that night; the Paisanos stood in a great drunken circle in the middle of the black living room, screaming Pie, Pie, Paisano, and stamping their feet; in the back room, people were shoveling mountains of THC up their noses; Garrity was distributing some brown liquid cocaine; the bathtub was filled to the top with beer cans; people were fucking in heaps in all three houses, on the back seats of cars, under the steps, in all the beds. In the midst of all this, the law students persistently queried witnesses, struggling to save the lives of seven people who were doing everything in their power to have themselves put away for life. One of the law students tried to question me; I thought he was a pig, and went running to Anne; I found her kissing Garrity. I stopped, shocked, but the anticipated jealousy didn't come. Anne was, after all, Anne; she knew a good thing when she saw it!

There were about twenty law students working on our case; they never got paid a cent, and they did their work on top of the demands of their own school work. They worked for six months prior to the trial, all through it, and right through the appeal. I never even bothered getting to know any of them until after I was out of jail, almost two years later.

Then there was the defense collective. It formed out of a collective Lerner organized in early September. It was composed of people entirely new to politics; this trial was their introduction to the political left. They were the shit workers par excellence. If ever a group of people were abused and exploited, it was the defense collective. We had discovered that it took lots of money to run a trial, and that also like a Broadway show, sponsors wanted to be sure of success before they would part with some dinero. The defense collective arranged for money; they wrote letters for contributions, put ads in newspapers and magazines, helped organize fund-raising speeches for the defendants. The boys were very good about meeting with the defense collective; I was very bad about it. I never once sat through an entire meeting; claiming illness, I would leave at the first opportunity. As with the law students, I barely recognized the existence of the defense collective; I hardly knew their names until after the trial was over and they hated almost all the defendants.

The show must go on. That's what happens when you're a star. Get your period, get a headache, fall in love, fall out, get no sleep, get no dinner, get no rest, get no time to yourself, get no time alone. Get up, get dressed, look ravishing, look happy, look energetic, look as though you aren't scared to death. Drive to make this speech; race to talk to that class; tell it like it is. Make it sound so exciting, so groovy that everyone will go out and tear apart a federal courthouse and get charged with conspiracy. Pretty soon there will be so many conspiracy trials, the government won't know what to do with all of them. Bong up the works, let's all be the conspiracy.

Go to meetings with lawyers, and meetings with the defense collective; go to meetings with just defendants. Go to fundraising functions; go to demonstrations. Go-Go-Go-Go-Go.

I whirled on the merry-go-round. The pace was brutal. On May 1, Air Force ROTC was attacked and set on fire; I helped to organize the demonstration. Then Joey and I took off for a three-day tour of Washington State to organize new liberation fronts and start riots. My rallying cry was "Sex, dope, and violence." Wherever I went the people loved me.

On May 6, thousands blocked the Seattle Freeway in response to Kent State, the culmination of a week of demonstrations and actions to protest the invasion of Cambodia.[1] Joey and I rushed home from eastern Washington in time for a nighttime rally. I made a speech in an attempt to provoke a riot at the U of W. I was out of my head with militancy; there was nothing but the struggle. Arrest, imprisonment didn't seem to threaten me or any of the other defendants with the exception of Lerner.

On May 21 the Weatherman underground issued its first communiqué. Chip played it during a fund-raising rock-and-roll concert. I held Anne's hand and cried as I listened to the tape of Bernardine's voice. I had goosebumps. It was like a voice from heaven, from the future, a voice that no American law could silence. Anne and I looked at each other deeply; we were proud to have been Weatherpeople.

The end of May the boys went East on a speaking tour. I went to Berkeley and made my first bigtime speech. I spoke to ten thousand students along with Lerner, Jerry Rubin, and Bill Kunstler. Everybody was mightily impressed with me and my speech.

On June first Joe Kelly was found guilty in Chicago of six counts of aggravated battery for a Weatherman action and was sent to Cook County jail for three months. His cellmate was Russ Neufeld. Russ

Neufeld told Joey that he was very sorry that he had once kicked me out of Weatherman.

At nine o'clock the morning of June 9, I woke up to some noise out in the living room. I got out of bed wearing nothing but a tee shirt, and without my glasses. I walked into the living room. First I saw Bé-Bé. He was wringing his hands and saying, "I'm sorry, Susan, I'm sorry." Then I saw Sidney, with his gun drawn, and his hand shaking, sweating. "Oh, no, not again," was all I could say. But it was again. Another federal conspiracy bust, this time for organizing the May 1 attack on the ROTC building. There were seven other defendants; among them were Abeles, and Garrity. The mother-fuckers wouldn't even let me get dressed in privacy; a dozen of them stood there stupidly with their guns drawn, looking green, and jumping nervously whenever I flickered an eyelash. Apparently the word was that I was a super-dangerous criminal, capable of any number of maniacal and sadistic tricks, an escape artist on a par with Houdini, with a streak of cruelty comparable to Aleister Crowley's. They watched me dress, cuffed me, frisked me, checked the cuffs, took off my glasses and drove me downtown, booked me, and brought me to the same cell. All the prostitutes thronged around me. "Ain't that the shits, girl—you mean they done bust you *agin?* You too much, bitch. You too fucking much."

From my perch on the top bunk of the now familiar cell, number 603, I didn't think I was too much. I thought I was done for. It was all beginning to catch up with me. My white-skin privilege was wearing thin. My days were numbered.

But my spirit was undimmed. They made me wait several hours on the day they released me. I sang freedom songs at the top of my lungs; I started a fire, and smoked out the entire FBI office. The pigs told Anne they were terrified of me. "There's this awful look in her eye; we never turn our back on Susan Stern." Anne drove me home; it was the first of a dozen times that she would pick me up from jail, drive me home, and pull me back together. Anne's love followed me into courtrooms and jail cells from coast to coast; it pervaded my thickest rhetoric, and my deepest depressions. Throughout the whole tumultuous episode, it was the one stabilizing thing in my life. Anne and Seattle; safety, love, home.

I was undaunted by the second arrest. More than ever I pretended that nothing was wrong with my life.

In the middle of June, Sundance finally dissolved completely. Anne and I moved into a little house on Brooklyn Avenue near Ravenna Park just at the edge of the U District. It was a quiet street, and a precious house. Garrity and his new girl friend moved in with us; Georgia had returned to Seattle from New York; she also moved in with us. Indian and a bunch of his wild friends made our home their pleasure dome. I got myself a boy friend and spent my nights with him, my days with Anne. I got another dog, a black and white ball of fluff named Go-Go, after my profession. My life was a frantic round of activity.

Anne and I lived in two separate realities that summer. To the world at large we were the Macho Mamas. We drugged. We drank. We roared. We swaggered. We were crude and vulgar. We fucked everything we could get our hands on. We took a hit of acid and THC every day. We cooked food for hippies on the hill; that was our contribution to politics. We went to as few meetings as possible. We took nothing seriously. We had forgotten the revolution. Everything was boggy, boggy, more reds. That was the image we sent out to the world. Then there was the reality.

We purchased a hundred-pound sack of fertilizer containing a lot of nitrates. We took the bag to the deserted Sundance house and spent hours drying it slowly in the oven. Then we mixed it carefully with diesel fuel and put it into gallon jars. We found a chemist who knew something about demolitions. He introduced us to detonators, to timing devices, to dynamite, to theory on demolitions. I ordered a dozen copies of the *Bombers Handbook,* and read it three times. I read government manuals on bombing; I learned everything there was to know on the subject.

The chemist drove us to the mountains once a week. Anne and I planted our fertilizer under bridges and tree stumps, under rocks and beside streams. In the still mountain darkness, we lit homemade fuses, and detonators, then we ran and hid. Great explosions rent the air, and big craters replaced the rocks and bridges and tree stumps. We had visions of IBM and Boeing going up in pieces; we hated America. We wanted to raze it and start all over again.

We never told anyone. No one. It was our secret world; the hub of our friendship. We were Weatherwomen, leading dual lives. Let them think we were the Macho Mamas, let the pigs think we did nothing but party and take dope; our hearts were in the hills, with our bombs; our hearts were underground, with the Weathermen.

Meanwhile, two collectives in Seattle had been formed with politics similar to Weatherman. It was all very confusing. Basically they did nothing but bother Anne and me about not being political enough. They were led by Roger and Robby. At one point Anne and I were almost ready to join, but then we were informed by Robby and Roger that we had to be in separate collectives because we were monogamous.

Anne and I couldn't take it. We refused to be separated, and not by Roger and Robby. We felt we had made a major breakthrough with our friendship; it was a beautiful example to women everywhere in Seattle of what two women could be to each other, of how to build a life without men as the major focus. We were not about to let Roger and Robby destroy it.

Some of those people from the two new collectives I had known in New York. Now they were in Seattle with different identities. One day I walked into my house and there was Barbara from Columbia, except now her name was Sally. Another day, a man was sitting in my living room; his name was Tim, only now it was Tom, and so on. Robby was part of the identity crisis. His thinning hair was dyed a ludicrous henna, which was growing out, so that an inch from the scalp was light brown; dozens of others walked around with bleached heads, for no special reason except that everybody thought everyone else was a pig, and they didn't want to be visible. Their very attempts at disguise made them as obvious as a purple star.

Anne and I lived through the summer high on the hog. Our lives were full, although politically we did little. Basically, we were vacationing.

But we were frenzied. Umpteen million meetings, legal research, fund raising, press work. Vague involvement with work other collectives were engaged in. There were still over a dozen functioning SLF collectives, although most revolutionary fervor had evaporated after Kent State. These collectives were organizing women's centers, building a free medical center on Capitol Hill, organizing against I-90, a freeway scheduled to run through the Central District, working with GIs at Fort Lewis, pulling together a union of the unemployed, working on welfare rights, running a free store in Georgetown, a white industrial slum on the outskirts of Seattle, planning a theater group, and circulating an anti-war, anti-tax initiative. Abeles still had his high school Rebel collective, which did little but steal to live, and Chip was stuck in Ballard with Stone Rage which was a stone drag; Joey went hiking a lot, and Dude was getting stoned in the Grode house. My house became known as the Fifty-sixth Street Gang, and once a week, we cooked up a great meal for the hippies on the Ave.

At night the collectives would gather at the Century Tavern, and smoke dope, drop acid, drink, and dance until the bar closed, when they would pour into my house around the corner to continue the festivities. For many of the people in those collectives, the summer was a long, unrelieved, unrewarding stint of hard work. For Anne and me it was Party City.

At the end of August SLF sponsored a rock festival. Sky River 3 was a good idea that boomeranged into a political debacle. Following on the heels of Altamont, rock festivals were already in ill repute. But this one, according to the men in the Seattle 7, was going to be political; that would make the difference. Every person who purchased a ticket, would be purchasing a piece of the lovely land the festival was to be held on. When all the land was bought, over a hundred thousand dollars' worth, the people would begin to build a socialist community. In the middle of America. Sky River was planned to last for ten days; part of the time there would be the traditional rock music and gang-bang; the rest of the time would be spent in political discussion.

The Fifty-sixth Street Gang took off for Sky River. On the surface it looked like every other rock festival to me, and I was happy to be there in the surging, stoned, drunken crowds of kids. But I was also frustrated; I thought there must be some key to transforming all the raw energy into revolutionary directions. All these kids seemed content just to hang in the sun, as they had in previous years.

There were differences which I noticed immediately as I meandered. One was the number of people passed out or lurching on reds; they looked ugly and sloppy, and I felt a twinge of remorse about my own ever increasing consumption of barbiturates.

Then there were the bikers hired to police the festival. My own dear Garrity had helped to make these delicious arrangements, since he was now a biker pledge. Everywhere were behemoth bikers with roaring bikes, tearing crazed and brutal through throngs of dazed, drugged kids; I had the feeling, as I walked around, that I had to be constantly wary.

And flying everywhere, to make the scene more bizarre, were Vietcong flags, testimony to the political spirit of the rock festival.

The music was mostly from local bands, and they weren't very good. The boys worked hard backstage, but I was already bored by the evening of the first day. In desperation I dropped two hits of acid, and began to roam again as night fell. I began to peak just as it got dark. Everywhere I went it was absolutely menacing. The bikers were still careening around; several times I pitched to the ground as they roared past me; men, lurching and disgusting, were grabbing at me from all directions; it was a constant struggle to escape their groveling hands. This had never happened to me at a rock festival before. Festivals used to represent to me a little oasis of my kind of life; I could wander naked and carefree among my people. Now I felt terrified; a piece of meat in the middle of a throng of ravening animals.

The acid was coming on too strong; I began to get frightened. There was too much going on around me. I saw a man selling reds; four for a dollar. I bought four, and popped one in my mouth. Over the loudspeaker, I heard a warning, one of many to come that night: "Beware of Mexican reds—they can contain ten times the normal dosage in a pill, while some contain very little barbiturate. Stay away from Mexican reds," and he went on to say they looked just like Lillys, but didn't have the tiny white Lilly trade name on them. In the dark it was impossible for me to read the tiny capsules anyway. I turned to head back up the hill to where SLF was camped.

I was jostled and slobbered over constantly on the long trek back to camp, and by the time I got there, it had begun to rain. I was so nervous and upset, so harried that I took the remaining three reds. For an hour I didn't feel anything, then suddenly I was being dragged down into that soggy barbiturate sleep. Like drowning.

I would half wake up, but I couldn't talk. I was aware of light, then of night; I was aware of heat, then of cold. Somebody was tugging at me, getting me up, slapping my face.

I had lain there for two days in the rain. Someone had thrown a blanket over me, and finally decided that I had better go home. My reds, it had turned out, were Mexican, and one or all of them had overdoses in them.

It took me a week to recover from my OD. During that time Sky River dragged on; Anne returned, sour and sniffling. The bikers had caused nothing but trouble; there had been a number of rapes. There were rumors that some of them had been gang rapes. She said everyone was disgusting and the whole rock festival thing had just disintegrated. SLF, and Sky River's sponsors lost thousands of dollars. The land was never bought. The people who paid their ten dollars felt cheated, since so many had gotten in free.

To me it signaled the end of an era. Dead the flower generation. Dead rock festivals. Dead the SLF. But I didn't stop to ponder it long. Too many parties, too many drugs, too many sunny Seattle days. Then suddenly it was too late.

The Fanshen Statement hit us like a ton of shit, shattering the frivolity of the summer. Circulated nationally by the female SLF dropouts, it was a castigation of the male members of the Seattle 7 for their role in Sky River, their manipulative and arrogant role in SLF, and their general brute characters. It was a vicious, scathing indictment of the boys, which was totally justifiable. The boys had a way of charming women with their political chic, treating them to epic fucks and the festival of life among the conspirators, taking their money—for the cause, of course—and then dropping them like hotcakes, frequently to pick up where they left off with their best friends. Like all other men, they had no idea how offensive they were. "How can you oppress someone when you're socking it to them?" pondered a bewildered Abeles when faced with Fanshen.

The problem with the Fanshen Statement was not with its contents but with its timeliness and the people it chose to censor. Singling out the Seattle 7 men did nothing but take the pressure off other men who were just as guilty of using politics as a sexual bait. It also made it almost impossible for the conspiracy men to function at a time when their lives depended upon it. Stupefied, depressed, insecure, and depleted, the men sat in our living room while Anne and I tried to placate them. But they seemed frozen. We were all packed in ice. The manic summer had passed; then a dreary, weary, dispirited fall was hurtling toward us, bringing rains, trials, and prison in its wake.

Suddenly we awoke from our sunbath, and we were alone. After Sky River, there were no more women in SLF; in fact, there was no more SLF. Everyone had wearied of the parties. The scene at the Century was getting stale. Everyone had hounded the heels of the men from Ithaca when they came, fresh and new to Seattle, bursting with energy and life, abounding in laughter and merriment. Everyone had followed willingly enough the motion as it splashed over Seattle ecstatically; everyone had stayed as long as the wine and laughter flowed; Seattle had followed the Pied Piper like thousands of rats, urging them constantly to greater revelry, because it meant more for them too.

Then, when the current began to ebb, the rats changed their tune. "These people have cheated us," they said. "They said the revolution would be fun, and it's not fun any more. They promised us the world and took our money. We've been had. Well, they won't get away with that." And they were gone, and all there was was the Fanshen Statement with its black and white castigation of the men, and a conspiracy trial that was scheduled to begin in two months.

It pours in Seattle. When the weather turns bad, it's bad. Anne and I were asked by our landlord to leave our little house. Our landlord had also rented the Sundance house; he had been subpoenaed to testify as a hostile witness at our trial. He felt he could not have us living in his house under those circumstances. We had a week to move.

I caught the flu that week. It was a strange flu, spreading through my entire body, exhausting and depressing me. I was constantly nauseated, and constantly famished. I was nervous and edgy. The flu hung on, and I didn't totally recover for weeks. Sluggish and cranky, I was forced into a new schedule; we were finally facing the trial.

Anne and I got jobs as barmaids at the Century Tavern early in September, just prior to the Fanshen Statement. We each worked there three or four nights a week. We enjoyed our work. At that time, the Century was still an SLF and Freak hangout, and we had plenty of ass and plenty of dope and wine. We ran the place. It was our turf. Many nights we showed up on MDA, the new psychedelic, which was animal tranquilizer, I think. Floating and speeding, I would serve beer and wine to all my friends; puffing on joints in the poolroom, drinking wine flips behind the bar, singling out my fuck for the night, corralling him, dragging him home along with Anne and her catch, getting them stoned, amazing and terrifying them with our Macho Mama routine, then dropping a couple of reds so that I could fuck them. In the morning I would stagger out of bed disgusted and sick, retch into the toilet a couple of times, and go to the Coffee Corral for breakfast.

The work load was staggering. The umpteen million meetings tripled. So did the speeches and fund-raising events. I spent a month organizing a speech for Bill Kunstler, we made $1,500.00 on his marvelous speech. Each member of the Chicago 8, one by one, came to Seattle to help us raise money by giving speeches. We gave a couple more rock concerts. We sponsored boat-ride parties around Lake Washington. At one party, SLF and Seattle 7 members were arrested; just for partying. The meetings were endless and monotonous. Most of the time was spent arguing either with Mike Lerner or Roger Lippman. Nobody agreed on anything. Everybody had their own idea about everything. According to communistic principles everybody had to be heard. You couldn't order someone to shut the fuck up, and slug him, like I wanted to do to Lerner and Lippman just about every meeting.

Early in the fall Lee Holly and Jeff Steinborn, the two younger lawyers, began to feud; they were always disagreeing at meetings. Carl Maxey disagreed with all the defendants about trial tactics; Mike Tigar had ideas of his own. The lawyers were afraid of a circus, like the Chicago 8 trial; the defendants wanted to go down with a bang and not a whimper.

We were audacious, stupid, bungling, brilliant, insensitive, insane, arrogant, and uncontrollable. We made a wreck of Jeff's conservative and respectable office, until they wouldn't allow us to hold our legal meetings there any more. Wherever we went, we impressed people either with our genius or our lunacy. No one was left unaffected.

In the middle of September, Anne and I moved our retinue to Seventh Avenue, right off the freeway. Garrity went to live with the bikers, and was replaced by a handsome, indolent man named Greg. Georgia remained with us. My flu still hung on, and I was generally run-down and depressed. But I never stopped the whirlwind of activities.

As the trial date drew near Lerner grew increasingly nervous, feeling that the rest of us were irresponsible and wouldn't focus on a rational trial strategy. He was for political confrontation in the courtroom, but he seemed unwilling to trust our collective wisdom on how to go about it. More and more meeting time was required to placate Lerner.

Other tensions developed. The defense collective became incensed at the outrageous activity of Abeles and Dude, as did every other house we went to. Led by Dude and Abeles, but followed by Bé-Bé, Joe, and Chip, the boys would stampede through the defense house, scavenge it for dope, raid the refrigerator, and, when the meeting had ended, leave the empty beer cans, wine bottles, and overflowing ashtrays and scraps of food in heaps all over the living room.

Sometime in October, I sat up in the middle of a particularly long and boring meeting, and told Joey I just had to have some gefilte fish with red horseradish. He gave me a weird look. The craving would not go away, so I sneaked out of the meeting, and went to the store and purchased it. I became a food addict. I would hoard food to eat when

I woke up ravenous at dawn, I ate myself through nights when a half a dozen barbs wouldn't put me to sleep, I would make huge breakfasts every morning for the house, escape to the Ave for immense lunches, and steal food for even bigger dinners. I ate steadily through meeting, after meeting, at work at the Century, and at two-thirty in the morning, when Anne and I would sit alone in our living room, smoking dope and cigarettes and go over the day's events.

One day it occurred to me that I hadn't spied a drop of menstrual blood in a long time. I tried to calculate how long, but time had lost all meaning. I had stopped using my birth control pills over the summer, testing out some theory I had about the accumulatory effects of birth control pills. Now, with the trial a mere month away, it suddenly dawned on me that I might be pregnant. A quick look in front of the mirror added to my growing suspicion; my breasts were big, very big. And I was fat, quite fat. I had been gorging for over a month now; and then there was that unexplained flu, lingering for six weeks. It all too clearly began to make sense.

I went to a doctor, was given a rabbit test and an internal. Negative. Anne insisted I see another doctor. I did, getting another internal, and two more rabbit tests. Both negative. If my calculations were correct, I would have been at least three months pregnant at that time; surely pregnant enough for two doctors to tell.

I dismissed the pregnancy theory. Yet my breasts continued to swell, and became so painful, that Anne finally gave me one of her bras. I began to wear it, for it hurt me to walk. I continued to gorge, and gained more weight. I got sleepier and sleepier, and more and more depressed. My back began to hurt. My feet began to ache. My body was telling me in a million different ways that it was inhabited by an invader, but I refused to listen to it. Medical science had said negative, not pregnant. I continued working, making speeches, taking speed when I was exhausted, taking acid and MDA, THC, downers, marijuana and drinking. I put on more and more makeup to cover the growing rings under my eyes; Anne made me a floor-length black skirt because I had outgrown all my other clothes, and I wanted to hide the growing bulge of my belly.

Anne was as busy as I was. She went to all the meetings, and stayed through them, while I went home to eat and sleep. She compiled most of Lee Holly's mountainous research, and Xeroxed it. Plus she worked at the Century, frequently filling in for me when I had to make a speech, or begged off because of illness. The house was going to ruin. Georgia was continuously traumatized and never cleaned. The boys would rampage through the house, eating all our food, leaving the usual mess. As the pace got more exhaustive, Anne and I had less time to clean. The signals began to flash; we were going down slow.

One day in the middle of October, I got up at six-thirty in the morning, and with Chip drove to Tacoma to make a speech at a community college. I had worked until two o'clock the night before, and had stayed up until three-thirty talking to Anne. Once at the campus, everybody listened mutely and stone-faced as Chip and I told them all about the conspiracy, and about the SLF, and the revolution, and so on. As I talked, I got angrier; they weren't moving a muscle. What a bunch of nurds. Not moving a fucking muscle. In desperation, I began to sing a freedom song; I began to sing and clap and dance around. Everybody looked shocked, and then slowly a little light burned in their eyes, and they began to clap with me. For a minute it looked as though they might get it on, but then that old glazed look spread over their eyes, and they slumped back into their seats, and turned off.

Before I'll be a slave
I'll be buried in my grave
And I'll fight
For my right
To be free.

The American people were already dead. They were past caring about freedom. Standing up there I suddenly felt that I had wasted my life, my youth; that as corrupt as my attempt had been, it had been an attempt nevertheless, and it had meant nothing. Nothing.

We drove to another campus, and another speech. I gave the speech, and then we spent the afternoon at a long, tedious meeting, during which Lerner argued that he no longer wanted the defense collective present. He thought some of them were pigs. A big argument commenced. The lawyers took the stance that democracy and justice entitled all to be present. Dude sided with Lerner. Abeles and Joey thought they had to be present; after all, they were doing most of the work. Chip vacillated as always, unwilling to offend anyone. I didn't want them present either, not only because I thought most of them were pigs, but because they complicated the entire proceedings by talking endlessly and knowing nothing. I was arrogant beyond description.

Nobody won completely. Sometimes they came to meetings, sometimes just the defendants met with their lawyers. Hard feelings and bad vibes were created all around. I detested Roger Lippman, I detested Mike Lerner. I detested Mike Tigar, and Lee Holly, I detested the defense collective, those peons. I myself was detestable, but I was too drugged to realize it.

After that meeting, which I ate and doped my way through, the boys and I dropped acid, and with a couple of terrified hangers-on, Joey drove us, careening in the pouring rain, to see *Woodstock*. We tripped though the movie, hit the Century around midnight, en masse, danced, drank and doped some more, and then went to KRAB radio station for a taping session on the developments in our conspiracy.

The boys dominated the taping for the first half hour; they were terribly boring and what they said had absolutely nothing to do with people starving in ghettos or the horrors of racism and war. A lot of theory, a lot of jive. Lerner finally spoke up, and began a longwinded treatise on the Weimar Republic. I watched his mouth moving; the boys were listening to him raptly. What the hell did the Weimar Republic mean to the nigger on the street, to the junkie copping his fix, to the prostitute under some stinking lump of male flesh, to a baby bitten by rats, to a lesbian, to anyone living in the here and now with real live problems of their own?

I broke in angrily, shaking, unnerved.

"My name is Susan Stern, and I am the only woman in the Seattle 7. I would like to say first of all that I think there is only one conspiracy in this country and that's led by Nixon and his gang and it is a conspiracy against the people of the world. It is a conspiracy to oppress the black people in this country, and keep them in the ghettos, it is a conspiracy to bomb the Vietnamese people back to the Stone Age, it's a conspiracy to build bigger and better stoves and refrigerators and irons and ironing boards for women so that they are bound to the kitchen; it's a conspiracy to separate the races, a conspiracy to separate the sexes, a conspiracy to separate the youth from the adults, a conspiracy to separate our bodies from our minds, a conspiracy to fuck us over, fuck us inside and out, keep us down, beat us, defeat us and make us into the automatons that call themselves Americans. That is the conspiracy we must fight, so that we don't become part of it too.

"What are we about? We are about building a different and better culture; becoming a whole human being, proud of our bodies, our minds, of the world we are going to create.

"We are audacious. But when we are so offensive that we stink, who is it that we stink to? We stink to the laws and administrators who run this country, who have corrupted it and made its people intolerable. Audacity means that we want to fight, that we will stand up, up tight, out of sight, and say exactly what we think about things.

"We are dropping out. But we are dropping out in a special way. We don't want to drop out and sit and smoke dope all day, and let the people in Vietnam take care of themselves. No, we want to drop out and then turn against our heritage. I don't want to be part of white America any more; I want to create a new America. I think I can do it, and let me tell you, the government thinks I can do it, and that's why they call me a conspirator. They think you can do it too, man, believe me. They think you can do it. And you're going to think you can do it too.

"One of the things this country propagates in a very big way is defeatism. Like, that's why they have competition, because somebody always got to get defeated. So that if somebody gets an A and you get a D and he gets a scholarship and you don't get to go to college, then you're defeated so you float around thinking, man, what a bum I am, I'm defeated, what can I possibly do? And you feel real unhappy and terrified and you feel alienated. So you go on leading a bummer of a life and you don't know what to do about it.

"Well, we're beginning to pull our heads together and find ways of doing things about it. We have time, we're young. That's another thing the government hates—youth. You know, they're all old men. Ted Kennedy, he's the youngest of them and that's why he got into trouble with that secretary. He was so terrified of what he was doing, he drove off a bridge.

"I know I'm an outlaw when I'm in jail and when I'm not in jail. I identify with prostitutes. They are some of the most right-on women I know. I identify with thieves and murderers, and all the alienated people who stand on the edges of society and look around, not knowing where to turn.

"I want to join with the black liberation movement, and struggle with the Vietcong. They are all building a new kind of life in the midst of war and they sing while they work, because their life has meaning. They're not cogs in the wheel any more; they are the wheel and they are rolling onto their own heritage, and those are the people I want to identify with.

"People are afraid of being beaten by police; they are afraid of being thrown in jail or perhaps killed. And there are good reasons for such fears. The reasons stem from fascism. Che Guevara said we are living in the middle of a monster. This country is a monster, this country will deal with us like a dinosaur deals with a bird. It will crush the wings of that bird so that it can no longer fly, and we have to fight against that, even though we are afraid.

"We have to understand that our violence is the last outcry, the ultimate end of frustration of a people, whether black or white or Vietnamese or women, who can no longer contain themselves, because they have tried in every way possible to fight their oppression, and they have been unsuccessful. Nothing remains but violence.

"Finally I'd like to say that the struggle will be very long, and many times it will seem hopeless. But I think we can win, not only because we're right, but because we're young and beautiful and strong, and because we're following the example of some of the most beautiful people of the world. I think we can win because we want to win, because we are revolutionaries and the revolution is our life."

I arrived home about four in the morning, exhausted but still strobing on the acid. Anne was in bed with a man; the light was out in the bathroom and there was no toilet paper and I had to shit. I went to the kitchen; the light was out in the kitchen; I tried to find some coffee; the can was empty; I wouldn't have found a clean cup anyway; the dirty dishes were piled all over the counter. I went back upstairs to the bathroom, trying to see myself in the dark room, feeling furious, and impotent, my life, my body, my house falling to pieces around me. Then taking my eyebrow pencil, I wrote thickly across the mirror:

SHAPE UP OR SHIP OUT — NOW.

I don't know if I intended the message for Anne, myself or both of us. But when I came home late the next afternoon after a day of speech making and fund raising, the house was gleaming and dinner was on the table. Anne never mentioned the scribbling on the mirror.

The end of October I began to notice a pain in my vagina. When it continued, I started feeling around down there, and encountered a lump as big as a golf ball. Terrified, I raced to Anne, who drove me to the hospital. What I had was a Bartholin gland which had become clogged, and instead of draining, was filling with pus. The Bartholin glands are generally invisible, and secrete a fluid in the vagina.

At the hospital they gave me a local anesthetic and lanced the Bartholin gland, and then stuffed it with gauze, told me to take several sitz baths a day, and come back to have the gauze removed. It was very painful and they gave me a vial of painkillers.

Now besides my exhausting schedule, and my outrageous eating, my painful breasts and my swollen stomach, I had a wound in my vagina and couldn't fuck. I became more frenetic than before. I was continuously drugged, but I continued with the meetings and speeches and fund raising.

Then, on the first of November, I was getting undressed, when Anne walked into the room. She took one look at me and paled.

"You're pregnant," she said. "Look at your stomach, Susan. It's just sticking out!"

I looked down and it was sticking out. Anne insisted on driving me to the doctor, so I got dressed again, and she drove me the few blocks to Open Door Clinic.

I waited there for an hour, and had an internal and still another rabbit test. This time the result was positive.

"You're almost four months pregnant," the doctor informed me. I called Anne in a state of shock, and she came to get me. That night, the boys, feeling very sorry for me, took me out to the movies. I cried all the way through the movie.

The lawyers were summoned post haste to deal with this new crisis. I wanted an abortion.

"Listen, Susan," Carl Maxey told me in his fatherly manner, "if we postpone the trial now for you to have an abortion, then the judge might sequester the jury over Christmas vacation and those people are going to be pretty damned mad at you defendants if they can't be home for Christmas. Think of the others; why jeopardize their freedom." Jeff, whom I loved and trusted, seemed to agree with him.

"But I don't want a baby," I pleaded with them.

"It will look good in the courtroom to have you come in, glowing and pregnant, maybe with some knitting," Carl told me benignly. We were sitting in a car in front of the house; Carl and I in the back seat, and Jeff in the front seat with his secretary who was taking notes.

"But I don't want a baby. I don't want it," I said desperately.

Carl was the picture of patience. "Come on, now, Susan, you'd probably make a darn good little mother. You only have another five months to go."

Nothing I said seemed to matter. Carl and Jeff insisted that if the jury was sequestered over Christmas vacation, it would be cookies for the defendants. In the end I agreed with them that it was too selfish of me to risk the men's lives, when I could always give the baby away if I didn't want it.

I left the car and walked into my house feeling sick from the inside out. I told Anne what had happened. Her reaction was immediate and violent.

"Bullshit," shouted Anne. "You don't have to have a baby if you don't want to. If the jury is sequestered, then it will be sequestered. The boys will understand. I know they will."

That night I demanded a meeting of all the men, and all our lawyers, with the exception of Tigar, who was in Los Angeles. We met in Anne's room upstairs. Very slowly, containing my anger, I addressed myself to the men: "I have decided, against the advice of Steinborn and Carl to have an abortion. I will arrange to have it as soon as possible, but I want two weeks to recuperate before beginning the ordeal of the trial. My body and my mind need the time. If you want to sever me from the trial, I won't object, although I think I would be of no benefit to the group. You guys have had each other for support all through this thing; as the only female defendant, I haven't had that luxury. Now, with all the tensions of building for the beginning of the trial, I have to cope with an unwanted pregnancy, which could have been taken care of a month ago, except that twentieth-century doctors can't even tell when women are pregnant.

"Carl has told me that if I delay the trial, there is a danger of the jury being sequestered, and that would be bad for all of us. I'm sorry, but my life, and the life of this unwanted child, must be taken into consideration as well."

All the boys started talking at once; they all said about the same thing, without hesitation. How stupid of me not to go to them in the first place. The law, the trial had as little meaning to them as it had to me. Carl and Jeff saw everything legally; how would the jury feel; how would the judge react; what would be the best strategy. To the boys the trial was secondary; the primary issue was whether or not I wanted the baby.

We talked some more over tactics, and it was decided that Jeff and I would visit the judge's chambers the next day, and privately ask him for a brief postponement so that I could have my abortion and recuperation period.

The next morning I dressed in my long black skirt, a black sweater, and wore a big black hat; I looked as though I was going to a funeral. Jeff, looking ravishing in a tight blue suit, got me stoned on the way to Tacoma. I was giggling by the time we reached the judge's office.

Judge Boldt was sitting white-haired and rosy-cheeked behind a massive desk in his chambers. He smiled when we walked in and asked us informally to sit down. Stan Pitkin, the U.S. Attorney who had taken over the case for Guy Goodwin, was present.

Jeff, with a glance at Pitkin, told the judge that this was a highly personal matter, and that his client, meaning me, would prefer it kept from the press.

"Mr. Pitkin, I'm sure that can be arranged," the judge commanded Pitkin, who nodded yes. "Now, young lady," said Boldt, smiling sweetly at me, "what can the court do for you?" Even in his chambers the judge thought of himself as the court.

"Your honor, I'm pregnant, and I must have an abortion. I can't endure this trial, and the possibility of imprisonment and carry a baby. If I should be found guilty, then what would happen to the infant?" I asked in my most angelic voice. "I am requesting, your honor, that you grant a postponement of this trial for three weeks, so that I may have my abortion, and then recuperate."

The judge haggled a bit about the pressures of time, and his jammed calendar, and the length of the trial, but finally acquiesced. The new trial date would be November 23, 1970.

The next day the headlines read, "Seattle 7 trial postponed"; the article said I had to have an operation of a "private nature."

On November 5 I had my abortion, a bare month before they became legal. Anne drove me to Portland, where I spent the night in the hospital; the operation was performed at eight o'clock and by two o'clock that afternoon I was sitting sleepily in the car, while Anne drove back to Seattle. When I arrived home that evening, about twenty-five people were in the house, concerned about my well-being. I sat and talked to them for several hours, and finally went to sleep. The next day there was no pain from the abortion, but I felt again the sharp pain from the Bartholin gland. With a quivering hand, I searched around down there, and immediately felt a hard lump.

For a couple of days I tried to ignore it, to pretend there was nothing wrong, but it continued to swell and the pain became intolerable. Finally, in utter depression, I called Dr. John Greene, and he recommended a female doctor to me, who worked at Planned Parenthood. He told me not to worry about expenses.

Dr. White was young, attractive, composed, confident and efficient. I liked her immediately, and although I was hysterical and neurotic when she examined me, I basically trusted her. She had to lance the gland again. It had been done improperly the first time, and it had healed leaving no draining point. She told me to continue the sitz baths. I had to return to her three times a week so that she could pry around in the minuscule hole, and keep it open as the wound healed. It was all exceedingly painful. I couldn't sit comfortably, and I couldn't walk without pain. I still couldn't have intercourse, and I was practically raving with sexual frustration.

The postponement turned out to be a godsend because we would have been totally unprepared for the trial on the original date. We made good use of the extra three weeks, however. With a new seriousness, the defendants finally settled down and began to make elaborate plans for the trial; strategy for defense, roles for each defendant, position of seating, roles for Chip and Lerner, the pro se defendants, and responsibility of the lawyers. There were meetings with Robby, who wanted to organize a huge protest. There were meetings with people preparing shuttle service from Seattle to Tacoma for our supporters. There were meetings with defense collective people for last minute fund-raising drives. We worked around the clock, doing what each of us did best. Chip and Lerner researched their defenses; Steinborn and Carl spent hours working with Roger and me; Lee worked with Joe and Abeles, and Tigar worked with Dude. We all read the briefs that Lee, Tigar, Steinborn and Maxey and the law students had so carefully submitted over the months. There were endless details to see to and the days sped by as November 23 approached.

It was like the opening of a Broadway show. All the defendants were especially concerned about their dress; image was very important. The boys finally decided to go as themselves; Lerner in a suit and tie, the rest in jeans and hippie belts and beads. I alternated between my long black skirt and black hat and knitting like Madame DeFarge, and my miniskirt for a little shock therapy. We were all aware of our charm and beauty, with the exception of Lippman; we intended to use these as weapons to seduce the jury.

As the Big Day drew near, we became hysterical in different ways; but the effects of the strain were apparent in all of us. Our use of dope escalated unbelievably those last three weeks, even though it was now contained to the few hours during which we weren't actively preparing for the trial. Lerner became intolerable; several times he was on the verge of tears during meetings; he was so visibly terrified that I felt sorry for him, even though I despised him. Even Roger's usually expressionless face became drawn, and he began to look green as the rest of us joked and laughed about Judge Boldt and Stan Pitkin, and tried our best to treat the whole thing casually. Chip was very serious, and did a lot to pull us all together; he was the center, the strength. Dude broke out in pimples and became chaotic; he would mumble incoherently and pace constantly. Abeles looked more insecure and bewildered than ever. Joey spent all his free hours pursuing one woman after another, unable to talk to any of them, grabbing my hand and assuring me that when my ship went down, he would be with me, that I was not alone. But the words rang hollow. Each of us was alone. Each of us coped with the terror of the law, the monster, the dinosaur in our own way. Pinioned by pain, deadly depression, the trauma of not being able to fuck, loneliness and fear of the actual trial itself, I tossed in bed all night before the first day, wondering what my life would have been like if I had not returned to Seattle on April 16, just in time to be arrested.

Six o'clock in the morning the alarm rang. I stumbled into a sitz bath, bleary with barbiturates, and, because we would be choosing the jury, dressed in my first-day costume, simple and severe and modest—my long black skirt, a black velvet blouse, a shawl, and the big black hat. Carefully I applied my make-up. I looked pathetic. But the make-up eased away all the pimples, circles, unhealthy pallor, and made me look younger and vibrant. Amazing.

By six-thirty I was in the kitchen cooking bacon and eggs for the entire house; a good breakfast under our belts would give us strength for the grueling ordeal. Halfway through breakfast Truman from the defense collective arrived; what would we have done without Truman. I never liked him; he always reminded me of the matrons in jail, or camp counselors. Seven-thirty in the morning he was awake and motivating and responsible and always interrupting our breakfast.

Truman had rented a bus. Every subsequent morning of the trial he would stop at all the defendants' houses, pry them out of bed or away from coffee and into the bus. My house was the last stop because Anne and I were always late. We were working at the Century until two o'clock in the morning throughout the trial. Then into the bus; Lerner, pleading silently with me not to bong up the works; Lippman, nodding to sleep, trying to giggle with the rest of us; Anne, dimpling and smiling; the boys, toking on a lid provided by Truman, and me, squirming to find a comfortable position, my Bartholin smarting, wise-cracking with Anne and the boys. We were always stoned by the time we reached Tacoma, where Truman dropped us in front of the Tacoma Federal Courthouse and then went to park the bus. Almost like the Rolling Stones!

It was drizzling that first morning, as it would be every morning of the trial. Nevertheless, about five hundred people had made the thirty-mile trip from Seattle and were standing noisily hunched in the rain and cold, waiting to gain entrance to the spectacle. Some of them loved us; many of them were just curious; all of them were drawn to the action which we were surely going to provide.

The defendants were hustled in by Steinborn who assured the pigs guarding the entrance that we were indeed the defendants. The courthouse looked like the Bastille; armed guards everywhere, all the windows had been boarded up, all the glass on the door covered with planks and steel bars, special people hired to search every bundle coming into the courthouse, except those things carried by the defendants themselves.

I was given an admittance card to my own trial. It said:

ADMIT No. XX 5 P
subject to available space or cancellation.
show card when entering or leaving.
SUSAN STERN

The card was issued by the United States Federal Marshal Charles Robinson, who would help to keep order in the courtroom throughout our trial, and who would shuttle us around to various prisons in the country over the next two years, and who would sign us in and out whenever we wanted to travel anywhere at any time during that period.

We could see there would be trouble about admitting people into the courtroom. Judge Boldt had allotted room for a hundred people; the first morning, half of that room was taken by prospective jurors, and another third by reporters and TV men, leaving only thirty seats available. Boldt had originally said that people could wait in the lobby, but now he had decided that there were too many people, and they would be too obstreperous.

The marshals in the lobby kept the door locked. Only lawyers and defendants were allowed in. Several of the people out in the rain made bitter remarks to me as I pressed through, and gave me dirty looks. "But it's my trial," I said. "I'm a defendant, you wanna take my fucking place, you can have it."

The courtroom was specially designed for Boldt, who had been made a judge for life years ago. I guess he thought he was something of a deity. The bench was built at the far right corner of the room, on a pedestal, so that the deity could look down on his domain. Beside the bench on its lofty stand was an American flag. The defense table was on the same side of the room as the bench, about seven feet away from it; the prosecution table was opposite the defense table. There were ten chairs around the defense table for defendants and lawyers; there were three around the prosecution. One for Stan Pitkin, the U.S. Attorney, one for Billinghurst, his assistant, and one for Lou Harris, the FBI man who had been handling our case.

To the left of the prosecution table were two rows of empty chairs enclosed in a box; the jury seats. There were sixteen chairs in all; twelve jurors, and four alternates. Then the room was cut by a wood divider, with a gate, and in back of it were the rows of wooden benches for our gallery, except that one complete side of the room was filled with middle-aged and old white men and women who looked grumpy and irritable and stared at the defendants with pure disgust smeared over their faces and nervously avoided our eyes and smiles and nods. From this group our jury would be chosen. I felt my heart sink as I looked at them. We didn't have a hope in hell of convincing those people how nice, lovable, and framed we were.

The entire two front rows were filled with reporters and artists who were already sketching away. Steinborn was chatting amiably with the enemy; the boys were harassing Charlie Robinson and his sidekick, the immense, dumb-looking federal marshal we called Lurch. Federal marshals, Charlie's storm troopers, were clustered at both entrances to the courtroom, were marching up and down between the corriders, were near the elevator, and were stationed at various points throughout the courtroom. Once again I had the feeling that this was a movie set; now the cast was in its place, nine-thirty had arrived, and the court clerk was timorously telling us to be quiet and come to order, the judge was about to enter.

A hush fell, the defendants noisily scrambled for their seats at the defense table, and then the judge came in. Feeling like a traitor, I rose with everyone else. The judge bowed his silver and pink head, pursed his lips, adjusted his glasses, clonked his gavel, and said. "This court is in session," and like a train moving down a track according to schedule, the trial had begun.

The first three days of trial were consumed in *voir dire*—the jury selection. There were 150 people from whom we could pick. The judge denied us the opportunity to question prospective jurors about their attitudes and biases; the judge decided to voir dire the jury himself.

Sixteen dour-faced individuals slumped into the empty chairs and were asked as a group, "Now if any of you have prejudice against black people, please raise your hand." If a person had been honest enough to raise his hand, he more than likely would have been a person we would have liked to keep; but admitting such a bias meant automatic dismissal.

Stan Pitkin systematically threw out any prospective juror who was under sixty, nonwhite, or who even vaguely admitted some sympathy with the defendants' views. One man in particular, queried about his views on Vietnam, said, "I don't agree with the war in Vietnam, but I also don't agree with violent demonstrations to oppose it." The man, a fifty-year old businessman, was dismissed as a prospective juror. Two days later he was fired from his job of many years.

I sat and watched our one hope, that of a fair and impartial jury, vanish, and what remained at the end of three days represented as much of a cross-section of the American population as President Nixon's Cabinet: staunch middle-class Tacomans, aged forty or above, pure white, three of them females, all of them having sworn on oath that they were for our boys, had no opinion about the war in Vietnam, were not racist, not prejudiced against youth with long hair, and not opposed to voices of dissent. It was a jury of my mother's peers.

Hopeless as it appeared, we decided to play to the jury; our strategy would be for them to get to know us, see how sincere we were, learn that long hair and promiscuity does not automatically mean bad—different perhaps, but not bad.

We had also decided early in our preparations for the trial that we didn't want a "circus" such as the Chicago 8 trial had appeared to be, that we would conduct a serious and orderly trial, without failing our politics. This became immediately impossible. I could not restrain myself from objecting when Pitkin threw out the one prospective juror in his twenties who had sideburns coming down past the top of his ears. I stood up very upset and interrupted the proceedings:

"Your honor, may I make one statement before you continue?"

"You are not a counsel of record. No."

"But I'm involved in the case."

"You're not a counsel in the case."

"In juror excuses," I persisted, ignoring the judge, "don't we have any way of challenging them at all?"

"Please, Miss Levy," Boldt said, mistaking me for one of the legal assistants sitting near the defense table.

"My name is Susan Stern. I'm the female defendant in this case."

"I'm sorry," Boldt said.

"I'm very concerned that one of the youngest jurors has been dismissed. I think it's specifically because of his youth, because he comes closest to being a juror of our peers, which we are entitled to under the Constitution."

Behind me the spectators clapped, and Judge Boldt looked displeased and told me irritably that there was nothing the defendants could do. Boldt always got irritated when he mistook one of the defendants for another, which he was constantly doing. Our judge was a perfect example of that legal American phenomenon, blind justice!

It was impossible to sit in that courtroom and not see it as a circus. George Boldt was the lion tamer, and we were the lions, our lawyers the acrobats, performing in front of an audience. And watching it all, the jury, those twelve strangers so suddenly elected to pass judgment on our lives. Boldt was a stern and efficient tamer. He knew how to make the lions jump through hoops and go precisely through their paces. Our trial was not so much a presentation of evidence as it was a lesson in bowing to authority. It was so surreal, that I constantly had to pinch myself to make sure I wasn't having a nightmare.

I found out what it means when they say the courts in America adhere to the "adversary system." You battle it out with your adversary, the bad guy, the enemy, the other side. On both sides heaps of evidence are arranged to make each side look better to the jury; the truth lies somewhere between the extreme of each side's version. The truth gets lost in the fight for jury approval. The truth is distorted not for the sake of justice, but for the sake of winning. One side has to win. The jury, in the final analysis, holds the power. Based on what they are as people, they regard the evidence. In our case, we were part of the evidence. They regarded us with one arched eyebrow, as they might a pornographic movie. They regarded us with a danger signal for their own kids buzzing in their heads. We were the people our parents had warned us against. As J.J. had said, the incubation of your mother's nightmare. For this jury, we were a nightmare materialized.

Perhaps they went home each night and looked at their own sweet angels, thinking, "There but for the grace of God. . . why, if it weren't for men like Judge Boldt, this country would be overrun by wanton, brutal, sadistic people like those defendants, destroying federal property, luring children into their fiendish orgies, addicting them to dope, encouraging them to drop out of school, making them turn away from the Church, from God, from cleanliness, from everything good, decent and American. Dirty commies."

For three weeks I watched that jury eight hours a day. I knew just how each one of them settled into his or her chair, how they would hold their hands, how the succession of expressions would pass across their faces as they listened to the opening statements, then to the witnesses. I saw the shock and horror in their eyes, the fear in their hearts that their own little darlings would catch the dread disease, and one day would be standing in some court, in front of some jury . . . we might, indeed, be their children.

The defendants' strategy was to make this bond between the two sets of children palpable to the jury; to show that we were children with a dream for the betterment of humanity; a voice of the future, out of place now only because it was premature.

Early in the trial Mike Abeles was to pop up too fast for Boldt to stop him and, laughing, point to his hair and ask the jury, "You think this is awful," and, his eyes rolling, turn around in a circle so that the jury could catch the full effect of his coiffure. One of the jurors would smile for a second, then catch himself, and drop his eyes nervously. Had he remembered a second in his almost buried youth when he had sprung out in all directions like Mike's woolly mop?

Several people on the jury could not repress a smile when Lerner, clothed in respectable suit and tie sauntered into court one day with a telephone hanging around his neck. When the judge ordered him to remove it, Lerner replied, 'Well, your honor, this is just symbolic of my crime," and, turning dramatically to the jury, "I am charged with using the phone, you know," he said conversationally, and they tittered slightly, and the spectators yowled and thumped, and the judge pounded with his gavel and thundered angrily until order was restored. What little secrets did those housewives tell over the phone? What would be revealed if the government had ever tapped your mother's line? What would your father say, what?

A courtroom is a rather dry place. The facts are aired like so many clothes on a line; some articles are more colorful than others, but they are all rather removed from life. The jury must look at this distortion of life, this jumble of facts, this refurbished truth, and decide upon guilt or innocence. Now in a crime like theft, you have some unalterable facts; object A, B, C was heisted. Defendant A did it, did not do it, check which one you think.

But conspiracy. Not as cut and dried. The truth even harder to ferret out. Did they meet? Of course they met, dodo, they all live in the same house. Oh yes, well did they meet for the explicit purpose of organizing this demonstration? Of course they did. They met with as many people as were possibly interested, in public places, and with the greatest amount of fanfare and publicity possible. With leaflets, spray paint, TV, newspapers and even a telegram to the mayor to make sure everyone would know exactly what they were doing.

The first actual day of the trial, when the government presented its opening statement, and Lerner, Chip and Carl presented ours, the jury was made to listen to two science fiction stories, each designed to make the side presenting it look good. Pitkin ran down the facts of the case as he saw it; "TDA began when two groups of protesters joined together in front of the courthouse and spilled over into the lawn. The group coming from the South was led by Lerner, Marshall, and Dude. The Northern group was led by Abeles, Lippman, Stern and others." Real point number one. Roger Lippman was in San Francisco at the time of TDA. Point number two. I was nowhere near Abeles when the Northern group began to move. Point number three. I was too busy handing out iron pipes to lead it anywhere. I don't know who led it. Garrity, Justesen, Ray, and I were in a small group, and were trying to convince everyone around us to trash, quite unsuccessfully, I might add.

Chip's statement said, "There was no conspiracy because there was no need for one. People didn't have to be manipulated into rioting. TDA, in cities all over the country, was the direct product of years of struggle and frustration around Vietnam and Black Liberation. It was the direct product of rage against the conduct of the Chicago conspiracy trial. Stop the Courts was not a secret password whispered from conspirator to conspirator, but a slogan shouted at rallies and painted in big red letters on walls across this country."

"The evidence will show," said Maxey, "that this was a demonstration called by the people of these United States."

Fact one: only a very small minority of this country demonstrated in TDA demonstrations; the rest probably agreed with the demonstrations on a scale of somewhat to not at all. Fact two: although the defendants didn't whisper in back rooms and huddle under bridges planning TDA, and although it more than likely would have happened without Sundance, we were largely responsible for organizing the demonstration, and, with the exception of Lerner, we wanted a militant demonstration. Joe, of course, was another fact; he simply wasn't in Seattle prior to TDA, and had no part in organizing it, and didn't participate in it.

The government's first witness established that Chip and Dude did leave Ithaca around December 5, headed for Seattle; the second established that we paid electricity on time for the Sundance house, a fact which astonished me. The Sundance landlord was called; he said we were average tenants, except that "I didn't like the color they painted the living room. They painted it black," he told the jury, who looked at us quizzically. Fortunately he omitted mention of my nude woman with the American flag coming out of her cunt!

Then a U of W pig testified that he had seen us practicing karate, or perhaps it was judo, "You know, somethin' like that," and that he had seen the defendants at meetings, but couldn't remember whom he had seen talking to whom.

The minutes ticked by those first few days. I had trouble staying awake. It was so boring. I looked constantly at the jury; they always looked as though they were nodding out. When I sat near Joe, we giggled, bolstered each other up. Most of the time I sat with Steinborn and, terribly sexually attracted to each other, we frequently were unable to restrain ourselves in front of the jury. I would lean to ask him a question, and end up by nibbling on his ear. Maxey and Tigar and Lerner complained to both of us repeatedly, but we never stopped. Of course my Bartholin refused to heal, so we could never fuck, although I went home with him several times. As the days of the trial passed, our lust increased.

One day Steinborn came running up to me, grabbed me, and propelled me into a seat. "Susan, you were bending over the table, and your ass was sticking up at the jury." I glanced over at the dirty dozen; they were looking down at the entire scene with something akin to pleasure on their faces.

"Well, they don't look very upset, Steinborn," I told him, and, standing up, leaned carefully over the table again.

Boredom threatened to overwhelm us, threatened to put the jury to sleep. The government's case dragged on. One morning I brought in some grape Kool-Aid to put in the water pitcher on the defense table. Stan Pitkin, Lou Harris, and Charlie Robinson smelled it, and we even offered them some, but they declined. Germs, you know. The next day, we brought wine and put it in the water pitcher; we offered them some, but again they declined, this time *sans* smelling. We got stoned in our defense room. We didn't even worry about the smell, surrounded as we were by judges, federal marshals, and other pigs. Maxey tried to restrain us, Tigar protested, but we ignored them; it was after all, our trial.

Someone at the Century gave me a piece of rubber that looked like a pile of shit for Stan Pitkin. The next day, I put it in front of his chair. He didn't think it was very funny. The judge asked the defendants to remove the "ornamentation."

Joey smiled, blue-eyed and rosy-cheeked, at the jury; several times the women averted their eyes. Chip looked straight at them when he talked; the defense certainly had it all over the prosecution when it came to looks.

We were, more than anything else, ourselves. We never fudged on the issues which were important to us: the war in Vietnam, racism, justice and repression in America, and our right to a fair trial. It got in deviously, but we got it in. The jury might see us as demented and destructive, but they would know we were sincere.

We consistently demanded admittance for our supporters; the judge steadfastly denied them admittance. We complained again and again about government electronic surveillance of our defense offices, tapped phones, FBI and police cars hovering in the vicinity of our homes, parked across the street from my house. Twice during the three weeks of the trial Lerner's house was broken into and ransacked; both times materials relating to the trial were stolen and nothing else. Stan Pitkin and Lou Harris repeatedly denied that they or any other government agency had anything to do with the thefts; in any event the judge maintained that such episodes were not within his jurisdiction.

At one point during the trial, Chip asked that we recess early to commemorate the anniversary of Fred Hampton's death; the judge said no.[1]

We asked him to arrange for another room with a speaker system for our supporters who could not fit into the courtroom; the judge said no, no other rooms were available.

As pro se defendants, Lerner and Chip had a little more leeway than the rest of us. In their cross-examinations of witnesses, opening and closing statements, they would mention Vietnam, and the judge would rule them out of order; they would broach the subject of the increasingly restrictive nature of the courts and judiciary, and the judge would order them to pursue another line of questioning. Time and again the judge admonished us that such issues were not germane to our conspiracy charges, and had no bearing on our defense.

Our lawyers fared only slightly better. Many times they were cut off when they approached political subjects; they were overruled on ninety per cent of their objections to Pitkin's misleading questioning, and were frequently asked to make their clients refrain from any outbursts or disturbances.

The judge, frightened by youth, displayed his dislike of our supporters throughout the trial, threatening at the slightest provocation to have them removed from the courtroom, and frequently admonishing them for laughing, but ignoring the loud guffawing of the prosecution and several of the federal marshals.

The eye of the judge was astigmatic; it saw what it wanted to see, heard only that which pleased it, allowed a great deal of latitude for the government's case, and defined as "overreaching" the greater part of the defendants' case.

I was in agony throughout the trial. My Bartholin healed partially, and began to swell again. I couldn't sit squarely on a chair, but reclined on three chairs, propped up uncomfortably by an elbow, craning my neck to see what was happening with the jury. Some days I loaded myself with Demerol to ease the pain, wore my miniskirt and sat up gingerly; no matter how many drugs I took, I was always uncomfortable. The pain, the drug consumption, the dehumanizing atmosphere of the trial, the long meetings each night after the trial, the job at the Century four nights a week, sometimes after four hours of meetings, the sexual frustration and loneliness, and the never ending tension of dealing with the male chauvinism of my codefendants, my lawyers, male admirers, drawn to a notorious Seattle personality, exhausted and depleted me. Although I took great pains to hide my misery and anguish, I remember those weeks of trial as the beginning of the greatest and most extensive depression of my life.

If the trial was difficult for the men, it was harrowing for me. Tentatively accepted by my co-defendants as an Auntie Mame figure with an eccentric fascination for violence which they labeled Weatherman tendencies, the lawyers primarily viewed me as a major obstruction to their idea about running orderly trials. Michael Tigar's attitude toward me was that of a big strong hero who would take care of a frail, sickly, impulsive heroine. Most of the time he addressed himself to Chip or Lerner, as the two defendants who came closest to his intellectual level. Carl Maxey treated me like a lovable but unruly daughter. Steinborn was my lover throughout the ordeal, although we couldn't fuck.

If I felt my isolation as the lone woman defendant generally, it was intolerable in the courtroom. Everything in the legal system seemed geared for men; male marshals, FBI agents, bailiffs, prosecutors, and then Judge Boldt. Throughout the trial I suffered because I was a woman in ways the men couldn't comprehend. All the male defendants spoke out of turn, asked questions, caused disruptions. I wasn't allowed the same freedom. In a patronizing manner I was frequently cut off, and admonished. Whereas the judge referred to the male defendants as Mr. Marshall, etc., he frequently referred to me as "young lady," rather than as Mrs. Stern.

Another time the judge complained that the defendants weren't coming into court on time. "If you fellows will keep an eye open and come in promptly, because we cannot proceed without every one of you in the room." I objected that I wasn't a fellow and the judge condescendingly replied, "Well, I think you are well cared for." When I repeated to him again that I was not a fellow, his eyes twinkled and he smiled and said, "Well, one of the prospective jurors emphasized that the other day rather humorously, you will recall." That was his manner with me throughout the trial—oh, that little sex kitten who got mixed up with those bad men. He never once understood my protestations, or those of the attorneys on my behalf.

Pitkin was no better. He frequently made sexist slurs, although he treated me a bit more seriously, since he was trying to prove that I was a brutal and violent subversive. My fury was finally sparked by an unconscious statement Pitkin made.

He was talking about a woman who had spoken at an organizational meeting for TDA, and he used the word "gal" several times. I was half-reclining over three chairs, unable to sit up straight because of my Bartholin. It was also difficult for me to stand every time I had an objection to make. Instead of rising, I yelled out, "From now on, please refer to a female as a woman, not a gal." Pitkin smirked and I repeated what I had said, this time more loudly. The men around the defense table were all standing, irately glaring at Pitkin.

Just as I made my second statement to Pitkin, Anne was entering the courtroom, having initially been barred from it because prospective witnesses weren't allowed to watch the proceedings, but then given special admittance because of her position on our defense team. The judge, seeing a standing female, assumed the interruption to Pitkin's statement had come from Anne, and ordered her to leave the courtroom. Poor Anne was dragged out before she even had a chance to sit down.

"But, your honor, I sat here and said that to Mr. Pitkin," I said, now attempting to get up from my clumsy position. The judge mistook my protest for that of another woman sitting in the rear of the gallery, and ordered that woman also to be removed.

At this point Dude couldn't contain himself and started shrieking, "You're deaf, dumb, and blind. I refuse to be judged by somebody that can't hear and probably can't understand the testimony." The judge snapped, "Sit down and be quiet, Mr. Abeles," and scribbled on a pad. By this time I was on my feet, still trying to be heard. The judge finally allowed me to speak, as he generally did when he was highly confused and needed some time to collect himself.

"Your honor, I would like to explain once and for all why I interrupted Mr. Pitkin so that it will be clear.

"In the Movement we have something called Women's Liberation that men and women take very, very seriously and Mr. Pitkin's reference to a woman as a gal would be the same thing as calling a black man a nigger. That is the way I feel about it and a lot of people in the gallery feel about it so that I don't wish to hear that kind of slur.

"I could not stand up, your honor, because of my illness and I was sitting down and it was my voice very clearly interrupting Mr. Pitkin. The woman that came into the courtroom had just been let in and had no time to know what was going on."

The court refused to accept the fact that he had made a mistake with Anne, and refused to readmit her into the courtroom. "There isn't the faintest, remotest, reasonable or any other doubt that it was that woman who spoke," he said firmly. The next day, when both Seattle newspapers reported the judge's mistake, Boldt apologized and, highly embarrassed, admitted Anne to the courtroom.

The worst shock came when Pitkin announced he was calling to the stand an undercover agent for the FBI. The few minutes while we were waiting for the witness to make his appearance were awful; who of our friends, lovers, acquaintances, was an informer, a pig, while acting under the guise of revolutionary comrade, friend. The thought that anyone could be that base made me so angry, that by the time the witness appeared, I was ready to kill.

Horace (Red) Parker. The dirty, stinking, motherfucking son of a bitch. In he walked, cool as a cucumber; a vegetable for a government grown so corrupt, that it has no heart; only eyes and ears with which to tap the heart of those who seek to maintain their own dignity and humanity.

He sat down guided by Stan Pitkin's triumphant smile, reassured by the grin on Lou Harris' face, reassured by the friendly nod of the judge, reassured by the presence of two protective FBI agents standing near him to guard him from the wrath of those he had informed against.

Just like any other man, he walked in and sat down, and my senses revolted. With all my soul, I wished I had a gun at that moment; to take his life would have been worth my own. But I sat and gaped as the redheaded man sat down, and I turned to look with stunned horror at Robby, who was ashen-faced.

Robby had been closer to Red Parker than I had; he had brought the man into our house, had him to dinner with his wife and child, and had even been close enough to him to give him one of our puppies—Parker had named the puppy Corky, after a Young Lords leader. Parker had shown an extreme interest in working to end the war in Vietnam; professing admiration for Robby, he had made arrangements for him to speak on more than one occasion at local coffeehouses. Although he had not been an intimate of Robby's, he had been considered a friend.

Now his hair was much shorter than it had been when he had masqueraded as a Movement person, and he had exchanged his jeans and leather jacket for a suit and tie. He smiled at me from the witness chair, as if he had won some kind of victory. Sickened, I got up and left the courtroom, without asking permission. I felt eyes upon me as I walked out, but the prosecution and the judge said nothing. I vomited, and returned to the courtroom in time to hear Boldt intone: "Mr. Pitkin, are you ready to begin direct of the witness?"

Just another circus act; the show must go on. The judge was, after all, used to informers; a highly religious man, he realized that Judas Iscariot was just a fact of life.

It took Pitkin two days to air Parker's testimony. Most of the time he concentrated on providing background for the jury on how he had become an undercover informer, and how reliable he was as an infiltrator of Weatherman.

Parker testified that he had joined SDS in July of 1969, and then had gone into Weatherman in March of 1970. He had been invited to join SDS by Robby, whom he had met along with me soon after we had arrived in Seattle. In a monotone voice he described his development as an informer.

"I went to an SDS meeting in July of 1969, because I was upset over the war in Vietnam. But I was disappointed with what I saw there. I told Robby that I objected to the Marxist ideology they were laying out, that I didn't dig Marx. I told him I would think about joining SDS, and he gave me some literature by Karl Marx and some little red books by Chairman Mao Tse-tung, and told me to keep in touch. I took the literature home and read it, but didn't like what I read. So I telephoned the CIA, who instructed me to contact the FBI, and they invited me downtown to meet with them. I told them there was a collective being formed on the U of W campus, and in

my opinion these people were Communist revolutionaries, and that
the FBI might be interested in knowing about it, and I left the literature with them."

"What happened next?" asked Pitkin.

"I received a phone call from an FBI agent who asked me to meet
him for lunch. I met him, and during lunch, he told me that the FBI
was interested in people who intended to damage government property ... he said that I had an opportunity to be of service to my country."

"In what way?"

"By infiltrating SDS."

"Did you tell him you would?"

"I told him I would think it over. Then I talked it over with my
wife and decided to go ahead and do it. I contacted the FBI a week
later and told them I was interested in working for the FBI. Then I
contacted Robby and told him I wanted to join SDS."

"And did you thereafter report what happened at SDS and other
radical left meetings to the FBI?"

"Every meeting and every encounter and every conversation that
I ever had with them I reported to the FBI," answered Parker
smugly.

Parker testified that he had been an undercover agent from July
of 1969 to November of 1970, and that during that time he had spoken to the FBI at least once and sometimes twice a day. He said that
when Weatherman emerged from SDS, he had been directed to stay
close to the Weatherman and to ignore the other groups. He claimed
to have infiltrated a Weatherman collective named Maxwell Silver
Hammer. They lived at the Fortress. Then he blandly identified
each of the defendants, stating that he knew Roger and myself best.

Parker went on to read reports that he had written of meetings
called to organize for TDA. Three of these meetings were Overt
Acts on our conspiracy charges. One of the reports, *The Making of a
Riot—1970*, read like a Grade Z detective story:

"The meeting began as Lerner offered a fourteen-point program
to those present. This program laid out the basic ideology for the
Seattle Liberation Front or SLF. After the manifesto had been read,
the meeting was thrown open to hear reactions from the audience,

who had been personally invited by Lerner. But the Weathermen did not have advance knowledge of the program and reacted strongly against it. Other groups were strongly in favor of the program. The Weathermen were attacked for having a hard line of violence as the only answer.

"Susan Stern consistently interrupted Lerner in a loud voice as he presented the program. He told her, 'Shut up, you goddam bitch.' When she continued to interrupt him he finally said, 'Oh, let the bitch talk.' Susan condemned the SLF for not dealing with the scheduled visit of a Marine recruiter on campus the next day. She denounced the SLF program for saying nothing about armed struggle or about racism.

"While being attacked by the Weatherman, Lerner yelled, 'Sue, if you don't like the program, get the fuck out of the room.' He was ready to back it up with his fists. Lerner apparently is very able to take care of himself. In my experience, no one has ever spoken to a Weatherman in this manner and gotten away with it. Something very unusual happened there; leaders of the Weathermen were being eclipsed by three new and highly intelligent leaders: Mike Lerner, Chip Marshall, and Jeff Dowd.

"It was obvious that Dowd and Marshall were professional organizers. They urged people to form collectives to begin their struggle against American fascist judicial system.

"Roger Lippman was the only Weatherman to realize that SDS had been overtaken by these new people, and he made a successful effort to ally Weatherman with SLF by agreeing with Lerner that the group should break down into smaller discussion groups.

"Justesen tried again to get support for driving the Marine recruiter off campus.

"Stern asked people present to 'really raise hell after the Chicago trial ended.' This was the first hint of a planned massive action aimed at the American judicial system, and in particular, at the Federal Courthouse in Seattle . . ."

"You liar," I muttered rather loudly.

"Mrs. Kelly," said the judge, looking straight at me, "please restrain yourself."

"I'm Susan Stern," I said forcefully, standing up so he could see me clearly. "He's Kelly," and I pointed to Joey, who stood up saying, "I'm Joe Kelly."

"I'm Abeles," said Abeles, jumping up, smiling.

"I'm Lerner," said Lerner, waving his telephone.

"I'm Marshall," said Chip, bowing to the judge.

"I'm Dowd," spit the Dude, "and here's a pair of binoculars to help you out, judge," and the Dude presented the binoculars to the judge to the titters of all the spectators. Boldt reddened, and scribbled some more on his pad.

Roger kind of halfway stood up, and whispered his name, looking embarrassed.

The judge banged his gavel, and admonished us please not to interrupt the proceedings.

"Well, please get us straight, your honor," I said. "I mean, I don't look anything like Joe Kelly—he has curly hair."

The spectators stamped, clapped and roared with laughter. The jury stifled giggles, and even Pitkin and Charlie Robinson had to suppress their laughter.

That night, we had a long meeting. The defendants were still having a hard time reconciling themselves to the fact that Red Parker was real. We realized that discrediting Parker was the key to our case. He was all the government had, and his story was so full of bullshit, that we were sure we could break it. Like chess players mapping out their moves, the lawyers, Chip and Lerner, built a strategy to tear Parker into shreds.

We visited old Weatherpeople after the meeting ended, and got the true stories from them of Parker's relationship to Maxwell Silver Hammer and the Fortress. SLF, former RYM 2 people, some of the anarchists appeared out of the woodwork with tidbits of information about Parker.[2] By two o'clock that morning we had a dossier of a man who had committed so many crimes in the name of patriotism, that our clean, religious, middle-class, respectable Tacoman jury would blanch at the story.

The next day Pitkin resumed his questioning of Red Parker, still trying to establish how close he was to the Weathermen, how well he knew the defendants, and how ugly, sordid, and debased the Weathermen were. Repeatedly our lawyers interrupted to remind Pitkin, Parker, and the judge that Weatherman was not on trial, nor were members of Weatherman; SLF members were being tried for TDA. But Pitkin had Weatherman fever; it was almost as if he believed that if he could prove we were Weathermen, then we would be guilty by association. He never spent much time asking questions about the Sundance house, where most of TDA was planned; he mostly was interested in the Fortress, where the would-be Maxwell Silver Hammer lived.

"I was recruited into the Weatherman collective in March," Parker said, "but I wasn't allowed to live with the collective members at that time because they had a higher revolutionary consciousness than I did, and I would hold them back. They began working with me constantly, eight, ten, twelve hours a day, trying to get 'pig' ideas out of my head."

I scrambled to my feet and shouted, "They didn't do a very good job."

The judge did some scribbling and said sternly, "Mrs. Dowd, I will have to admonish you again about making remarks of that kind."

"I'm Susan Stern," I said, and all the men stood up one by one to show the judge who was who once more. Boldt scribbled as we all popped up, peering at us, trying to discern who was who. Stan Pitkin waited with a martyred air, and when we had finished identifying ourselves, he continued his questioning.

"How long did you actually live at the Fortress?"

"Two to three months—March, April, and May 1970."

"Have you participated in the life style of the Weathermen, Mr. Parker?"

"Yes."

"Have you used drugs?"

"Yes."

"What drugs?"

"Acid, grass, speed, methedrine, cocaine."

"Did you have any instructions from the FBI about that?"

Carl Maxey objected vehemently, "If he used drugs, he used them on his own."

"Overruled. You may answer," replied the judge.

"I had instructions to do anything that was necessary to protect my credibility," Parker answered.

"Did you get arrested?"

"Yes. On November 6 and December 1, 1969."

"When you were living at the Fortress, how did everybody support themselves?"

"Selling dope, selling food stamps, ripping off money from their parents, wherever you could get it, beg it, steal it, borrow it."

"How did you support yourself?"

"I had a job at the paint store, and then of course . . . well, you know . . . I was paid . . . you know . . . for my other work."

"All right then. Now Mr. Parker, do you have any personal knowledge of the views of any of the defendants regarding the use of violence?"

"Yes. I have explicit quotes in my report, *The Making of a Riot*."

"Could you give the jury some idea of what these defendants said?"

"The Weathermen were always preaching violence. Susan Stern made some of the most vicious verbal attacks on high schools I've ever heard in my experience with campus radicals. She was especially rabid about the high schools, urging the organizers for TDA to tell students that 'Schools are fucked up. They are shitty. Drop out. Tell your teacher he is a pig. Don't go back to school—ever.' Things like that.

"Justesen talked a lot about armed struggle; said that people had to pick up the gun and off the pigs and not wait to be attacked.

"Roger Lippman was the theorist; he would always talk a lot about Marxism, and then tell people to fight the pig.

"Chip Marshall was always talking about collectives."

Chip interrupted. "Are you implying that I was a Weatherman? I ask that that be stricken from the record; that's his opinion."

"Overruled, Please continue, Mr. Parker," said the judge.

"Abeles urged violence as the only answer to a fascist court. At one meeting he passed out red armbands with the letters TDA printed on them in ink. He said, 'If the pigs try and stop us—kill them.'"

Pitkin smiled at the jury, who were looking at us expressionlessly. I tried to see us from their point of view, absorbing that list of incitement and violence. If my father or mother had been on the jury, our goose would have been cooked right then. I could see that we must look pretty horrendous to these staunch, middle-class Tacomans, who had had to work all their lives to get their rinky-dink houses, to send their kids to some community college, and here were we, children of the upper classes, spoiled brats from Ivy League campuses who had never had to worry about anything, living on food stamps, stealing, and dragging unsuspecting innocents into our den of iniquity. I couldn't blame these Tacomans for being middle-class, for being swallowed up in American propaganda, for being afraid of everything they didn't understand and understanding nothing because the system had been arranged that way purposely so that they couldn't grow and change. I understood them so well because I had been so much like them once, so deadened by the same views and values, so afraid and frigid and repressed. If I had not met and married Robby Stern, I might be just like any of the three women in that jury, hooked on *Redbook* and canasta.

I had changed. But it had taken years of agonized struggle. I had wanted to change. Could we expect these people to change in a few short weeks, to open up their minds enough to see that we were not their enemies, but victims, just like them?

The distance from the jury box to the defense table was immeasurable; it was the distance between two cultures. The judge and the prosecution, with whom the jury could most easily identify, were capitalizing on the differences between the two cultures. The defense would attempt to shrink the cultural gap. There were, after all, certain beliefs common to both; or rather, the defendants built their case on this assumption. In a real sense, our belief that we could reach the jury because we were right, was based on the same ideals that made us revolutionaries—a basic trust in humanity. We believed that if given an alternative, most Americans would choose to do the right thing. We built our strategy on the faith that Americans wanted to be good and just. We gambled on the integrity of a people despised by most of the world, because without that faith, we would have been no different than those we called our enemies. "Trust the people." It had been a meaningless Movement motto for years; we made it real. And we won; a small, shallow victory, but a victory none the less.

Carl Maxey began the cross-examination. Expertly building his questions, he made it clear that Red Parker was not always so reliable in his reporting. Re-examining his report, *The Making of a Riot,* he noted several mistakes. Parker had sworn that Abeles had said, "If the pigs try to stop us—kill them," yet in his report, he had attributed that quote to another man. He had reported that Mike Lerner's telephone conversation, which was one of his conspiracy charges, had been with Tom Hayden of the Chicago 8; it had actually been with Rennie Davis. Claiming that he was very close to the defendants, he admitted to Carl that he barely knew the men from Ithaca, and had really only known Roger and myself. Claiming intimate knowledge of Weatherman, he testified that the SDS split occurred in November when it actually occurred in June. He included several RYM 2 people in his list of Weathermen.

But Maxey's cross-examination only preluded Chip's; it was Chip who exposed Parker to the jury as a liar and a criminal.

Parker admitted that he had furnished the spray paint for people to use at TDA; the FBI had paid for the paint. "I was asked by the FBI to check the Fortress for explosives and weapons and to spend some time there just prior to TDA," testified Parker, "and I had to have a good excuse for spending some time there and it would increase my credibility to bring paint, so I brought paint."

"You needed an excuse to stay at the Fortress? I thought from your testimony that you were very close to these people," queried Chip.

"Well, being close can mean a whole lot of things."

"Well, these people, did you feel that they trusted you?"

"I was never sure," said Parker.

"What exactly was it about SDS that was so appalling that you went directly to the FBI after being so opposed to the war in Vietnam?"

Parker thought for a minute, and then said, "Probably the violence, the *strategy of building a fascist state for America*."

The spectators giggled; Pitkin flushed, some of the federal marshals shook their heads. Parker looked around nervously, unsure what the murmuring was about.

Chip quickly said, "Who had the strategy of building a fascist state? Are you talking about the FBI?"

"The Weatherman," answered Parker.

Chip looked incredulous. "The Weatherman strategy was to build a fascist state?"

"That's correct," Parker said firmly. "That's their strategy whether you know it or not."

The courtroom was in hysterics. One of our lawyers observed that even Lou Harris was laughing during the testimony. The judge tried unsuccessfully to bring the court to order.

"So you felt that you were opposed to these people," Chip pressed, "and you felt the people of SDS to be a threat of some sort, and you went to the FBI, right?"

"Yes."

"And you didn't like their violence, or the way they were using the war and racism for their own means, correct? You felt they weren't sincere about it?"

"Yes."

"But you felt no compunction yourself about using illegal means to get these people?"

"Sometimes it bothered me a little bit."

"But you were willing to do illegal things, and you were willing to use the same tactics as you deplored in these people, correct, for a higher good?"

"Right, I felt that my credibility was synonymous with survival."

"Now, you say you were close to the Weathermen?"

"As close as I could get."

"Well, just how close was that, would you tell the jury?"

"I lived with them, ate with them, shared their life style. I was a Weatherman, for all practical purposes. They seemed unable to detect that I was anything else."

"Well, now, in fact, isn't it true that you were never a Weatherman?" said Chip, looking absolutely menacing. I was surprised that Parker was holding his cool as well as he had.

"No," he answered, licking his lips. "I was an actual member of Weatherman, even though I was on another level."

"And you were very close to Weatherman, and knew what was going on?"

"Yes."

"Well, in your earlier testimony, you claimed that you had spoken to Roger, and that he had professed to be favorable and friendly toward Lerner. Is this true?"

"Yes. I think what impressed Roger was that Lerner said that he wanted to get people together who were tired of talking about revolution, and wanted to do something about it."

"You say Roger was friendly toward Lerner, and yet you say you were close to Weatherman. Weren't you aware that there was bitter antagonism between Lerner and Weatherman?"

"No."

"But you were close to them?"

The witness said nothing, and stared at the judge, who smiled encouragingly at him.

"Okay. Let's pursue this first meeting, January 19, which you so aptly describe in your report, *The Making of a Riot.* You heard me talk at that meeting, right? Would you please repeat again what I said."

"You said, 'We've been watching the Seattle scenes. We watched it on the Huntley-Brinkley report, we saw you out at Sea-Tac Airport slugging it out with the black brothers, and we thought this looks like the place to make things happen, so we came out here, and you know what? This is the deadest goddam town we've ever been in. Can't even find the ghetto. . . .'"

"You've said this four or five times—have you memorized this speech? Now are you absolutely certain this is what I said?"

"Positive," said Parker, looking relieved.

"You were arrested at that demonstration, I believe?" asked Chip.

"Yes."

"But with the exception of your arrest, wasn't that demonstration nonviolent?"

"Basically."

"Mr. Parker, if I were to say to you that I never mentioned in my whole speech the words 'Sea-Tac,' what would you say?"

"I wrote your remarks as best I remembered them."

"Wasn't I, in fact, referring to Seattle Community College of the spring before?"

"I don't remember it that way."

"But you're not positive now."

"To the best of my ability . . ."

"Do you remember me talking about dancing in bars in that speech? Talking about how this town was very lively, and that people were dancing in the bars and there were a lot of parties over Christmas time?"

"No, I remember your talking about this being the deadest goddam town . . ."

"Didn't I say in fact, it was the liveliest town I had ever seen?"

"No, I don't remember."

"Do you remember me talking about the potential of this town, for instance, talking about unemployment?"

"I think I do, now that you mention it."

"So there was more in the speech than you just remembered or wrote in your report?"

"I just remembered certain parts."

"And certain other parts that you think perhaps might not be inflammatory you have forgotten?"

"I didn't write down everything, I guess."

"Well, is it your job to write down things that are inflammatory? Isn't that what the FBI wants?"

"Well, we are interested in violations of federal laws and bombings and attacks against human life, anything that would cause injury to human life."

"So that you would only take down certain things that might be of use to the FBI and ignore other things in your report?"

"I put down what I remembered."

"Speaking of inflammatory remarks, isn't it true that you urged people to use the paint you brought to the Fortress? Didn't you say something to this effect—'Didn't you people hear what those fuckers did to the people in Chicago? Don't you think we should do something about it?'"

"I don't remember."

"In fact, wasn't this part of your policy regularly, to try to goad people by talking militantly?"

"I had to take kind of a hard line once in a while."

"Didn't you talk particularly about bombings and violence and fighting cops? Didn't you encourage a number of people and say, 'These kind of actions were good actions and necessary'?"

"It's possible." Parker looked pale by now. "I was trying to infiltrate them, so I had to say things they'd agree with."

"Did you ever try to recruit people to Weatherman?"

"That was part of my job."

"To recruit people into violent acts so that they could be busted or trapped, in other words?"

"No!"

"What did you tell these people?"

"I talked to them about a minority revolution in America, and about building a class war based on an article by Eldridge Cleaver."

"So in other words, you actively—to keep your cover—you had to say certain things to Weatherpeople. But you also talked to people who were not in the Movement—maybe trying to make up their minds about the Movement, about the necessity for armed struggle, violence, et cetera, you yourself? Yes or no?"

"Yes."

"You testified earlier today that you were opposed to the violence of SDS but you didn't find that your talking to these people who might not even be in the Movement about violence in any kind of contradiction with that?"

"Yes, so I stopped doing it."

"You stopped doing it? Then you didn't have a conversation some time in the end of April with anybody in the SLF in which you said that the Seattle conspiracy indictments were outrageous, and that you thought something should be done, perhaps burning a campus building down?"

"No."

"Never? You are under oath now."

The judge interposed, "He knows it."

"I doubt it," said Chip, his eye on the jury. "But you insist you never encouraged anyone to attempt to burn down a campus building?"

"No."

"Mr. Parker, are you familiar with the term 'agent provocateur'?"

"Yes."

"What does it mean?"

"Well for years the C.P. has used the word 'provocateur' to mean anyone who infiltrates them or, you know, opposes them, especially people that oppose them directly."

"Have you ever heard of police agents inciting people to do actions so that they will later be trashed?"

"Yes. But I don't think there is any fact behind it."

"Have you ever encouraged people, anyone, since you have become part of the FBI, to violate a law; yes or no?"

"Yes."

"Did the FBI direct you to do this?"

"Yes."

"Did the FBI encourage you to give drugs to people in the Movement?"

"No."

"You did that on your own?"

"They asked for it."

"But you would supply drugs? In fact, didn't you supply even this summer a number of high school students with marijuana?"

"That's a lie."

"Are you aware of any nicknames that you had among people other than Red—like Speed, for instance?"

"No."

"Speed Parker? You have no idea what it could refer to?"

"No."

"Didn't you tell a number of the Weathermen during the spring that you were afraid of being addicted to codeine?"

"I was concerned about it."

"Were you also concerned about being addicted to speed?"

"I was worried about it, so I quit taking it."

"Weren't you in fact, mainlining it?"

"No, I took it orally."

"Was this taking speed part of the life style of the revolutionaries that helped your credibility?"

"I took it to keep going."

"Speed is what is known as a hard drug, is that correct?"

"It's a pretty bad drug."

"And isn't it a point in the SLF program that we have to discourage people from using hard drugs?"

"I don't remember."

"Doesn't it say specifically that 'as a loving community, we will discourage and try to stop the use of hard drugs in our community'?"

"Now that I think about it, I guess it does."

"Were you taking hard drugs because you felt some sort of pressure?"

"Yes."

"Was it perhaps a contradiction between always having to lie to people?"

"No, it was the hours I was putting in."

"You didn't feel any pressure about lying to people?"

"None whatsoever."

"It didn't bother you at all?"

"No."

Chip waited a minute to let Parker's answer sink into the jury. They were staring intently at Parker, a strange look on all their faces. There was a tension in the courtroom. Pitkin looked green; Lou Harris looked sick; the judge was frowning deeply. I held my breath as Chip expertly lined Parker up for the kill.

"You testified previously that you first contacted the CIA? And not the FBI? Did you first call the CIA because that appeared more glamorous to you?"

"No."

"Did you ever exaggerate in your reporting?"

"NO."

"You testified previously that you lived in the Fortress. Isn't it a fact that you never lived in the Fortress, that maybe you stayed there one or two nights?"

"I lived in—an apartment across the street, but I stayed in the Fortress quite often."

"But you never lived there?"

"I ate there, I slept there. What else do you call it?"

"But did you actually live there? There's a difference between living and crashing."

"I lived between the Fortress and the apartment."

"In the street," said Chip, smiling, and the jury smiled with him; the spectators applauded.

"I lived there for about a week," said Parker, beginning to perspire, beginning to look desperate.

"When?" snapped Chip.

"In March."

"After TDA?"

"Yes, for three or four days . . ."

"It's starting to get smaller," said Chip. "First three months, then a week, now three days. All right. Now you testified the other day that the people living at the Fortress lived by lying and ripping off, and things like that . . ."

"Yes."

"You didn't know that four people that I know were working during that period?"

"No."

"But you lived in the Fortress and were close to the Weathermen?"

Parker seemed to shrink in his chair. I looked at the jury; on the faces of one or two I thought I saw the barest traces of hostility.

"Going back to the spring again, didn't you last spring take a number of people shooting, supply these people with ammunition, and talk a lot about sniping, and your experience in the Green Berets?"

"I didn't supply ammunition."

"But you did talk about the Green Berets?"

"Yes."

"Isn't it a fact that you were never in the Green Berets?"

"Yes."

"You did it to make yourself look big for these people?"

"Right."

"Some of these people had never shot before? And you encouraged them to learn how to shoot? Was that going along with your FBI duties taking people out who didn't know how to shoot, and teaching them how?"

"I wanted to find out how much they knew about shooting, and the only way I could find out was to be with them when they were shooting. I was convinced that they couldn't hit the side of a barn."

"Is this your normal practice, to find out things about people by pushing them into it?"

"Well, I was constantly trying to find out how competent these people were who claimed to be urban guerrillas."

"You were opposed to these revolutionaries and violence, but you thought nothing wrong with giving them guns and teaching them how to shoot? You tried to help them, and encouraged them to become urban guerrillas, didn't you?"

"Only to find out how much they knew."

"You were continually lying to these people, right?"

"Right."

"You would do anything to protect your cover?"

"Right."

"It's very important to you that people like us be brought to justice? I mean, you feel very strongly that we are bad people and should be brought to justice?"

"Yes."

"So you would go to almost any length, short of killing somebody, but almost any length of trickery to bring us to justice?"

"Yes, any length."

"Any length—and for months and months you lied to people who thought you were their friend in order to get us, isn't that correct?"

"That is absolutely correct."

"You are willing to go, as you say, to any length to get us?"

"That's correct," answered Parker.

"Do you still feel that way?" asked Chip.

"Yes."

"You were willing to lie to get us?"

"Yes."

Chip turned to the jury, and, looking straight at them, said, "That's what he said."

The spectators shrieked and applauded, the judge banged with his gavel, Pitkin shuffled some papers, then put his head in his hands, as Chip, trying not to gloat too much, sat down. And in the jury box, twelve people sat stunned, knowing that Red Parker had not been telling the truth; that he would do anything, say anything, to get us, even lie under oath.

That was the end of the prosecution's case. But just for good measure, Tigar's cross-examination, which followed Chip's, brought out that Parker had purchased potassium chlorate for self-igniting Molotov cocktails in April of 1970, and had accepted money to buy dynamite. Around that time, which was the time we were indicted, Parker also offered to sell dynamite, guns, plastic explosives and an assortment of dope to people in and outside of the Movement.

The cross-examination of Parker ended at the noon recess on December 8, sixteen days after the trial had begun. It was now the prosecution's turn to produce another witness. We waited all that afternoon, while Stan Pitkin paced back and forth, nervously telling the judge that his witness had been delayed but would come as soon as possible. Meanwhile we sat in court and waited. The jury sat in the jury room and waited. The spectators sat in the gallery and waited. We all waited for the witness, but none arrived.

As the day passed, my Bartholin gland, which had never healed, began to swell again, until at midday, it was once more the size of a golf ball. I swallowed several painkillers, but it was impossible for me to sit or walk; during that entire tedious day I half lay across some chairs, groggy from the Demerol, and almost in tears from the pain. Finally, in desperation, I called my doctor, and she told me I would have to come the following day to have it operated on. It could not wait. In a panic, I called Steinborn to the phone; he conferred with my doctor, and when he hung up, he steered me into the judge's chambers, where we explained to the judge that I had a serious personal illness, had to have an operation immediately and since Pitkin was stalling with his next witness, this appeared to be a good time for me to undergo surgery.

Boldt reluctantly granted permission. It was not proper procedure to dismiss a defendant from her case, but he was convinced of the utter necessity of it. I would be excused from court December 9 and December 10; I would have to be present on Monday the fourteenth. With the weekend to recuperate, I agreed.

The operation was minor but painful. The doctor lanced the gland once again, drained the pus, and then sewed the flaps of flesh flush against the wall of my vagina, with melting stitches. Then I was wadded with gauze, given more painkillers, and told to sitz constantly. When the local anesthetic wore off, the pain in my vagina from the lancing and the stitches was intolerable. I went home and went to bed.

The boys came home that night exhausted and frustrated; Pitkin had stalled another day—still no witness. He refused to admit the fact that he had no case; Parker had been his ace in the hole and he had been smashed. The boys complained about the increasingly poor treatment of our spectators, and the systematic exclusion of many of them from the courtroom. Everybody was nervous and touchy from waiting for the prosecution.

Around ten-thirty the next day I was awakened by the insistent ringing of the telephone, which had been installed upstairs because I could not walk very well. I answered it—Joey was on the line.

"Susie," he said in a quavering voice, "it's cookies. I only have a few seconds, and then they're taking us to jail."

"To jail," I shrieked. "What happened?"

"Fucking Boldt called a mistrial, I can't go into it now, but he said we had prejudiced the jury, and called a mistrial, and refused to give us a trial or a hearing, and said he was going to send us all right to jail today. I ran out, and went into another building to call you, to say good-by, to tell you I love you, to keep on trucking."

"But, Joey, what happened . . ."

"Listen, baby, I got to go now, we're having a press conference and we got to get our shit together. Don't worry about me. See you in six months. I love you."

"Joey, Joe . . ." but he had hung up.

Panic! Hysteria! Then the calm of crisis, cold as steel, methodically doing what had to be done, routine after years of living on the line between sanity and insanity, balancing precariously for survival.

I called a boy friend, and asked him to come over. Then I roused a girl who was crashing in the house; she had just started using smack, and was groggy, but she helped me to dress. Over my puffy face, my brown circles, my bluish eyelids, I smeared my mask; with shaking hands I brushed my hair until it stood out electrically. Then into my courtroom fancies—long black skirt, flowing shawl, black hat, and I was hobbling down the stairs to meet my old boy friend and be driven to Tacoma to kiss the boys good-by, to be with my people, anything, just not to be alone.

It was pouring rain. We drove to Tacoma, and could only find a parking space two blocks away. My old boy friend, an ex-football player, picked me up and carried me the two blocks to the courthouse, up the steps, into an elevator and then down the hall. Dozens of federal marshals parted, Charlie Robinson stared, Lou Harris' mouth fell open, Stan Pitkin paled. Rain-drenched and tear-drenched, pale and frail, I was carried into the pressroom. The door flung open, and three TV cameras turned like robots to take in the picture. It was very bright in there from all the spotlights for the cameras, and I didn't have my glasses on. I wanted Joey, Anne. Unable to speak, I stretched out my arms, and the boys surrounded me, while the cameras ground away. Then finally, gently, I was lowered to a chair, and Joey was pressing my hand, and Anne was kneeling beside me. I could not stop crying, and I thought I was going to faint. In the background, I heard Lerner saying, "The railroad has stopped today, and we say the railroad in this court is not going to start again." Then there were applause and chants.

It turned out that Boldt had decided to wait until Monday to sentence the defendants; they were free to return home until that time.

Carefully Anne and Joey led me out of the courthouse and out into the rain, with the cameras flashing away, the reporters hovering like vultures. For once I didn't feel like playing to the press; I was almost being carried by Joey and Anne. One of those photographs was reprinted on the front page of the New York *Post*; in between a radiant Anne and a handsome, somber Joe was a drawn woman with wasted eyes, her chin thrust out defiantly, in sad contrast to the wreckage of her face. When I first saw that photograph, I thought, "They're destroying me." And then I thought, "No, I won't let them. They won't defeat me. I won't let them. I *won't!*"

Riding back to Seattle, the boys told me what had happened.

When they arrived in the courthouse at eight-thirty the morning of the tenth, a crowd of fifty people was huddled outside the courthouse door, drenched. They protested to Charlie Robinson, who refused to let the people into the vestibule of the courthouse and was keeping the door locked.

The defendants threatened Robinson, and soon a scuffle broke out around the courthouse door. One of the lawyers advised the Dude to approach the judge and notify him that a riot was about to occur.

The Dude, infuriated, raced upstairs to the judge's chambers and began pounding on his door; the judge refused him admittance, and Dude pounded away. When Boldt finally opened the door, it was to cite Dude with contempt of court for pounding on the judge's chamber door.

The Dude returned with the lawyers to the defense room, and the other defendants were summoned. At nine-thirty the only person the bailiff could find in the courtroom was Carl Maxey. Even though no one was in court, the judge ordered the jury to be brought in, something he had never done before. Then he sent the bailiff after the defendants and their counsel.

Five minutes passed and the judge was pissed!

Once more he sent the harried bailiff down the hall to the defense room; the bailiff notified the defendants through a closed door, and returned to court.

Finally the lawyers for the defense appeared. But no defendants.

"Where are the defendants?" Boldt thundered.

"They refuse to come, your honor," Tigar said.

Boldt turned pink. "Bailiff, go get the defendants. Tell them the court orders them to come immediately."

The bailiff galloped off again.

Boldt, frothing, lashed out at the lawyers: "The court has ordered the defendants to appear at their trial, the jury has been waiting for twenty minutes, and the defendants have not appeared. If they do not appear, I will have to take some action."

"Your honor . . ." began Tigar.

"I want them to follow the order of the court."

"Your honor, may the defendant Dowd have time for a hearing?"

"I wish the defendants to respond to the order of the court." By now Boldt was bright red. His eyes were bulging; the veins in his neck were standing out. He looked like a man in the throes of apoplexy.

The bailiff returned to inform the court that the door to the defense room was locked, and that the defendants refused to admit him.

That did it. Purple with rage, Boldt leaped off his pinnacle, and, with his robes flapping, flew across the courtroom and down the hall, followed by the puffing bailiff, and a dozen federal marshals and the defense lawyers, leaving the bewildered jury sitting there.

He arrived at the defense room just as the door swung open. Out poured the acrid odor of marijuana, an unction for the frenetic Dude.

"You are now, each and all of you, commanded to immediately come into the courtroom!" barked Boldt.

"We were just on our way," said Abeles.

"Why aren't our people allowed inside?" asked Joe.

But the judge had turned away and was proceeding down the hall. The defendants surrounded him, elbowing the federal marshals;

the judge walked faster. Chip began to trot to keep up with him; the judge, huffing a bit, began to jog. Chip increased his pace, and the judge, intent on being the first in the courtroom, bellowed with wrath and began a full gallop down the hall. With a trill of laughter, Chip, onetime track star at Cornell, burst into stride, and was in the courtroom in a second, and there, to his astonishment, sat the jury, looking bewildered.

Chip smiled and nodded his head to the jury. The jury smiled and nodded back. Chip approached the jury box, leaned against it and said, "I would like to explain to you why we refused to come in this morning. There are a number of people who have been kept outside every day in the rain, people who are getting sick, and all we ask is that the marshals allow these people to come into the lobby, which they have not done. Also, the judge has called Mr. Dowd in contempt for attempting to speak to him about the people in the rain . . ."

At this point the judge heaved into the courtroom, and there before his very eyes was Chip, having an amicable conversation with the jury. Not in all his years as a Judge for Life had this occurred in a courtroom of Boldt's.

"*Mr. Marshall,*" he shrieked as he climbed onto his pinnacle, "*be silent!*"

Chip, still addressing the jury, said, "I think we are entitled to a hearing . . ."

"*Mr. Marshall, Mr. Marshall, Mr. Marshall,*" the judge parroted and then, unable to restrain himself, ordered the jury out of the room, declared the defendants, with the exception of me, in contempt of court, and ordered a mistrial on the basis that the defendants had prejudiced the jury by their contumacious behavior. Although all the defendants objected, the judge refused to listen. Losing control, he was paying them back for balking at his authority. It was at that point that Joe had slipped out to phone me, believing that Boldt intended to cart them all off to jail that day.

The jury was dismissed by the judge. When they were polled, the majority of them said they had been very interested in the case, and had wanted to see it through, had witnessed very little disruption by the defendants, and did not feel prejudiced against them.

Pitkin had not produced a witness for two days. He had none to produce. The government's case was clearly lost; had the trial continued, there is no doubt that we would have been acquitted. Judge Boldt solved the government's embarrassing failure by calling a mistrial, although I'm sure he knew his reasoning was flimsy and that his reaction to the defendants was very personal.

The weekend passed in a frenzy of meetings, parties, drugs, and drink, marked by delirious hilarity. The boys were full of bravado, except for Lerner, who was constantly on the verge of tears. Their girl friends and friends clung to them, frightened, almost blaming them for going to jail and disrupting their lives. I felt more than ever that weekend what it was to be a star, how cruel a deception it is. Even the night before going to jail, we had to provide entertainment; it was expected of us, and we exacted it from ourselves.

I was in quite a dilemma. Because of my operation, I had missed the mistrial and I wasn't in contempt. Yet, it seemed clear that I too would go to jail. In a way I felt it was expected of me . . . not to go to jail would have made everything I had claimed about being a revolutionary meaningless. It's not that I wanted to go to jail; it's just that I wanted the judge to know I was just as contemptuous of him as the boys were, that women could hate just as much, could be just as disruptive and deaf to authority. I was caught up in the drama of it all. To be a defendant of a famous conspiracy case and not to go to jail— what a farcical anticlimax. I knew I would go with the boys. So did the boys. So did Anne. So did all our friends. I could not fail.

That Sunday, we had an all-day meeting. I can't remember much of it, because Joe and I dropped acid and giggled through the entire thing. During that meeting we did decide that all of us including myself would make a statement to the judge concerning the mistrial. We decided that since I was not cited for contempt, my speech could be more vitriolic. To leave a lasting impression as the lone woman defendant, I would speak last, the position of prestige.

Just before we left the meeting, Lerner called his mother; I heard my co-defendant say,

"Okay, Mom, yes, Mom, I'll wear my rubbers and carry an umbrella." I remembered an old Movement joke I'd heard about the mothers of Mark Rudd and Mike Lerner going to temple together and moaning about their lost sons.

Anne gave a good-by party in our house that night. About a hundred people were there; everyone was smashed. I sat on the steps with Anne, and we made plans. She would take over my job at the Century and keep the house, for when the boys and I got out of jail, we would need a place to live. Anne looked very solemn. All her friends were going to prison in one fell swoop. If that wasn't Nazism, what was?

I sat on the stairs with Anne, my darling friend, with a dead heart, lonely, lonely, lonely. My Bartholin hurt terribly; I had been going to my doctor every other day to have it perforated. I was in an agony of sexual frustration, but there were no tender arms to hold me that night. The party came and staggered away. A dozen people slept in our house that night. About three o'clock I went to my room alone; even Anne was fucking—so were all the boys. I took four reds, and two Demerols; they drowned out the acid, but didn't put me to sleep.

At six o'clock, I got up, staggering, unco-ordinated, and made breakfast for the entire house, then woke up everyone. After breakfast I sluggishly dressed, piled on my make-up, and, still wobbling from all the downers, sat quietly, waiting for Truman.

In the courtroom, everyone was tense, expectant. The judge came from his chambers, arranged himself, and read the contempt citation. Each of the defendants was given a copy; all of us, with the exception of Lerner and Lippman, ripped them up, and threw the pieces into the air. Dude and Abeles presented the judge with a Nazi flag that had been made the night before. The judge was white with repressed fury, but he contained himself and had the marshals remove the flag from his bench.

Then one by one each of our four lawyers addressed the court. Then one after the other, the male defendants spoke, concluding with Chip. Lerner spoke for the longest time, taking up twenty-four pages of court transcript.

Then I got up to speak, my mind a vacuum, my heart very full. I was still disoriented from the barbiturates, and in dreadful pain, but all I could think of was that I had to say something, that people still didn't understand; if I could just phrase it right, one more time, they would finally understand. I grabbed the lectern to support myself; the room was circling about me.

"Mrs. Kelly . . ." began the judge.

"I'm Kelly," and Joey once again stood up.

"Mrs. Stern, will you please sit down and be silent."

"I want to be heard."

"Please sit down."

"I insist on being heard."

"Mrs. Stern, please, young lady, listen. You have not been cited for contempt, and there is no reason for you to speak. If you do speak, it may result in a contempt citation . . ."

"You said all the defendants could speak," Joey interrupted furiously.

"You're supposed to protect freedom," Abeles shouted.

"Please sit down, Mrs. Stern."

"I intend to speak, your honor."

"Please sit down. Please sit down and be silent, Mrs. Stern. Please sit down."

"I'm not going to sit down, so stop repeating yourself like a broken record."

The Dude stood up, spitting and shaking his fists, his gigantic frame towering above the federal marshals who were beginning to move cautiously toward the defense table. "You can't understand it from a woman, can you, judge?" screamed the Dude.

"Mrs. Stern, I am going to take steps to impose a penalty for your defiance of my order. Now, if you want to speak in defiance of my order, you may do so."

"Your honor, let me advise you that I am fully aware that I may be held in contempt of court if I continue, but I must speak. I know you don't like to listen. Women in this society are to be seen and not heard. I am one woman who wants to be heard.

"I want to thank my attorneys, Jeff Steinborn and Carl Maxey; they both defended me and supported me as best as they could, within the limits of the law. It was impossible for these lawyers to

328 WITH THE WEATHERMEN

defend me, because there is absolutely no way that the gap could be
bridged between what I believe in and what you stand for in this
courtroom.

"In other words, there is no way that these lawyers could express
what I feel so that you could understand it.

"I couldn't express what I feel so that the jury could understand
it. I was not allowed to express any human responses, or emotional
feelings, or to explain my ideals. Even though all the defendants
were gagged by court procedure, because of our aggressive and persistent outbursts, the jury began to listen to what the defendants
were saying. If they were prejudiced, your honor, it most certainly
was not against us.

"Jeff Dowd said that this courtroom was not big enough to admit
everybody that should be admitted, that he would like the Woodstock nation in here. I would like them in here too. I would have
liked some of our peers in the jury box; it would have been less surreal to me to see some freaks on the jury. But that wasn't allowed.

"It's not possible to include the other people that I would include
in this courtroom, all the Vietnamese people that are dead, napalmed
by the system you purport to keep in order, napalmed by the system
that we purport to destroy, napalmed by the system that you say you
will uphold, and I say it is you burning those children, men, and
women. Give them back to me, give all the Vietnamese men, women
and children who have been killed back to me, and let them sit in this
courtroom, and let's ask them what they think; or the people of My
Lai.[3] Soldiers were instructed to destroy every living thing in My Lai
on sight; and you purport to uphold such a system, to give credence to
its law and order, and I purport to destroy it.

"I will destroy it because I cannot see one man, such as you or
Nixon, or the two thousand or so of you and Nixons in the world
destroying hundreds of millions who are suffering in this world.

"Give me back the people of My Lai, Judge Boldt, because the
onus is on you, their deaths are on your shoulders, not mine. You
can't possibly hold me in contempt, because I can't deal with the
word in the vernacular in which you use it; the word contempt
doesn't begin to express what I feel about Vietnam.

"Give me back the American troops that were killed there, help-lessly and hopelessly duped—forced, some of them by poverty, to enlist, because they couldn't get jobs in this country; forced to invade another country and be killed by people who repeatedly said they didn't want to kill American troops, but were forced to defend themselves. That is revolutionary violence, a term we were begin-ning to introduce to the jury, and you made sure they didn't hear any more about it, because revolutionary violence is different from the kind of violence that you perpetuate on this society, sir.

"Revolutionary violence means self-defense, it means what the Vietnamese people are doing for their children and their lives and their future and their land. What they are doing for themselves and for me, and all the people in this world, except for a few like you, unfortunately.

"Give the troops back and then maybe we can talk about con-tempt, and then you can bring in Bobby Seale, who in another court was bound and gagged when his lawyer was not there to defend him, and in his attempt to defend himself, was treated to the brutal-ity of justice in this country. Bring me Bobby Seale, and all the black kids right here in Seattle who are walking around with swollen bel-lies because they don't have any food to eat at night.

"Why you go home each night Judge Boldt, and very much like Pontius Pilate—and I understand you are a religious man who believes deeply in Christ—just like Pilate you wash your hands of what is going on in Vietnam and the ghettos of Seattle and around this country and Latin America and Africa, and all over this world; very much like Pontius Pilate, you wash your hand of it all, and you say, 'Bravo, they choose Jesus!'

"Well, Jesus was framed just like we were; the people didn't choose to persecute him, just as they didn't choose to persecute us; a grand jury voted to indict us, and you and Pitkin will make sure we lose.

"But your dishonesty is not enough, your honor, because even while I am talking, outside I can hear the chants of my people, of people who know where you are, where your head is at, where you stand, who know that you are on your last leg, that you are dying and that this country is dying with you; of people, young people, and a growing number of middle-aged and older people who are beginning to understand that there is a different kind of justice, that there is a different kind of law and order, that there is a new Renaissance, which we call the revolution that is going to create a new humanity, and someday, although I doubt that I will live to see it, it won't include people like you."

I spoke quietly, they told me later. Forcefully, and with great dignity. Chip said everyone in the courtroom had tears in their eyes; even the federal marshals were listening sympathetically.

I attempted to conclude my remarks by talking about the unfairness of the mistrial, but Boldt, upset by the effect of my speech, was vehement about my not mentioning the mistrial. As I tried to speak, he continuously interrupted me, ordering me to sit down. I repeatedly refused until there was a shouting match, with the defendants, except for Roger and Lerner, all shouting at the judge, who shouted back.

The judge, quivering with rage, called me in contempt. People from the gallery began to shout as Boldt ordered me again to sit down and keep quiet.

"They will have to drag me off to stop me," I finally said, angered because I could not conclude.

Beside himself, the Dude screamed, "Come on, let's see them drag her off. I want to see the sight of those killers dragging off a woman who has just gotten out of the hospital two days ago, and you, you old killer, you're so bloody it's unbelievable."

Chip demanded a jury trial for our contempt.

Abeles shouted that Boldt should let me speak.

The Dude, totally out of control now, was jumping up and down shouting, "Kill the kids, kill the kids, kill the kids," over and over again.

The courtroom was in bedlam. From nowhere a group of thirty behemoth federal marshals appeared with black gloves on their hands and blackjacks. In no time they were around me. I was grabbed from behind around my chest and neck, and they began to drag me out of the courtroom. I struggled wildly, choking. I heard Tigar screaming, "Let her go, she's sick," and I saw him race across the courtroom; then I saw him stop short, and fall forward, crying in agony, "I've been maced, I've been maced."

I was swinging with my arms; Steinborn told me later that I broke a pig's nose. I saw a hulking marshal grab Joe by the balls and drag him across the courtroom. I saw another slug Abeles and drag him away. Then I got very dizzy and didn't struggle as they pulled me out of the courtroom.

An hour later we appeared before the judge; Chip and Joe were handcuffed. He charged all the men, with the exception of Roger and Lerner, with another contempt, and then handed out six-month maximum sentences. For Chip, Joe, Abeles, and Dude this meant a year in prison; for the rest of us, six months. No hearing. No trial. Go directly to jail.

The Honorable George Boldt told us that he was serving justice by punishing us so, and that he had personally forgiven us, because his Christian faith required it of him.

"I have no doubt my daily prayers for strength and guidance to be calm, understanding and patient in this case, and to do that which is fair and just in the sight of our heavenly Father have been answered," the judge said very devoutly. "I believe Divine Providence may have given this court, and others, guidance to an effective solution of disruptive trials. I pray it may be so."

DECEMBER 14, 1970

Anne came into the defense room crying.

"Annie, what are you crying for?" I asked, upset.

"Susan, you're going to jail—how can you be so calm?"

I hadn't realized it. For some reason I expected to go home. I was very tired and wanted to lie down. The lawyers were arguing that I should be taken to a hospital instead of City Jail until I sufficiently recovered from my operation.

I clutched Anne convulsively when the federal marshals finally came to get me. They drove me to a hospital. I was put into a tiny room with no windows, and two guards were stationed outside my door. I undressed and gratefully crawled into bed and slept

I was awakened a few hours later by a doctor, who wanted to check my Bartholin gland; I followed him into an examining room, and the two federal marshals followed me, and waited outside the door.

The doctor wasn't a doctor at all. He was an intern who had studied "women's problems" for six weeks as part of his over-all medical education in medical school. He was "vaguely acquainted" with the Bartholin gland, and ecstatic that he had a real live one to examine.

He decided my gland was filling again and required another lancing. I was duly lanced, and returned to my hospital bed in agony.

A couple of hours later a different intern came to examine me; the same procedure was repeated. I screamed bloody murder when he started scraping my vagina with his little knife. I was given some painkillers and sedation and allowed to sleep through the night.

First thing in the morning, I was summoned by still another doctor, who told me that I had to be examined still again. I was positioned on the examining table and three new interns gathered around. First the doctor scraped with the sharp, tiny knife; I began to whimper. When he had finished, I started to get up, but one of the interns wanted to look at this incredible Bartholin. I was pushed back down on the table, my legs were held open, while the intern probed with the knife. Now I didn't whimper. I was terrified, and beyond myself with pain. I shrieked, and the startled doctor let go of my legs. I leaped off the table, and plunged toward a window, jammed myself against it and screamed, "If any of you touch me again, I'll jump," and began to howl at the top of my lungs for the federal marshals. They came bursting in, went white when they saw me; apparently they were supposed to deliver me to prison alive.

"I want to go to jail," I yelled. Unsure of what they should do, one of them called Charlie Robinson, who gave permission. I was dressed and driven to City Jail, still in terrible pain.

I had been in City Jail five or six times before, yet I had to suffer the same procedure. I was signed in by a matron, my possessions and clothes were taken, and I was given a uniform. It was a faded blue cotton wrap-around which hung to my knees. Then I was taken for mug shots; one facing forward, one profile, one without my glasses. Then fingerprinted; each finger, an extra thumb print, then all the fingers of each hand at once. They never came out the first time, so the process had to be repeated. Then into a holding cell, to await processing and reassignment to a permanent cell. In the holding cell are the transients; those waiting bail, those not yet booked, those sleeping off a drug or a drunk. Exhausted, I fell asleep on top of the rough wool blanket of a bunk bed. In the holding cell you can't read or write; you're not let out into the corridor; you just wait. Sleep is the best friend a prisoner has.

DECEMBER 20

I am in cell 603, Seattle City Jail, Public Safety Building, Third and James Street, Seattle, Washington 98104. I have paced my cell dozens of times. Lengthwise it's eighteen steps. Widthwise, ten steps. On one wall there are five bunk beds; only two of them are empty. Opposite the bunks is a rectangular iron table with attached iron benches on either side of it. A few feet to the right of the table is a toilet and a sink and a shower stall. There is no privacy; everything is painted a ghoulish mint green.

Along with two uniforms and a white cotton nightgown, each week I get two sheets, one pillow case, two towels and one washcloth. I have the top bunk because I'm afraid I will get raped on a lower one; this way, I'll have some warning if anybody tries to climb up to reach me. One of my two gray wool blankets is tucked carefully into my bed. The other is folded like a bedroll at the foot of it. My nightgown is under my pillow and my towels and extra uniform are on a hook between my bunk and the next. My few toilet articles and personals are in a box on the floor. We're allowed undies and sox, face cream, shampoo, toothpaste, and a hairbrush; no make-up. From the library I have gotten several books. I read an average of twelve hours a day. I can't stand the fucking TV. And I can't sleep more than six hours a night.

I think I'm withdrawing slightly from the barbiturates. I have a strange runny nose, but no other cold symptoms. I feel very nervous and anxious, but that may just be my environment. I have trouble sleeping and am frequently nauseated.

All the women in my cell are here for drug violations, mostly heroin. The black women pronounce it "heron." They all admire my veins, especially after I take a bath and they stick out on my hands and feet. They tap my veins and pine for such sweet virgin lines to bliss. Their arms are striated with thick track marks. Some show me tracks on their temples, others scars from boils where they missed the vein. When they get out of jail they tell me, they'll cop a fix before they do anything else. Smack is their life. What else is there?

To support their habits, most of the women were also prostitutes. To pass the time I participate in what is known among jail women as "whore talk." The whores mostly talk shop and I listen wide-eyed and with a growing respect for professional prostitutes. They are certainly more liberated than most Movement women I know.

Today is visiting day. Everyone is excited. Contraband make-up is passed around, and uniforms, carefully hemmed to miniskirt length, are donned. The matrons will confiscate them after visiting hours, but by next week new uniforms will be hemmed again in time for visiting.

I look at myself in the tiny mirror above the sink in our cell. My hair hangs lifeless, my skin is sallow. The faded uniform is too large for me, and the hem is uneven. I am embarrassed to greet my visiting friends in such condition.

Visiting hours are from eight o'clock to eleven o'clock on Sunday morning, and then from two o'clock to five o'clock Sunday afternoon. I know Anne and the rest will come in the afternoon; they will visit with the boys who are being held in County Jail in the morning.

At two o'clock I am on pins and needles. The matrons blare out the names of women who have visitors. One by one my cellmates race from the cell to contact with the outside world. I wait and wait, but my name isn't called.

At two-thirty I finally go to the front and peer out into the receiving room.

"Matron, don't I have any visitors? I'm expecting several."

"The federal marshals informed us this morning that you aren't allowed to have visitors," snapped the matron. "Now get back to your cell."

I began to cry. I didn't want to, but those fucking tears just plopped on out. I had wanted to see Anne's face so much, hear her voice, even for twenty minutes.

Rage followed the tears. How could they be so cruel! They knew what visitors meant to prisoners. I had waited all week for visiting day. It was just to harass me that they hadn't told me.

I jumped down from my bunk bed, and ran down the hall. I was going to give them a piece of my mind. I flew out into the receiving room, and there, standing at the receiving desk, being processed, was Anne. She turned as I ran in, and running to me, flung herself at me; we hugged intensely, holding to each other for life.

The matrons, horrified at this public display of affection, pulled us apart.

"Annie, what are you doing here?" I asked.

"Well, Stern, we all came here to visit you, but when we arrived they said you weren't being allowed any visitors. Everyone else left, but the matron wanted to speak to me. She opened the door to the jail, and asked me to come inside for a second. I didn't want to, but she said it was just to speak to me. So I walked in, they closed the door and arrested me for traffic warrants I had never paid. Steinborn is on his way. See, they wouldn't let me see you so I had to get busted."

Steinborn arrived, and Anne and I went with him into the tiny conference room reserved for lawyers and their clients. There Anne told me the news. SLF had fallen apart; everyone was dispirited. The house was fine, work miserable, life a drag without all of us, she missed me very much.

Steinborn had little information. Our lawyers had filed for an appeal with the Ninth Circuit Court of Appeals in San Francisco, but they hadn't heard anything yet. I would just have to sit tight and wait. Steinborn was sure bail would be granted eventually. The boys were doing fine; they all sent love.

DECEMBER 22

The boys were clandestinely moved out of County Jail. The newspapers speculate that some of them may be in prisons outside of Los Angeles. Not even the lawyers know for sure where they are.

DECEMBER 23

My Bartholin is causing me so much pain that Charlie Robinson has arranged for federal marshals to take me to Planned Parenthood to see my doctor and have it cared for. I am dressed in my street clothes, handcuffed, and a matron and two marshals escort me to Planned Parenthood.

When we walk in the door, the first thing I see is Anne, who leaps up, embraces me and kisses me. The marshals, immediately convinced this is a Weatherman escape plot, close in, wrench Anne and me apart, and stand holding me and looking nervously around. My doctor, after explaining to them that Anne was there purely by coincidence, checks me and agrees to care for me. Charlie Robinson agrees that it is better for me to have my doctor than the prison doctor. The federal marshals will escort me there three times a week, so that my Bartholin can finally heal.

I am lanced again, and returned to my cell; no painkillers this time. I toss all night. I hear the moans of tortured women. They give aspirin to a woman in my cell who is coming down from heroin and about to have a baby. She cries through the night. They finally take her upstairs to the doctor, but she loses the baby. Probably better; it would have been born an addict. In the holding tank, several drunks, howling a cats' chorus of curses and cries, beat on the door. The noise reverberates through the jail. On this one floor in the Public Safety Building, hidden away from all the moral, honest citizens of Seattle, are compressed unspeakable fears, agonies, and suffering. Awake or asleep, life is a nightmare.

DECEMBER 26

Steinborn visits me to tell me that Judge Boldt refuses to grant us bail even though it has been ordered by the higher court. Boldt put off enforcing the higher court order that we be released on bail because he feared that we would attack potential witnesses, officers of the court, including himself, and the community in general. We were to be held pending action by the court of appeals.

"You'd better settle in," Jeff said matter-of-factly. "You may be here for a while." And he kissed me, signed out, and walked out. I think all lawyers should spend some time in jail before they are allowed to practice!

DECEMBER 31

Happy New Year. Still in jail. I went to sleep at nine o'clock, when the lights went out. At midnight one of the women in my cell woke me up, and asked me to give her a New Year's kiss.

"Please," she whispered, "just close your eyes and let me kiss you for a minute, I'm hurtin' so, honey."

I closed my eyes and kissed her, feeling nothing. I wished for the hundredth time that I was a lesbian. I loved the prison women so. There was a gentleness in these barbaric conditions that simply doesn't exist in the outside world, the world of men. Women have it all over men; why don't I want to fuck them?

JANUARY 6, 1971

Jailtime means time. Endless time. Rows and rows of bars representing minutes, hours, days, months, years of empty time; there is always more time to come, floating, suspended, inching along, broken only by sleep, and then more time.

Jailtime means waiting. Waiting for morning, then waiting for night, waiting to eat, waiting for visitors and begging for sleep; waiting as time inevitably passes.

Jailtime means the blues, black and blue, growing deep and mean out of your soul. Blues because you aren't with the people you love, because life is going on outside but you are in here, separated from your life.

Jailtime is life being buried alive. You can't breathe, can't escape from the others in your coffin. You suffocate sitting for three hours on your bunk, and then lying for three hours on your back staring, and then pacing around and around the cell, until you pray that you will go insane or really die.

"Please let me out." The scream overwhelms you from within and you can hear your guts howling and you can see clocks in everything and they're all stopped, but tick on loudly, for ever. An eternity. And there's no way out.

JANUARY 8

I am getting institutionalized. I can hardly believe it happens this fast; I've only been here a couple of weeks. But all the women tell me it's happening. I can sleep now, not as much as the other women, but I fall asleep as soon as lights are out at nine, and I have trouble getting up when the matrons wake us at five-thirty.

I eat all the food now; I even store extra bread smeared with yellow grease and sugar for later in the evening. I am constantly hungry. I am always thinking about food, and salivating by the time the next meal arrives. I voraciously finish off my tray, and scavenge food from other trays. Perhaps a sick junkie can't eat; we divide her tray. Occasionally a trustee who likes me will shove an extra tray in under the door. I am gaining weight.

I have my schedule down pat now, and I lead a very orderly, regulated life. Up at five-thirty, change into my uniform, help to clean the cell, make my bed, and be sitting at the iron table waiting for breakfast. It's gruel with raisins in it generally; on Sundays, besides the gruel, we get some orange-tainted water they call orange juice, and a stale roll.

Breakfast is finished by seven o'clock and most of the other women go back to sleep. I read or play solitaire. One day I played thirty-two consecutive games of solitaire before I ripped the cards to shreds.

Lunch at eleven o'clock; thin sandwich, soup. Gulped down without chewing, leaving me hungry. Then more reading, embroidery I'm working on, some knitting, more solitaire, a mid-afternoon nap, and then finally, supper. Some mystery meat with thick gravy, powdered potatoes, some slimy vegetables and tepid tea, and two slices of bread. It tastes epicurean to me.

Then the endless evening. I now go to watch TV. I never lift my eyes from the screen. Commercials, "The FBI," "The Partridge Family"—whatever garbage is on, I watch it fastidiously. Then back to the cell, countdown and sleep. Sundays my visitors come and once or twice a day visits from Steinborn or a law student. Most of the other women don't have visitors lining up to see them. Some of them never have visitors. Several women have never seen a lawyer. They wait month after month for their trial. Who misses them?

JANUARY 10

Dear Mom—

Life in here is one long, boring minute that never ends. When I think of time in terms of one hundred and eighty days it seems less, but when I think of months, time seems endless. So I have come to think of it as lost time, as if I was sick and in a delirium, and at the end of several months, I will get well and start living again. All is suspended animation.

Although I would love to see you, I won't have you visiting me. You could not touch me or kiss me or hardly see me, because I am on one side of a steel-enclosed room and you would be on the other. There is a six-inch window for us to see each other through, and we would have to talk over a phone. Besides, I don't think you realize the horror of prison; the ghastly green walls, drab atmosphere, reality of steel and bar cages; it would break your heart to see me this way in my ugly, formless blue uniform, with my washed-out skin, you wouldn't be able to stand it, and it would make me suffer too much.

Prison is the harshest reality in life. I won't have you see me caught like an animal. It's no memory for a daughter to give a mother.

JANUARY 12

wearegettingbail wearenotgettingbail wearegettingbail wearenotgettingbail wearegettingbail wearenotgettingbail Boldt has made himself inaccessible, has withdrawn with his family, will not discuss the issue of bail. As far as he is concerned, we are in for the duration.

Tigar senses the demise of all constitutionality and in desperation phones Justice William O. Douglas at his retreat in Goose Prairie, Washington; Douglas has been closely following the case and thinks Boldt is totally out of order. Meanwhile, I am still here. Our only chance, Steinborn tells me, is if the Ninth Circuit Court ignores Boldt and orders bail set in spite of him.

Jailtime reminds me of being in college—I read a lot, write a lot, think a lot, am bored a lot, horny a lot and I am told what to do all the time by people I don't like a lot.

Some notes on jail: everything iron and steel, changing smells, continuous noise, racism, paternalism of matrons; cold food, diet never varies, same routine day after day. Boredom.

JANUARY 13

There's a butch in here named Johni. She wanders in and out of my cell every day to visit other prisoners. Every woman in the place wants her head between their legs. She is handsome and beautiful at the same time. From the back she looks like a man, from the front, a masculine woman. She wears her hair like the Elvis greasers of the late fifties; a cigarette hangs perpetually from the corner of her mouth. Her eyes are a clear peacock blue; her smile is lovely.

When Johni comes to visit, she stares at me on my perch on the top bunk; she nods hello, and smiles at me, and always asks me what I'm reading. She has a way of looking at me that makes my heart beat. I always get flustered when she enters the cell.

JANUARY 16

The boys have been sent to several different federal prisons; they can't send me anywhere because of my Bartholin gland. It looks as though I'm stuck here for six months.

For the past week I've been going upstairs to recreation. We play ping-pong and listen to records; we are allowed to use the phone occasionally. The black women hog it. The white women never interfere, because the black women run it. When a white woman gets out of line, all the black women attack her. She gets the shit beaten out of her because the matrons take their time about breaking up fights among inmates.

Today I am irritable, and when this one black woman is about to make her third phone call, I say, "Please get off the phone and give somebody else a chance." She ignores me, so I repeat it. Just then a matron walks by, hears me, and tells the black woman that her phone privileges are revoked for a week. The woman slowly puts the phone receiver down, and looks at me. Her eyes read very clear—KILL.

I phone Anne and speak for a minute. Then I sit in a corner of the recreation room reminding myself that in the war between black people and white people, white people are the bad guys. When recreation is over, we all are herded back to our cells. I perch on top of mine, carefully remove my glasses, and wait to be killed. I have been cautioned many times this month that if I should ever get into a fight with black women, the best thing to do is nothing, if I hope to live. I have been told to lie still and let them kick and punch me, and pull out my hair; but I won't die. I am prepared to be humble.

Just as the black woman saunters into my cell, a matron barks out my name. Grateful for the reprieve, I put on my glasses and run to the receiving room.

"Stern, clean up your bunk and get your street clothes on; you've been bailed out."

Maybe there is a God. It's times like this . . .

The infuriated black woman curses me from a distance, tells me she'll be waiting for me.

But she O.D.'d herself before I had to spend any length of time again in Seattle City Jail.

My bail was $25,000. My father refused to help, so my boss at the Century put up the bread for me.

JANUARY 20

Huey P. Newton once said that when he left prison he'd "be going from maximum to medium security." I found out almost immediately that he was right.

Eyes were everywhere. Friends showing concern, men wanting action, FBI agents, federal marshals, photographers, undercover pigs, and beat pigs; everybody in the world was staring at me. A clear case of oversell.

TV men interviewed me as I ate my dinner my first night out of jail; I was hot stuff, big news.

With the attention came paranoia. All the pigs tailing me barely attempted to hide themselves; I was constantly aware of being observed.

Tonight I was at a meeting for my second conspiracy trial, coming up in May. The meeting was downtown in Steinborn's office. Around nine, I had to leave to go to work at the Century. In a hurry, I made a left-hand turn from a right-hand lane; in a flash, the pigs stopped me. I hauled out my I.D.

"Well, lookee who we have here," said one gloating pig. "If it isn't the notorious Susan Stern. We'd better take her in."

"What," I said, astounded, "for a traffic violation?"

"Goodness knows what else there is on you," and they dragged me into the patrol car, and took me back to City Jail. The matrons gave them a withering look when they brought me in; I called Anne, who went to work for me, and sent Steinborn over.

They held me in the library. It only took a few hours, but it unnerved me; my paranoia was real; they were harassing me. Steinborn finally arrived, paid the ticket, which was twenty-five dollars, and drove me to the Century.

I worked for an hour, and then Anne and I visited with a couple of men hanging at the bar. We called them "cuties." They meant nothing to us at the time, yet Anne and I would allow one of them, a dark, brooding man who called himself Snake, to come between us. That night my relationship with Anne began to disintegrate, although it wouldn't become obvious for many months to anyone but me.

JANUARY 24

Since my arrest on the twentieth, I refuse to go anywhere alone. Anne usually goes everywhere with me.

My Bartholin won't heal; I still can't fuck. I depend more and more on barbiturates to sleep, and tranquilizers to calm me through the days. I am a nervous wreck; I live in constant fear of the pigs. I feel they are closing in for the kill.

Today, Anne and I went grocery shopping. I jaywalked on Forty-second Street, from the Orange Julius to get into our car across the street. We hadn't driven two blocks when a pig car stopped us, pulled me into the squad car, and before Anne's horrified eyes, drove me to City Jail. The charge—jaywalking.

I was crying when they brought me into the receiving room. The matrons were very kind; they were enraged at the pigs.

My fine was fifteen dollars. Anne went home, got fifteen dollars, and came to bail me out.

"Sorry," the clerk told her, "we found some unpaid traffic warrants—it will be forty-five dollars to get her out."

Anne went to Steinborn's office, and he gave her the money. She walked back to the Public Safety Building.

"Sorry," the clerk said blandly, "she is being held on a murder charge—her bail is now $100,000." Anne blinked, and, stunned, returned to Steinborn's. They both hurried back to the Public Safety Building.

Meanwhile, upstairs in the receiving room, the FBI was telling me they were going to extradite me to Chicago immediately, where, supposedly, I had robbed a bank and murdered a guard in the process. I was terrified; I was sure it was a plot to kill me. I began to moan and cry; the matrons made the FBI leave.

I was hysterical when Steinborn arrived. He was very efficient. In a matter of hours, the entire mistake was cleared up. "The computer made a mistake," smiled the FBI, and Steinborn carried me, babbling, out of City Jail.

But the worm had turned. I had had it. My dam had burst, and my mind had drowned. My thinking was soggy, and I saw and heard through layers of mud. Outside my head, everything grew dark and muted. I walked through a continual hum. I answered when no one had asked questions. I heard my voice, high and garbled, talking to an empty room. I saw people looking at me funny; I hid out so that they couldn't laugh at me. I laughed too loudly. I spilled more drinks than I served at the Century. And I was almost twenty-eight. Anne reminded me continuously how old I was getting, how young she was, how sick I looked, how old, how drab, how ugly, how old.

"Susan's almost thirty," she said to dozens of people. She got especially vociferous about it when we were with Snake.

JANUARY 31

It was my birthday. Joey called people to our house for a meeting. When they all arrived, they all shouted Happy Birthday. I dropped some acid, and we went in a large group to see John Lee Hooker.

For me it was the birth of the blues.

I still couldn't fuck, so I went to sleep alone that night. It's so lonely not to have someone hold you on your birthday. Anne was with Snake. I had managed to fuck him one night, but it inflamed my Bartholin gland. Anne got him the next night. She kept him. Why not—I was out of commission anyway.

FEBRUARY 1971

TERRIFIED. DEPRESSED. WIPE THIS MONTH OUT!

MARCH 1

The past few days have been bizarre! On the twenty-fifth of February, I was notified by my Chicago lawyers that my trial for the Days of Rage was definitely being held on Friday the twenty-ninth. My lawyers were plea-bargaining for me. This means that I admit my guilt, throw myself on the mercy of the court, and save the state of Illinois the expense of a jury trial; in exchange, the judge tends to be more lenient. This doesn't always work, but the People's Law Office, where my lawyer worked, had had a lot of success with plea-bargaining for political cases.

On the twenty-eighth, I prepared to fly to Chicago. I had borrowed a youth-fare card from a friend, which would reduce the fare by half; a stupid thing to do. I thought I was still anonymous Susan Stern. Times had changed. I was stopped from boarding the plane and detained. I had to call a disgruntled Anne to race to the airport with the additional money. And I was on my way to a trial, no less!

On Friday, in court, our lawyers plea-bargained all the other Weatherwomen down to suspended sentences with some probation, with the exception of me.

"You know, Susan, the judge read about the Seattle 7 case, and feels that perhaps you need some time in jail to think about breaking the law," my disappointed and apologetic lawyer told me. "He demands that you do a month. I'm sorry, I did my best."

A month. I had already done a month in jail, so I wasn't too upset. Nevertheless, I called Seattle with a show of histrionics, and tried to make everybody feel sorry for me. Then I called Joe, who was visiting his parents in New York with Bé-Bé; they immediately flew to Chicago. I was given the weekend free; I had to turn myself in at nine o'clock sharp Monday morning.

We all stayed at one of the PLO lawyers' houses. A couple of other Weathermen were there as well. Mourey, the head of the Chicago Red Squad kept a careful perusal of the house, and had his men follow us to numerous bars and cafes, and to see Andy Warhol's *Trash*, and to visit old friends, hoping to ferret out a mystical, magical underground Weatherman.

I was very lonely, even though Joey stayed right by me; but the night before I went to jail, I slept on a couch by myself; my Bartholin was still raw.

At seven o'clock on Monday we got up, and Joey offered to drive someone in the house to the airport, which was only a little out of the way from Cook County jail; halfway to the airport, her eyes got very wide, and she interrupted an amicable conversation saying, "You're going to jail today, I had forgotten." And stared at me as though I was a Martian.

I had almost forgotten too. Joey was chattering and squeezing my knee, and I couldn't imagine walking into jail and saying, "Here I am, lock me up."

But that's what I did. At nine o'clock sharp. I kissed Joey good-by, followed a matron upstairs, and began my month in Cook County.

MARCH 4
Dear Annie,

I thought I was tough but I wasn't prepared for Cook County! This place makes Seattle City Jail look like a country club.

My cell is minuscule; the size of a small bathroom. A double bunk and a sink are squeezed into it. It is so hot in here that I'm constantly sweating; five minutes after I take a shower, I stink again. We are let out of our cells for meals, and during the afternoon and evenings into a larger room which serves as an eating place and recreation—recreation consists of cards, TV, reading, writing letters, and chatting.

The meals are disgusting; some deadly gruel for breakfast, with eight cups of powerfully sweetened coffee, some gloppy soup with bread for lunch, and maggoty meat or beans for dinner. I try to eat as little as possible and get fresh fruit from commissary, but I am already getting the jailhouse chugs.

The worst thing about the joint is that there are no toilets in the cells. Three toilets sit side by side along with a big box with three showers in it, opposite three sinks. So if you happen to be brushing your teeth, somebody may be shitting right behind you. And if it's after lights out, and you have to go, you have to scream down a long corridor for the matron. You scream, "Knockdown, cell—" until you're hoarse; sometimes she hears you, sometimes she is snoring too loudly. Sometimes you shit in the sink, and quietly wash it up so your cellmate (cellee) doesn't notice. Of course my colitis is great in a situation like this, with all the beans and other starches, I have the runs constantly. I'm always asking for a knockdown, and the matrons hate me.

The Seattle City matrons are half human; these matrons are murderous. Not only are they enormous, but they have sadistic looks planted on their faces. They especially hate us four Weatherwomen in here because we hate pigs.

The high point of the day is when the mail arrives. I swear, if it weren't for the thought of future letters, I'd be awfully depressed. So please write, baby.

I was pretty anxious about meeting the three imprisoned Weatherwomen; you know, I never was very popular with leadership. But June, Lila, and Candy are very nice, and although I have the feeling they are "organizing" me when we talk, I am grateful for their company. To think that they were underground. They seem so strong, so definite; they make me feel once more that Weatherman was so right, that our feelings last summer were not misplaced.

Listen—Seattle seems as far away as Mars. I can't stand to write these stupid letters because I can't swear and I can hardly express myself without swearing, and I can't write what's really on my mind, etc. I also can't spell.

I am meeting beautiful women in here, like an eighteen-year-old girl accused of murder who writes poetry that just stuns me. But it's not like being with you and Joe and everyone else. At night, when we can't sleep, I tell my cellee about our life in Seattle, and it's almost creepy how sentimental you get.

I read *Woodstock* and decided that if Abbie Hoffman could write a book in three days, so could I. So I wrote the first page which was out of sight, but unprintable!

MARCH 12

Dear Beverly, Erin, Julia, and Shelly—

In here, behind the endless rows of bars, behind the heavy clang of iron green doors that shut out air sun rain clouds trees grass space, we have created a life, my friends and I, all the criminals who are too dangerous to be allowed free, the prostitutes, junkies, thieves, murderers, and Weatherwomen, black, yellow, red, and white women, young and old—and we lean softly and tentatively, at first, upon one another, knowing that our bodies have been caged but our minds souls hearts wander with all our sisters and brothers in wild freedom.

I know that I am not behind bars for nothing, that my beliefs are not a contradiction to all that's beautiful, to all that's love in this world, but only to that which maims beauty and kills love. Sometimes when the bars choke me, or when the iron doors seem about to crush me, I think of all of you, each of you so differently beautiful, and I know beyond a doubt that I am right, that I am not a criminal—or you could not love me, or I you. I don't believe freedom can be bartered or sold or stolen—it is a state of mind that we must transform into a reality. If I dance a war-dance in my heart, it is only against those who threaten the music makers and gentle people all over the world, who bring the Blue Meanies into Pepperland,

and make a funeral out of festivity; if I must dance a war-dance, the driving force of my rhythm is love. I love you all so much. I believe that you, Julia, Shelly, and Erin, will grow to be all the things I will never be. . . .

MARCH 15
Dear Joey,

I remember when you were in Cook County last summer I never wrote to you once; and I have been here two weeks and you've written me three times! I love you so much; I can't figure out why you love me, I'm such an idiot.

I have only two weeks left; then I will be free free free and sleep with beautiful men and eat until I burst and feel cool air on my face even if it is polluted, I don't care. I'll catch a pale ray of Chi-town sun, and hear my Joplin and Hendrix and buy some new threads and put on make-up, puff out my hair, throw out my breasts, swing my rounding-out hips and TRUCK, TRUCK, TRUCK.

There is so much I have to tell you, but I don't think I can express myself enough in writing, so it will have to wait until I get home.

What's happening on May Day? I hope to hell you're not planning a peace march. By the way, how did you like the Weatherman bombing to commemorate the town house? Give the Senate building a touch of Vietnam. The FBI over the country are going berserk looking for suspects. They'll never catch the Weathermen; we are everywhere!

MARCH 17—FOURTEEN DAYS TO GO TILL FREEDOM!
Dear Annie:

I WANT SEX, HAMBURGERS, COKE & COKE, FRENCH FRIES AND A NEW VAGINA FOR STARTERS! FREE SUSAN STERN!

It's very interesting to be here with Lila and June and Candy—they are radiant, much involved with Women's Liberation, emphasizing the closeness of women, women depending for support only on each other, women turning to women for sex, and concentrating on women when organizing. . . .

By the way, Joey and I had a long talk while he was here about the way you and I relate to men, you know, referring to them as cuties, or cocks, whistling at them when they walk by; in part I am satisfied with our approach, you know, reverse chauvinism, but maybe we are overdoing it a bit.

Did I write you my great discovery about Bugler's tobacco (important only when not in Vietnam, parts of Mexico, or free in your own living room)? You roll Bugler's like a joint, light it after fasting preferably, inhale deeply, hold breath as long as possible, exhale real slowly—you get high! You probably get cancer real fast too!

I'm going to F———k like crazy when I get out of here—that is, if I don't have leprosy of the vagina! Since summer is on the wing, there should be a lot of new traffic flowing with love juice through Seattle.

At last I must pay homage to that wonderful black bomber, Muhammad Ali. The entire prison listened to the Ali/Frazier fight on the radio—despair city! The moon must be bad for Ali, or Allah got drunk or stoned. But don't worry, Muhammad will beat Frazier's ass on the return match and maybe I'll be around to see that one.

MARCH 20
Dear Annie,

Since getting Joey's letter, and spending time with him here in Chicago, I began to get excited about the possibilities for May first. Yet, with all the letters I've received, nobody has said a thing about it. Does that mean nothing's happening?

During my political life, I was able to generate a great deal of excitement, to keep myself and others going. But too much lately, I have been thinking I was all burned out, getting old, part of a political way of thinking that was obsolete, or, even worse, destructive to the revolution, and I began to feel weak and neurotic. So I looked to you thinking, well let the younger, stronger, newer ones take over and give me a rest, let this old mare out to pasture, and I kept thinking that you would inspire me by your actions but it never happened.

I'm not sure why—maybe you weren't that interested—whatever the reason, somehow the war was getting farther away from me, right at the time when the Vietnamese were turning to ask, were demanding that Americans become human beings again. Joe's face and a couple of lines in his crazy letter brought it all joltingly back to me, and with the jolt, I feel like myself again.

Apparently the situation in Seattle, with many women old and new getting involved on many different, mostly conflicting levels, is true across the country; yet it is also true that the strongest moving force for revolution in the white movement comes from women and women's groups. The thing that largely upsets me is the liberalness and passivity which characterize too much of the work being done by women in general and by women specifically around May 1. It's as if the women are afraid to assume leadership, and instead keep on talking about elitism and as a result turn people away because they aren't afraid to get anguished, emotional, freaked out about the war, or criticize people who get enraged.

It seems to me, Annie, that with your life and enthusiasm, you could do much more than you do to regenerate the life once bounding around Seattle at the time of TDA, and I know your imagination is limitless. May 1 is not going to be the ultimate or last demonstration—whatever it turns out to be. There are no new forms of organizing, but there are always new ways of approaching things with the same total spirit that most people in this country just don't have on the surface.

Listen, we say "Keep on boogying, keep on smiling, keep on trucking and smash the state," so we might as well boogy and truck onto May 1, with all the endless tools of our trade—buttons, matches and shirts with May 1 printed on them, psychedelic posters, street theater, symbols sprayed on windows, walls, doors, bumpers, jackets; smoke-ins, intercourse-ins (can't curse), be-ins, dance-ins, free suppers, food-ins—splatter the city with insignia, signs, and trifles that indicate the BIG EVENT is coming, AND THE WHOLE WORLD WILL NOT WATCH, IT WILL PARTICIPATE! Put signs on Go-Go's tail . . . well, I could go on forever.

It's often easier to write about things than to do them. If this letter misses the mark, then make a good fire out of it, toke up, play Janis for me, and take from it what you can.

MARCH 25

I was released this morning. I couldn't believe it—five days early. I called Anne immediately, then prepared to fly to New York. I would then go to Madison, Wisconsin, to attend a Yippie Convention to plan for May 1. There was going to be another National Action in Washington, D.C. Hopes were to shut the city down.

APRIL (SEATTLE)

There is something wrong with me. I thought it went away in jail, but it's here again, and worse than before. I can barely talk to Anne, who, contrary to her easygoing attitudes, has suddenly begun hyperventilating. She and Lisa, another woman in my house, have gotten very close while I was away; Lisa doesn't like me. They have an established routine in the house and are telling me what to do.

I spend a lot of time in my bedroom, watching the clouds move across the sky. Sometimes I wish I was back in Cook County—I knew what to expect there. All I had to hope for was mail.

I have done nothing for May 1—I have done nothing period. You could say I was wallowing in self-pity, but it's more. Maybe it's my concussion. I went back to Dr. Greene, who told me my brain was all right, but that I would be subject to periods of blackouts for the rest of my life—perhaps I was going through one now.

MAY 1

Two days ago, Joey pulled up in a snazzy drive-a-way and said, "Get in," and like a mannequin I obeyed. He, Bé-Bé, Lisa, Robby Stern, and I drove to Washington, D.C., for the May Day demonstrations.

I was petrified; I was facing three years' probation, and here I was in D.C.—exactly where I shouldn't have been.

That night there was a rock festival but my mind was too weird for me to drop acid. I got pretty bored wandering around. I knew hundreds of people there, but somehow I didn't feel like talking, I wasn't sure what I would say from time to time. Joey would come bounding from every direction to ask me how I was, squeeze my arm, and bop off in pursuit of another woman.

The next day, just before we were going out to do it in the streets, Lerner comes rushing in, white-faced; "The FBI knows we're here—we didn't sign out." So while all the freaks are shutting the courts down, Chip, Lerner, and Joey and I are inside a courthouse with a lawyer, trying to sign in with a D.C. federal marshal, so bench warrants from Seattle won't be put out for us.

That scared me! That afternoon at a meeting, they needed a woman to chair, you know, female leadership, so Chip volunteered me. It was a meeting to decide where the next area of attack would be. When the meeting was over, dozens of people, sensing a leader, came up to me asking questions, as if I knew something. That scared me! That night, Chip insisted on me going to a meeting. I began to make suggestions—you know, can't break old habits. People dashed up to me when the meeting was ended, I saw pigs everywhere, I was nervous, uptight, paranoid, and convinced I was going to be discovered breaking probation, and be sent back to Cook County for three years. That thought really scared me!

I borrowed a hundred dollars, and five o'clock in the morning, had a friend drive me to the airport and flew back to Seattle. Back to an empty house—all the boys, et al. were in D.C., and Anne had flown to Chicago for her brother's wedding. I was alone in that house for three weeks. It didn't matter. I could talk to myself out loud now without having people look at me funny.

I barely dressed for those three weeks, only leaving the house when I ran out of food. I discovered this dope that was almost as powerful as smack; I chain-smoked it. I took downers. I hardly saw anyone, although Robby stopped in occasionally to ask me to stay with him, he was worried about me. I smiled, no need to worry. I was doing just fine. Just couldn't talk, is all.

I decided to surprise Anne and paint the living room; she had wanted it green and white. But the green paint I got was just the color of Seattle City Jail and Cook County, and when I did the living-room trim, the living room looked like a jail cell. It was ugly as hell, and I tried to remove some of it with paint remover, making a bigger mess, and ended up leaving it.

I wanted to take a bath finally, but I forgot and let the water overflow. I realized it when I saw a stream trickling down the stairs; I didn't bother mopping it up; the air will dry it, I thought.

I tried to iron some clothes, but burned a hole in everything; one day I noticed that all the dog food I had bought two days ago was untouched—poor Go-Go, he was a good garbage dog. When the phone rang, I never answered; I never looked in the mailbox.

SUMMER 1971

My house is a madhouse. People are coming out of the woodwork. Chip and Lisa, Joe, and now Karen from the defense collective has moved in with Joe; Abeles has built a bed in the cellar, Anne and myself, Gary from Ithaca; Harlowe, a Movement hippie whom I had known vaguely when I lived in New York, her daughter Peach, and her old man. Everybody is bopping all the time. I still can't talk, Anne only growls at me now, and I can't seem to throw off this melancholy.

The last week in July, I was arrested, along with Harlowe, for credit-card forgery. We spent three days in a cell in City Jail together; she offered to take the rap from me because I was on probation from Cook County. Harlowe creates a way of life out of that kind of generosity. Steinborn handled the case and we never did any time; he also took care of my second conspiracy charge that summer—it was dropped.

SEPTEMBER 1971

The house is quieting down somewhat, since Harlowe and clan got a home of their own, just around the corner. Bé-Bé has moved in with them. Chip and Joe and Abeles spend a lot of time over there. I don't get along with Lisa or Karen. Anne doesn't get along with Karen, and whispers constantly with Lisa. I am sure Anne is saying nasty things about me, too.

My hands are shaking. I am talking compulsively now, in a high, shrill stream; I can't stand the sound of my voice; I can't shut up.

The Snake has reappeared in my life. I hate wanting him. But whenever I think about him, he appears; it's almost psychic. He has started me on Yoga . . . it's disgraceful. I am slipping. I know I am having a nervous breakdown, have been ill for months. What shall I do? Commit myself to a hospital? Ex-Weathermen all over the country have had trouble readjusting to a normal life. I mean, when you're a Vietcong one day, and then the war is over the next, what do you do, all geared for death, and you got to go on living?

OCTOBER 1971

Joey saves me once again. He takes me to Vermont to visit his sister for two weeks. She lives in a log cabin in the woods; my first experience with country living. I sort apples for an orchard for $1.75 an hour eight hours a day; I get up at six each morning; no electricity, an outhouse. Joey's sister says us city meat-eaters have stunk up her outhouse with our poisoned shit!

In the quiet of the woods, I heal strangely and swiftly. There is a guitar which I play; only the trees hear my voice, deep with confusion. I stop smoking, cigarettes and dope; I refuse to take barbiturates, even though I can't sleep; I begin to sing constantly; I buy a harmonica and blow into it; I begin to run in the woods; I stop eating meat, I stop drinking soda; I begin to relax and stop talking so much and so fast. I decide to buy a piano, teach myself how to play it, and sing and write songs. I am not going to die. I am not going to go insane. The revolution will happen, but it will take a long time; I have to survive until then. Is that the end of youth? Have I finally made a mature decision? Am I copping out? Has jail so frightened me that I will become reactionary?

WINTER 1971–72

Gray, drizzling Seattle winter. I feel like winter inside and out, but my mind is clear. Anne and I still estranged; but around my birthday, we begin to draw closer. I don't really know why, but the bad period slowly faded, and we began to talk to each other again.

I sit at my old upright piano eight, ten, twelve hours a day; I have all kinds of books, and I picked up the blues on my own. My voice is getting clear again now that I'm not smoking.

The Seattle 7 are wasted; they are no longer interested in putting on a good show. The political gains of an aggressive trial are unclear at the moment. Our attorneys assure us that we will get off lightly if we go nolo contendere. That translated means no contest. We admit our guilt, and waive our right to a jury trial, and throw ourselves on the mercy of the court. Essentially it's plea bargaining.

We had to pay Maxey five thousand dollars to handle the case. During the month of March I did nothing but work on setting up a good-by, fund-raising party to be held at a local tavern, and invited Country Joe MacDonald up to play for us. He was very generous and came.

That month I got nervous again and started taking barbiturates; I also took a new interest in cocaine, which seemed to grow in proportion to the scarcity of marijuana. Cocaine, the great, white bitch, flowed freely in Seattle. A discreet little sniff almost anywhere, and you felt like a million, and had a lot of poise and charm and energy.

The fund raiser was a huge success in many ways. We raised over a thousand, which I gave to Maxey, and everyone had a good time. I left very early, to get fucked.

At the end of the month, Anne moved into a house around the corner; she couldn't stand the mess the boys made all the time. I didn't move because I wasn't sure if I was going to jail or not.

MARCH 28

Judge Smith listens to all our stories. One after another Chip, Joe, Abeles, Dude, Lerner, Roger, and myself tell him how guilty we are, how idealistic we were, and how reformed we will be. We are the picture of obedience. We are deplorable. It's a disgrace, but we grit our teeth and go on with the farce.

Judge Smith does not hate us, and probably thinks we have been through enough. However, he must defend the honor of the courts and Judge Boldt. All our contumacious behavior is excusable—but the presenting of an American judge with a Nazi flag is insufferable.

Six months for all defendants except Lerner, who gets off, and Lippman, who gets one month. Lerner's father, a New Jersey judge, came to tell how Lerner always wanted to be a rabbi; Lerner also had his wife and child seated under the judge's nose. He made it seem as though he had been manipulated into our group but had not realized we were all Weathermen until it was too late.

I asked the judge for a day off to take care of some "pressing matters," and was granted it.

Everyone was in tears; all the boys, all their girl friends, and myself. It was very passionate and emotional. I went home, found someone to fuck and the next morning, Gary and Go-Go drove me to jail.

APRIL—SEATTLE CITY JAIL
Dear Annie,

Things have improved in here since last July; still, I have a groovy schedule which wouldn't keep a droll occupied; still up at the ghastly hour of five-thirty, scrub the cell, eat breakfast (I am always famished) which is decently good (generally eggs, sometimes bacon, toast, and several cups of coffee thickly sweetened), and then I play cards with my friend Rosie, who solemnly beats my ass every time.

After cards, and an hour of work on my book, which I have begun to keep me from going insane, I exercise like crazy. I am now up to twenty-five situps and fifty jumping jacks plus a lot of relaxing yoga stuff, a great deal of stretching. I jog miles around my cell each day, and up and down the corridor, working myself into a sweat, whereupon I leap into a broiling bath, and perfume myself up, by which time we have reached the astounding hour of ten o'clock. Soon after that it's time for lockup, where I read until lunch. After lunch I begin working on the book in earnest, and don't move until four o'clock, when they unlock us again and I exercise some more, and I read until dinner at five-thirty, and then comes the worst hours of all—night. It bears in on me like a smothering pillow, heavier than anything else, long, endless minutes which drag into more long, endless hours, until the lights go out at ten and then, honey, I pray for Treasure Sleep.

From six to ten are the longest, most intolerable years of my life, and each day I wake up dreading when those hours will start. That's when I miss you and everyone the most, that's when the awful SEX monster gets to me, and nothing helps, nothing can take my mind from it. I watch TV, strain my eyes to read some more, drink some coffee, read the papers, ponder my book, but generally give up and roll and flop on my bunk. It's stifling hot in here at night, and I try to remember what air smells like. So far I have been falling asleep easily, and sleeping straight through until the morning, unless some roaring drunk sets up a bellowing boo-hoo in the drunk tank next to cell 603, or some poor junkie pukes through the night, or any of the personal tragedies of some fifty-odd women become so unbearable that they cry or scream until the matrons come and take them upstairs and sedate them.

And this is jailtime and let me tell you it's hard time, lonely time, endless boredom, and unrelieved depression.

APRIL 7

Tonight is one of those nights. I feel it will never end. It's dragging on and on, and I am so restless. I feel predatory; Christ, now I finally know how a tiger feels pacing in his cage. My heart is pounding me to pieces; my teeth are gnashing, and every once in a while I slump from the tension and get the whirlies, round and round, everything in circles, closed in. SUFFOCATING, I CAN'T BREATHE. LET ME OUT OUT OUT. I want to throw all the windows open and jump. I can't think, can't believe past tonight.

I am quivering apart. Five eternal minutes ago I tried to count seconds and by seconds I counted first one hour-long minute and then another, and then I lost count because the seconds flood like ants over spilt honey.

I tried to do what Lila, June, and Candy and I did in Cook County—food trip: Oh when I get out of here it will be a rare sirloin smothered in onions, a shrimp cocktail, and a lobster, and raw, screamingly fresh celery and a cold, dripping, brilliant glowing strawberry, and bacon and twin yellow suns of eggs done lightly and gooey marmalade on cream cheese.

I try to sex-trip, and there is a deep and curious void; I try to think of some man, but that doesn't do it. I'm inventing a fictional love because I need it so badly, but what I want goes deeper than my need for sex, always has.

I want to finish this book, then it will have been worth it. I only hope it isn't banned as revisionist when the revolution comes.

In *Ada*, this book by Nabokov that I am reading, there is a sentence I must use, because it sums up exactly how I feel. The main man, Van, says of his life, having lived well past the age of ninety, "My long life, my too long life, my never-long-enough-life." And it's all those contradictions I so acutely feel. My twenty-nine years, my too too long twenty-nine years, my never-long-enough. Sometimes I desperately want out, and at other times the pendulum swings and I want every day to be a month long. Sometimes all the treasures of youth and health mean nothing; but now a leaf on a vine they have in the outer office is compelling as a whole forest; green, translucent, earthy-smelling, living, and working its tendrils magically across the wall of a prison.

One thing I know, I want to be free. I want fresh air, I want to walk in a straight line and not constantly be folded into myself like an egg into batter. I want to make love to some raw, young man, I want to see the flash of Anne's smile; I want to kiss the furry stench of Go-Go, I want to brush my mother's sweet soft lips. I want to climb Mount Rainier, and stand there with my Vietcong flag and piss on Seattle below and say, "Here at last, free at last, Good God Almighty, free at last."

APRIL 20

Dear Mom,

I guess all my radical rhetoric is true; we are reliving the McCarthy era, and Mitchell and Nixon will shut up any voice that even attempts to speak up for freedom or truth. If I can't speak for such things, then I don't want to live at all. Being in prison intensifies everything I ever felt about revolution; jails are such stupid, criminal places. How can you "rehabilitate" a person by shutting them into a dark cage for a given amount of time? What is rehabilitative about boredom? It leads to insanity, and a bitterness so far-reaching that nothing ever again can shake or alter its foundations.

I am reading George Jackson's prison letters. He was put in prison for stealing seventy dollars from a gas station, and because his skin was black, they gave him a year to LIFE! And then they shot him in the back after he spent ten years in prison, and now he's dead. Mom, ten years for seventy dollars—doesn't that seem wrong to you?

I still say that if I had it to do all over again, I wouldn't hesitate. Like all the impoverished of soul and spirit, I have no choice. I don't want to get married and have children; I want to be free to lead my own life, and not do what generations of blind tradition have said I must do simply because I'm a woman. I don't want to be a teacher or a social worker; it's ridiculous to think of helping people in a society bent on the destruction of everything human.

Listen, to put me and most people in jail, is murder in the truest sense of the word. It warps and maims and kills like a slow but lethal poison. There is no escape from its outcome. My life from now on will be at least partially the result of these months here; every beat of time, every year will in some way be distorted by the brutality I have been subjected to by being caged.

Being treated like an animal has made me begin to think like one.

END OF APRIL

Charlie Robinson is trying to have me transferred to Purdy State Institute for Women; Maxey is pushing him. I have phoned him a couple of times, but he is out of his office right now. I don't think he was ever a treacherous pig like Boldt; I think, in a better society, he might become a better man.

BEGINNING OF MAY

Dear Mom,

I am writing this letter from Purdy State Institute for Women, and am I grateful to be here. This prison is paradise. When we win the revolution, we should model prisons after Purdy.

It's reminiscent of a small, new community college. The single-story brick buildings are attached in a rectangle, which form a natural boundary for the prison. Four of the buildings are housing units; every woman has her own room, and wears her own clothes from home, and decorates her room with her own belongings. Everything is new and spotless.

The food is delicious, and we are allowed as much as we want. Everyone eats in a large, pleasant cafeteria. There are also cooking facilities in each housing unit.

We are allowed to roam free until nine o'clock at night. Within the prison circumference, there are grassy areas bordered by flowers; there are nice walkways, and a large area for bicycling. There is a recreational room in the chapel building, along with a library. Then there are classrooms. Classes largely fall into three categories: high school curriculum, secretarial and computer training, and arts and crafts. All the art supplies are free, so I have taken up pottery and macrame. I also am taking sewing classes, but I hate to sew.

Visiting days are on Saturday and Sunday, from one to five; Anne has already brought all my clothes and belongings.

MIDDLE OF MAY

Johni, the butch I met a year ago in City Jail is here on a heroin charge; every woman in Purdy has a crush on her. My heart flipped the first day I was here, when I went to buy something at the commissary, and looked straight into her brilliant blue eyes across the counter.

"Well," she drawled in a Mae West voice, "you can't hide up on that top bunk of yours no more," and grinned broadly. "What unit are you in?" I told her, and she said, "Well, ain't that a coincidence? I'm in the same unit." Then she suddenly froze; I turned, as her hulking girl friend approached the counter.

Johni was sought after by every woman on the campus. The prison was her domain; here she could be the stud society would not let her be. I was very infatuated with her, and as the days passed, my infatuation quickly became lust. The wheedling want in my vagina would not let me be; I wanted Johni as much as I had ever wanted any man.

I began to put on make-up, and wear sexy clothes. She noticed, and when her girl friend wasn't around, she whistled loudly. Several times when we were in the cafeteria, I would brush lightly against her, almost as if by accident; but she would stare at me, and we both knew it wasn't an accident.

She began to come to my side of the unit. She would stop at every door, peer in, jive a bit, and pass on. Eventually she came to my room; I would hear her coming and stop breathing until she arrived. When she looked in she would say hello, smooth down her pompadour, and gaze at me deeply. I would always blush, but I managed to stare right back.

One night I put on a nightgown Harlowe had given me; it was very sheer. I carefully put on my make-up. Two months without drugs, and with good food and plenty of sleep had improved my appearance greatly; I was plump and sassy!

I waited for Johni to make her nightly rounds. When she reached my room, I was waiting. She took me in at a glance, stopped, flabbergasted.

"Johni," I said, moving up to her, and putting my hand right on her breast, "will you sleep with me sometime?"

She nodded yes, and then slowly, firmly, took me in her arms and kissed me. It didn't seem strange to kiss another woman. The swell of her breast felt good against mine, the curves of her body familiar. I was weak-kneed when she drew away, and brushing my hair softly, left the room.

Dear Annie,

I have come, at the age of twenty-nine, to measure my existence in terms of history, and how I fit into history. And when I think about existence, I think about dying, and I am pleased that I will die having done the historically correct thing; i.e., live and identify with the poor and oppressed of the world, and attempt to lead a revolutionary life. I know I fall far short of my expectations, but at least I'm trying. If I waited until I was a perfect revolutionary (what's that) then I might never do anything. People often err in trying to do the right thing; does that mean they should stop and do nothing, or continue to change themselves as they change history?

Still, I am unhappy in my role as revolutionary, because it is not enough for me; I want to stand out in the history I am trying to make. My existence will have meaning only if lots of others know about it. Call it fame, immortality, call it what you will, until I have it, I will always be unhappy. I guess that's the saddest thing about me, my fatal flaw.

In a real sense, then, I exploited the revolution for my own personal ends. Still would the Movement have been better off without me? Would the hundreds of people I convinced be better off unconvinced? Now that you know the awful truth, do you respect me less?

I tried for a long time, especially in Weatherman, to change. During that time I came closest to being selfless. But I couldn't change. My desire for immortality, my need for fame is perhaps the essence of my life; it alone can give meaning to my existence. I am helpless in the face of it, even though it tears me to pieces and makes a charade of my finer instincts. It is the reason for my great depressions, for my restless, painful, persistent driving of myself, and only as by-products do I achieve some measure of female liberation.

I have often looked at people and been amazed that they were so content to be commonplace; to be so many cogs in the endless wheel, faces in the crowd. I have often hated myself for wanting more, felt I have missed much in life because I am discontent with so much of it. And what is more the pity, I shall probably never get what I want so badly, and will grow old ungracefully, longing for the release of death and hating its insistent approach, and never really know peace. Sounds awful, but it's me; I have to accept what I can't change.

Love, I almost hate the word. I have always been an abysmal failure at it. I have often thought if I could find love I would not crave fame so, but it seems I lose on both scores.

I am at that point in my love life where each new intelligence on the subject makes me more ignorant. I can't understand a thing about it. All I know is that some people are more suited in this world to love and be loved than others. Let me tell you what has happened to me in prison.

I have fallen in love with a woman and slept with her, my first homosexual encounter. I am not interested in any other women, and don't think much about men. With Johni, I am like a fourteen-year-old going through my first crush. I have learned nothing in the past fifteen years, nothing. I am just as unequipped to deal with love now as I was then. It hurts just as much, means just as much, is just as brilliant and insufferable. I'm not at all liberated; I'm just a quiet prisoner, inside and out of jail. I try so hard to keep my feelings locked up that when they finally assert themselves they do so with a fury that astonishes me.

When I see Johni kiss another woman, I feel the same stabs of jealousy that I did as a girl, and I'm walking around now in the same perturbed state of mind that I did before my first date. Absolutely nothing have I learned from all those years except that there is a pattern; but alter it, stop it, improve it, impossible.

JUNE 1972

Apparently I am very desirable to other women. It amazes me that I am more of a coquette with women than I ever was with men. But the lesbians in here like sexuality in all forms, including dress.

In many ways I have been freer here than I am allowed to be outside. With no men around, I don't think about sex. If I enjoyed women, I would have plenty of it. But I am very content to play the piano, do my pottery and macrame, and work on the book.

Anne has visited me every Sunday; it's an hour trip here. I will probably move into her house when I get out.

I have a black girl friend named Cobra; I don't sleep with her, but I spend time with her. She shows me off to other women who desire me. Everybody is suspicious of Johni and me. We spend little time together, but her enormous girl friend beat the shit out of some poor jealous butch who snitched on us. Johni denied it and went out and beat up the girl a second time.

Maxey has worked hard on getting me out a month earlier. I will also get a month for good behavior. So my out date is June 29.

JUNE 29

I did some fast walking out of that prison. I never turned once after waving the last time to the two women who stood plastered against the other side of the glass door that separated me from them and them from freedom. It was eight-thirty in the morning, and I, Susan Stern, was free.

It was the beginning of the summer. The long, clear beautiful Seattle summer, and I was a summerchild.

I laughed fast walking out of that prison, and I laughed right through the summer until the fall, when the rain began again. And I knew that morning when I walked out of Purdy with that summer feeling stealing in my bones, making me want to yelp, leap, fly, surge for joy, I knew as early as that morning that autumn would come again, and bring with it the rain and the pain of settling in for the winter.

I fast-stepped out of Purdy and there was Anne waiting for me, shining in the morning sun, her hair flying in all directions, her smile wide and her teeth flashing, and her eyes filled with joy when she saw me.

Immediately we began giggling and gossiping as she drove down the winding road away from Purdy.

"Harlowe and Fritz are still fighting, but oh, Susan, you should see how big Peach and Joy are getting. Chip and Lisa are getting along fine. Joe and Karen about the usual."

"Oh, Annie, look at the mountains." And all about us loomed the mountains; the Cascades, the Olympics, and the white, towering, elegant Mount Rainier. I felt as though I were coming home from Mars, but Purdy had only been an hour out of Seattle. Actually, I felt that I had never left home; only some time had mysteriously elapsed, and suddenly now it was summer, and I was warmed from the inside out.

"Annie, what's the man situation like? You know I haven't fucked a man in three months."

"Don't worry, Susan, there are plenty of men, we'll find you a man, just don't worry about anything. They always turn up when you need them, don't they?"

"You know, celibacy wasn't so bad, Annie, not after the first three weeks. You kind of lose the real keen desire, you know, you just stop thinking about it so much. Especially in there with no men, I just stopped thinking about men. It was nice living without men; it wouldn't be so bad if they all vanished. They ain't such great shakes anyway."

Anne flashed me a smile.

"I know, listen, I know. There simply aren't that many good men. Believe me, I never stop looking. And every time I think I've found one, I get disappointed. Like Paul this spring, while you've been away. Good-looking, intelligent, rich, all he ever wanted to talk about was law. And he always had to work. Finally after two months, he tells me he's actually in love with another woman. It took him two months to get around to telling me that."

Anne was hot on the subject of Paul. With both of us it was a generally established fact that vis-à-vis men you were damned if you did and damned if you didn't. But somehow, we had both managed to retain some objectivity about the whole matter of men, so no matter how many times we were fucked over by them, we rolled with it, and came back again for more.

We had had endless discussions about men, and our relationships to them, and how come if we were so beautiful and smart and witty, etc., we didn't have billions of groovy, handsome men just crawling all over us; how come some nice man just didn't fall in love with us? Why were we seemingly destined to lives of loneliness? What was wrong with us?

Through the years we had finally evolved the theory that there was nothing wrong with us; that the problem lay with the men. There simply were not enough men around who could ever appreciate women of the caliber of Anne and myself. Anne and I didn't want children; at least not right now. And I was twenty-nine and that wasn't no spring chicken, so when was I going to have children? We wanted freedom, independence; we were used to calling our own shots, making our own plans, earning our own money. I guess we really were liberated in a sense.

But we never fooled each other or ourselves for an instant. We both were looking for the MAN, the LOVE, the same old white knight, only our list of qualifying characteristics had grown while the type of man who could fill them was swiftly diminishing. We had always agreed in the past, and we agreed again that lovely morning driving home from Purdy, that we were lucky to have each other. Harlowe had once said that Anne and I were the best couple she knew. In a sense she was right. We loved each other, brought only pleasure to each other, took our petty jealousies and weaknesses out on the men we consistently had crushes on, and came back to each other again for more support and uplifting.

I looked at Anne as she was driving, chatting, smiling, and I really felt totally that instant how much I loved her. Her dimples were winking as she talked, unaware that I was scrutinizing her from behind my sunglasses. I thought fleetingly that she would leave me someday, that even though our friendship was strong and rich because we left each other free to do as we wished, someday it all would end, and Anne would go off with some man and leave me alone.

But the sun was melting me like butter, and Anne was making plans to go to my favorite tavern, and just at that minute the Smith Tower Building came into view and I started laughing, howling, gleefully wiggling in my seat.

"What're you laughing at?" she asked.

"Annie, remember two summers ago when Robby and Roger formed those two collectives, and told us that to join them, we would have to separate because we were a monogamous couple?"

It cracked me up. Here were two women who hung with each other more than men, who loved each other, and who were good to each other, and who were not particularly bitter or warped about men. What the hell was Women's Liberation about if not Anne and myself?

The car was turning down the Forty-fifth Street exit onto Forty-fifth Street, past the Blue Moon, our neighborhood tavern, and then right to Seventh Avenue, and up Seventh and stopped in front of the ramshackle green house with the red flag still waving over the sagging front steps and my dog, Go-Go sitting with all his dog-friends on the front porch, and I was jumping out of the car and into the sun and Go-Go was all over me, furry and crying and jumping and licking, and so were all the other dogs and Anne kept saying, "Look, Go-Go, Susan's home," and boy, was I ever!

SUSAN STERN . . . . Released from prison June 29, 1972. Susan Stern fell immediately in love. For the next three months she loved and played and was happy. She took a lot of drugs and became addicted to cocaine. When her romance ended in the fall, she became even more dependent on the cocaine. She began topless dancing again to support her habit, eventually began stripping, and actually turned a trick one night at a stag party but was so befuddled she forgot to collect her thirty dollars.

In December 1973, she decided to go to New York and attempt to publish the book she had begun in prison.

She went with Anne to Florida over Christmas, and rested, and took no drugs. She looked very old and tired. She looked at the end of things. In January she gathered her courage and visited a friend, who read her manuscript and was impressed enough to introduce her to a literary agent, David Obst.

On Inauguration Day 1973, Susan followed agent Obst to Washington, D.C. He read her manuscript and introduced her to a Doubleday editor, who also read and liked the manuscript, and purchased it.

Susan signed her contract just after her thirtieth birthday. A photograph that a friend took shows a long-haired, attractive woman with sunglasses, slim and shapely, and proudly smiling.

In her heart she was singing a little Weatherman ditty:

YOU CAN GET ANYTHING FOR FREE
IF YOU STEAL IT FROM THE BOURGEOISIE
COMMUNISM IS WHAT, WHAT WE WANT
COMMUNISM IS WHAT, WHAT WE WANT.

WEATHERMEN BOMB ROCKS HEADQUARTERS OF GULF OIL

Pittsburgh, Pa. (AP)—An explosion rocked the upper floors of the Gulf Oil Corp.'s international headquarters last night, moments after a telephone caller claiming to be from the radical Weather Underground warned that a bomb had been placed.

Police said the blast left the 29th floor "all messed up," and a newsman reported a gaping hole in the ceiling of the 28th floor of the 38-floor building.

There were no reports of injuries and police said there was apparently no fire in the wake of the blast.

Assistant Police Supt. Robert Coll said the explosion was "apparently dynamite," and caused extensive damage to the 29th floor, which is occupied by the Gulf Asian Co., a Gulf subsidiary.

It was the second time in two weeks that someone claiming to be from the Weather Underground warned of a bombing minutes before a bomb went off.

On May 31, a bomb damaged the Los Angeles office of the California attorney general. In that case, as in the Pittsburgh explosion, members of the news media were directed to telephone booths where they found letters signed "Weather Underground" and bearing the sign of the radical group—an arrow piercing a rainbow.

But the Los Angeles letters said the bombing was an expression of sympathy with the Symbionese Liberation Army, the terrorist kidnappers and converters of newspaper heiress Patricia Hearst.

The Pittsburgh letter was eight pages long, addressed mainly to Gulf's alleged "crimes" against peoples around the world.

Moments before the explosion at 6:43 p.m., PDT, The Associated Press received a call from a woman who claimed she was a member of the Weather Underground and said the group was bombing the building.

Seven men were trapped for 40 minutes in an elevator by the blast.

S.L.A. IN SPOTLIGHT, BUT WEATHERMAN STILL TO BE RECKONED WITH

Los Angeles (AP)—While the spotlight is on fugitive members of the Symbionese Liberation Army, the revolutionary Weather Underground has surfaced again and served notice it is still to be reckoned with.

Ten days ago the group left word with authorities that they planted a bomb in the Los Angeles office of California Attorney General Evelle Younger.

Ten minutes later the explosive detonated, causing considerable damage but no injuries. The Underground said it was in solidarity with the six S.L.A. members killed last month in Los Angeles.

The Underground, called Weatherman when it broke off from Students for a Democratic Society in 1969, remains the subject of widespread investigation by the Federal Bureau of Investigation.

The agency concedes it has learned little about the revolutionary group. Small, tight-knit "new left" underground groups have been especially difficult for the agency to infiltrate.

A spokesman said the bureau hasn't been able to find the Weatherpeople, doesn't know much about the way they live, and can't be sure what crimes they've actually committed.

Friends of the Weatherpeople say the group is alive and well and still active.

The group is believed comprised mostly of young, white radicals. Most are college educated, many are children of rich families.

The best known of those identified by the F.B.I. are Bernardine Dohrn, whose name adorns most important communiques; Mark Rudd, active in the S.D.S. strike at Columbia in 1968; and Katherine Boudin, whose father, Leonard, defended Daniel Ellsberg.

They are among 28 Weatherpeople sought on various federal warrants by the F.B.I. Many others are also underground and active with the group, but are not sought by law enforcement agencies.

Miss Dohrn was on the bureau's Ten Most Wanted list for months until charges were dropped against her and several others for conspiracy to engage in terrorism and sabotage.

The group formed in the summer of 1969, when a faction of S.D.S. wrote, "You Don't Need a Weatherman to Know Which Way the Wind Blows," a pamphlet explaining their radical political philosophy.

That phrase, and the group's name, is derived from the lyrics of a Bob Dylan song, "Subterranean Homesick Blues."

In July 1969, the group took over leadership of S.D.S.—probably the most influential of all New Left organizations, comprised at its peak in 1968–69 of an estimated 70,000–100,000 persons on campuses across the country.

Weatherman political strategy was the most action-oriented in the history of the New Left, including fist-fights with youth gangs to prove their courage, and street-fights with police in Chicago.

After a number of indictments were brought against the Weatherman members in 1970, the group disappeared. They have been burrowed in the underground ever since; few members have been caught.

Aside from the bombings, the Weather Underground's visibility has been limited to written and sometimes taped communiques, and the infrequent cracks in the armor of secrecy.

Two former members apprehended in 1970 are now above ground and active in other radical work.

"The Weatherman is still a threat," said an F.B.I. spokesman, "although a lot has been neutralized by the charges."

The 28 Weather fugitives are all charged with at least one of the following:

Interstate flight to avoid prosecution; anti-riot violations; destruction of government property; violation of the national firearms laws, or conspiracy to violate any of the above.

The F.B.I. said the oldest known Weatherperson is Miss Dohrn, who is 32, while the youngest members sought by police are several young men now 23.

The Weather Underground has been staunch in its support for the S.L.A. and has called for the rest of the radical left to face up to the new group's challenge. However, in a letter by Miss Dohrn, the group stops far short of embracing the S.L.A. tactics of kidnapping Patricia Hearst and assassinating Marcus Foster, Oakland, Calif.'s prominent black school superintendent.

"We do not understand the killing of Marcus Foster, and respond very soberly to the death of a black person who was not the recognized enemy of his people," wrote Miss Dohrn.

The group is best known for its bombings, directed usually against government or police agency facilities. The first Weatherman bombing was directed against the New York police department in 1970.

Also in 1970, three Weatherpeople were killed in an explosion in a New York townhouse, apparently while fashioning explosives.

The best known Weatherman bombing perhaps was an explosion in the United States Capitol Building March 1, 1971.

The group also engineered the 1970 prison escape of Timothy Leary. He took asylum in Algeria, fled to Europe, but was later recaptured.

Despite the dramatics, the Weather Underground has maintained strict security and a low profile. The group tried to avoid the charge directed against the S.L.A. by radicals, that the group is "adventurist." Many have made that charge against Weatherman also.

"Adventurism is when you don't believe you can organize the people and lose confidence in the people," said Bill Ayers, a Weatherman founder, now underground.

He is one of several persons whose parents grace the upper class. His father is chairman of the Commonwealth Edison Co. in Chicago.

Many of the others' backgrounds are similarly imposing. One of the original Weatherman cadre was James Mellon of the Pennsylvania banking family. The F.B.I. said he is no longer sought.

One of three persons to die in the townhouse tragedy was Diana Oughton, a Bryn Mawr graduate and descendant of the founder of the Boy Scouts of America.

The Weatherpeople, unlike the S.L.A., keep their names and acknowledge their background:

"We are the sons and daughters of the enemy. Our political objective is the destruction of honkiness. We have to force the disintegration of society, creating creative strategic armed chaos where there is now order," the group once wrote.

Former acquaintances of Weather Underground members are generally unaware of their present lives. They discuss the group in the most general terms.

—Seattle *Times*, June 11, 1974

LEARY LIKELY TO TESTIFY AGAINST THE WEATHERMEN
by Lacey Fosburgh, Special to the New York *Times*
SAN FRANCISCO, Aug. 21—Dr. Timothy Leary, the former Harvard psychologist now serving a 20-year jail sentence on various drug charges, is expected to testify before a Federal grand jury in Chicago against some of his former colleagues in the revolutionary Weatherman organization, according to sources here and on the East Coast.

In return for his information, the 54-year-old Dr. Leary reportedly expects to avoid further prosecution and obtain a speedy parole.

John Russell, a spokesman for the Department of Justice, confirmed that Dr. Leary was cooperating with the Federal authorities in the hope of making a "deal."

He said the case was "being handled by the general crime section" in Washington, but refused to discuss Dr. Leary's information or the possible indictments that might stem from his testimony.

Among the information Dr. Leary has reportedly turned over to the authorities are the details of how the Weathermen helped him escape from the United States.

They allegedly took him through California to Seattle, where he met with a number of revolutionary leaders, including Bernardine Dohrn, leader of the group. Finally, he went to Chicago, where they allegedly helped him get a false passport, and he then flew to Paris and Algiers.

January 31, 1943	Susan Harris born Brooklyn, New York.
1951	Parents divorced after bitter and protracted courtroom battles.
1952	Goes to live with father and brother in small town in New Jersey.
1961	Begins Syracuse University as Liberal Arts major.
November 1964	Meets Robby Stern.
February 1965	First abortion.
July 1965	Marries Robby Stern.
September–December 1965	Teaches sixth grade in ghetto school in Syracuse.
September 1966	Enters School of Social Work in Seattle, Washington.
August 1967	Attends New Politics Convention with Robby; meets national SDS organizers.
Fall, 1967	Joins SDS.
June 1968	Receives Master's Degree in Social Work; leaves Seattle and Robby Stern.
August 1968	Works at Los Angeles Regional SDS Office. Attends Democratic Convention in Chicago.
Fall–Winter, 1968	Works in SDS at Columbia University in New York.
December 1968	Attends SDS Convention in Ann Arbor, Michigan. Progressive Labor Party fac-

tion within SDS, and other SDS members in violent conflict. Resolution *Toward a Revolutionary Youth Movement* (RYM) passed.

March 1969   Attends SDS Convention, Austin, Texas. Meets Joe Kelly and Chip Marshall. Gap between Progressive Labor and rest of SDS widens. Differences appear in group favoring RYM resolution passed in December. SDS struggles toward alliance with Black Panthers.

April 1969   Mark Rudd airs Weatherman paper to Columbia SDS leadership.

June 18–22, 1969   SDS National Convention. Split between Progressive Labor and SDS. RYM 2 statement presented as refinement of original RYM proposal. Weatherman paper presented by those who emerge as Weatherman leadership. Weatherman take over SDS National Office.

Susan makes plans to return to Seattle, rent a house, and wait for Joe Kelly, Chip Marshall, and others to arrive from Ithaca.

End June 1969   Attends United Front Against Fascism Conference called by Black Panthers in Oakland, California. Panthers criticize SDS, especially Weatherman. Split between RYM 2 and Weatherman broadens. Proposal for National Action in Chicago in the fall passed by SDS.

July 26, 1969   Returns to Seattle.

August 12–15, 1969   Participates in Ave riots in Seattle's University District.

August 22, 1969   Seattle Weatherman formed with eight members including Susan. A few days

	later Robby Stern leaves Seattle, totally opposed to Weatherman.
September 1969	Organizing for Days of Rage.
October 8–11, 1969	Attends Weatherman Days of Rage in Chicago; arrested for feloniously assaulting an officer of the law. There are hundreds of arrests and major felony indictments; all Seattle Weathermen are arrested; many injured.
October 21–25, 1969	Weatherman collective slowly returns to Seattle.
November 14, 1969	Mark Rudd arrives. Heavy criticism of Susan.
November 15, 1969	Susan suffers severe concussion during Mobilization demonstration.
November 16–17, 1969	Criticism session of Susan resumes. Reorganizing of collectives. There are now twenty-four Seattle Weathermen.
December 1, 1969	Weathermen attack University of Washington ROTC.
December 11, 1969	J.J. arrives. Susan criticized again; demoted from Weatherman leadership.
December 15, 1969	Two closest friends in collective go underground.
December 28–31, 1969	Attends Weatherman War Council in Flint, Michigan. Weathermen decide to go underground as a group. The Sundance collective, including Chip Marshall and Joe Kelly and Anne Anderson leave Ithaca bound for Seattle.
January 17, 1970	Jerry Rubin speaks in University of Washington Hub Ballroom at invitation of Mike Lerner. Weathermen attempt to precipitate action but fail. That night, two Weathermen arrested for trying to bomb

	Airforce ROTC on U of W campus. Bail set at $50,000.00.
January 19, 1970	First meeting of Seattle Liberation Front. First overt act of Seattle 7 conspiracy.
January 20, 1970	Susan leads attack on Marine recruiters' office; arrested for assaulting an officer of the law.
January 20–22, 1970	Held in Seattle City Jail.
January 25, 1970	Kicked out of Weatherman.
January 26, 1970	Attempted suicide; taken to boy friend's farm.
January 31, 1970	Twenty-seventh birthday.
February 2, 1970	Leaves farm and joins Sundance collective to organize for Seattle Liberation Front and The Day After demonstration.
February 16, 1970	Flies to Chicago for pretrial hearing for Days of Rage. Returns that night to Seattle.
February 17, 1970	The Day After demonstration.
February 21, 1970	Kicked out of Sundance collective.
March 6, 1970	Greenwich Village town house explosion in which three Weathermen killed.
March 11, 1970	Divorced from Robby Stern.
March 25, 1970	Leaves Seattle to go underground. Soon after named co-conspirator in Weatherman conspiracy charges stemming from Days of Rage.
April 16, 1970	Returns to Seattle. Arrested for conspiracy for organizing The Day After demonstration; jailed.
April 21, 1970	Released on bail. Meets Anne Anderson.
May 1, 1970	Attack on Airforce ROTC for May Day demonstrations.
May 3–5, 1970	Tours Washington state with Joe Kelly, making speeches about the conspiracy.

May 6, 1970	Thousands in Seattle block freeway, protesting invasion of Cambodia, and Kent State.
End May 1970	Speaks on Berkeley campus with Jerry Rubin, William Kunstler, and Mike Lerner.
June 9, 1970	Indicted and arrested for second conspiracy for May 1 attack on U of W ROTC.
June 15, 1970	Sundance collective dissolves. SLF stresses summer programs.
End June 1970	Robby Stern and others form two collectives calling themselves Weathermen.
Summer–Fall, 1970	Mostly party. Cursory work on conspiracy trial.
November 5, 1970	Second abortion. Beginning of six months of illness.
November 23, 1970	Conspiracy trial begins in Tacoma, Washington.
December 1, 1970	Begin testimony of Horace (Red) Parker, undercover FBI informer.
December 9, 1970	Susan excused from court for minor surgery.
December 10, 1970	Judge George Boldt declares a mistrial and cites six male defendants for contempt of court.
December 14, 1970	Defendants return for sentencing. When Susan makes a statement, Boldt places her in contempt. A riot begins in the courtroom when federal marshals attempt to drag her out of the courtroom. Defendants sent to jail.
January 16, 1971	Released from jail; $25,000 bail.
January 20, 1971	Arrested and jailed for making a left-hand turn from right lane.
January 24, 1971	Arrested and put in jail for jaywalking.
January 31, 1971	Susan's twenty-eighth birthday.

March 1, 1971	Put in Cook County Jail in Chicago for one month for assault charges stemming from Days of Rage.
March 25, 1971	Released from Cook County Jail—three years' probation.
Begin April 1971	Attends Yippie Conference in Ann Arbor, Michigan, to plan for May Day demonstrations in Washington, D.C. Returns to Seattle.
May 1, 1971	Drives from Seattle to Washington, D.C. for May Day demonstrations.
July 25, 1971	Arrested for credit card forgery. Three days in Seattle City Jail.
Fall–Winter, 1971	Very depressed.
January 31, 1972	Twenty-ninth birthday.
March 26, 1972	Seattle 7 return to prison for contempt charges.
June 29, 1972	Susan is released from Purdy State Prison for Women.

Explanatory Notes

CHAPTER 1. LEAVING

1. Free University: The Free University of Seattle (FUS) was a countercultural organization that offered classes on a variety of subjects.

2. New Politics Convention: Between August 31 and September 4, 1967, three thousand delegates from two hundred progressive organizations assembled at the National Conference for a New Politics to discuss an electoral strategy for 1968.

3. Founded in 1960, Students for a Democratic Society (SDS) was the best established of the student protest groups at the time.

4. The Congress of Racial Equality (CORE) was founded in 1942 by an interracial group of students at the University of Chicago to further the cause of civil rights through nonviolent protest. By 1968 CORE had become increasingly militant, inculcating the ideology of Black Power.

The Black Panther Party (BPP), founded in 1966 by Huey P. Newton and Bobby Seale, was known for its socialist ideology and its doctrine of armed resistance as well as for the free breakfast programs and community-based schools it ran.

5. Betty Friedan, *The Feminine Mystique*: This best-selling 1963 book, which described the stultifying effects of women's role as housewife, was an important impetus to the women's movement of the 1960s.

6. Paris revolts: The 1968 Paris riots, which brought together students and workers, culminated in a two-week general strike that almost brought down the French government.

7. Eldridge Cleaver: Minister of Information for the Black Panther Party and author of the controversial 1968 best-seller *Soul on Ice*.

8. Huey P. Newton's murder trial: Accused in 1967 of killing a police officer, Newton was convicted the next year of voluntary manslaughter. His conviction was reversed in 1970.

9. Mao Tse Tung: Leader of the 1949 revolution that established the People's Republic of China, Mao was responsible for the Cultural Revolution (1966–1976), which resulted in the death of millions.

10. DNC in Chicago: The 1968 Democratic National Convention had become notorious for the frequent and bloody clashes between protesters and police. In the aftermath of the convention, prominent protest leaders (the Chicago Seven) were charged with conspiracy in a trial that received national attention.

CHAPTER 2. CHICAGO

1. Yippies: Founded in 1967, the anarchistic Youth International Party was known for its politically oriented street theater. Two of its most prominent members, Abbie Hoffman and Jerry Rubin, were numbered among the Chicago Seven.

2. National Mobilization Committee: The National Mobilization Committee to End the War in Vietnam, better known as Mobe, was responsible for organizing mass protests against the Vietnam War.

3. Eugene McCarthy campaigned for the Democratic Party's 1968 presidential nomination on an antiwar platform. Despite the wide support he enjoyed among progressive voters, McCarthy ultimately lost the nomination to Vice President Hubert Humphrey.

4. New York Motherfuckers: Active in the Lower East Side of Manhattan, the anarchist group Up Against the Wall Motherfuckers took its name from a poem by Amiri Baraka. Inspired by the Dada and situationist art movements, the group was prominent in the countercultural scene in New York in the late 1960s.

5. Ho Chi Minh: Communist president of North Vietnam, 1955–1969.

6. Malcolm X: Prominent black nationalist leader and national spokesman for the Nation of Islam, assassinated in 1965.

7. Rennie Davis: One of the Chicago Seven and a leading antiwar protest leader.

8. March of the poor people: The Poor People's Campaign, led by Martin Luther King Jr. and other members of the Southern Christian Leadership Council (SCLC) in 1968, culminated with a march on Washington to dramatize the problems of economic inequality. Reverend King was assassinated before the march reached its conclusion.

9. Algerian women: In the hugely influential 1966 film *The Battle of Algiers* (dir. Gillo Pontecorvo), which depicts the struggle of Algerian guerrillas to free themselves from French colonialism, women are shown having a pivotal role in the insurrection.

10. Dick Gregory: African American comedian and civil rights activist.

11. Columbia University strikes: Under the leadership of Mark Rudd, the Columbia University chapter of SDS organized a student occupation of classrooms and administrative buildings on April 23, 1968, during which three school officials were held hostage. Although the demonstration was violently suppressed by the police, SDS saw it as a success and a model for future student actions.

CHAPTER 3. NEW YORK

1. Liberation News Service: A left-wing alternative news service, active 1967–1981.

2. PL: Progressive Labor Party, a Marxist-Leninist-Maoist political party that attempted to take over SDS. PL, in opposition to Weatherman, believed that the industrial working class was the catalyst to revolution.

3. Bill Ayers: Weatherman leader.

4. Kathy Boudin: Weatherman leader.

5. Panther 21: A group of Black Panthers arrested and accused of conspiring to plant bombs around the New York City area; all were acquitted.

CHAPTER 4. WEATHERMAN

1. White Panthers: A group founded by Detroit-area activists John and Leni Sinclair and Lawrence (Pun) Plamondon as a support wing of the Black Panthers. Their ten-point program included a call for the "Total assault on the culture by any means necessary, including rock n' roll, dope and fucking in the streets."

2. Mao's *Little Red Book*: This collection of the quotations of Chairman Mao was widely read by U.S. leftists during the 1960s and early 1970s.

CHAPTER 6. HANDLE-VANDALS

1. Che Guevara: Argentine-born guerrilla leader, with Fidel Castro, of the Cuban Revolution. Captured by the CIA in Bolivia in 1967 and executed by the Bolivian Army, Che became a worldwide socialist icon.

CHAPTER 9. LAST-DITCH EFFORT

1. Vietcong: North Vietnamese guerrillas.

2. Moratorium Peace March: A series of peace marches held across the United States on October 15, 1969, involving an estimated two million people.

3. Vietnam Mobilization Committee, otherwise known as the Mobe. See chapter 2, note 2.

CHAPTER 10. DISINTEGRATION

1. "the sabotage of the imperialists' office buildings in New York": Weatherman engaged in a series of bombings of corporate and government buildings as a means of spreading disorder.

2. Palestine Liberation Front: A militant Palestinian group founded in 1964.

Tupamaros: Also known as the MLN (Movimiento de Liberación Nacional, or National Liberation Movement), a guerrilla movement in Uruguay in the 1960s and 1970s noted for staging political kidnappings and assassinations.

CHAPTER 11. WAR COUNCIL

1. Huks in the Philippines: The Hukbalahap Rebellion was a communist-led peasant uprising, 1946–1954, ultimately defeated by the Philippine government with the assistance of U.S. military supplies.

2. Sundance Kid: *Butch Cassidy and the Sundance Kid* was an Academy Award–winning 1969 Western featuring Robert Redford and Paul Newman as glamorous outlaws.

CHAPTER 12. KICKED OUT

1. narodniks: A Russian revolutionary society of the 1870s and 1880s, the Narodniks believed that peasants were a revolutionary class, but that they required charismatic leaders from outside their class; the Narodniks turned to terrorist tactics after their movement was crushed by the government in 1877.

2. Jerry Rubin: Yippie leader (see chapter 2, note 2).

3. Russ Neufeld and Cathy Wilkerson: Weatherman leaders.

CHAPTER 13. SUNDANCE

1. Seattle Liberation Front: An antiwar organization led by Michael Lerner, founded in 1970 and disbanded in 1971.

2. John Mitchell: U.S. attorney general under President Richard Nixon, convicted in 1975 of conspiracy in the Watergate scandal.

3. H. Rap Brown Act: A law against "interstate conspiracy" that was used

against the Chicago Seven defendants. Brown was chairman of the Student Non-Violent Coordinating Committee (SNCC), but joined the Black Panthers in 1968 and became the Justice Minister of the Black Panther Party. He appeared on the FBI's Ten Most Wanted list on charges of carrying a gun across state lines and inciting riot.

CHAPTER 14. SEATTLE 7

1. Kent State: On May 4, 1970, the Ohio National Guard shot to death four Kent State University students during an antiwar protest. The shootings sparked international outrage and led to a nationwide strike involving eight million students.

CHAPTER 15. TRIAL

1. Fred Hampton: The twenty-one-year-old deputy chairman of the Illinois chapter of the Black Panther Party, killed in 1969 by a police SWAT team while he lay asleep in his Chicago apartment.

2. RYM 2: The Revolutionary Youth Movement (RYM) was a faction within SDS that opposed the PL, or Progressive Labor Party, faction. RYM later split into two groups: one became Weatherman and the other, RYM 2, formed into a collective of small Maoist cells.

3. My Lai: On March 16, 1968, U.S. troops massacred hundreds of unarmed Vietnamese civilians, including women and children in the North Vietnamese village of My Lai. News of the episode leaked, despite attempts by the military to cover it up, leading to an international scandal.

About the Editor

Laura Browder is an associate professor of English at Virginia Commonwealth University and the author of *Her Best Shot: Women and Guns in America*.